CYBERLAW
Your Rights in Cyberspace

Gerald R. Ferrera

Stephen D. Lichtenstein

Margo E. K. Reder

Ray August

William T. Schiano

THOMSON

LEARNING

Australia • Canada • Mexico • Singapore • Untited Kingdom • United States

Cyberlaw: Your Rights in Cyberspace by Gerald R. Ferrera, Stephen D. Lichtestein, Margo E. K. Reder, Ray August, William T. Schiano

Printed in Canada
1 2 3 4 5 04 03 02 01

For more information contact Thomson Learning, 5101 Madison Road, Cincinnati, Ohio, 45227 or find us on the Internet at http://www.westbuslaw.com

For permission to use material from this text or product, contact us by
• telephone: 1-800-730-2214
• fax: 1-800-730-2215
• web: http://www.thomsonrights.com

Library of Congress Cataloging-in-Publication Data
Cyberlaw : text and cases / Gerald Ferrera ... [et al.].
    p. cm.
  Includes bibliographical references and index.
  ISBN 0-324-07473-5
  1. Computer networks—Law and legislation—United States. 2. Electronic commerce—Law and legislation—United States. 3. Internet (Computer network) I. Ferrera, Gerald R.
  KF390.5C6 C93 2000
  343.7309'944—dc21
                                                        00-033841

For Judith, David, Vinita and Boulder
—GRF

For my wife, Cindy, our children Jeff and Julie, and my parents, Max and Frances.
—SDL

For all of my family, friends and colleagues
—MEKR

This book is for two dedicated and inspiring teachers: Fred and Libby Schneider
—RA

Contents

Preface

You are holding in your hands the first Cyberlaw book written specifically for business readers. Information technology is no longer merely intersecting with business, but has become an integral part of our economy—as the business news media will not let us forget. What business oriented readers are asked is to prepare themselves with a legal competency suitable for the e-commerce business manager of the 21st century.

Cyberlaw: Your Rights in Cyberspace builds on the principles of law and the legal environment of business already taught in business schools. After all, laws that apply to real space also apply to cyberspace. Shrink-wrap contracts are still contracts. Federal registration of domain names, web pages, and business methods in the United States Patent and Trademark Office are still governed by intellectual property law. Case decisions on jurisdiction of an e-business are analyzed on a sliding scale based on a company's interaction with the end user, but the law continues to require satisfaction of the long-arm statute and compliance with the due process clause. Privacy has taken on a new significance with digital profiling, but the legal analysis remains the same.

It is the authors' intent to illustrate throughout this book how cyberlaw builds on the offline analysis of traditional principles of jurisprudence. This book contains the leading cases and statutes in Cyberlaw explained in a clear and comprehensive style. It is the authors' sincere hope that you thoroughly enjoy this text and the experience of learning about the exciting and dynamic discipline of cyberlaw.

Subject Matter and Basic Organization of the Text

The subjects covered follow a logical application of the legal issues surrounding e-commerce. The book's focus is on the needs of business managers working, in some fashion, in the online environment.

Features

Manager's Checklist. Each chapter provides a Manager's Checklist that offers suggestions useful to business managers working in online environments in an effort to reduce their companies' liability exposure. The authors wanted to blend the practical with the necessary theoretical legal analysis found in the case decisions.

Cyberethics. Readers should continue to discuss ethical dilemmas found in business transactions. Online business has its own set of unique relationships that often develop into potentially unethical business conduct. The cyberethics boxes in each chapter should lead to lively discussions.

Web sites. Throughout the book Web sites are noted that apply to the subject matter and can be used for additional reading, legal resources, and topics of interest.

Appendixes. Several abbreviated statutes relevant to e-business are found in the Appendix at the end of the text.

Acknowledgments

We would like to thank the following reviewers of this book for taking time from their demanding schedules and providing us with their helpful suggestions:

Christine Neylon O'Brien, Boston College
Michael E. Jones, University of Massachusetts–Lowell
Susan Demers, St. Petersburg Junior College
Lori Harris-Ransom, Caldwell College
Diana Walsh, New Jersey Institute of Technology
W. Ray Williams, Rutgers University
Robert Bird, Fairfield University
David Austill, Union University

We are thankful for the excellent work and advice of the West publishing team—Rob Dewey, Kelly Keeler, Michael Worls—and especially Susan Smart, whose patience and expertise were invaluable in this endeavor.

The Bentley College authors would like to thank President Joseph Morone, and Vice-President and Dean of Faculty, H. Lee Schlorff, for their enthusiastic support of this project, and chancellor and former President of Bentley College, Gregory H. Adamian for his support and encouragement over the years; Janice McMahon, administrative secretary of the Law Department, for her dedication; and Florence Jones, administrative secretary of the Department of Accountancy for assisting on portions of the manuscript.

The Washington State University author wishes to thank Dean Glenn L. Johnson of the College of Business and Economics, and Director Robert Greenberg of the School of Accounting, Information Systems, and Business Law for their encouragement and support; special thanks go to the faculty and students of the School of Accounting, Information Systems, and Business Law, for their suggestions, ideas, and materials that were included in this book.

Gerald R. Ferrera
Stephen D. Lichtenstein
Margo E. K. Reder
Ray August
William T. Schiano

PART I

Introduction
to Cyberlaw

1

Technology and Cyberlaw

"We reject Kings, Presidents and Voting. We believe in Rough Consensus and Running Code."

—Internet Engineering Task Force Credo

Introduction

Around the world, millions of people are using the Internet for information, research, retail purchases, finance, and correspondence without a thought to the legal issues involved in electronic communication and commerce. These issues are an important consideration of doing business in our free enterprise system. In the past, business managers had to know the basics of our legal system to understand the fundamentals of face-to-face business transactions. Now they must also understand the legal functioning of electronic commerce, or e-commerce, as creative online business models radically change the legal environment of business.

Before we discuss and explain the new legal developments of how the law applies to Internet transactions, it will be helpful for you to understand the material in this introductory chapter. As you read the chapter, try to visualize how technology has changed traditional ways of doing business. Our courts and legislators are crafting a distinct body of laws that will assist you in understanding the online business environment.

Cyberlaw—law governing the use of computers and the Internet—focuses on a combination of state and federal statutory, decisional, and administrative laws arising out of the use of the Internet. These new laws often build on traditional laws that apply to bricks-and-mortar companies. To discuss cyberlaw meaningfully, it is necessary to understand the potential and limits of the technology in question. This chapter establishes a brief background for the discussion of cyberlaw, from the history of the Internet to its current global use, and places this technology in a business context. To a great extent the material discussed in this chapter governs behavior and business transactions. Keep in mind that software and hardware can affect important cyberlaw issues such as privacy, contracts, and intellectual property rights.

2

History of the Internet

Most people think of the Internet as synonymous with the World Wide Web, but it is not. The Internet is a network of computer networks. The very name *Internet* comes from the concept of inter-networking, where multiple computer networks are joined together. In the business arena, electronic mail (e-mail), file transfer, and chat rooms take place through the Internet, while commerce and considerable information dissemination take place through the World Wide Web. Together they comprise a world of cyberspace where important legal issues are often raised.

The Internet began in 1969 as ARPANET, an effort by the U.S. Department of Defense to enable defense researchers at various sites across the country to communicate and collaborate. Many of these sites were large universities, and academics at those schools began using the Internet, especially e-mail, to communicate about nondefense matters. Other features included discussion groups, access to databases, and file transfers. In 1973 ARPANET began to be connected to more networks and to networks in other countries, and it evolved into the Internet. In the late 1980s, the National Science Foundation built its own network, and by 1990 ARPANET ceased to exist, although its functions lived on. Its history shows the Internet was never intended to be a commercial network, and until 1991, when the World Wide Web was developed, users were held to an acceptable use policy that expressly prohibited commercial applications.

History of the World Wide Web

The World Wide Web began in 1991 at CERN (www.cern.ch/Public), the European Laboratory for Particle Physics, as a way for physicists to exchange formatted academic and technical papers. While all had access to the Internet, a compatible software format was needed. In 1990 Tim Berners-Lee at CERN developed and named the World Wide Web program, which became available for universal use on the Internet a year later. It was not until the early 1990's that e-commerce was taken seriously by the business world. Keep in mind that Amazon and Yahoo, now household words, did not exist prior to this time.

How the Internet Works

To connect to the Internet, individuals and firms use **Internet Service Providers (ISPs)** such as America Online or Prodigy, for local and international connections. All users, whether commercial or individual, connect to their ISPs via communication lines—typically telephone lines, although increasingly other means such as satellite dishes and cable television lines are being used. The capacity, called the *bandwidth,* of the lines is determined by the needs of the business or individual. Slower connections use modems, while faster connections use other types of connectors, such as network interfaces.

Large ISPs are typically connected directly to the high-speed backbone of the Internet, and often establish their own international networks to improve security and reliability for their customers. Smaller ISPs connect to the Internet by connecting to larger ISPs. Some services, such as America Online, serve as an ISP while also providing services not on the World Wide Web, such as chat rooms, reference materials and other content.

Internet Addresses

Every computer on the Internet has a unique **Internet protocol (IP)** address that consists of four series of three numbers ranging from 0 to 256, separated by periods. These numbers are important because they are required for communication from one computer to another. However, a string of up to twelve digits would be a cumbersome way to access sites, so the **domain name system (DNS)** was implemented in 1984. The DNS matches the numerical IP addresses of computers with text names in a manner similar to a telephone directory, which matches names with phone numbers. Each domain name is associated with a unique IP number. When a text address is typed into a browser (such as Netscape Navigator) or sent as an e-mail message, the name is looked up (resolved) on a domain name server and the connection is made.

A domain name consists of a top-level domain name and a sub-domain name. When the DNS was established, each country was assigned a country code as its top-level domain name. As an example, a site in England would have the top-level domain name ".uk" and the sub-domain would be the specific site in the United Kingdom, such as "amazon.co.uk." In the United States, other top-level domains include .com for commercial sites, .gov for government sites, .net for networks, and .org for organizations. For example, www.ustreas.gov is the Web site on the Internet of the United States Treasury, and www.un.org is the Web site of the United Nations. In Great Britain, the top-level commercial domain name is .co (as in amazon.co.uk, or dmgt.co.uk, for the London newspaper the *Evening Standard*). Domain names have a significant application in cyberlaw because conflicts often emerge between trademarks and domain names used by a competing company. Chapter 3 on Trademarks will discuss this in detail.

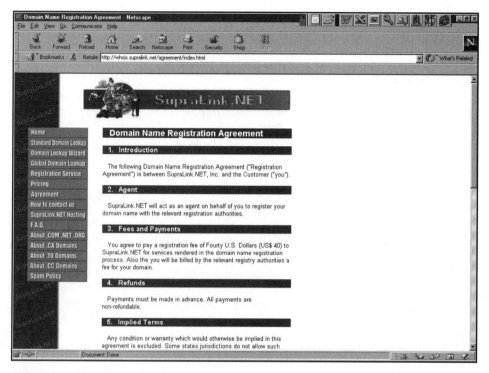

© 1999 SupraLink.NET

The Language of the Internet

Since many scientists used mainframe and UNIX workstation computers, file format compatibility was a major challenge. **Hypertext markup language (HTML)** was developed as a standard document format, and **hypertext transfer protocol (http)**, the http you see at the beginning of a web address, as the way of exchanging such files. This means that HTML can be viewed on any brand of computer using any operating system, with a viewer, or browser.

Accessing a Web Site

Within a given domain, there may be many different Web pages, each identified by a unique address called a **uniform resource locator (URL)**. A URL is simply the name of a file stored on a Web server. Accessing a Web page involves transferring files from a server computer to a client, or browser. Within a given Web page there may be many files, including pictures, sound, and video, for which the codes used to create them can be seen. This makes protecting the design of Web pages very difficult. For companies trying to protect their brand, the inability to control how these pages are found or the context in which they are displayed can be frustrating.

Transmitting Information

The Internet, like all computer networks, operates exclusively with digital transmissions, represented by zeroes and ones. All data on the Internet travels in small bundles called **packets,** and each packet includes a *header* with address information. A single e-mail message might be sent as several packets. Figure 1.1 shows the contents of an Internet packet.

The packets travel to the addressee by passing through many other computers, and each computer examines the address information in the packet header and sends it to the next node in the network. Not every packet will necessarily travel the same route; thus, each packet is numbered so that the sequence can be reestablished at the other end. The multiple connections were a deliberate effort to provide redundancy; if one connection fails, the other can be used to keep traffic moving despite congestion.

Packets allow many users to use the same connection and to reduce the amount of data that must be re-sent in the event of a network error. Figure 1.2 shows the route a test packet traveled from telestra.net in Australia to Bentley College in Waltham, Massachusetts. (Note the IP addresses in parentheses.) One packet traveling through eighteen connections gives one an idea of the sheer volume of data flowing through the Internet each day. This volume and the multiple connections make regulation of the Internet difficult.

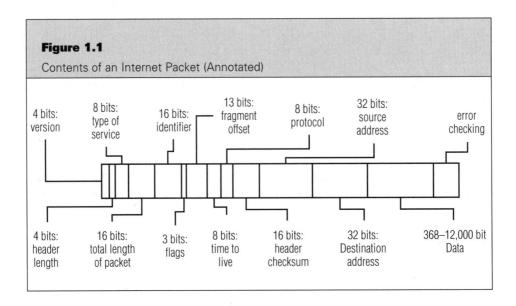

Figure 1.1

Contents of an Internet Packet (Annotated)

4 bits: version — 8 bits: type of service — 16 bits: identifier — 13 bits: fragment offset — 8 bits: protocol — 32 bits: source address — error checking

4 bits: header length — 16 bits: total length of packet — 3 bits: flags — 8 bits: time to live — 16 bits: header checksum — 32 bits: Destination address — 368–12,000 bit Data

Netiquette

The Internet's academic origins and prohibitions on commercial use created a strong culture on the Internet that survives today. Using intrusive or overly aggressive advertising, ignoring site or group policies, and asking questions for which answers are available in frequently asked questions documents are all considered breaches of *netiquette*. Such breaches are met with a variety of responses, from tolerance to vitriol.

Figure 1.2

Trace of the Route from Bentley College to Australia

```
traceroute to athena.bentley.edu (141.133.239.248), 30 hops max, 40
byte packets
  1  Ethernet0.dickson.Canberra.telstra.net (203.50.0.1) 1.439 ms
     1.704 ms 1.371 ms
  2  Serial6-5.civ2.Canberra.telstra.net (139.130.235.1) 3.188 ms
     3.179 ms 2.54 ms
  3  Fddi0-0.civ-core1.Canberra.telstra.net (139.130.235.226) 3.26 ms
     3.48 ms 2.058 ms
  4  Hssi0-1-0.pad-core3.Sydney.telstra.net (139.130.249.33) 33.954 ms
     171.456 ms 63.008 ms
  5  139.130.249.235 (139.130.249.235) 25.87 ms 20.75 ms 122.246 ms
  6  205.174.74.33 (205.174.74.33) 221.518 ms 230.233 ms 225.299 ms
  7  199.37.127.67 (199.37.127.67) 220.604 ms 323.975 ms 222.63 ms
  8  s2-0-0.paloalto-cr18.bbnplanet.net (4.1.142.253) 227.638 ms
     227.733 ms 325.946 ms
  9  p3-2.paloalto-nbr2.bbnplanet.net (4.0.3.85) 236.601 ms 223.836 ms
     226.26 ms
 10  p4-0.sanjose1-nbr1.bbnplanet.net (4.0.1.2) 303.175 ms 231.028 ms
     223.42 ms
 11  p1-0.sanjose1-nbr2.bbnplanet.net (4.0.5.86) 225.687 ms 226.534 ms
     238.566 ms
 12  p4-0.nyc4-nbr2.bbnplanet.net (4.0.5.98) 289.694 ms 296.001 ms
     292.647 ms
 13  p1-0.nyc4-nbr3.bbnplanet.net (4.0.5.26) 326.089 ms 296.495 ms
     292.014 ms
 14  p2-3.cambridge1-nbr2.bbnplanet.net (4.0.2.173) 396.145 ms 301.188
     ms 296.95 ms
 15  p3-0.cambridge1-nbr1.bbnplanet.net (4.0.5.17) 299.059 ms 296.572
     ms 295.969 ms
 16  p0-0-0.cambridge1-cr18.bbnplanet.net (4.0.5.74) 299.101 ms
     296.297 ms 313.018 ms
 17  s1.bentley.bbnplanet.net (4.1.130.214) 307.736 ms 326.592 ms
     331.458 ms
 18  athena.bentley.edu (141.133.239.248) 343.785 ms 302.765 ms
     307.842 ms
```

Regulation of Cyberspace

Because the Internet is a coalition of networks throughout the world, no one organization owns the Internet. The Internet Society oversees boards and task forces that deal with network policy issues. Among these are the Internet Engineering Steering Group, which is responsible for final approval of Internet Standards, and the Internet Engineering Task Force, the protocol engineering and development group. The Internet is largely self-policing—networks that do not conform to the norms of the Internet are cut off from the rest.

The Internet was designed as a collaborative environment, and therefore was not a high-security environment. Founded by academics, the open exchange of information became a basic tenet of the Internet. This is in direct contrast to corporate computer network environments, where the assumption is that all access is denied without explicit authorization, and where measures are taken to ensure security. In addition, the sudden expansion of World Wide Web commercial usage has raised numerous legal issues regarding privacy, security, and copyright and trademark infringement. This book will explain the relationship of these legal issues to e-commerce. It will be helpful as you read the text to keep in mind the technology that is used in e-commerce transactions.

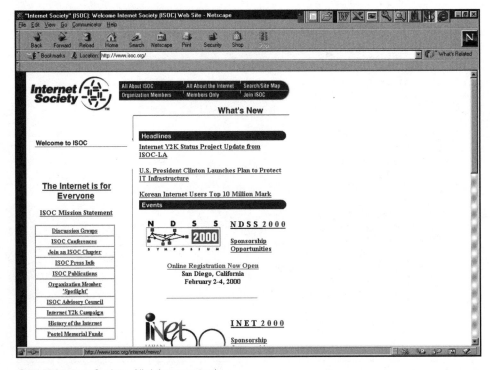

© 2000 Internet Society. All rights reserved.

Business and Individual Users

Security and privacy concerns on the Internet extend to both the individual user and the business user. The most straightforward way in which businesses obtain information from individual users is through a form completed and submitted by a user. However, many users fear more insidious, invisible data-gathering methods.

Currently, if a company wants to track a user's behavior over time without asking the user for data, the only way to do so is with **cookies.** Cookies are small text files that a server can store *on the user's machine.* When a user visits a site, the server may store up to twenty cookies on the user's machine, and when the user returns to the site, the server can request any cookies previously stored *by that server only* to see information from previous visits. Cookies can store information on which pages were viewed and when, or any information the user entered, such as username, password, age, sex, and so on, or simply contain an identification code that can be used to match the user to records stored in a database. Based on the information stored in the cookies or in its databases, the site may then deliver a page customized to the user.

Basic HTML is not sophisticated enough for a Web site to execute programs on a user's computer, so a common language for doing this was developed in a language known as **Java.** The Java language is run by a special program built into most browsers called the *Java virtual machine (JVM).* When the program is executed on the user's machine, the JVM is designed to protect the computer from harmful or malicious programs. However, hackers have found ways to permeate the protection of the JVM, and Java can be used to capture additional information about a user and transmit it to a server. Users can protect themselves by disabling Java. Chapters 8 and 11 on privacy and security will explain how this technology applies to e-commerce.

When a Web page is viewed, a copy is held in a temporary storage space on the user's hard drive called the **cache.** The browser will overwrite the oldest file in the cache each time a new page is loaded, but because users return to the same pages often, those pages are kept in the cache and not routinely deleted. This allows anyone with access to the user's computer a robust view of the recent browsing patterns of the user. Users can protect themselves by cleaning out their caches periodically.

Business Systems Security

Like users worried about the capture of sensitive data, companies hosting Web sites often want their sites to integrate with some systems in the firm while protecting other systems from unauthorized access from the Internet. To control access to these systems, **firewalls** are used. A firewall is a computer program that limits the access to other computers based on a variety

http://
www.isoc.org

http://
www.ietf.org

Ping of Death

The Internet Communications Management Protocol (ICMP) was developed to ease the diagnosis of network problems. ICMP provides a command called *Ping* to determine the speed of a connection to another machine on the Internet. A small packet is sent from one machine to another and then returned. The time of the travel is calculated. One way service was denied to machines was by sending much larger packets, called a *Ping of Death*.

of rules and techniques, including IP address, passwords, time of day, and type of request. Some Internet access is limited by filtering technology that prevents access of inappropriate material for minors or employees.

Risks come not only from exposure of the computer itself, but also during transmission. Since packets pass through myriad sites during transmission, they can be intercepted; therefore, encryption is used to prevent unauthorized access to the contents of sensitive packets. There are two types of encryption schemes commonly used: **private key** and **public key.** Private key is the simpler scheme. Messages are encrypted using a key known only to the communicating parties. Assuming the key is kept secure, the message is known to be authentic, because only someone with the key could have locked up the message.

Public key encryption avoids the cumbersome problems of private key encryption. With public key encryption, each party creates a pair of keys, one public and one private. The private key is never released, but the public key is distributed to anyone with a need for it. A good analogy is a night deposit slot at a bank. The bank builds a safe at the bottom of a chute. At the top of the chute is a locked door. Customers needing to make after-hours deposits are given a *public* key to the chute so they can securely deposit money, because only the bank has the *private* key to the safe. See Chapter 11 on security for a discussion of how this technology applies to cyberlaw.

Public/private key pairs can also prevent **spoofing,** where sites are set up to appear similar to other sites. One common method of spoofing is using common misspellings. For instance, Amazon.com is such a popular site that another site at www.*amazom*.com receives many hits due to misspelling.

There are a number of vulnerabilities throughout the Internet, in addition to the interception of transmissions and rogue Java programs. **Denial of service attacks** involve overloading a server to keep other users from gaining access. Viruses can be transmitted as attachments to e-mail, or embedded in files. Passwords can be stolen or guessed, allowing unauthorized access. Once hackers have entered a system, they may simply "look around," or vandalize the server, or make subtle changes in programs on the server that may not be detected by system administrators. The changes could be for amusement or financial gain.

Business Uses of Internet Technologies

The Internet can be used within an organization, such as a corporation, government agency, or university, in which case it is called an **intranet.** Sometimes companies open up their systems to a limited number of customers, suppliers or other business partners. This limited access is called an **extranet.** *Virtual Private Networks* use the public Internet, but secure it so that it behaves like a private network. **File transfer protocol (FTP)** is used to move files from one computer to another. FTP sites are often used for the transfer and exchange of pirated software or other electronic content (video, audio, etc.) on sites called *warez.* These sites are shut down by the hosting ISPs when they are located, and often last only a few hours. *Internet relay chat (IRC)* is a means of communicating via the Internet in real time. *Videoconferencing* is becoming increasingly popular on the Internet, requiring a camera and some additional software.

The predominant use of the Internet is electronic mail. There are many potential pitfalls for e-mail. E-mail addresses can be spoofed or made to look similar to more formal addresses. One pitfall is unsolicited commercial e-mail, often referred to as *spam.* Such messages clog e-mail systems and individual e-mailboxes; e-mail servers can also be overloaded by sheer volume of messages, a process known as *flooding.* E-mail addresses are harvested from a number of sources, including mailing lists and bulletin board systems. Email has been used to send vitriolic messages to individuals and firms, called *flames.*

Because businesses have begun to rely on e-mail as a way to conduct business, e-mail messages are routinely stored as a backup measure. This allows the company to easily retrieve all messages to or from a specific e-mail account.

Globalization

Much of the growth of the Internet in the late 1990s was outside the United States, and by 2000 most estimates showed that more than half of all Internet users were outside the United States. While web sites remain predominantly in English, sites in other languages are rapidly increasing in number. The world does grow smaller as the global use of the Internet and World Wide Web increases.

The legal concerns that affect us domestically are the same concerns that affect our use of the Internet internationally. Issues regarding privacy, security, jurisdiction, trademarks, and commerce are all affected by our expanding use of computers to communicate, collaborate, and trade. See Chapter 13 for a detailed discussion of international cyberlaw.

Law and Cyberspace

Some issues of privacy and security have been mentioned, but there are many other issues with which individuals and businesses must be familiar when using the Internet and the World Wide Web. Many potential legal issues may arise while doing commerce on the Internet. For example, do users approve of the insertion of anything into their computers without their knowledge and consent? Are cookies legal? Can sales made on the Internet be taxed? What constitutes defamation on the Internet? Is Web content protected by copyright laws, or can it be considered public domain information? How can laws related to the Internet be enforced? This book will answer some of these questions and others, and possibly raise even more.

Chapter 1 provides this introduction to cyberlaw, then moves on to jurisdiction in the next chapter. Because the legal environment of electronic commerce has no geographical boundaries, it must be determined who will have legal authority to hear cases in the event of a legal dispute.

Chapters 3 and 4 cover the intellectual property issues of trademarks and copyrights. Copyrights protect the creative content of Web pages, and trademark disputes are among the most common types of litigation involving the online environment.

Chapters 5, 6, and 7 discuss legal issues dealing with doing commerce on the Internet: online contracting, taxation, and online securities offerings. Laws that govern the making and enforcement of contracts and the legal remedies that are available in the event of a breach are covered, especially those aspects that most affect e-commerce. Sales and use tax on e-commerce is considered the most critical tax controversy confronting a Web-based business, as vendor companies face sales tax liability for failure to collect and remit sales tax on out-of-state sales. Finally, online securities are covered. These transactions traditionally conducted by investment banks and brokerage firms are now also conducted electronically. Although the same laws govern Internet transactions, adjustments to the traditional regulatory framework have had to be made.

Chapters 8, 9, 10, 11, and 12 discuss the social side of legal issues relating to the Internet. Topics include privacy, obscenity, defamation, Internet security, and computer crime. Laws exist currently that cover these issues, but adjustments must be made to these regulations in the unique environment of the Internet.

Finally, Chapter 13 covers the implications of international use of the Internet for commerce. It examines the organizations that regulate cyberspace internationally, the jurisdiction of national governments over electronic commerce and communications, and the national laws and international treaties that define and regulate cyber-commerce and communications.

Summary

This chapter reviews the history of the Internet as it applies to its current structure. The Internet's open, consensus-driven, academic roots clearly influenced the current configuration, creating challenges for commerce and law. The technology of the Internet and the Web are explained to clarify the basis of legal issues discussed throughout the book. The nature and extent of security issues are described, establishing that security is possible on the Internet, but not the default. Finally, the scope of business use on the Internet is described to establish the context for the myriad legal issues raised.

Manager's Checklist

- Determine what transmissions need to be protected from interception and alteration, and implement appropriate security measures.
- Weigh the benefits of customization using cookies and other technologies against possible perceptions of invasion of privacy.
- Balance the use of advanced technologies with security risks.
- Monitor the Internet to see if anyone is spoofing your site. This will require searching for your company on search engines and examining the results for impostors.
- Once you implement a Web site, your company becomes accessible globally. Determine the extent to which you will serve customers outside your country and prepare for the required compliance.

2

Jurisdiction

"[W]e realize that attempting to apply . . . law in the fast-developing world of the Internet is somewhat like trying to board a moving bus."
—*Judge Van Graafeiland in Bensusan Restaurant Corporation v. King*

Introduction

Did you ever think that launching an e-business could mean defending a lawsuit in any state or country where the end user resides? For example, your California Web company could be doing business with customers in Florida or in India. If a user is deprived of a legal right in the user's state, the user may be able to sue you in that state or foreign country if a court has jurisdiction over your company.

Once a company creates a Web site it has a continuous online presence in every state and foreign country where an end user can access the Internet. Internet technology continues to pose a threat to the jurisdictional importance of state and national borders. Of great concern to an e-business is the daunting possibility of being sued by a consumer or other aggrieved party in a remote state or foreign country. In the United States an e-business merchant may be required to defend a lawsuit in a foreign jurisdiction only if the court has **personal jurisdiction** over the e-business defendant. Personal jurisdiction is the court's authority and power to make the defendant obey a court order. E-business transactions transcend geographical boundaries and instantly reach global marketplaces formerly unavailable to most merchants.

E-commerce introduces the novel business arrangement of establishing an electronic presence outside its local jurisdiction. But the expanded market opportunities come with strings: "doing business" in other states or countries might make the e-business accountable to those regions' laws. A legally aggrieved plaintiff user in an on-line transaction may file a lawsuit anywhere in the world where the business violation occurred. In contrast to a mail order catalog company, which chooses the locations of its potential customers, an e-business does not choose its customers. They are wherever Web access is, and they bring their local laws with them.

Jurisdiction is the authority of a court to hear a case and resolve a dispute. Because the legal environment of e-commerce has no geographical boundaries, it establishes immediate long-distance communications with anyone who can access the Web site. Usually an online e-merchant has no way of knowing exactly where the information on its site is being accessed. Hence, jurisdiction issues are of primary importance in cyberspace. Engaging in e-commerce on the World Wide Web may expose the company to the risk of being sued in any state or foreign country where an Internet user can establish a legal claim. Legal counsel and insurance underwriters should carefully review this potential risk and its accompanying cost to the business. In each case, a determination should be made as to whether an online presence will subject the e-business to jurisdiction in a distant state or a foreign company.

When trial lawyers represent online clients who are being sued in a foreign court, they will always consider having the case litigated in the jurisdiction where their client's primary business is located rather than the plaintiff's state or country. Although the case could be litigated in a state court, it will more commonly be a federal court because cyberspace issues often involve federal statutes (e.g., copyright and/or trademark law) or diversity jurisdiction (i.e., a plaintiff from one state suing an e-business defendant from another state with damages of $75,000 or more).

This *home court advantage* is important for several reasons:

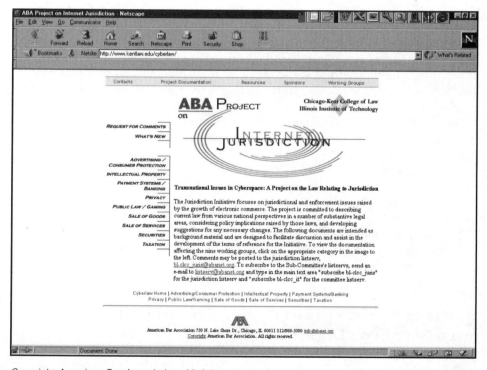

1. Local law will apply. This may be state law and or the federal law of that particular judicial circuit (see Figure 2.1).
2. A local law firm's attorneys will not have to travel to another jurisdiction for depositions and other kinds of pretrial discovery given by its client.
3. It will not be necessary to hire attorneys from another state to file pleadings and so on.
4. If the case is tried in the client's home region, the jury may be familiar with and sympathetic to the e-business.
5. The trial lawyer will be familiar with the local judges and their decisions. One could say there is a legal "comfort zone" in trying a case in a local court.

Keep in mind that jurisdiction does *not* resolve the issue of liability, but only the issue of the court where the case will be tried. The issues addressed by personal jurisdiction over a nonresident e-business defendant are discussed in this chapter. Succeeding chapters in this text will illustrate the vast liability exposure of electronic commerce in general.

Traditional Principles of Jurisdiction

Common law principles of personal jurisdiction have evolved by judge's opinions in their case decisions long before the online world existed. The cases that created our traditional principles of personal jurisdiction will be applied to e-commerce. When a nonresident e-business defendant raises the issues of lack of personal jurisdiction by a motion to dismiss, the plaintiffs must generally prove satisfaction of *both* the local state's long-arm statute and the due process clause of the U.S. Constitution (see Figure 2.2).

Since e-commerce on the Internet reaches unknown marketplaces, the aggrieved end user may file a lawsuit in any state (or country) where the court has personal jurisdiction over the nonresident defendant. Keep in mind that the term **personal jurisdiction** includes a "person" doing business as a sole proprietor, corporation, partnership, or other form of business organization. Since most e-businesses are corporations, a foreign court must have personal jurisdiction over it if challenged by a motion to dismiss.

Later in this chapter we discuss suggested legal safeguards to protect against lawsuits in a foreign jurisdiction. They should be included in every e-business's terms of use that commonly appear at the end of the Web site's home page.

State Long-Arm Statutes and Personal Jurisdiction over a Nonresident Defendant

Jurisdiction over a nonresident e-business is based on the local state **long-arm statute.** The metaphor of a *long arm* is useful if you think of a local state with a long

Figure 2.1

The Thirteen Federal Judicial Circuits

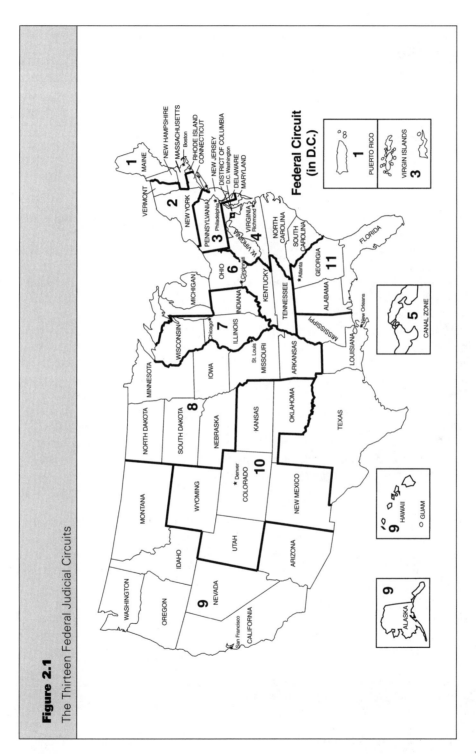

Figure 2.2

Plaintiff's Burden of Proof for Personal Jurisdiction

Personal jurisdiction over a nonresident e-business = Long-arm statute + Due process clause

arm reaching out to grab a nonresident e-business and bring it into the state to account to the plaintiff for its illegal acts.

State long-arm statutes authorize the courts to claim personal jurisdiction over a nonresident defendant whose principal business is outside the state. Although long-arm statutes differ from state to state, all have one thing in common: they establish personal jurisdiction over a nonresident defendant based on business transactions or torts committed *within* the state.

Always keep in mind that the statutory requirements of the long-arm statutes vary. Some state long-arm statutes assert jurisdiction over nonresident defendants who transact business, commit torts, or own or use property within the state. Other states (e.g., California, Oklahoma, Rhode Island, and Wyoming) simply assert jurisdiction if it is reasonable to do so, consistent with the due process clause of either the Fourteenth Amendment (if a state claim) or the Fifth Amendment (if a federal claim), as will be discussed.

Once the court is satisfied that the facts of the case apply to the long-arm statute over the nonresident e-business defendant, it must then determine if the facts comply with the requisites of the due process clause.

A 1985 U.S. Supreme Court case *Burger King Corp. v. Rudzewick* stated that when nonresident defendants reach out beyond one state and create continuing relationships with the citizens of other states, they are subject to regulations in that state and sanctions for the consequences of their actions. This case, and others to be discussed in this chapter, laid the groundwork for personal jurisdiction over a nonresident e-business resulting from electronic transactions that create continuing business relationships with citizens of other states.

Think of driving an automobile through different states. Imagine telling a traffic cop that stopped you for speeding, "That's not the speed limit where I live!" An online company doing business in foreign states (e.g., e.Bay) could be subject to the laws where the customers reside. An e-business could be accountable to its customers under the laws in all fifty states and numerous countries. This chapter will explain how to limit that vast jurisdictional exposure with a **forum-selection clause** in its **terms of use** displayed on its Web site.

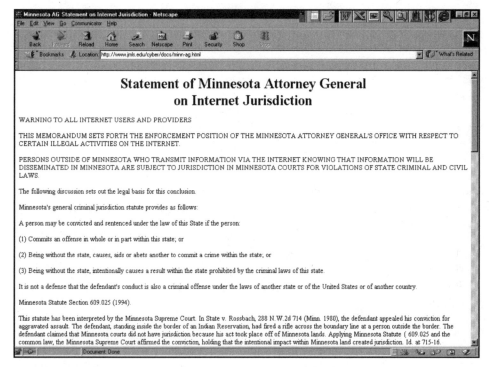

Application of the Due Process Clause over a Nonresident Defendant

A court is limited in exercising its powers over a nonresident defendant by the due process clause of the Fifth and Fourteenth Amendments to the United States Constitution.

The due process clause of the Fifth Amendment to the U.S. Constitution, which applies to the federal government, provides in part that ". . . no person shall be deprived of life, liberty, or property, without due process of law." The due process clause of the Fourteenth Amendment provides that " . . . no state shall . . . deprive any person of life, liberty, or property, without due process of the law." For a court to render a judgment (i.e., monetary damages) against a nonresident e-business defendant and thereby deprive that company of a property interest, it must do so within our traditional notions of due process. This property interest is the amount of money stated in the judgment issued by the court that an e-business owes the plaintiff. However, due process is not defined in the U.S. Constitution. Its meaning has been shaped by U.S. Supreme Court decisions.

In 1980, the U.S. Supreme Court in *World Wide Volkswagen Corp. v. Woodson*, 444 US 286, stated, "The due process clause of the Fourteenth Amendment limits the power of a state court to render a valid personal judgment against a nonresident defendant . . . We have never accepted the proposition that state lines are irrelevant for jurisdiction purposes . . . The states retain sovereign power to try cases in their courts."

An e-business, without geographical boundaries, remains subject to this pre-Internet constitutional principle of limiting a court's ability to reach across state lines. Remember, the nonresident e-business defendant has the constitutional right to due process before another court can assume personal jurisdiction over its company. Think of due process as a federal constitutional right that an e-business has before it is subject to a foreign court's jurisdiction.

Due process as it relates to personal jurisdiction is a constitutional requirement based on two criteria:

1. The nonresident e-business defendant had sufficient *minimum contacts* in the forum state where the case is being tried.
2. Jurisdiction in that court will not offend *traditional notions of fair play and substantial justice*.

These federal constitutional principles will be discussed throughout this chapter. However, it is useful to briefly explain minimum contacts before we look at the cases.

A nonresident defendant must purposely avail itself of the benefits of the state's economic market to establish **minimum contacts.** The court may exercise personal jurisdiction under the due process clause when the business transaction was such that a defendant's conduct and connection with a forum state are such that he should reasonably anticipate being hauled into court. This makes personal jurisdiction reasonably foreseeable by the defendant who elected to do business in the foreign state.

In *Burger King Corporation v. Rudzewicz*, 471 US 462 (1985), the U.S. Supreme Court has stated,

> If a foreign corporation purposely avails itself of the benefits of an economic market in the forum state, it may subject itself to the state's *in personam* jurisdiction even if it has no physical presence in the state. The substantial connection between the foreign defendant and the court necessary for a finding of minimum contacts must come about by an action *purposely directed* toward the forum state. The mere act of using interstate commerce does not of itself constitute a purposely directed act.

Keep this rule in mind as you think about e-business in cyberspace. Although a physical presence is not necessary for the court to find personal jurisdiction over a nonresident company, simply going online and "using interstate commerce" may be insufficient to establish personal jurisdiction. (See *Bensusan Restaurant Corporation v. King*, discussed later in the chapter.)

Figure 2.3

Motion to Dismiss for Lack of Personal Jurisdiction over a Nonresident Defendant

---

PLAINTIFF'S BURDEN OF PROOF WHEN DEFENDANT FILES A PRETRIAL MOTION TO DISMISS
FOR LACK OF PERSONAL JURISDICTION OVER A NONRESIDENT DEFENDANT

(P) End User	v.	(D) E-Business
P must prove: (1) The local state "long-arm statute" applies *and* (2) There is no violation of D's due process rights under the Constitution.		D files and argues a motion to dismiss for lack of personal jurisdiction.

Motion to Dismiss for Lack of Personal Jurisdiction over a Nonresident Defendant

The nonresident e-business defendant's lawyer will generally bring a pretrial **motion to dismiss** the case for lack of personal jurisdiction and attempt to have the case tried in the state where the e-business is headquartered. The lawyer will argue that the local state's long-arm statute does not apply to the facts of the case and that the due process clause will be violated if the case is tried in a foreign court (see Figure 2.3).

Judicial History of Personal Jurisdiction

Constitutional Framework for Due Process under the *International Shoe Company* Case

The judicial pre-online history of personal jurisdiction over a nonresident defendant has its origin in an 1878 U.S. Supreme Court case, *Pennoyer v. Neff*, 95 US 714. The Court, in order to establish personal jurisdiction over the nonresident defendant, required the defendant's physical presence in the state where the court was located. Before a court had personal jurisdiction over a nonresident defendant, the defendant had to be served a summons and complaint by a sheriff while physically present in that state. So after 1878, a nonresident defendant just remained out of the state to avoid being sued.

Of course one can easily see the impracticality of that rule as interstate commerce and communications developed. In 1945, the U.S. Supreme Court decided the landmark *International Shoe Company v. Washington State*, 326 US 310, 66 Ct. 154 case. The defendant, International Shoe Company, had its principal office in Missouri but transacted business in the state of Washington, where it took orders for shoes. It did not own an office, warehouse, or any property in Washington; its employees merely took orders on shoes where only one shoe was displayed—hence, the argument of no inventory in the state of Washington. The purchase orders were accepted in Missouri, where the shoes were shipped to customers in Washington.

When the state of Washington sought to collect unemployment taxes from the corporation, International Shoe argued the Washington court had no personal jurisdiction over it because it had no physical presence in the state. The court found that the business activities in the state of Washington established "sufficient contacts or ties with the state of the form to make it reasonable and just according to our traditional concepts of fair play and substantial justice to permit the state to enforce the obligations that incurred there."

Note that the court found personal jurisdiction even though the defendant had no physical presence in the state of Washington. This concept of doing business in a state without a physical presence will become important as the courts begin to analyze e-commerce engaging in electronic interstate activity without a physical presence.

At the time this case was decided, there were no state long-arm statutes. Hence, the U.S. Supreme Court in the *International Shoe Co.* case had to build its legal argument of finding personal jurisdiction over the nonresident defendant on constitutional fairness under the due process clause of the Fourteenth Amendment because the case involved the state's claim for taxation.

Two-Pronged Analysis for Finding Personal Jurisdiction in the International Shoe Company Case

The Supreme Court in the *International Shoe Company* case in finding due process considered the many business minimum contacts the shoe company had in the state of Washington. In deciding for the State of Washington, it found no violation of traditional notions of fair play and substantial justice. To prove minimum contacts, the plaintiff must persuade the court that the nonresident defendant purposefully availed itself of the privilege of doing business in the marketplace of the forum state. Both minimum contacts and traditional notions of fair play and substantial justice must be satisfied to find personal jurisdiction.

In cyberspace this would require more than a casual online presence. The defendant's e-business must have actively solicited business in the plaintiff's state. In addition, the exercise of personal jurisdiction over a nonresident defendant must be reasonable and not unfairly inconvenient to the defendant to travel to the foreign state where the case will be tried.

Since International Shoe used the state of Washington to sell shoes and developed substantial income from those transactions, it met the minimum contacts requirement. The traditional notions of fairness and substantial justice were not violated within that context so long as jurisdiction in the state of Washington was reasonable.

After the *International Shoe Company* decision allowing states to tax nonresident businesses that carried on substantial business within the state, various state legislatures seeking taxes from out-of-state businesses passed long-arm statutes that subjected out-of-state defendants to its jurisdiction whenever they do business within their state.

Personal Jurisdiction in the Online Environment

We have discussed personal jurisdiction as it applies to a traditional brick-and-mortar business, but the rules are also relevant to the online environment. When an e-business establishes and maintains a Web site and engages in electronic commerce, it is entitled to the protection of the U.S. Constitution, the State Constitution, and the local law where the company is located. Any person, including a distant user, who accesses the company's Web site is entitled to the same legal protection.

In *World Wide Volkswagen v. Woodson*, 444 US 286, the U.S. Supreme Court held that merely placing a product in interstate commerce does not of itself "purposefully avail oneself" to a forum state's jurisdiction. What is required is "additional conduct," defined as an intent to serve the market in the forum state.

In the following online trademark infringement case, a Massachusetts company (Digital) sued a California corporation (AltaVista Technology) in the Federal District Court in Massachusetts. The California e-business defendant argued a *motion to dismiss for lack of personal jurisdiction* that was denied in the Federal District Court because Digital's online search service satisfied the personal jurisdiction tests.

Notice how the plaintiff Massachusetts company, Digital, had to convince the court that the Massachusetts long-arm statute was satisfied because the California company, AltaVista, transacted business in Massachusetts. In addition, it had to prove that there would be no violation of the due process clause because of AltaVista's minimum contacts in Massachusetts.

Digital Equipment Corporation v. AltaVista Technology, Inc., 960 F. Supp. 456 (D. Mass. 1997) involved a trademark infringement case. The case was based on the theory that Digital, a Massachusetts corporation, contracted with Alta Vista Technology, a California company, that changed its corporate name to Alta Vista Corporation, not to use its trademark "AltaVista" in a product or serviced offering. Digital paid AltaVista for all rights to the trademark other than AltaVista Technology's right to use the trademark, as part of its corporate name and address. Less than two months after the contract was signed, Alta Vista Technology's Website used the trademark "AltaVista" at the top of its home page and later added banner ads. The California defendant, Alta Vista Technology, brought a motion to dismiss the case from the Massachusetts federal court for lack of personal jurisdiction. The court denied the motion and found jurisdiction since the Massachusetts long-arm statute was satisfied because there was evidence of AltaVista Technology doing business in Massachusetts based on its solicitations for banner ads.

This case has special significance to the e-business community because it involves a trademark licensing agreement between a company that owned a common law trademark, Alta Vista, and a company that wanted to use that trademark and was willing to pay a great deal of money to do so.

---

http://

See

www.altavista.com

and under its "Terms of Use" click on "Miscellaneous" for its choice of law clause and see under its "About Alta Vista" the information "where the name came from" is an interesting history of the AltaVista trademark

---

A trademark search may reveal that another company is using your mark. It may be worthwhile to explore the possibility of entering into an agreement allowing the company to continue using the trademark for its name and address but not for online purposes.

Passive Web Sites versus Interactive Web Sites

National or worldwide personal jurisdiction over a nonresident e-business does not automatically follow developing a Web site and going online with a service or product. A **passive Web site** that merely transmits information and does not solicit business will generally not incur personal jurisdiction in a foreign state or country. Consider the number of professional Web sites that merely advertise an accounting or legal service. Students often have a passive Web site that displays a resume and other information and does not solicit business. An **interactive Website** *does* solicit business. Table 2.1 highlights the differences between nonactive and interactive Web Sites.

The following case involved a Web site that was essentially informational. Although it did solicit some business in its own state of Missouri, it was not solicit-

Table 2.1

Personal Jurisdiction Analysis Based on Nature of the Web site

Passive Web site	Interactive Web site
• Provides only information • Does not solicit business • Is not usually subject to personal jurisdiction in a foreign country or state	• Provides information for users to make purchasing decisions • Actively solicits business • May be subject to personal jurisdiction in a foreign country or state

ing business in New York, and hence the court refused to find personal jurisdiction. Maintaining a passive Web site that posted information about its business was not enough to confer out-of-state personal jurisdiction.

Bensusan Restaurant Corporation v. King, 126 F.3d 25 (2d. Cir. 1997) is a leading jurisdiction case involving a trademark displayed on a Web site used by another company. Mr. King owned a cabaret in Missouri that used the name "The Blue Note" before the well-known New York jazz club used the same name. The New York club later federally registered the trademark, "The Blue Note". After the Missouri club refused to stop using the trade name on its Web site, this case was brought by the New York jazz club alleging, among other claims, trademark infringement. The defendant brought a motion to dismiss the case for lack of personal jurisdiction. The New York federal court allowed the motion and dismissed the case because the New York long-arm statute was not satisfied. The statute requires the tortious act of trademark infringement be committed within the state of New York. In this case the acts relevant to the law suit were performed by persons physically present in Missouri, namely the development of the Missouri Web site, use of the words "Blue Note" and the "The Blue Note" logo. Although Bensusan suffered injury in New York the alleged wrongful acts were not committed in New York.

This case illustrates the importance of the state's long-arm statute. A court in another state applying it's version of the applicable long-arm statute may come to a different conclusion.

http://
See
www.thebluenote.com
and view the logo of the Missouri club and compare it with the New York club's logo at www.bluenote.net

Note how the next leading case involving jurisdiction and electronic commerce illustrates that the "additional activity" requirement under the due process clause is satisfied by an e-commerce transaction where the defendant "purposefully availed" himself to the forum state law. Although "minimum contacts" were electronic in nature, they were sufficient to satisfy the due process clause. Be aware of how the court's analysis follows the "purposeful availment" requirement of the previously discussed off-line situation of *Burger King Corporation v. Rudzewicz.*

In *CompuServe v. Patterson,* 89 F. 3d 1257 (6th Cir. 1996) the federal court of appeals in Ohio reversed the district court's dismissal for lack of personal jurisdiction over the defendant. Mr. Patterson, a Texas attorney and software developer, signed a shareware agreement with CompServe, an Ohio corporation, to sell his software on its service. Mr. Patterson claimed he never was in Ohio and never did business in that state. The shareware agreement contained a law selection clause that stated Ohio law would govern any dispute under the contract. Patterson developed a software program that helped people navigate around the Internet. Shortly thereafter CompuServe marketed a similar product with a trademark "FlashPoint Windows Navigator" that Patterson claimed infringed his business name of "Flash-Point Development". CompuServe brought suit in Ohio asking the court to decide it had not infringed any common law trademark that Patterson might have owned. Patterson then brought a motion to dismiss for lack of personal jurisdiction that the federal district allowed. On appeal the court found personal jurisdiction based on the software contract's provision that Ohio law would apply. It also applied the analysis for personal jurisdiction based on the purposeful availment requirement that Patterson took actions that created connections with the state of Ohio and that he sold his software only to the Ohio company.

This case has special importance because the entire transaction took place over the Internet. The software agreement and Paterson's software were both sent electronically. An electronic presence is sufficient to establish a presence for doing business in a foreign state. The decision was not based on how much money was generated from the business arrangement or how many customers Patterson had in Ohio.

http://
See
www.compuserve.com
and under "Legal Notices" at the bottom of the page see the exclusive jurisdiction clause where all disputes will be governed by the state and federal courts of Ohio.

A clear analysis of online jurisdiction appears in the trial court's decision of *Zippo Mfg. Co. v. Zippo Dot Com, Inc.,* 952 F. Supp.1119 (1997). Zippo is the Pennsylvania-based manufacturer of Zippo lighters. It sued a California Internet news service for trademark infringement based on the defendant's use of the domain name "zippo.com." In finding jurisdiction over the nonresident California defendant, the court articulated a sliding-scale standard used in deciding subsequent e-business decisions that relates jurisdiction to the amount and type of online commercial activity. The court stated:

> The likelihood that personal jurisdiction can be constitutionally exercised is directly proportionate to the nature and quality of commercial activity that an entity conducts over the Internet. . . . At one end of the spectrum are situations where a defendant clearly does business over the Internet. If the defendant enters into contracts with residents of a foreign jurisdiction that involve the knowing and repeated transmissions of computer files over the Internet, personal jurisdiction is proper (e.g., *Compuserve, Inc. v. Patterson,* 89 F. 2d 1257, 6th Cir. 1996). At the opposite end are situations where a defendant has simply posted information on an Internet Web site that is accessible to users in foreign jurisdictions. A passive Web site that does little more than make information available to those who are interested in it is not grounds for the exercise of personal jurisdiction (e.g. *Bensusan Restaurant Corp., v. King,* 937 F. Supp. 296 S.D.N.Y. 1996). The middle ground is occupied by interactive Web sites where a user can exchange information with the host computer. In these cases, the exercise of jurisdiction is determined by examining the level of interactivity and commercial nature of the exchange of information that occurs on the Web site.

This sliding-scale standard is useful in illustrating that having only an electronic presence in a foreign state is insufficient to establish personal jurisdiction over an e-business (see Table 2.2).

For instance, an online consulting company's informational site that posts a newsletter free of charge and does not solicit business is not commercial activity and will not subject the owner to out-of-state jurisdiction. Remember that if there are grounds for a lawsuit, and there is no personal jurisdiction over the nonresident e-business, the case could be tried in the company's state. Lack of jurisdiction does not mean there is no liability.

A nonresident interactive e-business that solicits online business in a foreign state will be subject to its jurisdiction. Online cases that appear to fall between passive and interactive transactions are based on a perceived level of commercial activity. As the courts attempt to quantify the amount of Internet business, they appear to assert jurisdiction over a nonresident online defendant when the amount of commercial activity is high.

Each case is "fact sensitive" and requires a careful analysis to determine jurisdiction. Some of the uncertainty over jurisdiction can be resolved by the appropriate use of forum selection clauses.

Table 2.2

Sliding-scale Analysis of Personal Jurisdiction

Interactive e-business	Mixed Web site	Passive (informational)
Personal jurisdiction	Jurisdiction depends on the degree of interactivity	No personal jurisdiction

Forum Selection Clause

Most Web sites include at the bottom of their home pages their *terms of use,* which include a **forum selection clause** in the event that a lawsuit is brought against the online company.

It is important to note that not all courts will automatically follow the forum selection clause that requests to have the case litigated in a particular state and court. Since the forum selection clause is a unilateral, nonnegotiable jurisdiction clause, it is legally referred to as an **adhesion contract.** Such contracts are legal providing they are "reasonable" and "fair."

The U.S. Supreme Court in *Burger King v. Rudzewicz,* 471 US 462, 472 n. 14, 105 S. Ct. 2174 (1985) has stated that because a person can consent to personal jurisdiction, such clauses are in general valid and enforceable. However, in *The Bremen v. Zapata Off-Shore Co.,* 407 US 1, 92 S. Ct. 1907 (1972) the Supreme Court stated that these clauses must be "freely negotiated" and not "unreasonably unjust." One could question whether an electronic click to a Web site, with its terms of use buried at the end of the home page, satisfies that requirement.

http://

For an example of a forum selection clause, click on "Terms of Use" at
www.sidewalk.com

Cyberethics

Is it ethical that a user be legally bound by the terms of use (e.g., forum selection clause) that appear at the bottom of a home page and that are seldom read or understood?

However, the national trend follows a Massachusetts case, *Jacobson v. Mailboxes, Etc. U.S.A., Inc.* 419 Mass. 572 (1995). The court found that the unilateral and nonbargaining nature of a forum selection clause, accompanied by its undue inconvenience over the plaintiff litigating the claim in the defendant's state, argues in favor of the clause being unenforceable as an unfair and unreasonable adhesion contract.

Terms of use generally appear in small print at the end of the Web merchant's home page and consist of boilerplate (i.e., standard legalese) provisions. A typical clause may state " . . . *the parties agree that a condition of using this site is that any and all claims arising out of use of this site will be tried in Massachusetts and Massachusetts law will apply.*" The court in *Jacobson* held the "overreaching must be based on something more than the mere fact that the forum selection clause was a boilerplate provision on the back of the form." Since most major online companies are using forum selection clauses on their Web sites and it has become a trade practice to do so, it appears that the clauses will be enforced if they are drafted in a way that is fair and reasonable.

International Jurisdiction in Cyberspace

Online Web sites are electronically carried to international users. A transaction may require an e-business plaintiff to litigate in the United States against a defendant in a foreign country or be a defendant in a foreign country. An e-business should be aware of the possibility of being sued by litigants from a foreign country. Web sites that have a drag-down list of foreign countries where a customer may wish to purchase their products or services are inviting litigation in that country.

> **http://**
> A site that shows an example of a drag-down list to subscribe in foreign countries is at
> **www.NationalEnquirer.com**

Principles of international law apply to electronic commerce and generally permit a country to regulate only those activities that have a *substantial effect* in their country. The United States, Canada, and the European Union (EU) are working on universal laws that will be transnational and predictable to an e-commerce transaction. The EU is developing a "country of origin" principle that would apply the law of the country where the contract originated. For example, a United States law would apply to a contract dispute with an EU member if the e-commerce transaction originated in the United States. In opposition to the "country of origin" principle is the "country of reception" rule that would allow consumer end users to have the benefit of their country's own consumer protection laws. This principle would apply only to a consumer transaction and not to a business-to-business e-commerce contract.

Global solutions to international e-commerce transactions will depend on the revisions and developments of international laws to accommodate the Internet. Global organizations such as the United Nations Commission on International Law, the World Trade Organization, and the Organization of Economic Cooperation and Development are all working in this direction. See Chapter 13, Global Issues, for a detailed analysis of International Jurisdiction.

Summary

It should be comforting to the owners of both e-business startups and legacy companies with an e-business that they have constitutional rights that will protect them from a foreign court's jurisdiction. Under the *due process clause,* before an out-of-state court has jurisdiction over an e-business, the company must have purposefully directed its sales to the marketplace of the foreign state.

Pre-Internet cases have established the ground rules for personal jurisdiction in cyberspace. The U.S. Supreme Court as early as 1945 in the *International Shoe Company* case held that a *physical presence* was *not* required for a nonresident defendant to be subject to the court's jurisdiction so long as the due process clause was satisfied.

This decision, and subsequent cases that require compliance with *both* the state's long-arm statute and the due process clause, created a legal foundation for personal jurisdiction over a nonresident e-business with only an *electronic presence* in a state to be accountable to a foreign court.

Potentially, every dot.com business is subject to jurisdiction all over the country. As long as the state's long-arm statute and the due process clause of the U.S. Constitution are satisfied, the nonresident e-business must have the case tried in the foreign state.

The solution to this global jurisdictional exposure is for the e-business lawyer to draft a *forum selection clause* that appears on the dot.com's home page in its terms of use. The company should also consider limiting the product or services on the Web site to certain states and countries. Failure to take these precautions could lead to costly litigation in distant jurisdictions.

Manager's Checklist

- Be aware that an interactive Web site that solicits business worldwide may subject the company to personal jurisdiction in any state or country.
- Consider the use of technology that counts the Web site "hits" and have it audited by a CPA firm to document the number of sales in the foreign state or country. This may be useful in proving that the site does little or no business in the state where the plaintiff is bringing the lawsuit.
- Consider using a technological "filter" that prevents the Web site from being seen in certain states or countries where you do not want to do business. This will limit your liability exposure to those states and countries where you are soliciting business.
- Include a forum selection clause in the Web site as a condition of doing business with the company. The clause states: "In the event of a dispute, the laws of the state of . . . will govern and the case will be tried in that state." Be aware that not all state or federal courts will be obliged to follow that requirement.
- Review insurance contracts to ensure that you can cover the additional costs of defending lawsuits in remote jurisdictions.
- Consider disclaimers in the Web site's terms of use regarding not doing business in selected states and/or countries.

Additional Readings

- Kalow, Gwenn M. *From the Internet to Court: Exercising Jurisdiction Over World Wide Web Communications,* 65 Fordham Law Rev. 2241 (1997)

- Kurland, Philip B. *The Supreme Court, The Due Process Clause and the In Personam Jurisdiction of State Courts-From Pennoyer to Dencla: A Review,* 25 U. Chi. L. Rev. 569 (1958)

- Lessig, Lawrence. *Code and Other Laws of Cyberspace,* Chapter 14, "Sovereignty," New York, NY (Basic Books, 1999).

- Perchbacher, Rex R. *Minimum Contacts Reapplied: Mr. Justice Brennan Has It His Way in* Burger King Corp. v Rudzewicz, 1986 Ariz. St. L.J., 585 (1986)

PART 2

Intellectual Property Issues in Cyberspace

3

Trademarks

"Dozens of companies, including Taco Bell, MTV, Kentucky Fried Chicken and others have had to cajole, pay thousands of dollars or even sue to gain the rights to domain names that match trademarks that they have spent millions of dollars cultivating and protecting."
—"Miller, Cyber Squatters Give Carl's Jr., Others Net Loss"
Los Angeles Times, 1996, WL 11004750.

Introduction

Trademark disputes are among the most common types of litigation involving the online environment. As brick-and-mortar companies mutate into e-businesses and startups establish an online Web presence, they will select numerous domain names. A **domain name,** (e.g., www.ford.com) is merely a business address on the Internet. Domain names, discussed below, were designed for entirely different purposes than trademarks. This chapter will explain that difference and its consequent legal problems and how domain names and trademarks have acquired business value in cyberspace.

Most companies whose distinctive corporate tradename is a federally registered trademark with the **U.S. Patent and Trademark Office (PTO)** in Washington, D.C., will try to register the same name as their domain name with **Network Solutions, Inc. (NSI)** or its successor, the **Internet Corporation for Assigned Names and Numbers (ICANN),** or other certified domain name registrar.

NSI has been registering domain names since 1992 under an agreement with the National Science Foundation and the Department of Commerce. Prior to the creation of ICANN, it enjoyed a monopoly status and had registered more than six million Internet addresses. By agreement with the Department of Commerce, NSI has opened the registration of domain names to more than eighty international companies.

ICANN is a nonprofit public-benefit nongovernmental organization with an international board of directors. In 1998 ICANN was selected by the United States government to manage the domain name system. Its accredited registrars must agree to rules developed by ICANN such as the Uniform Domain Name Dispute Resolution Policy. In 1999 ICANN assumed management of the domain name system from

Network Solutions Inc. Its principle mission is to create new *top-level domain* (TLDs) names in addition to .com, .net, and .org (e.g., .firm, .info and .store). It has authorized eleven new independent companies as domain name registrars in different countries, including China, Singapore, Korea, Denmark, Sweden, and the United Kingdom. ICANN grew out of the U.S. government's decision to privatize the domain name system.

ICANN and its accredited registrars are responsible for the registration of second-level Internet domain names that appear with the top-level handle of .com, .org, .net, and .edu (*amazon* is an example of a second-level well-known domain name). They register the second-level name on a first-come, first-served basis and do not evaluate whether the second-level name infringes on the rights of a federally registered trade name owner. Hence, it is quite possible for a second-level domain name to be the same as, or deceptively similar to, a federally registered trade name. ICANN has authorized seven new top-level domain names to wit, .aero, .coop, .info, .museum, .none, .pro and .biz. See http://www.icann.org/tlds/. The new top-level domain names must be approved by The National Telecommunications Information Administration (NTIA) of the Department of Commerce. Only the NTIA can approve additions to the root file that will make the new top-level domain names available to the public.

The following trademark-infringement case was brought against NSI for allowing registration of domain names that were previously used by the plaintiffs who had similar federally registered trademarks with the PTO. In this case the court found no trademark infringement by NSI because it was only the registering agent for the domain names, not the user of the names.

In *Lockheed Martin Corp. v. Network Solutions, Inc.*, 985 F. Supp. 949 (Cal. 1997), the court held that NSI did not "use" the plaintiff's trademark as required for direct infringer liability, merely by registering the mark as a domain name. Since NSI had no unequivocal knowledge that the domain name was being used to infringe on the plaintiff's trademark, there was no contributory trademark infringement liability.

ICANN's domain name dispute policy between a famous trademark owner and the holder of the same or similar registered domain name has been established to resolve these conflicts, if possible, out of court. It accredited the National Arbitration Forum and Disputes.org to join the World Intellectual Property Organization (WIPO) as the dispute resolution service providers.

A computer user who knows the domain name will key in the URL (Universal Resource Locator) and view the company's Web site homepage. (See Chapter 1 for a technical explanation of the URL.) If the domain name is not known, the end user may use a search engine and type in a name or key word that will identify the company's Web site.

---

http://

www.icann.org/registrars/accreditation.htm
ICANN's Articles of Incorporation and bylaws are available at
www.icann.org/general/articles.htm and
www.icann.org/general/bylaws.htm

Since millions of companies are now online with more to come, the likelihood of consumer confusion of a trademark with another company's domain name will surely be a necessary concern of every online corporation.

An e-business's *brandname equity* is intellectual property, and it is considered one of the valuable elements of its goodwill that should be guarded and legally protected.

This chapter will examine the laws that provide legal recourse to a company whose distinctive trademark and/or trade name has been infringed in cyberspace.

Trademarks

A **trademark** is defined under the **Lanham Act** of 1976 as a word, name, symbol, or device or any combination thereof including a sound, used by any person to identify and distinguish goods from those of others. To be granted federal registration, the mark must be used, or promise a "good faith" intent to be used, in commerce. Displaying the e-business trademark online will generally automatically establish use in interstate commerce.

It is important that an online company register its distinctive domain name as a trademark with the U.S. Patent & Trademark Office (PTO). Keep in mind that different companies can use the same trademark for different classes of goods and services (e.g., Delta Airlines and Delta Dental), while only *one* company can register a particular dot.com domain name.

Federal registration of a trademark with the PTO will establish the applicant as the owner of the trademark and allow the owner to sue for trademark infringement and/or dilution in the federal court system. The distinctive domain name must be used to identify the product or service produced by the company to qualify for federal trademark registration.

Trademarks are classified into five categories:

1. *Generic marks* do not receive protection because they do not distinguish a business's mark from other products or services.
2. *Descriptive marks* will not receive protection unless the applicant can prove the mark is either inherently distinctive or has acquired a secondary meaning in the marketplace. A secondary meaning does not require that the trademark was inherently distinctive, as long as there was a change in the public perspective about the meaning of the trademark.

3. *Suggestive marks* suggest some quality of the product or service (e.g., Microsoft's "Where do you want to go today?").

http://
www.icann.org/udrp/udrp.htm

> **Table 3.1**
>
> Trademark Classifications: A Specific Example
>
> *Generic.* Apple Produce Mart cannot register *apple* as its trademark. It is too general.
>
> *Descriptive.* Apple, a company that sells computers, *can* register *apple* as a trademark because it is an *inherently distinctive* trademark for a computer.
>
> *Suggestive.* Apple may register the *apple logo* (an apple with a bite taken out) because it is suggesting that its product is as easy to use as eating an apple.
>
> *Arbitrary.* Since there is no relationship between a computer and an apple, this is a trademark that can be registered, as it is inherently distinctive.
>
> *Fanciful.* The trademarks *apple* and *macintosh* in relationship to a computer have no significance from a name perspective and are inherently distinctive.
>
> Apple Computer, Inc, can thus register the trademarks Apple, the Apple logo, and Macintosh. By applying a general word to an unrelated product, Apple Computer creates a distinctive image.

4. *Arbitrary marks* exist without any inherent relationship to the product (e.g., amazon.com).
5. *Fanciful marks* also have no inherent relationship to the product (e.g., the board game's trademark Candyland).

The last three categories receive protection because they are automatically inherently distinctive (see Table 3.1). This will be discussed in more detail in the next section.

Service Marks

Service marks are words, phrases, logos, or other graphic symbols that promote services and are also granted legal protection. Familiar e-business service marks are eBay, priceline.com, and Compaq's "Better answers." Service marks can be registered in the U.S. Patent and Trademark Office and are protected under the Lanham Act. Although it is not legally necessary to do so, it is a good practice to place an "sm" next to the service mark to confer ownership.

Trade Dress as a Trademark

Trademarks have been expanded to now include a **trade dress** that may be a *colored design or shape associated with a product*. Most franchises are known by their trade dress because the general public associates the color scheme and ambiance of a busi-

Table shown in browser window:

PTO/SB/61pct	1999/07	Petition for Revival of an International Application for Patent Designating the U.S. Abandoned Unavoidably under 37 CFR 1.137(a) [3 pages]
PTO/SB/64pct	1999/07	Petition for Revival of an International Application for Patent Designating the U.S. Abandoned Unintentionally under 37 CFR 1.137(b) [2 pages]
Trademark Related Forms		***ACCESS TRADEMARK ELECTRONIC FILING SITE***
The Below Forms are best viewed with the Latest Version of Adobe's free Acrobat reader.		
PTO/TM/1478	1999/12	**Trademark/Servicemark Application, Principal Register**
PTO/TM/1553	1999/05	**Statement of Use/Amendment to Allege Use for Intent-to-Use Application**
PTO/TM/1581	1999/12	**Request for Extension of Time to File a Statement of Use**
PTO/TM/1583	1999/05	**Declaration of Use of a Mark under Section 8**
PTO/TM/4.16	1999/12	**Declaration of Incontestability of a Mark under Section 15**
PTO Form 1963	1999/12	**Combined declaration of use in commerce/application for renewal of registration of mark under Sections 8 & 9**
PTO Form 1583	1999/12	**Combined declaration of use & incontestibility under Sections 8 & 15**
PTO/TM/4.8	1999/12	**Collective Membership Mark Application, Principal Register**
PTO/TM/4.9	1999/12	**Certification Mark Application, Principal Register**
PTO/TM/1478(a)	1999/12	**Collective Trademark/Service Mark Application, Principal Register**
PTO/TM/4-17a	1996/06	**Opposition to the Registration of a Mark**
PTO/TM/1618	1996/06	**Recordation Form Cover Sheet**

Last Modified: Monday, January 10, 2000 17:15:40

Courtesy the U.S. Patent and Trademark Office.

ness with the franchise (e.g., the McDonald's restaurant is red and yellow). A color design and graphics on a Web site's home page associated with a product or service should be registered as a trade dress. The trade dress then becomes part of the goodwill of the e-business and a valuable asset of the online company.

Registering a Trademark, Trade Dress, or Service Mark with the PTO

To register a trademark, trade dress, or service mark in the U.S. PTO an applicant e-business must be capable of *distinguishing the applicant's goods and/or services* from those of others. It no longer has to be first used to be registered, as long as no one else is currently using the trademark in business.

A trademark registration in the PTO will be allowed because of actual use or a good-faith intent to later use the mark in commerce. This "later use" provision is useful in building a Web site and business plan for a startup e-business that may apply for federal registration before using the trademark in commerce. The trademark may then be used on the Web site and business plan before the e-business is actually launched.

A search will be made by the PTO to determine if another party is using the trademark in the same or a similar business. If not, the trademark will generally be registered. Once registered, there is *constructive notice* to all businesses that the mark is now owned by a particular company. The owner should display the circled (®) and/or (SM) on its Web site home page to give *actual notice* of federal registration and its claim of ownership.

This is a valuable designation in an infringement lawsuit where the plaintiff must first prove *ownership* of the trademark. Federal registration with the PTO is prime facie evidence of trademark ownership. In the court's discretion, the plaintiff may be awarded up to three times the damages proved, court costs, and, in certain cases, reasonable attorney's fees.

The initial registration is for a term of ten years. This may be renewed. The mark will be automatically canceled at the end of the sixth year if the registrant does not file in the fifth year an affidavit indicating its continuing use of the trademark in interstate commerce. If the trademark is not used, there must be specific reasons, and the registrant must state that there is no intent to abandon the mark.

The renewal process is rather involved, and the e-business and its legal counsel must carefully follow the Lanham Act procedures to assure trademark renewal (see 15 USC sec 1058 and 1059).

Trademarks as Distinctive: Either Inherently or Through a Secondary Meaning

A trademark is deemed to be distinctive when it is either **inherently distinctive** or has an acquired distinctiveness through a **secondary meaning.** We have previously mentioned that suggestive, arbitrary, and fanciful trademarks are inherently distinctive. Trademarks that are made up of common or ordinary words are not distinctive. People's names, geographic terms, and descriptive names are generally not distinctive and cannot be registered. However, a person's name that has acquired a "secondary meaning" (e.g., Michael Jordan) may be protected by registration, as he has acquired great public recognition beyond the world of basketball. "Calvin Klein" was once a nondistinctive trade name that has acquired a valuable secondary meaning.

If a trademark is not distinctive and has not yet acquired a secondary meaning, it may be placed on the **Supplemental Register** in the PTO that provides constructive notice of ownership to companies in all fifty states. If the trademark remains on the Supplemental Register for five years with continuous use in commerce, it may then be placed on the **Principal Register** in the PTO under the *secondary meaning rule* and secondary meaning will be presumed.

This process of filing the trademark in the Supplemental Register is especially useful for an e-company that has a nondistinctive trademark and seeks national protection (e.g., "your name" .com, Inc.). Since domain names can be federally registered, the owner should consider the benefits of its registration in the Principal Register, or, if necessary, the Supplemental Register.

Common use of a circled ® indicates it has been registered with the Patent and Trademark Office. This should appear on the Web site's home page to indicate actual notice of ownership along with other intellectual property claims that have federal registration, such as the circled © for a copyright and "sm" for a service mark.

Trademark Infringement and Dilution

Businesses spend a lot of money protecting their names and building goodwill. They are therefore protective of their trademarks. But trademarks can be devalued without being duplicated or stolen. Trademark infringement and trademark dilution can do great harm to a company. As the commercial world enters e-business, companies should be aware that the online environment makes them even more exposed to trademark infringement and dilution.

Trademark Infringement

A **trademark infringement** occurs when a party uses a trademark that causes a "likelihood of confusion" between goods or the relationship between the parties that make the goods. It generally takes place between competing companies and causes an immediate likelihood of confusion with the consumers. For example, if Dunkin' Donuts were to use Starbucks' registered trademark and also use its own trademark, Dunkin' Donuts, it would give the confusing impression that Dunkin' Donuts has an affiliation with Starbucks. Starbucks would be entitled to sue Dunkin' Donuts for trademark infringement.

Trademark Dilution

The **Federal Trademark Dilution Act of 1996** (15 U.S.C. Sec. 1125) amended the Lanham Act to protect companies against dilution of *famous and distinctive marks* in the United States. The Federal Trademark Dilution Act defines a dilution as "the lessening of the capacity of a famous mark to identify and distinguish goods or services, regardless of the presence or absence of (1) competition between the owner of the famous mark and other parties, or (2) the likelihood of confusion or mistake or to deceive." See Table 3.2.

The Federal Trademark Dilution Act can be found online at www.uspto.gov.

It is important to note that a trademark dilution creates a new statutory remedy and differs from a trademark infringement.

A **trademark dilution** occurs when a trademark is used by another company in such a manner as to cause its identity to diminish over a period of time. It need not cause immediate confusion in the mind of the consumer. Dilution can take place without consumer confusion regarding the identity of the goods, even when the mark is used on unrelated noncompeting goods or services. Although trademark dilution is actionable under about half of the states' statutory laws, it was not actionable under the

Table 3.2

The Plaintiff's Burden of Proof and Defenses in a Trademark Dilution Case

Plaintiff	Defendant's defenses
1. Must prove it owns the trademark (e.g. registered in the U.S. PTO) 2. The mark is *distinctive and famous* 3. The defendant's use is *causing* dilution	1. Ownership of a registered trademark 2. *Fair use* of the mark in promoting its goods or identifying competing goods 3. Noncommercial use of the mark 4. Any form of news reporting or commentary

Lanham Act prior to the 1996 amendment. You can expect trademark dilution to be used extensively in domain name disputes by *famous trademark* owners against any party using a registered domain name that will lessen the value of their mark.

A trademark dilution will allow a registered trademark owner of a famous mark to bring a claim against the registered owner of a similar or identical domain name used for commercial purposes. When a domain name in some fashion causes a dilution of a "famous" registered trademark, there could be a violation of the act.

In a dilution case there is no requirement that consumers be "likely confused" that there is an association between the unauthorized using company and the trademark owner, or that the user be a competitor. The defendant may be an unrelated business using a famous trademark online. The trademark owner who has the "famous mark" may bring a claim against the unrelated business causing dilution of the distinctive quality of the mark.

"Famous" Trademarks.   In order to be eligible to sue under the Federal Trademark Dilution Act the plaintiff company must first prove its trademark is a **famous trademark.**

When a court must determine whether a mark is distinctive and famous, it applies guidelines to the facts of the trademarks use. (See Table 3.3 for guidelines to determine when a mark is famous.)

The burden of proving the mark is famous is often accomplished in court by an expert witness testifying about surveys made in response to questions based on the guidelines in Table 3.3. For instance, the trademark *Oracle,* although relatively new, may qualify as a "famous" trade name because it is readily recognized in the computer world. Note that the best method in qualifying a trademark as famous should be to register it in the Principal Register at the PTO and then to engage in an extensive advertising campaign.

Table 3.3

Guidelines to Determine If a Trademark Is Famous

- The degree of inherent or acquired distinctiveness of the mark
- The duration and extent of use of the mark in connection with the goods or services with which the mark is used
- The duration and extent of advertising and publicity of the mark
- The geographical extent of the trading area in which the mark is used
- The channels of trade for the goods or services with which the mark is used
- The degree of recognition of the mark in the trade
- The nature and extent of use of the same or similar marks by third parties
- Whether the mark was registered on the Principal Register

In *Washington Speakers Bureau, Inc. v. Leading Authorities, Inc.*, C.A. No. 98-634-A, 1999 U.S. Dist Lexis 980 (E.D. Va., 1999), the Court held that the defendant's use of the domain name "washingtonspeakers.com" infringed on the plaintiff's name and caused a likelihood that consumers would be confused by the defendant's use of a "colorable imitation" of the plaintiff's trademark in its domain name. The services the parties offered the public were virtually identical, and the Court found the defendant adopted the domain name in bad faith to attract the plaintiff's business. However, the Court also found that there was no trademark dilution because the plaintiff's trademark was not famous. Note that a trademark dilution claim cannot be brought unless the plaintiff can prove the trademark is famous within the guidelines already stated.

Dilution by Tarnishment. **Dilution by tarnishment** occurs when the plaintiff's mark has been associated by the defendant's conduct with unwholesome, unsavory or shoddy quality products, or when consumers are likely to associate the lack of prestige or quality of the product with the plaintiff's unrelated goods.

A 1996 case, *Hasbro, Inc. v. The Internet Entertainment Group*, pitted the maker of a child's game against a pornographer. The famous family board game Candyland was being used as a domain name by a pornographic Web site. The plaintiff sued for trademark infringement, trademark dilution, and unfair competition of its federally registered trademark "Candyland" for use with its board game, alleging the toy maker's wholesome image was being tarnished by the adult-oriented site. The court enjoined the defendant from using the domain name because the defendant's use of the pornographic Web site was a trademark dilution by tarnishment and would degrade the quality of the Candyland mark.

The following case discusses how the use of the domain name "Adults R Us.com" on its Web page in connection with adult-oriented toys constituted a violation of the Federal Trademark Dilution Act of 1996 of the famous Toys "R" Us and Kids "R" Us trademarks.

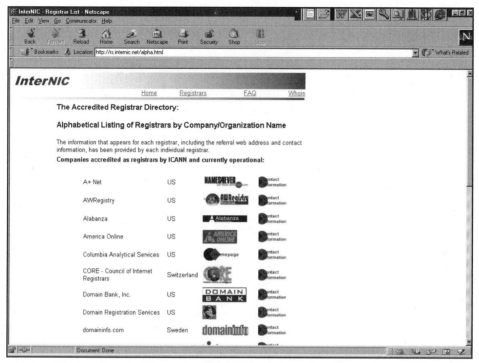

Courtesy U.S. Department of Commerce. InterNIC is a registered service mark fo the U.S. Department of Commerce.

In *Toys "R" Us v. Akkaoui,* 1996 U.S. Dist. LEXIS 17090 (N.D. Cal. Oct. 29, 1996) the plaintiff, Toys "R" Us, discovered that the defendant was using Adults "R" Us as a domain name to sell sexual products online. It immediately notified the defendant to shut down its operation. After defendant refused the plaintiff

See
www.toysrus.com
that will bring up
www.amazon.com
and then click under "about the store" to read how
toysrus.com has teamed up with **amazon.com** for online toy-shopping

brought suit alleging trademark dilution. Since Toys "R" Us is a famous trademark the court held it would be tarnished and diluted by allowing the defendant to continue to use its name. Notice how trademark dilution need not cause immediate consumer confusion. The court held that the defendant's use of the mark in association with sexual products was inconsistent with the image that Toys "R" Us had acquired in the commercial market.

A trademark dilution claim allows the famous trademark holder to sue for monetary damages as well as injunctive relief. To be awarded monetary damages the trademark holder, as Toys "R" Us , would have to prove the defendant acted willfully. The court may then award treble damages, attorneys' fees and court costs. In the Toys "R" Us case it would appear the defendant was acting willfully. Managers should consider having their lawyers send a "cease and desist" letter to the diluting company to build a legal record of willfulness.

Dilution by Blurring.   **Dilution by blurring** occurs over an extended period of time when a famous trademark's value will be diminished by its use on dissimilar products. For example, if an online clothing company were allowed to use "www.fidelity.com" as its domain name, blurring would eventually dilute this world-famous trademark. Although the consuming public can distinguish mutual funds from a noncompeting clothing e-business, over a period of time the Fidelity trademark would be diminished.

In *Toys "R" Us., et al. v. Richard Feinburg, et al.*, 98 Civ.2780 (AGS), 1998 U.S. Dist. Lexis 17217 (S.D.N.Y.) 1998, the Court held defendant's use of the domain name "gunsareus.com" for an e-business selling firearms neither infringed or diluted the famous plaintiff's Toys "R" Us trademark and trade name. Note that there were two claims in this case: one for trademark infringement and the other for trademark dilution. The infringement claim failed because the Court found that consumers were not likely to be confused by defendant's use of the domain name "gunsareus" with the "R" Us company. The defendant sold firearms out of a small retail store, and on their Web site defendant's domain name would neither blur nor tarnish plaintiff's name because consumers could not relate the defendant's business to the plantiff's.

This is a weak argument with respect to the trademark dilution. The "R" Us family sells children's toys, and any parent that sees the "gunsareus.com" Web site could easily believe that there is an affiliation with the plaintiff. Remember that the likelihood to deceive or confuse the consumer is not necessary in a trademark dilution case. Further, there is no way of knowing the size of the retail gun store by viewing a Web site. This case was later overruled on appeal.

Trademarks in Cyberspace: Cyberpiracy and Internet Technology

Anticybersquatting Consumer Protection Act (ACPA)

Domain names have become valuable commodities, so *cyberpirates* have registered domain names with Network Solutions, Inc. or other domain name registrars that are famous trademarks. The cyberpirates then attempt to sell the registered domain name to the trademark owner for a large amount of money. Keep in mind that the first person to register a dot.com domain name secures all rights to use the name as a URL.

http://

See

www.jmls.edu/cyber/cases/toysrus1.txt

The 1999 U.S. **Anticybersquatting Consumer Protection Act** made several changes to the Lanham Act (federal trademark law) to protect trademark owners from online cyberpiracy.

The ACPA states in part "A person shall be liable in a civil action by the owner of a mark, including a personal name which is protected as a mark . . . if that person has a bad faith intent to profit from the mark." The Act does not define *bad faith,* although is does define nonexclusive factors as guidelines in determining bad faith (see Table 3.4).

The Act also makes it illegal to register the domain name of a living person without the person's consent with the specific intent to profit by selling the name for financial gain.

Under the Act, a plaintiff may elect *statutory damages* in lieu of *actual damages* (loss of profits) in the amount of at least $1,000 but not more than $100,000 per domain name, as the court considers just (see Table 3.5). It may also order the transformation of the domain name to the owner of the trademark, as well as reasonable attorney fees. The intent of the law is to make cybersquatters accountable to the holders of famous trademarks who have spent years and large amounts of money in advertising the federally registered trademark.

Internet Technology and Trademark Infringement

Internet technology, the code used in software, provides three areas of concern with respect to trademark infringement and dilution. They include *deeplinking, metatags, and framing.* (See Chapter 1 for a technical explanation of these terms.) Surfers seeking information about a product or service without having the correct URL often use a search engine that generates a list of sites based on a key term provided by the user. The following explains various ways that a Web designer may violate a trademark right by using Internet technology.

Deep Linking. The very culture of the World Wide Web involves a process known as **hyperlinking** that allows a user to conveniently move from one site to another by a predetermined highlighted area on a Web page. A hyperlink is created by the Web designer inserting a URL (universal resource locator) into HTML (hypertext markup language) code that, upon a left click of the mouse, allows the user to automatically access the new linked site. The home page of this new Web site is called a *surface link.* Because a surface link is merely an address of a site and does not

Table 3.4

Bad Faith Guidelines Under the ACPA

Any of the following may constitute bad faith by the domain-name holder:

✓ The trademark rights of the owner of the federally registered trademark will be diminished.
✓ The domain-name owners intend to cause consumers to divert the goodwill represented by the trademark, either for profit or to tarnish or disparage the trademark, by creating a likelihood of confusion in the minds of the consumers.
✓ The domain-name owners offer to sell the name to the trademark owner or a third party for financial gain.
✓ The holder of the domain-name applied for it by providing false information.
✓ The holder applied for multiple domain-names registration that were known to be identical or confusingly similar to others.

Table 3.5

Remedies of a Trademark Owner against a Cyberpirate

Sue for *actual damage* (i.e., loss of profits to the company) and reasonable attorney fees plus cancellation of the domain name.
or
Sue for *statutory damages*—minimum of $1,000 up to $100,000 per domain name and reasonable attorney fees and cancellation of the domain name.
or
Transfer the domain name to the plaintiff trademark owner.

involve a copying, there is generally no copyright violation and may usually be provided without the owner's consent. (See Chapter 4 on Copyrights.)

A **deeplink** goes beyond the home page to other pages within the Web site. In most cases only the home page will show a banner advertisement and the Web site owners' trademark. Since a home page often displays "banner ads" that pay the Web site owner a fee based on the number of "hits," a deeplink can result in an enormous amount of lost income. This is especially true for a noncommercial site that often depends on "banner ads" as its sole source of revenue. Deeplinking that bypasses the home page may give the end user the false impression that the product or service described or shown belongs to the wrong company.

Metatags.   A **metatag** is an invisible code imbedded in the hypertext markup language (HTML) used to create Web sites. Its primary use is to assist a search engine to index and summarize sites. For example, a person looking for a bookstore would type in "amazon" and find its URL. When a user seeks information on a search engine about a company (e.g., Amazon.com), a competing company (e.g., Barnes & Noble) with an invisible metatag on its Web site could lead the user to believe there is

> **Cyberethics**
>
> Is there an ethical justification for surface linking to another company's Web site without the site owner's permission?
>
> Assume that your Web site was linked to a pornographic Web site. Would that change your answer?

an affiliation with that company. An unethical Web site owner can easily use a competitor's trade name with a similar product or service by placing the competitor's name on its metatags. This could constitute a trademark infringement, trademark dilution, or unfair competition.

An e-business can determine if a corporation is using its trademark as a metatag by entering its trademark as a search term on a search engine, such as *www.yahoo.com*. It could then note the Web site listed as a "hit" upon which the trademark does not visibly appear. If it views the HTML version of those pages on a Netscape Navigator by right-clicking the mouse on View and then the Document Source, it will illustrate the key terms included in the metatag. The infringing company can be using a registered trademark that has nothing to do with the company and simply attempts to lure users to its site. This is often referred to as *invisible trademark infringement.*

In a 1999 decision, *Brookfield Communications, Inc. v. West Coast Entertainment Corporation,* the court described a metatag trademark infringement this way:

> Using another's trademark in one's metatags is much like posting a sign with another's trademark in front on one's store.
>
> Suppose West Coast's competitor (let's call it "Blockbuster") puts up a billboard on a highway reading—"West Coast Video: 2 miles ahead at Exit 7"—where West Coast is really located at Exit 8 but Blockbuster is located at Exit 7. Customers looking for West Coast's store will pull off at Exit 7 and drive around looking for it. Unable to locate West Coast, but seeing the Blockbuster store right by the highway entrance, they may simply rent there. Even consumers who prefer West Coast may find it not worth the trouble to continue searching for West Coast since there is a Blockbuster right there. Customers are not confused in the narrow sense: they are fully aware that they are purchasing from Blockbuster and they have no reason to believe that Blockbuster is related to, or in any way sponsored by, West Coast. Nevertheless, the fact that there is only initial consumer confusion does not alter the fact that Blockbuster would be misappropriating West Coast's acquired goodwill."

One can question the ethics of an e-business using metatags to entice consumers to a Web site and thereby steal its hard-earned goodwill.

International Protection of Trademarks

Remember that federal registration in the PTO does not grant

Complaint may be found at:
www.ljx.com/internet/tktmaster.html

http://
www.bna.com/e-law/cases/totalset.html

international protection. Since e-business is global by nature, a company that intends to do business in foreign countries must take legal steps to protect the trademark in those countries. (See Chapter 13, "Global Issues," for a discussion of the international protection of trademarks.)

- *E-business objective:* To protect the e-business's trademarks from trademark infringement and trademark dilution
- *Legal strategy:* Federal registration in the PTO of the e-business corporate name, domain name, company logo and advertising slogans, and constant vigilance to determine if they have been infringed and/or diluted

Summary

Yahoo, AOL, and Amazon.com are household words that did not exist a short time ago. They are now famous trademarks that have acquired a special meaning on the Internet. A successful e-business must establish a dominance on the Web by brand-name recognition. This business strategy requires a great deal of money and a legal strategy to protect the domain name, company name, its logo and advertising slogans from being infringed and/or diluted by others.

Our legal system provides for federal registration of trademarks granting the owner federal statutory rights against infringers and dilutors. These rights extend to certain technological devises such as the wrongful use of metatags, deeplinking, and framing. A sound legal strategy of federal registration in the PTO must protect the trade name, domain name, its logo, and advertising slogans as valuable intellectual property of the e-business.

Manager's Checklist

- Register a company's domain name with the U.S. Patent and Trademark Office. If possible, it should be the same as its trade name.
- Be aware of what constitutes a "famous" trademark and consider doing whatever is possible to acquire that status. Remember that a claim against an online noncompetitor for trademark dilution requires that the plaintiff's trademark be "famous."
- Constantly review, with your lawyer, the duration of the trademark, and any renewal that may be necessary.

- Register with an accredited registrar of Internet Corporation for Assigned Names and Numbers as many derivative domain names relative to your product and/or services as possible to prevent others from doing so. Consider federal registration of these derivative domain names with the PTO.
- Be aware that the online use of a "famous" trademark by your company or another noncompeting company, may constitute "blurring" or "tarnishment" under the Federal Dilution Trademark Act.
- Display the circled ® on your Web page wherever the registered trademark appears. For a service mark, use the sm initials. Although not required by law, this provides actual notice of federal registration.
- Be aware that federal registration of a trademark does not grant international protection. This is a very real problem because an online company using its trademark has a global presence and may have to register the mark in every country in which it is doing business. This can be a very costly process.
- Be sure your Web designer avoids deeplinking and framing and does not use another company's trade name in its metatags.

Additional Readings

- Quick, Rebecca. *Can't Get There from Here May Be Web's New Motto,* Wall St. J. (July 2, 1997), B6.
- Beatty, Sally Goll. *Alta Vista Alters Its Vision of the Market,* Wall St. J., Dec 18, 1996, at B9.
- Lessig, Lawrence. *Code and Other Laws of Cyberspace,* Chapter 10, Intellectual Property, Basic Books, N.Y. 1999.

4

Copyrights

"For the holder of the copyright, cyberspace appears to be the worst of both worlds—a place where the ability to copy could not be better, and where the protection of law could not be worse."
    —*Lawrence Lessig,* Code and Other Laws of Cyberspace, *(Basic Books, 1999), p. 125*

Introduction

Imagine having paid a Web site developer hundreds of thousands of dollars to launch a killer application and acquiring millions of dollars from a venture capitalist firm, only to then discover that another e-business is using your online material. What kind of legal recourse do you have in this situation?

Or consider a scenario where your Web site is linked to an e-business that displayed copyrighted material without the owner's consent. Could your company be liable under a theory of copyright infringement? This chapter will address these and other issues relevant to copyright protection and liability.

It is a common mistake to lump copyrights and trademarks as the same kinds of intellectual property. Think of a copyright as an original work of authorship—for example the drawing of Mickey Mouse—versus the trademark of Walt Disney (www.disney.com), including the entire Disney enterprise and associating in the consumer's mind all of the works that accompany its productions. Chapter 3 discussed trademarks in detail.

E-business Web sites are a composition of materials, often consisting of words, graphics, audio, and video, that are expressed to the consumer as information content. The owners and Web site developers carefully select the content to sell the company's product or service. The subject matter expressed in the site is an electronic publication of this content. Registration of the entire e-business Web site as a copyright in the U.S. Copyright Office is permitted if it is original and creative. http://lcweb.loc.gov/copyright

As will be discussed in this chapter, registration in the copyright office provides the owner of the copyright work with exclusive statutory rights. The copyright subject matter may take the form of software, music, literary works, or databases

http://

See, for example,
www.amazon.com, www.ebay.com, and
www.priceline.com

that are not merely factual. When federally registered, the plaintiff copyright owner has special statutory remedies in the federal court against an infringing defendant.

Since designing, producing, and maintaining a sophisticated Web site is very expensive, protecting content ownership is extremely important. Electronic commerce will continue to be highly competitive. As Web sites become more and more interactive with consumers, their creation, design, and maintenance place enormous demands on innovative marketing techniques that should be legally protected.

Framers of the U.S. Constitution knew the value of protecting exclusive rights in the owner of creative works. The authority of Congress to enact copyright laws is found in Article I, Section 8, clause 8: The Constitution grants power in Congress *"to promote the progress of science and useful arts, by securing for limited times to authors and inventors the exclusive right to their respective writings and discoveries."* This exclusive property interest gives the copyright owner of a Web site a monopoly in the work. The free flow of information that is the very culture and value of the World Wide Web may conflict with this copyright interest. The First Amendment's history of freedom of speech encourages the currency of ideas and their expression, no matter how controversial. Creative information and, indeed, commerce itself, depends on the development of commercial expression. Balancing these competing interests is the purpose of the U.S. Copyright Act (Lanham Act, 15 USC sec. 1051, *et seq*) and the federal courts.

Never before has it been so easy to violate a copyright owner's exclusive right to copy the material. Common copyright violations are employees forwarding or attaching copyrighted e-mail without the consent of the author. Both methods may violate the owner's exclusive statutory right to copy the document. The uploading of information and making multiple copies of online material could also be a copyright violation, as well as the downloading of MP3 files (www.mp3.com). Companies and

Figure 4.1

E-Business Copyright Objective and Legal Strategy

E-business objective: Protect the Web pages of the company's Web site from being copied by other companies and protect the company from any copyright infringement suits.

Legal strategy:
- Register the copyright of the Web pages.
- Include appropriate disclaimers in the terms of use for copyright infringement by linked companies.
- Monitor bulletin boards and chat rooms for known copyright infringements by third parties.

individuals that are not aware of these copyright infringements may find themselves liable under legal theories discussed below.

The Lanham Act, discussed in Chapter 3, covers copyrights as well as trademarks. It is a strict liability statute. This means that it is possible to be liable as an unintentional infringer, and hence the importance of an e-business working closely with its lawyers cannot be overestimated. This chapter will review the copyright laws of e-commerce and acquaint you with some of the copyright problems relative to the online environment. Suggestions will be made throughout the chapter as to how an e-business manager can legally protect copyright ownership and limit a company's copyright liability (see Figure 4.1).

Copyright Act of 1976 (Lanham Act)

In order to implement the congressional authority as stated in the U.S. Constitution of granting exclusive rights to copyright owners, Congress adopted in 1790 the first U.S. copyright law. The statute has gone through numerous amendments, resulting in a comprehensive revision in 1909. As our mass media evolved from radio to movies to VCRs, to audio and videotapes, Congress again saw fit to amend the Copyright Act in 1976. The act took effect on January 1, 1978.

The federal courts' function is to interpret the Copyright Act within the context of our current environment of information technology. As stated by the U.S. Supreme Court, "From the beginning, the law of copyrights has developed in response to significant changes in technology." (*Sony Corp. v. Universal Studios, Inc.,* 464 U.S. 417 (1984). The role of the court, however, remains constant. It must maintain the delicate balance between the exclusive rights of copyright owners and the public's right to have access to information.

Subject Matter of Copyrights

Copyright ownership can be registered for (1) literary works, (2) musical works, (3) dramatic works, (4) pantomimes/choreographic works, (5) pictorial, graphic, and sculptural works, (6) motion pictures and audiovisual works, (7) sound recordings, and (8) architectural works.

In order for this material to be registered in the Copyright Office as a copyright, it must be "*an original work of authorship* fixed in any tangible medium of expression from which they can be perceived, reproduced, or otherwise communicated either directly or with the aid of machine or device." 17 U.S.C. Sec. 102 (a). This requirement fits the application of the material found on Web pages, allowing them to federally registered with the U.S. Copyright office (see Figure 4.2).

The nature of its originality requires the work be a creative document not copied from another source. It must be the independent work of the author. Under the Copyright Act a **fixed creative work** is fixed "when its embodiment in a copy or phonorecord . . . is sufficiently permanent or stable to permit it to be perceived, reproduced, or otherwise communicated for a period of more than transitory duration" (17 U.S.C. Sec. 101). **Fixed creative works** must be fixed in a tangible medium of expression in order to be copyrighted. Web pages fit this statutory requirement and may be federally registered. The Copyright Act clearly states that an original work of authorship does not extend to any idea, procedure, process, system, method of operation, concept, principle or discovery, unless fixed in a tangible form (17 U.S.C. Sec. 102(b)). Copyright law protects the expression of an idea and not the idea itself. Although you cannot copyright a creative and original idea, once the idea is expressed in a fixed, tangible form, it may acquire copyright protection. For example, the contents on a Web page were once original and creative ideas, but when coded and fixed in floppy disks, compact disks, or other digital storage devices, they may be sent with the application to the Copyright Office for federal copyright registration. Notice that a system or method of operation is not a subject matter for a copyright. However, an appropriate "business method" may be patentable.

Original and creative digital works fixed in a tangible medium of expression will receive exclusive statutory rights under copyright law. This is the basis for Web site federal registration in the PTO.

Requirements for Registration in the Copyright Office

Registration of a copyright in the copyright office requires a completed registration form and a submission of the original work. The copyright office will accept a floppy disk of the Web site as the "original work." The Copyright office will then issue to the owner a certificate of registration. In a copyright infringement case the plaintiff will submit this certificate to prove copyright registration and ownership. The certificate of registration constitutes *prima facie* evidence of the validity of the copyright and allows the owner to sue an infringer in the federal court and pursue

---

Figure 4.2

Criteria for Copyright Protection of a Web Page

✓ *Originality*—The Web site may not copy a similar site and should strive for a unique presentation (e.g. www.consumerreview.com).
✓ *Creativity*—The Web site need not be novel, as in a patent requirement, but should be an independent creation (e.g. www.landsend.com).
✓ *Fixed form*—The application of the content to the Web site is sufficient to create a fixed form for copyright protection purposes.

statutory remedies. So the importance of federal registration of the e-business Web site cannot be overestimated. It provides the e-business with a property interest in the Web site that is legally protected.

Duration of Copyright

In October 1998 Congress enacted the **Sonny Bono Copyright Term Extension Act (CETA)**. It extends the term of most copyrights by 20 years. These changes harmonize U.S. law with European copyright laws.

Thus, copyrights for works created prior to January 1, 1978 generally endure for a term of 28 years with the option to renew for a further term of 67 years. (Prior to the CTEA the renewal term was for 47 years.) 17 U.S.C. sec. 304.

Copyrights for works created on or after January 1, 1978 generally endure for a term consisting of the life of the author plus an additional 70 years after the author's death. (Prior to the CTEA the term after death was for 50 years.) 17 U.S.C. sec. 302.

Exclusive Statutory Rights of a Copyright Owner

E-business owners of a federally registered copyright work have the following **exclusive statutory rights** that collectively define the scope of the copyright:

- To reproduce the copyrighted work
- To sell, rent, lease, or otherwise distribute copies of the copyright work to the public
- To prepare derivative works based on the copyright work
- To perform and display publicly the copyright work

Right to Reproduce the Work

Copyright infringement in the online environment often involves a violation of the reproduction right that occurs by transferring data from one computer to another.

An early 1984 case, *Apple Computer v. Formula International*, 594 F. Supp. 617, held that copies stored in random access memory (RAM) were temporary, and running a computer program from RAM does not create an infringed copy.

However, in a 1993 case, *MAI Systems Corp. v. Peak Computer, Inc.* 1991 F. 2d 511 (9th Cir. 1993), software was downloaded into RAM when the defendant turned the computer on in the course of performing maintenance. In doing so, the defendant was able to view the software program to assist him in diagnosing the problem. The court found that the copy created in RAM was sufficiently permanent and "fixed" to satisfy the Copyright Act and cause an infringement of the software. This case should alert the e-business manager that an unauthorized downloading of software onto RAM and using it for personal gain constitute both a "copying" and infringement.

Other instances of an unauthorized reproduction and copyright infringement are "scanning" a copyrighted printed document into a digital file, and uploading and/or downloading a digital copyrighted file to a bulletin board system.

Right of Distribution: Selling, Renting, or Leasing Copies

Since a copyright is the exclusive property of the owner, the right to exercise property interests such as selling, renting or leasing the copyright, is protected by the court. A person who does not own the copyright and makes it available on a bulletin board service, can be liable for copyright infringement.

In *Playboy Enter. Inc., v. Frena*, 839 F.Supp. 1552 (M. D. Fla. 1993), the court held that when unauthorized photographs of Playboy Enterprises were downloaded

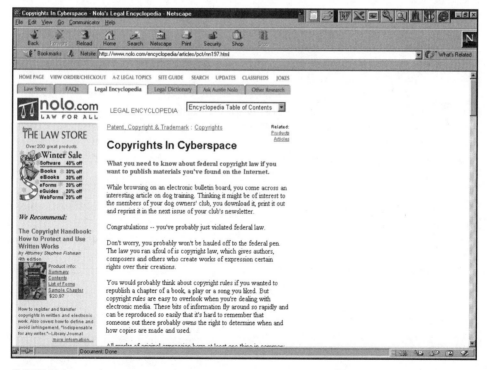

© 2000 Nolo.com, Inc.

to a bulletin board system by the defendant's subscribers, the plaintiff's exclusive right of distribution was infringed by customers of the defendant. Notice how a bulletin board operator, as the defendant in this case, has an obligation to monitor its system to ensure that copyrighted documents are not being displayed and "downloaded" by its customers.

The same rationale regarding the copyright owner's exclusive right of distribution applies to e-mail *attached* or *forwarded* without the permission of the copyright owner. This has become common company practice and managers should be aware of the potential employer's copyright infringement liability.

In a 1997 case, *Marobie-Fl. Inc. v. National Ass'n of Fire Equip. Distribs.*, 983 F. Supp. 1167 (N.D Ill.), unauthorized copies of the plaintiff's electronic clip art files were placed on the defendant's Web page. The court held that this constituted an infringing distribution because the files were available for downloading by Internet users. Since this has become a common practice, Web designers as well as managers should be careful in obtaining permission from the owner of clip art if they want to use it on their Web sites.

Linking to a Web Site.   Linking to a *surface page* (i.e, a home page that often displays the Web site's trademark, copyright and "banner ads") by listing its URL (Universal Resource Locator) is similar to giving directions to the listed site and is not a "copying" within the Copyright Act.

Hence, a surface link to a home page does not generally require permission. This position is based on the theory that going online creates an implied license for anyone with a computer to view the Web site.

However, the terms of use published in many sites restrict the user to making only one copy for personal use of any information displayed. This interactive feature of the WWW to hyperlink defines its very culture distinguishing it from any other communications medium. E-business Web sites often link to other sites that provide the user with merchandise, helpful information, or resources related to the product and/or service being offered.

It would be a prudent business practice to obtain permission to link. Entering into a Web-linking agreement with the linked site will avoid any misunderstanding regarding a copyright infringement.

Creators of a Web site who wanted assurance that it was not linked to a pornographic or shabby site could place a prohibition in its 'terms of use' similar to, "Do not link to this site without our express consent." This could negate any implied license to link by merely going online.

http://
See
www.collegehire.com or **www.mapquest.com**

Databases.   Databases may be subject to copyright registration if the author is creative in selecting and arranging the data and does not merely display the data as facts. In a copyright infringement suit before the U.S. Supreme Court, defendant was the publisher of a telephone directory that reproduced over one thousand of the plaintiff's telephone numbers without its consent. The court found for the defendant and held that the plaintiff's mere arrangement of facts lacked originality because "there is nothing remotely creative about arranging names alphabetically. . ." (*Feist Publications, Inc. v. Rural Telephone Services Inc.,* 499 U.S. 340 (1991)) Note that the court denied copyright protection on the basis that the mere alphabetical listing of names and telephone numbers lacked originality.

A federal court in deciding an online case involving the "Red Book" that listed the retail value of used automobiles held that the book would be granted copyright protection. The listings in the defendant's "Red Book" were found to be original because the compilation included the selection of optional features in a unique fashion, made an adjustment for mileage in five-thousand-mile increments and used the concept of an "average" vehicle as the subject of evaluation (*CCC Information Services, Inc., v. McAllen Hunter Market Reports, Inc.,* 44 F. 3d. 61 2nd Cir. 1994).

This case is especially important in the online environment because information acquired from consumers is often compiled in a database, and in some instances it is sold to other merchants. (See Chapter 8, "Privacy"). To acquire copyright protection for the consumer database, it must be an original coordination and arrangement of the data. You could accomplish this by dividing the information into regional areas based on customer preference, and so on. Managers should be careful of being in compliance with the privacy policy posted on the company's Web site that makes representations to the users how the information will be used.

Right to Prepare Derivative Works

Web designers will often examine various Web sites and select their most attractive features. The designers must be careful not to infringe on the copyright of another site by preparing a derivative work based on the original presentation.

The Copyright Act defines **derivative work** as "a work based upon one or more preexisting works, such as a translation, musical arrangement, dramatization, fictionalization, motion picture version, sound recording, art reproduction, abridgment, condensation, or any other form in which a work may be recast, transformed or adopted." (17 U.S.C. sec. 101) A derivative work includes "a work consisting of editorial revisions, annotations, elaborations, or other modifications, which, as a whole, represent an original work of authorship. . . (17 U.S.C. sec. 101).

> **http://**
> See
> **www.ebay.com**
> for a "privacy policy" statement on a web page.

A federal court held that a "Game Genie" device that altered features in Nintendo's videogame cartridges did not create a derivative work. The "Game Genie" enhanced the audiovisual displays without incorporating the underlying work in any permanent form (*Lewis Galoob Toys, Inc. v. Nintendo, Inc.*, 964 F. 2d. 965 9th Cir. 1962).

To avoid a possible copyright infringement suit based on it being a derivative work, the Web site should not be an adaptation of another site. Managers should consider an indemnity contract with the Web site designer that will repay them for any loss sustained from this potential liability.

Right to Perform and Display Publicly a Copyright Work

The Copyright Act defines **public performance** as when the performance occurs at a place open to the public. It also includes a semipublic place or any place where a substantial number of persons outside of a normal circle of a family and its social acquaintances are gathered (17 U.S.C. Sec. 101).

In *Columbia Pictures, Ind. V. Aveco, Inc.*, 800 F. 2d 59 (3d. Cir. 1986), the defendant improperly authorized public performances by renting videotapes and allowed customers to see the tapes in viewing rooms. The court held that this constituted "a place open to the public" within the meaning of Sec. 101, on the theory that the rooms were open for "any member of the public to avail themselves of this service."

Business managers who display Web material on a computer monitor in employee training programs, without the consent of the owner, may be opening this to the public. Within the statutory definition of a *public place,* you should obtain permission from the owner before doing so. Courts have held making available videotape over the Internet without authorization and posting unauthorized copies of electronic clip art on Web pages could violate the copyright owner's exclusive statutory right of public display (*Michaels v. Internet Entert. Group, Inc.*, 5 F. Supp. 2d 823 C.D. Cal. 1998).

Theories of Liability for Copyright Infringement

There are three theories of copyright infringement liability: direct, contributory, and vicarious.

Direct Infringement

The direct infringer is the direct actor who, with or without a specific intent to infringe, is the primary party that violates one of the copyright owner's exclusive statutory rights. This is the person or company that actually carries out the infringing copying.

The Copyright Act is a strict liability statute, meaning that knowledge or intent of infringement need not be proved by the plaintiff. However, under the Digital Millennium Act of 1998, (discussed later) an online service provider is not liable for **direct infringement** without some element of volition or

> ### Cyberethics
>
> Is it ethical for copyright law to hold a person liable as a direct infringer if she had access to the original copyrighted material and her work was substantially similar?
>
> With easy access to the WWW, almost everybody has the original copyright material available. Does that necessarily mean that a similar work was copied?

causation. If the defendant's work, as the direct infringer, had a substantial similarity to the original copyright work and the defendant had access to that work, the court will presume an intent to infringe.

Bulletin board operators may be liable for the unauthorized distribution and display of images uploaded to and downloaded from their systems. A Florida court held that it was irrelevant that the bulletin board system operator did not make the copies itself and thus found it liable for direct infringement. (*Playboy Enters., Inc. v. Fern*, 839 F. Supp. 1552 M.D. Fla. 1993).

A California court took a more realistic position and held there was no direct infringement of the statutory exclusive rights under the Copyright Act when the infringement was initiated by a third party. In now-famous legal language, the court stated "although copyright is a strict liability statute, there should still be some element of *volition or causation* which is lacking where a defendant's system is merely used to create a copy by a third party." The court reasoned that it would be inappropriate to apply direct infringement liability to a party such as an Internet service provider that acts like a conduit of information. (*Religious Tech. Ctr. v. Netcom On-Line Communications Servs., Inc.*, 907 F. Supp. 1361 N.D. Cal. 1995, discussed in full later in this chapter.)

In 1998, Congress enacted the **Digital Millennium Copyright Act (DMCA)** that provides "safe harbors" from infringement liability to online service providers (OSP). In effect, the DMCA codifies the rational of the *Religious Tech v. Netcom* decision. The theory is to view the OSP as a mere conduit of posted copyright material by others, similar to a library or bookstore. It would be almost impossible to monitor the millions of messages posted on the Bulletin Board Services of an OSP's system.

OSPs are immune from copyright liability so long as they (1) adopt and implement reasonable policies providing for the termination of users who repeatedly infringe upon the rights of others and (2) accommodate and do not interfere with copyright owners' standard technical measures used to protect and identify copyrights.

Under the DMCA there are "safe harbors" for an OSP for the following:

1. *System storage and information locating tools:* This application applies to storing bulletin boards provided by an OSP system. If the OSP has no knowledge or rea-

son to know of direct infringement by subscribers, it will not be liable for copyright infringement.

2. *System caching:* OSPs are not liable for temporary copies of infringement materials in their possession placed online by someone other than the OSP.

3. *Transmission and routing:* The OSP is not liable for transient storage of copyrighted information routed through its system as long as it is without modification and it makes no copies of the information.

Contributory Infringement

Contributory infringement is the tort (civil wrong not based on contract) of contributing to the direct infringement of another. Although not mentioned in the Copyright Act, the legal theory developed by court decision supporting contributory infringement liability is based on the fact that a person with knowledge or reason to know of the infringing activity causes or materially contributes to the conduct of the direct infringer. For there to be a contributory infringement claim *there must first be a direct infringement* by another person.

In the following leading e-commerce case the court *did not find direct copyright infringement* by the operator of an electronic Bulletin Board Service but, nevertheless, found him liable for contributory infringement. The users of the Bulletin Board Service were the direct infringers.

The *Sega Enterprises Ltd. v. Maphia* case is one of the leading cases on contributory infringement that held if a person has knowledge that a user is copying a document or could monitor such activity and carelessly avoided doing so, there is contributory copyright infringement. E-business managers must be aware of direct infringing taking place by their subordinates. For example, a company could be liable for contributory infringement if a manager knows that an employee is consistently using e-mail to forward or attach copyrighted material to others and allows this to continue.

Vicarious Infringement

Vicarious infringement occurs when a company receives direct financial benefit from the infringement by another party and had the right and ability to supervise the infringement activity. Courts have held that vicarious liability requires neither knowledge nor participation in the direct infringement.

In the following case the court dismissed a claim of vicarious liability against an Internet service provider because the plaintiff could not prove any evidence of direct financial benefit received by the provider from posting the infringed material.

Limitations on Copyright Owners' Exclusive Rights

Limitations on copyright owners' exclusive rights include fair use, the first sale doctrine, public domain use, and other statutory exemptions on copyright owners' exclusive rights.

In *Religious Technology Center v. Netcom On-Line Communication Services, Inc.* 907 F. Supp. 1361 (N.D. Cal. 1995) the plaintiff, Religious Technology Center (RTC) brought this suit alleging copyright infringement on the theory that Netcom engaged in direct, contributory or vicarious infringement. RTC held copyrights in the works of Dr. Hubbard, the late founder of the Church of Scientology. Ehrlich, a former Scientology minister used an online forum for criticism of the church and posted copyrighted material without permission of the plaintiff owner on a bulletin board service connected to the Internet through the facilities of the defendant, Netcom. The court had to decide whether the Internet access provider, Netcom, that allowed the bulletin board service to reach the Internet should be liable for copyright infringement caused by another person. The court found the Internet access provided of a bulletin board service similar to the owner of a copying machine owner that allowes the public to make copies on its machines. It held an Internet access provider should not liable for copyright infringement it could not reasonably deter.

This very practical decision was necessary to allow the free flow of information over bulletin board services and Internet access providers. The decision in no way exonerates the direct infringer, Mr. Erlich, from direct copyright liability.

> **http://**
>
> See
> **www.loc.gov/copyright**
> and view the FAQ for a quick review of copyright law.
> Also see
> **www.benedict.com**
> for a readable explanation of all phases of copyrights.

Fair Use Doctrine

The **fair use doctrine** is a statutory limitation on the exclusive rights of a copyright owner. Think of fair use as the first cousin to free speech. It is a policy position taken by Congress that the public interest is best served by placing statutory limitations on the copyright owner's monopoly to its original work. Certain fair uses of a copyright are authorized by law and do not require the consent of the copyright owner. They may even be used over the owner's objection and are a defense to a copyright infringement lawsuit. For example, limited copyrighted material may be used as handout material in a college classroom over the objection of the copyright owner.

Congress has set out in the Copyright Act (U.S.C. 17, Sec. 107) the following four nonexclusive factors to be considered in determining whether the defense of fair use is appropriate.

1. *The purpose and character of the use, including whether its use is of a commercial or educational nature:* The first test is to determine if the purpose of the use was *commercial* or *nonprofit educational*. In *Sonny Corp. v. Universal City Studios, Inc.,* 114 S. Ct. 1164 (1994) the U. S. Supreme Court stated that commercial use of copyright material raises a presumption of unfair use that must be rebutted by the defendant.

   Although nonprofit educational institutions that distribute copyright material are inclined to have the benefit of fair use, they must be aware of its limitations. Courts have found copyright infringement for teachers distributing substantial photocopies of portions of books in class and the classroom unauthorized use of videotaped material (*Marcus v. Rowley, 695 F. 2d 1171 9*[th] *Cir. 1983*) and *Encyclopedia Britannica Ed.. Corp. v. Crooks, 558 F. Supp. 11247 W.D.N.Y. 1983*).

2. *The nature of the copyright material:* Courts will examine the nature of the work to determine if it is merely informational or factual. Newsworthy events and mere information are generally subject to fair use.

3. *The amount and substantiality of the copyright material in relation to the copyright work as a whole:* This criterion is quantifiable and relates to the number of pages used. Distribution of a page or two may be appropriate, but a small critical portion may implicate infringement liability. (*Harper & Row Publishers, Inc. v. Nation Enter., 471 U.S. 539 1985*). This limitation may be of special importance if a user in a nonprofit institution should download an entire program.

4. *The impact of the use on the potential market value of the copyright material:* The courts will be unwilling to find fair use if the plaintiff can prove that due to the defendant's copying, the value of the copyright material will diminish. This economic loss can occur either currently or potentially. Even with the first three criteria satisfied, there will not be fair use if the potential market of the copyright material is lost. (*American Geophysical Union v. Texaco, Inc. 37 F. 3*[rd] *881 2*[nd] *Cir. 1994*).

   The U.S. Supreme Court has stated, "Fair use, when properly applied, is limited to copying by others which does not materially impair the marketability of the work copied." (*Harper & Row Publishers, Inc., v. Nation Enter., 471 U. S. 539 1985*).

First Sale Doctrine

The **first sale doctrine** (Sec. 109(a) of the Copyright Act) limits the copyright owner's exclusive right to distribute publicly a copy of the work when the copyright material was lawfully acquired by another. Under the Copyright Act, "the owner of a . . . copy . . . is entitled, without the authority of the copyright owner, to

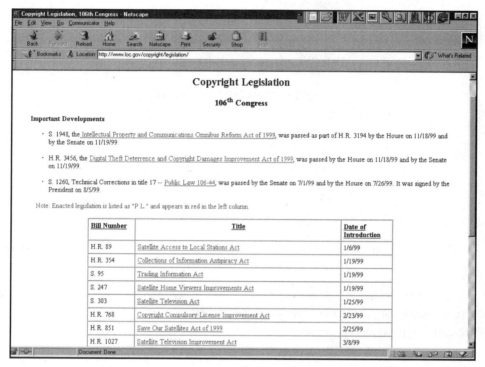

Courtesy United States Copyright Office/The Library of Congress.

sell . . . that copy." (17 U. S. C., Sec. 19). You could and probably will sell this textbook, and can do so without violating its copyright. However, the sale, rental, or lease of a licensed computer program without permission of the copyright owner may constitute an infringement.

Consider the case of a textbook purchase in electronic form, transferred and delivered to a student through the Internet. If the student electronically resold the textbook, it would involve the infringing acts of reproduction and public display of the textbook that are not permitted under the first sale doctrine. The first student who owned the book also retained a copy, so the first sale doctrine does not permit the distribution and reproduction of a copy through the Internet.

Public Domain

Materials in public domain are not subject to the exclusive statutory rights of the copyright owner. Public domain falls into two categories: (1) all works of the United States Government (e.g., the Congressional Record and court decisions) and (2) works whose copyright term has expired (refer back to the explanation of the duration of a copyright).

Figure 4.3
Burden of Proof in a Copyright Infringement Case

COPYRIGHT INFRINGEMENT LAWSUIT

PLAINTIFF   v.   **DEFENDANT**

A. Owner of the registered copyright
B. Violation of an exclusive statutory
   right under copyright law
C. Theory of liability
   (1) direct infringement
   (2) contributory infringement
   (3) vicarious infringement

doctrine of fair use applies
or
public domain

Other Statutory Exemptions on Copyright Owners' Exclusive Rights

The owner of a copy of a computer program may make a copy as an essential step in using the program in a computer and may make limited copies of that program unless prohibited by the terms of the license. (Copyright Act, Sec. 117). See Figure 4.3 for burden of proof in a copyright infringement suit.

Since 1989, under the Berne Convention Implementation Act, there is no longer a requirement that the copyright owner display use of the copyright material by the symbol ©. Although it is now optional, copyright owners should use the circled © with online activities. This will assist the owner in proving that the defendant had knowledge that the content was copyrighted.

Remedies for Copyright Infringement

A plaintiff in a copyright infringement lawsuit has a number of remedies available against the defendant.

1. *Monetary damages.* The plaintiff may sue for actual damages and for the return of any profits made by the defendant by its use of the copyright material.
2. *Statutory damages.* If the copyright has been registered in the Copyright Office prior to the commission of the infringement, the plaintiff is entitled to statutory damages in lieu of actual damages. **Statutory damages** under the Copyright Act are set at $500 to $20,000 per work infringed. *Willful* infringement may result

in damages up to $100,000 per work infringed. *Innocent* infringement may be reduced to a minimum of $200 per infringed work. Under the Intellectual Property and Communication Omnibus Reform Act 1999, S. 1948, statutory damages will be increased to $750 to $30,000 per work infringed and willful infringement has been raised to $150,000.

3. *Attorney's fees.* A successful plaintiff in a copyright infringement case may recover reasonable attorney's fees from the defendant.

4. *Preliminary Injunction (PI) or a Temporary Restraining Orders (TRO).* A plaintiff in a copyright infringement case may ask the court for a PI or a TRO in the event there would be irreparable harm in allowing the infringement to continue pending the upcoming trial. This is important because of the long wait before a trial in the federal courts is available.

In 1997 Congress passed the **No Electronic Theft Act.** The statute establishes criminal copyright liability, even without economic gain to the user, when the copyrighted material consisted of one or more works with a total retail value of more than $2,500. The Act was based on a 1994 case involving a Massachusetts Institute of Technology undergraduate student who was acquitted of criminal charges after he offered copyrighted software for free on his electronic bulletin board. This is one of many statutes that could make *hacking* a crime even without economic gain.

Patentable Subject Matter

Patentable subject matter is defined as "any new and useful process, machine, manufacture, or composition of matter, or any new and useful improvement thereof." (35 USC Sec.101) An e-business may have a business model that commonly includes original ways of doing business. (For example, see *State Street Bank v. Signature Financial Group,* 149 F. 3d 1368 (1998), cert. denied, 119 S. Ct. 851 (1999) which affirmed a lower court that held software-enabled business methods and processes are patentable as long as they are novel, nonobvious, and produce tangible results. An example of a novel, nonobvious business method that produces tangible results is Amazon's "one-click" ordering system. This was the basis for a patent infringement lawsuit against Barnes and Noble, where a federal judge ruled in favor of Amazon.

"Methods of Business Operations" as a Patent

Although patent law is distinct from copyright law, its application to e-commerce has become especially important regarding the patentability of an e-businesses *method of business operation.*

http://
Visit
www.amazon.com, www.bn.com

Advantages of Obtaining a Patent on a Business Method.   An e-business should work with its patent lawyers to determine if the business model could include a business method that may be the subject matter of a patent. Any systematic manner of organizing business activities is potentially patentable. This can prove to be a competitive advantage as it will prevent a company from using your business method and could thereby increase your market share. A business method that has been registered as a patent is especially useful for a startup e-business. The new asset may be used as security for debt financing and could provide the company with a legal remedy against a larger company that uses its patented business method. There is always the possibility of obtaining royalty income from licensees that may use the business method in noncompeting enterprises.

Search to Determine a Preexisting Patent of the Business Method.   Original methods of business operations that are not subject to copyright protection may be patentable with the PTO. To avoid patent infringement, an e-business should question if the Web site method of doing business has created a system subject to a preexisting patent. A patent lawyer will make an extensive search of existing patents to be sure the business method is original. If it is original, the e-business should investigate taking out a patent on its unique business methods.

The following are recent examples of patented methods of doing business in e-commerce:

1. "A system and method for conducting a multiperson, interactive auction without using a human auctioneer to conduct the auction" (Pat. No. 5,835,896—Nov.10, 1998—to Onsale, Inc.).
2. "A method of automatically matching sellers of property with potential buyers through a communications network, preferably the Internet" (Pat. No. 5, 664115—Sept. 2, 1998) to Richard Fraser.
3. "A merchant system for online shopping and merchandising to create electronic orders" (Pat. No. 5, 897622, Apr. 27. 1999) to Microsoft Corporation.
4. "A method and system for providing a fully automated electronic bill processing capability that is integrated with banking institutions and their customers" (Pat. No. 5, 885, 288-Mar. 16, 1999) to Sun Microsystems, Inc.

International Copyright and Patent Laws

http://
Each of these patents is used in commonly recognizable Web sites.
www.priceline.com, www.ebay.com

Keep in mind that the federal copyright of Web pages and patent registration of e-business methods do not always protect the works in foreign countries. Recognizing that e-commerce is global in nature, there is an attempt by international organizations to address the issues of global protection on intellectual property.

Copyrights, patents, and trademarks are protected under the Agreement on the Trade-Related Aspect of Intellectual Property (the TRIPs Agreement), administered by the World Trade Organization (WTO), which has 135 members. All intellectual property violations, including those relevant to e-commerce transactions, are adjudicated through the trade dispute resolution process administered by the WTO. Article 17 of the TRIPs Agreement protects patents rights and gives international recognition to the basic patent principles of law. See Chapter 13, "Global Issues," for a discussion of international intellectual property laws.

Summary

An e-business's Web site is a composition of content that is unique and constantly being revised. It represents a large capital investment and must be legally protected from those that would copy and use it without the owner's consent and payment of royalties. Our legal system provides a process for federal copyright registration of the Web pages that grants the owner exclusive statutory rights. These rights are limited by the fair use doctrine, which has guidelines that must be complied with for the doctrine to be upheld in court.

Since most e-business Web sites have a bulletin board or chat room to interact with the customer, it is important to monitor the material posted to ensure that there is no known copyright violation. The e-business could be held liable as a contributory infringer if it knew of the copyright material posted by the customer and actively allowed it to remain online.

An e-business must have its lawyers review and register with the Copyright Office its Web pages and have a patent lawyer review the business model to determine if any business method may be patentable.

Manager's Checklist

- Employee training programs that use videotapes and display Web sites on a computer monitor may be violating the copyright owner's exclusive right to display the work publicly. Managers should obtain the authorization of the copyright owner.
- When linking to a Web site, consider entering a "Web-linking agreement" with the linked site owner to avoid any possible violation of a term of use that may prohibit this practice.
- Web designers and their clients should be careful not to violate the copyright owner's exclusive right to prepare a derivative work.

- Databases should be arranged in an original and creative manner in order to qualify for copyright registration.
- Managers should be aware of the theories of contributory and vicarious liability.
- Managers should obtain an indemnification contract from the Web site designer in the event of a copyright infringement suit against the company.
- Managers should review with a patent lawyer the possibility of taking out a patent of its method of doing business.

Additional Readings

Rivette, Kevin, and David Kline. *Surviving the Internet Patent Wars,* (The Industry Standard, Dec. 13–20, 1999) pp. 180–82.

Lessig, Lawrence. *Code and the Other Laws of Cyberspace, Ch. 10 Intellectual Property.* Basic Books, NY 1999.

"Web Posting of Book Portions Can Be Contributory Copyright Infringement." *E-Commerce Law Weekly,* vol. 1, 9(1999): 216.

PART 3

Business and Finance Issues in Cyberspace

5

Online Contracting

"The overriding purpose of any commercial code is to facilitate commerce by reducing uncertainty and increasing confidence in commercial transactions. We believe that [the Uniform Computer Information Transactions Act] fails in this purpose. Its rules deviate substantially from long-established norms of consumer expectations. We are concerned that these deviations will invite overreaching that will ultimately interfere with the full realization of the potential of e-commerce in our states."

—The Attorneys General of Connecticut, Idaho, Indiana, Iowa, Kansas, Maryland, Nevada, New Mexico, North Dakota, Oklahoma, Pennsylvania, Vermont, Washington and the Administrator of the Georgia Fair Business Practices Act

Introduction

A contract is an agreement to exchange property or services that is legally enforceable in a court of law. For business, the value of a contract cannot be overestimated. Without contracts, businesses could not dependably buy, sell, employ, lease, license, or do any of the other things that businesses do.

Business on the Internet, or *e-commerce*, similarly depends on contracts. The prediction made by the Organization for Economic Cooperation and Development that e-commerce will exceed $1 trillion by 2003 is really a prediction that more than $1 trillion worth of property and services will be contractually exchanged over the Internet by 2003.

More importantly, while e-commerce is less than a decade old, contracting law is as old as business. And the rules and procedures for making, performing, and enforcing a contractual promise in the real world also apply, with very few exceptions, to the virtual world of electronic commerce.

Almost any kind of property and service can be contractually exchanged. The following are examples of property:

- Money
- Negotiable instruments (stocks, bonds, checks, etc.)
- Goods (movable tangible things such as computer hardware, fax machines, automobiles, etc.)

- Real property (immovable tangible things, including land and the fixtures attached to land)
- Intellectual property (software, copyrights, patents, trademarks, etc.)

Services can be ordinary employment agreements, agency arrangements (such as hiring a lawyer or an independent auditor), commercial service arrangements (engaging an Internet Service Provider), and so on. Similarly, there are many ways in which property and services can be contractually exchanged. Most commonly, these involve a sale, a lease, and a license of property, or an engagement of services. Of course, not all exchange agreements are enforceable. For example, some agreements are illegal (such as the sale of contraband or the hiring of a hit man), some are contrary to public policy (agreeing to monopolize trade), some are made by persons who lack capacity (the insane or young children), and some are merely social engagements (a date).

This chapter will discuss the laws that govern the making and enforcement of contracts, the requirements (or legal elements) for creating enforceable contracts, the consequences of not keeping (or breaching) contractual agreements, and the legal remedies that are available in the event of a breach. Those aspects of contract law that most affect e-commerce will be emphasized.

Laws Governing Contracts

Contract law is a matter of both common law (judge made) and statutory law. The common law contract rules are summarized in the *Restatement Second of the Law of Contract* (cited later in this chapter as "Restatement"). This is an unofficial but highly respected synopsis of the rules set out in U.S. court cases prepared by the American Law Institute.[1]

Statutory contract law—the contract law enacted by the U.S. Congress and state legislatures and federal and state administrative agencies—is remarkably similar throughout the United States. In part, this is due to the efforts of the National Conference of Commissioners on Uniform State Laws (NCCUSL), which has drafted model uniform state codes. Although the drafts must be adopted by state legislatures before they come into force in a state, nearly all states have done so. The NCCUSL draft law for commercial transactions is the *Uniform Commercial Code* (UCC), which has been adopted by all fifty states (although Louisiana has adopted only part of it), as well as the District of Columbia. Article 2 of the UCC sets out the rules governing the sale of goods and Article 2A the rules governing the leasing of goods.

[1] The American Law Institute was founded in 1923 by a distinguished group of lawyers, judges, and law teachers with the goal of preparing "an orderly restatement of the general common law of the United States, including in that term not only the law developed solely by judicial decision, but also the law that has grown from the application by the courts of statutes that were generally enacted and were in force for many years." Wolkin, "Restatements of the Law: Origin, Preparation, Availability," 21 Ohio B.A. Rept. 663 (1940).

http://

Laws, case decisions, and other materials about contracts are available online at Cornell Law School's Legal Information Institute at
wwwsecure.law.cornell.edu/topics/contracts.html

In 1995, the NCCUSL and ALI undertook a joint four-year project to draft Article 2B governing licenses and, in particular, the licensing of software. Ultimately, this could not be accomplished. Many of the ALI's members were critical of the provisions of the draft, which are generally more favorable to software licensors than consumers. The NCCUSL, however, was satisfied with the draft, and in April 1999 it redefined the draft to make it a separate freestanding act independent of the UCC. This allowed the NCCUSL to approve the act independently of the ALI. The result is the *Uniform Computer Information Transactions Act* (UCITA), promulgated by the NCCUSL in July 1999 and offered to the states for enactment.

Many of the provisions in the UCITA have proven to be controversial. Within days of its adoption, a letter from thirteen state attorneys general, later joined by another fourteen state attorneys general, asked the NCCUSL to withdraw and revise the UCITA. The main objection the attorneys general raised to the UCITA is that it preempts existing state consumer protection rules. (It does so by defining consumer software as nongoods.) Additionally, they objected to provisions that allow a merchant to withhold almost all of the contractual terms in its sale of software to a consumer until after the sale is completed.

Because of the controversy, it seems unlikely that the UCITA will be adopted in its current form.[2] As a consequence, the rules currently governing the licensing of software are those in UCC Articles 2 and 2A. Nevertheless, the main provisions of the UCITA as it would apply to software licenses will be discussed in this chapter.

In addition to the UCC and the UCITA, several other statutory laws currently apply to the making and enforcement of contracts. These include federal consumer protection laws, especially the *Federal Trade Commission Act* (which forbids deceptive and misleading practices by sellers) and the *Magnuson–Moss Warranty Act* (which requires sellers to disclose information about their written warranties), and similar state laws.[3]

Of special importance are electronic signature acts that have been adopted in most states and by the federal government. The Washington State *Electronic Authentication Act,* for example, provides for the licensing of authorities that certify to the authenticity of encrypted digital signatures.

---

[2]Since this book was written, Maryland and Virginia have adopted the UCITA.

[3]One such state law, California & Bus. Prof. Code, § 17538, was recently amended to apply to sales transactions consummated over the Internet.

The Requirements of a Contract

In order for persons to enter into a valid and enforceable contract, several requirements must be met. These are:

1. **Mutual Assent.** The parties to a contract must manifest by words or conduct their intent to enter into a contract. This is usually done by one of them making an offer and the other accepting it.
2. **Consideration.** Each party to the contract must exchange something of value.
3. **Capacity.** The parties must have the legal ability to enter into a contract. Persons judicially declared incompetent lack contractual capacity. Others, including minors and intoxicated persons, have limited contractual capacity.
4. **Legality.** The object of a contract cannot be criminal, tortious, or otherwise against public policy.
5. **Form.** A few contracts must be in a particular form. That is, they must be in writing and signed.

In the materials that follow, each of these elements will be discussed in more detail.

Mutual Assent

The *Restatement Second of the Law of Contracts,* § 3, defines the making of an agreement that constitutes a contract as: "the manifestation of a mutual assent on the part of two or more persons." In other words, the parties to a contract must give some outward indication of their intention to be bound.

Ordinarily, the parties show their mutual assent through an offer and an acceptance. One party proposes (offers) by words or conduct and the other agrees (accepts) by words or conduct. A contract that is expressed in words (whether oral or written) is an *express contract.* A contract that is formed by conduct is known as an *implied contract.*

Whether express or implied, all contracts involve either (1) the exchange of one promise for another or (2) the exchange of a promise for either an act or a forbearance to act. The first of these, involving two promises, is known as a *bilateral contract.* The second, involving a single promise, is known as a *unilateral contract.*

In determining if the parties have manifested mutual assent, the law applies an *objective standard.* That is, it looks to see if the intent of each of the parties can be ascertained from that party's words or actions. The law is not concerned with subjective intent (i.e., with what a party may have thought at the time of expressing an intent).

http://
See "Survey of State Electronic & Digital Signature Legislature Initiatives" posted at
www.ilpf.org/digsig/digrep.htm

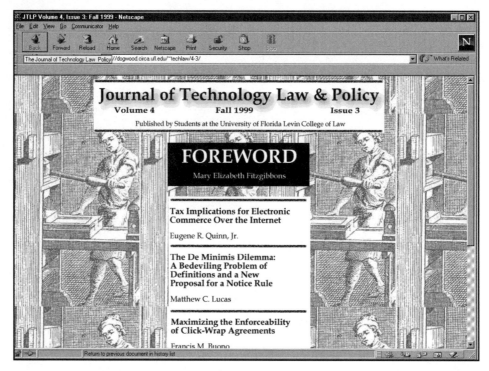

Offer.   An offer does not have to be in a particular form. However, it must (1) manifest an intent to enter into a contract, (2) be communicated (by the person making the offer—the *offeror*—to another—the *offeree*), and (3) be definite and certain.

- *Intent.* An offer must convey the offeror's intent to enter into a contract. A proposal that is made in jest ("Ha, ha. You bet, I'll give you $10,000 for your old 8086 computer!") is not an offer. Similarly, a preliminary inquiry ("How much is that Pentium III laptop?") is not an offer.

  An advertisement on an Internet Web page does not constitute an offer. If it did, the merchant might not be able to deliver the promised property or services if too many people were to accept. Recognizing this, the law treats advertisements, newsletters, quotation sheets, merchandise displays, and the like as informational notices rather than offers.

  A company that runs an auction is likewise not making an offer to sell goods, software, or other property that it lists for sale. It is, rather, soliciting offers. The persons placing bids are offering to buy the listed items. Only when the auction company declares that the auction is closed and that a bid has been accepted is there a binding contract.

If an auction is advertised or announced as being *without reserve,* the auction company may not withdraw an item put up for sale unless no bid is received within a reasonable time. If there is no advertisement or announcement of this sort, then the auction is *with reserve* and the auction company may withdraw the items put up for sale at anytime, even after several bids have been made.

- *Communication.* An offeror must intend to communicate an offer to an offeree and must actually do so. In other words, the offer is ineffective unless the offeror means to communicate it to a particular offeree. For example, Ann may send an e-mail to Bob offering to sell him her laser printer for $200. She likes Bob and wants to give him a special price. Bob doesn't need the printer, but he knows that Charlie does, so he forwards Ann's e-mail to Charlie. Charlie's acceptance of Ann's offer would not be effective, because Ann made the offer to Bob, not Charlie.

  Additionally, the offeror must actually deliver the offer to the offeree. For instance, assume that Dale sends an e-mail message offering to sell his cell phone to Elvira. Because of a server error, the message never gets to Elvira. If Elvira were to call Dale on the phone and tell him she wants to buy Dale's cell phone, she would not be accepting the e-mail offer, because it never got to her. Instead, she would be making her own offer to Dale, and the terms of that offer would govern their contractual relationship, not the terms in Dale's e-mail message.

- *Definiteness.* The terms of an offer must be reasonably certain and complete. This is so that a court will be able to enforce the resulting contract it if asked to do so.

  If too many terms are missing, a court may hold that the parties did not intend to form a contract. Because contracts take many forms, it is not possible to list the essential terms necessary to form a contract. However, for most contracts, the material terms would include the subject matter, quantity, quality, price, payment terms, and duration.

Duration of Offers.   An offeree may accept an offer until the offer terminates. An offer will terminate (1) when it is accepted, (2) when the time within it is to be accepted lapses (or, if no time is specified, within a reasonable period of time), (3) upon the offer's revocation by the offeror, (4) upon its rejection by the offeree, (5) when the offeree makes a counteroffer, (6) whenever the offeror or offeree dies or becomes incompetent, (7) upon the destruction of the subject matter of the offer (such as the accidental erasure of all the data in a database), or (8) if the type of contract involved subsequently becomes illegal.

Sometimes an offeror will promise to keep an offer open for a specified period of time. UCC § 2-205 provides that such a promise is enforceable, but only if the offeror is a merchant (one who deals in goods), the subject matter of the offer is goods, the period of time does not exceed three months, and the promise is made in a signed writing. Various other statutes make certain nonmerchant offers irrevocable. These include offers made to government bodies and offers to subscribe to stock prior to a business's incorporation (which cannot be revoked for six months). Otherwise, nonmerchants may revoke their offers any time before they are accepted.

Acceptance.   An acceptance is a positive and unequivocal expression of an offeree's intent to enter into a contract on the terms set out in the offer. Only when an offer is accepted does a contract come into existence.

The requirements for making an acceptance depend on the kind of contract involved. If the contract is *bilateral* (a promise exchanged for a promise), the offeree must intend to accept and must communicate acceptance to the offeror. If the contract is *unilateral* (a promise exchanged for an act or an act of forbearance), acceptance usually does not have to be communicated.

Silence as Acceptance. An offeree usually is under no legal obligation to reply to an offer. The offeree's silence or inaction, therefore, will not constitute an acceptance.

Consider this problem, however. Suppose Chancy Software Company sends you unsolicited e-mail with a software program attached. The program promises to make you rich and famous in thirty days. You decide to install the program to see what it is all about. When you do, a small window opens on your monitor with 140 lines of small type. Among the terms is a promise to pay Chancy $100. Beneath the window is the query: "Do you accept all the terms and conditions of this offer?" There is a button that says "yes" and one that says "cancel installation." If you click on the "yes" button, are you accepting the offer?

The answer is unclear. Most states and the federal government have laws that allow a recipient to keep unsolicited merchandise as a gift. On the other hand, if you click on the "yes" button, an argument can be made that you are accepting the terms of Chancy's offer and that you do not regard the program as a gift. The courts have yet to decide a case dealing with this situation, so we will have to wait to find out which way they will rule.

Silence or inaction can constitute acceptance if the parties agree in advance that it will, or if custom, usage, or a prior course similarly so provide. For example, when a person becomes a member of a mail-order book club, the person agrees that failure to return a notification card rejecting offered goods will constitute acceptance of the club's offer to sell the member the goods.

UCC § 2-208 allows for silence to serve as acceptance only where a single contract involves "repeated occasions for performance." UCITA § 112(f) expands on this, allowing the parties in one transaction to agree that acceptance by inaction will apply to any "future transactions between the parties."[4] Needless to say, if the UCITA comes into force, consumers and other purchasers will want to carefully read the fine print of every software license they are offered before they agree to be bound by its terms. If they do not, they may be agreeing to accept the offeror's future software products unless they respond negatively to them.

Time When Acceptance is Effective. Unlike an offer (as well as a revocation, counteroffer, and rejection), an acceptance is ordinarily not effective when it is received. Rather, it has effect *from the moment of its dispatch by the offeree.* This is so unless at least one of the following conditions apply:

1.   The offer specifically provides otherwise.

---

[4]The state attorneys general who object to the UCITA cite this provision as being one that invites abuse.

2. The offeree uses an unauthorized method of acceptance (such as mailing a response by ordinary mail when the offer requires that the response be by e-mail).
3. The acceptance is sent after the offeree sends a rejection (in which case, the communication that gets to the offeror first will be the one that is effective).

Acceptance with Modifications. It is not uncommon for an offeree to want to change or add terms to an offer. Under the common law, the *mirror image rule* applies. That provides that an acceptance must exactly mirror the offer. *Any change or addition will constitute a rejection of the offer and the making of a counteroffer.*

Lack of Mutual Assent.   An essential element of every contract is that both parties must intend to be bound by it. This mutuality of intent is sometimes referred to as a *meeting of the minds.* If there is no meeting of the minds, there will be no contract. Therefore, even if both the offeror and the offeree sign a document that is labeled a contract, they will not have a contract if they both believe it involves something different.

• *Shrink-wrap Licenses.*   Software sold on discs in retail stores frequently comes with a contractual license that can only be viewed by opening the plastic wrapper in which the disc is enclosed. Commonly, the purchaser does not open the package until after paying for the software and taking it home. Have the parties in such a case really entered into a contract governed by the terms of the **shrink-wrap license?** Has there been a "meeting of the minds" at the time the software was purchased?

According to the trial judge in the case of *ProCD v. Zeidenberg*, 980 F.Supp 640 (W. D. Wis. 1996), a shrink-wrap license violates a basic notion of contract law: that both parties have to know what they are agreeing to. This decision, however, was overturned on its appeal to the U.S. 7th Circuit Court of Appeals (86 F.3d 1447 (7th Cir. 1996). According to the 7th Circuit, shrink-wrap licenses have to be enforceable because they have the beneficial effect of reducing the cost of software for consumers.

The Court of Appeals' decision also upheld the validity of the shrink-wrap license in question in the *ProCD* case, because the license allowed the purchaser to return the software if the terms of the license were unacceptable. The new *Uniform Computer Information Transactions Act* approves such an approach to shrink-wrap licenses, which it calls **mass-market licenses.** UCITA § 210(b) provides that "[i]f a licensee does not have an opportunity to review a mass-market license or a copy of it before becoming obligated to pay and does not agree, such as by manifesting assent, to the license after having that opportunity, the licensee is entitled to . . . return [the licensed software]. . . ."

• *Click-wrap Licenses.*   Software downloaded from the Internet is commonly sold with a **click-wrap license.** Such a license appears on the screen of the purchaser's monitor the first time the software is being installed and the purchaser is asked to accept the terms of the license before installing the software. UCITA § 210(b) would make such a license enforceable.

One of the objections made to the UCITA by the state attorneys general is that it would make shrink-wrap and click-wrap licenses enforceable. Click-wrap licenses, according to the attorneys general, are too easily subject to abuse. For example, a vendor's Web site may instruct the purchaser to view the license terms, but then distract the purchaser with a variety of special offers and other information. After having been distracted, the software may automatically be installed on the purchaser's computer before the purchaser can review the license. As a consequence, the purchaser might be unwittingly billed for software and ancillary services.

Contrary to the state attorneys general's view, the validity of one click-wrap license was upheld in the case of *Caspi v. Microsoft Network*, LLC, 732 A.2d 528 (New Jersey Superior Court, Appellate Division, 1999). In that case, Caspi, a New Jersey resident, filed suit in New Jersey against Microsoft after subscribing over the Internet to the Microsoft Network (MSN). He argued that he was not bound by a forum-selection clause requiring any lawsuit against Microsoft to be brought in Washington State because he did not get adequate notice of this clause. The clause was one of a number that had appeared on Caspi's computer screen in a scrollable window next to blocks providing the choices "I Agree" and "'I Don't Agree." Because Caspi clicked on the "I Agree" choice, the court held that he got sufficient notice. According to the court "We discern nothing about the style or mode of presentation, or the placement of the provision, that can be taken as a basis for concluding that the forum selection clause was proffered unfairly, or with a design to conceal or de-emphasize its provisions." Caspi's complaint against Microsoft in New Jersey was therefore dismissed.

• *Fraud.* If a party intentionally misrepresents a material (important) fact that induces the other party to rely on that fact and enter into a contract, the injured party may avoid the contract. For example, in a recently filed criminal case, *New Jersey v. Crespo*, (*Essex County Sup. Ct., filed Dec 2, 1999*), the defendants allegedly set up an Internet Web site that claimed to represent a well-known Australian financial services company when it did not. In addition, the defen-

> **http://**
> The *New Jersey v. Crespo* case is described in the Perkins Coie Internet Case Digest at
> **www.perkinscoie.com/resource/ecomm/netcase/Cases-03.htm**

dants are alleged to have used the moneys sent to them by investors for personal purchases, including personal travel. If this is true, the investors are entitled to get their moneys back, plus any additional losses they may have suffered, such as lost profits on the investments they thought they had made.

Fraudulent misrepresentation does not always have to be stated. Sometimes it can be implied from a person's failure to speak up. For example, if Linda sells a software program to Mary knowing that it contains a virus that will harm Mary's computer, Linda has to disclose that fact to Mary. Mary can properly assume that the software is virus free, and if Linda knows otherwise, she must speak up.

• *Misrepresentation.* Misrepresentation is a misstatement without intent to deceive. A contract entered into through a misrepresentation, like a contract induced by fraud, is avoidable by an injured party.

• *Mistake.* If both of the parties to a contract are mistaken as to some material fact that induced them to enter into their contract, they really have not had a "meeting of the minds" and therefore they do not have a contract. Either party may rescind such a contract. To do so, there must be a *mutual mistake* (i.e., it must be made by both parties) and the mistake must relate to a *material fact* (i.e., the parties would not have entered into the contract if they had known about it). For example, suppose there are two software programs known as "Omega 13," one manufactured by Company X, the other by Company Y. If the Online Auction Company thinks it is selling a Company X version of Omega 13, and so does the buyer, when in reality the software is the Company Y version, there is a material mutual mistake, and either party may rescind the transaction.

Consideration

In order for a contract to be enforceable it must be supported by consideration. Consideration is a legal obligation assumed or a legal right surrendered. If a contract is bilateral, the promises exchanged by each party are the consideration. If a contract is unilateral, the consideration of one party is its promise; the performance of an act is the consideration of the other party.

Consideration Must Be Bargained For. In order for consideration to exist, the parties must have bargained for it. That is, the parties must really intend to exchange one thing for another. Most exchanges involve a bargained-for exchange. However, some do not. Transactions the law does not consider to involve an exchange of consideration include: (1) gifts, (2) something given in exchange for a service already performed by the other party (this is known as *prior consideration*), and (3) something given in exchange for a service that other person is already obligated to do (this is known as a *preexisting obligation*).

Exceptions to the Requirement of Consideration.   There are several exceptions to the requirement that a contractual promise be supported by consideration:

- *Modification of a sale of goods contract.* UCC § 2-209(1) provides that "[a]n agreement modifying a contract [for the sale of goods] needs no consideration to be binding." For example, if Yancy agrees to sell a laptop to Zeek for $1,000, but then changes his mind, and demands $1,500, Zeek cannot later complain if he goes ahead and pays the $1,500 because the sale of the word processor is the sale of a good. (A good being a tangible and movable thing.)
- *Firm Offer.* UCC § 2-205 provides that a merchant's assurance to keep open an offer to buy or sell goods for a stated period of time is enforceable even though it is unsupported by consideration. This *firm offer,* however, must be made in a writing signed by the merchant, and it will be valid for no more than three months.

   Anybody, however, may enter into an *option contract* that promises to hold open an offer to buy or sell anything for a period of time. This is because an option contract involves a payment by the person for whom the offer if kept open. For example, News Company may pay $10,000 to Data Services to have the option to buy Data Services' trademark name anytime during the next six months. During that six-month period, Data Services could not sell its trademark. However, if News Company does not exercise the option during the six-month period, then Data Services would be free to sell the trademark to someone else. On the other hand, the $10,000 is only a payment for the option to buy. If News Company chooses to buy the trademark, it will have to pay an additional price for it.
- *Promissory estoppel.* The doctrine of *promissory estoppel* says that a person who reasonably and foreseeably relies to their detriment on the promise of another may estop (prevent) that other person from revoking the promise, even if the promise is unsupported by consideration. In order to prove promissory estoppel, three things have to be shown: (1) a clear and unambiguous promise, (2) a reasonable and foreseeable reliance by the party to whom the promise is made, and (3) an injury sustained by the party who so relied. For example, suppose an Internet Service Provider tells a client that it is welcome to set up a Web site for free on the ISP's Web server. Because of this, the client spends several thousand dollars to have a Web site designed. The ISP cannot later change its mind and refuse to let the client put the Web site on its server.

Capacity

Persons who enter into contracts must understand that they are doing so. Someone who does not understand the consequences of what he or she is promising to do lacks contractual capacity.

Ordinarily, the law assumes that everyone has the capacity to contract. There are three main exceptions to this rule. Minors, intoxicated persons, and the mentally incompetent are often held to lack contractual capacity.

Minors.   In most states, a minor is anyone under the age of eighteen. Minors are allowed to avoid contracts they have entered into, unless the contract is one for *necessaries*. Necessaries are those things a minor needs to live, such as food, clothing, shelter, and medical care. Although minors may not *disaffirm* contracts supplying them with necessaries, the courts in many states will hold that minors are only obliged to pay their "reasonable" price for such things.

In addition to limiting a minor's ability to avoid a contract for necessaries, the courts in most states will not allow minors to disaffirm a contract if the minor misrepresented his or her age at the time of entering into such a contract. Of course, the other party must reasonably have been able to believe that the minor was actually an adult. So, for example, if a seven-year-old states in person or over the telephone that he is twenty-one, it is highly unlikely that anyone could believe him, and therefore he will be able to disaffirm the contract, despite his misrepresentation. On the other hand, many online sites rely on circumstantial criteria for determining if a customer is an adult. Commonly, they require a customer to provide an employment address, a credit card number, and a statement that the client is an adult. Even a seven-year-old may not be able to disaffirm the contract in such a circumstance. However, there is currently no court decision on this question.

Minors may disaffirm a contract anytime before they become adults, and for a reasonable time thereafter. If they don't disaffirm within a reasonable time after becoming an adult, they are said to have impliedly ratified the contract. On the other hand, the adult who enters into a contract with a minor may not disaffirm it at any time.

Intoxicated Persons.   A person who is so intoxicated that he or she is unaware that they of entering into a contract is not bound by the promise. This is so whether the intoxication was self-induced or caused by someone else. In the context of e-commerce, however, intoxication is likely to be very difficult to prove. You would have to show, for example, that you had turned on your computer, connected to the Internet, logged on to an auction house, chosen a product, entered a bid, read the disclaimer stating that all bids are final, and reentered the bid, all while so high on liquor or drugs that you had no idea what you were doing.

Mentally Incompetent Persons.   Persons declared incompetent in a court proceeding lack the capacity to contract, and any contract they enter into is said to be void. Persons not yet declared incompetent, but who are unable to appreciate the effect of their contractual promises, have the right to disaffirm such a promise.

Legality

Contracts must be legal to be enforceable. If they require a party to commit an illegal act, they are said to violate public policy. That is, they violate accepted standards of behavior and they are *void*. When a contract is void, courts will generally take no action, leaving the parties in the situation they have put themselves.

Not all illegal contracts are void. Sometimes, one party is unaware of the illegality, and sometimes a law making conduct illegal is meant to protect one of the parties. The innocent party, in such cases, may rescind the contract and require the other party to return any consideration the innocent party gave him or her. For example, Horace may hire Imogene as his lawyer, not knowing that Imogene has been disbarred. In such a case, Horace can demand that Imogene return any money he paid her.

Following are examples of illegal contracts that the courts regard as void:

- Contracts to commit a crime or tort
- Gambling contracts (unless authorized by law)
- Contracts charging usurious interest (interest greater than that specified by law)
- Contracts violating a licensing statute (a statute requiring a person—usually a professional—to be licensed before contracting to provide a service)
- Exculpatory contracts (contracts that attempt to limit the liability of a person who sells goods or services to the public)
- Unconscionable contracts (contracts in which one party uses bargaining power to take advantage of the other party)
- Contracts meant to restrain or restrict trade

Of these illegal contracts, those involving a restraint of trade are the most likely to affect online contracting.

Section 1 of the Sherman Antitrust Act, the principal federal law dealing with the regulation of competition, prohibits contracts, combinations, and conspiracies in restraint of trade or commerce. The most common contract in restraint of trade is *price fixing:* an agreement among competitors to set the same price for their products. Because an agreement to set prices in advance rather than letting the forces of the marketplace determine the price is anticompetitive, injurious to consumers, and a restraint of trade, it violates the Sherman Antitrust Act and is illegal.

Other arrangements that amount to restraints of trade are *noncompetition agreements*—agreements not to sell competing products or services; *tying agreements*—agreements to purchase one product or service as a condition or prerequisite to purchasing a second product; and *grant back agreements*—agreements requiring one party to turn over to a second party any improvements the first party makes to a technology licensed to it by the second party.

One very prominent example of the use of tying agreements involved Microsoft. In the early 1990s, Microsoft used licensing agreements to require personal computer manufacturers who were purchasing its operating system software to also purchase and install its office and other software, and to keep them from purchasing or installing similar software from Microsoft's competitors. When the US Justice Department and the European Union's competition authority objected, Microsoft entered into a consent decree in 1994 that forbade Microsoft from using "tying agreements" of this sort. To get around this prohibition, Microsoft began integrating its other products into its operating system. The Justice Department then brought suit—the case is *United States v. Microsoft Corporation*, 147 F.3d 935 (District of Columbia Circuit Court of Appeals, 1998)—to enforce the consent decree. In particular, it wanted to keep Microsoft from integrating its Internet Explorer web browser into its Windows 95 operating system. The court dismissed the Justice Department's complaint, ruling that the consent decree was worded in such a way that Microsoft was not forbidden from integrating its products together so long as the integration added significant value over what the separate software products offered. Although it was clear that the effect of Microsoft's decision to integrate its products was to require personal computer manufacturers to purchase what had previously been two or more Microsoft products (contrary to the intent of the original consent decree), the court ruled in favor of Microsoft because the language of the consent decree specifically allowed for Microsoft to "develop integrated products."

Soon after the Justice Department lost in its attempt to enforce the 1994 consent decree, it sued Microsoft for anticompetitive behavior. On essentially the same facts, the trial court in that case—*United States v. Microsoft* (Docket No. 98-1232, 2000)—held that Microsoft had sought to restrain trade and act in a monopolistic manner, and it ordered that the company be broken up. The order is currently on appeal.

Form

Most contracts do not have to be any particular form. As a general rule, they may be written, oral, or even unstated, and still be enforceable.

There are certain contracts, however, that must be in writing. These are contracts described in a law known as the *Statute of Frauds*. Originally adopted by the

English Parliament in the seventeenth century, all of the U.S. states now have their own statutes of frauds. These statutes require that following contracts be in writing:

- Contracts involving the sale of an interest in land
- Contracts that cannot be performed within one year
- Collateral contracts to pay the debt of another person
- Contracts made in consideration of marriage
- Contracts made by an executor or administrator of an estate to personally pay the debts of that estate.

The Uniform Commercial Code, which has its own Statute of Frauds provisions (UCC §§ 2-201 and 2A-201), requires that these additional contracts be in writing:

- Contracts for the sale of goods for $500 or more
- Contracts for the lease of goods for $1,000 or more

Additionally, the *Uniform Computer Information Transactions Act* (UCITA § 201) requires a writing for:

- Contracts for the licensing of informational rights for more than $5,000.
- Contracts for the licensing of informational services that cannot be performed in less than one year.

It is important to note that the writing requirements in the UCC and the UCITA apply only in the United States. Most international sale of goods transactions are now governed by the *United Nations Convention on Contracts for the Sale of Goods* (CISG), which does not have a writing requirement. Similarly, most other countries only require a writing for the sale of goods when a nonmerchant is involved.

Form and Electronic Commerce.   The requirement that certain contracts have to be in writing has long been a concern for persons engaged in commercial transactions. Some thirty years ago, before the advent of the Internet, companies began entering into contracts based on an exchange of data that was in a computer-processable format. Known as **Electronic Date Interchange (EDI)**, this involves the electronic exchange between companies of pricing schedules, purchase orders, acknowledgments, order status inquiries, shipping schedules, delivery conformation, invoices, payments, and other business information. Originally, EDI data was physically delivered on computer tapes or discs. Later it was exchanged on dedicated telephone networks and most recently, of course, over the Internet.

> **http://**
> For information about the development of EDI standards see the Data Interchange Standards Association (DISA) home page at
> **www.x12.org**

In 1979, the American National Standards Institute began developing uniform national and international standards for the interindustry electronic interchange of business data. The development of these standards, which now constitute some 275 transaction sets, facilitates business transactions by establishing a common, uniform business language for computers to use to communicate with each other.

A major concern for U.S. companies using EDI is whether the EDI contracts are enforceable. The UCITA specifically validates such contracts, but until it (or something like it) comes into force, doubts remain. The most important of these doubts relates to the *form* of EDI contracts.

EDI contracts typically involve a sale of goods, and most of these sales are for large sums of money. The UCC's Statute of Frauds, of course, requires contracts for the sale of goods for more than $500 be in a signed writing. EDI contracts, however, are not contained in a "paper" writing and they do not involve a human signature.

We will talk about the writing and signature requirements shortly. Before doing so, however, we need to point out the practical procedure that companies currently use to ensure that their EDI contracts are enforceable.

The practical way to make sure that EDI contracts are legally valid is for the EDI trading partners to enter into an **EDI Trading Partner Agreement.** Such agreements are written on paper and signed by the partners. They state that the trading partners intend for their EDI transactions to be as valid and as enforceable as conventional paper contracts. In addition, they address the apportionment of risk, security procedures, the use of electronic signatures, the definition of what constitutes a receipt of a communication, and the various business issues contained in a standard purchase order (such as delivery and payment schedules and dispute settlement arrangements). See box below.

Complying with the Statute of Frauds.   The writing requirement of the statutes of fraud does not require that a writing be in any particular form, that it describe the entire agreement, or that it even prove that the contract is binding. All that is required is that a writing or memorandum prove that a contract was made. It must do the following:

1. Specify the parties to the contract
2. Specify with reasonable certainty the subject matter and the essential terms of that part of the contract this is not yet performed

> **http://**
> For more on EDI Trading Partners Agreements see
> "Electronic Data Interchange and the Law" at
> **www.cl.ais.net/lawmsf/articl3.htm**

3. Be signed by the party against whom the contract is to be enforced

• *The Writing or Memorandum.*   A writing or memorandum may be any permanent record showing that the parties entered into a contract. The federal government and most states have adopted electronic signature acts that define writings so that they include information stored in an electronic medium that is retrievable in a perceivable form. Similarly, UCITA § 106 provides that an electronic record is to be regarded as a writing and § 107 states that "[a] record . . . may not be denied legal effect or enforceability solely because it is in electronic form."

- *The Signature.* The **signature** that is required on a writing or memorandum may be a person's name, initials, or any other symbol, as long as the party intends for it to authenticate the writing. The electronic signature acts that have now been adopted in most states establish procedures for making valid electronic signatures or establish criteria for determining if a signature is valid. For example, the Washington State *Electronic Authentication Act,* mentioned earlier in the chapter, establishes a procedure for creating valid digital signatures through the licensing of certifying authorities. By comparison, California has enacted rules for identifying electronic signatures (California Code § 16.5(a) (1995). This provides that an electronic signature is valid under these conditions:

1. It is unique to the person using it.
2. It can be verified.
3. It is under the sole control of the person using it.
4. It is linked to the data in such a manner that if the data is changed the signature is invalidated.
5. It conforms to regulations adopted by the appropriate state agency.

On the other hand, the federal *Electronic Signatures Act in Global and National Commerce Act*, which applies to interstate and foreign consumer transactions, validates electronic signatures if the consumer consents in advance to their use.

In line with the California and federal rules, the UCITA would provide for the authentication of an electronic record both by human action and by means of an electronic agent (i.e., by a program that can independently initiate an action or respond to an electronic message or request without review or action by an individual). UCITA § 107(d) states:

> A person that uses its own electronic agent for authentication, performance, or agreement, including manifestation of assent, is bound by the operations of the electronic agent, even if no individual was aware of or reviewed the agent's operations or the results of the operations.

Exceptions to the Statute of Frauds' Writing Requirement

There are several exceptions to the Statute of Frauds' requirement that some contracts have to be in writing.

The *doctrine of part performance* applies to contracts for the sale of an interest in land. This says, that when a purchaser of land makes value improvements to it, or when the purchaser takes possession of the land after having paid part of the purchase price, that a writing is not needed to make the contract enforceable.

There are several exceptions to the UCC Statute of Frauds rules that sales of goods for more than $500, and leases of goods for more than $1,000, have to be in writing. UCC §§ 2-201 and § 2A-201 state that a writing is not required for the following:

- Contracts for goods specially manufactured for the buyer on which the seller has begun performance
- Contracts for which payment has been made and accepted or for which the goods have been received and accepted
- Contracts in which the party being sued admits in a court or in the pleadings that the contract was made

In addition, for sales of goods (but not for leases of goods), a writing is not required for contracts between merchants, if the merchant being sued received a written notice from the other merchant confirming the existence of the contract and if the merchant being sued did not object to the confirmation within ten days of its receipt.

The exceptions in the UCITA are analogous to those in the UCC. UCITA § 201 says that a writing is not required for the following:

- Contracts for which payment has been made and accepted or for which the information has been received and accepted
- Contracts in which the party being sued admits in a court or in the pleadings that the contract was made
- Contracts between merchants, if the merchant being sued received a written notice[6] from the other merchant confirming the existence of the contract and if the merchant being sued did not object to the confirmation within ten days of its receipt.

The Parol Evidence Rule.   The **parol evidence rule** applies to contracts that are in writing, whether or not they are required to be so by a Statute of Frauds. This rule states that the parties to a complete and final written contract cannot introduce evidence in court to change the meaning of the terms of the contract. See UCC § 2-202 and § 2A-201, and UCITA § 301.

The parol evidence rule only excludes evidence of oral or other agreements made at the time of, or prior to, the making of the written contract. It does not exclude evidence of a modification made after the written contract was agreed to, or which is introduced to explain (but not change the meaning of) a contractual term.

---

[6]UCITA § 201 uses the term "record" rather than "writing." It defines a "record" as "information that is inscribed on a tangible medium or that is stored in an electronic or other medium and is retrievable in perceivable form." UCITA § 102(58).

For example, suppose Imogene, a seller, told Jake, a buyer, that the computer system he wanted to buy included a 16-gigabit hard drive and a DVD drive. Later, when Jake signed the contract to buy the system, the written contract said that there would be a hard drive, but it did not specify the size. Also, instead of a DVD drive, it said a CD-ROM drive would be provided. Jake may testify in court to explain that the hard drive was meant to be a 16-gigabit drive, because his testimony would help the court understand the meaning of the term "hard drive." However, he may not testify that the CD-ROM drive was suppose to be a DVD drive, because this would change the meaning of that term.

Third Parties to Contracts

In addition to the parties who enter into a contract, third parties may acquire a contractual interest by assignment, by delegation, or as an intended beneficiary.

Assignment of Contractual Rights

A person who owes a duty under a contract is known as an *obligor,* and the person to whom he owes a duty is known as an *obligee.* Of course, when a contract is bilateral, each party is both an obligor and an obligee.

For example, assume that Jane promises to sell a copy machine to Kirk and Kirk promises to pay $5,000 for it in monthly installments over the next two years. Under this contractual arrangement, Jane is entitled (as an obligee) to receive the monthly installments from Kirk and is required (as an obligor) to deliver the copy machine to Kirk. Kirk, accordingly, is entitled (as an obligee) to receive the copy machine and required (as an obligor) to pay Jane the monthly installments. This is illustrated in Figure 5.1.

An assignment of contractual rights is the voluntary transfer to a third party of an obligee's rights arising under a contract. In the preceding example, if Jane decides to transfer her rights under the contract (the right to receive monthly installment payments from Kirk) to Lucia in exchange for a payment of $4,500 from Lucia, this would be a valid assignment of Jane's rights (see Figure 5.2). Jane, in this case, would be known as an *assignor,* Lucia would be an *assignee,* and Kirk would continue to be an *obligor.*

After a valid assignment is made, the assignor's right to have the obligor perform comes to an end. At that time, only the assignee is entitled to have the obligor perform.

When an assignor assigns rights, the assignor impliedly warrants that the rights are valid. If the assignee is unable to enforce these rights against the obligor because of incapacity, illegality, or breach of contract, the assignee can sue the assignor.

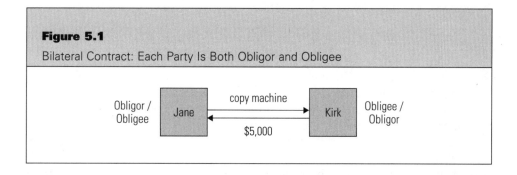

Figure 5.1

Bilateral Contract: Each Party Is Both Obligor and Obligee

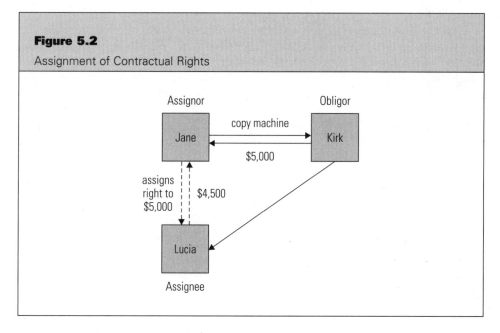

Figure 5.2

Assignment of Contractual Rights

Notice of Assignment. As soon as an assignment is made, an assignee should promptly notify the obligor of the assignment. Otherwise, the obligor may continue to pay the original obligee (now the assignee).

As a practical matter, notification is the best way to avoid the problem of an obligor/assignor carelessly or dishonestly transferring rights to more than one assignee. The law in most states provides that the first assignee to notify an obligor has priority, regardless of which assignee received the first assignment of rights.

Contracts That Cannot Be Assigned.   Most contractual rights can be assigned. However, an assignment that increases the burden of performance to the obligor cannot be assigned. For example, suppose that a New York retailer has agreed to ship a computer to a buyer in New Jersey. The buyer would not be allowed to assign the right to receive the computer to a third party in California because the retailer's shipping costs would increase.

A contract provision that expressly prohibits an assignment will be strictly construed by the courts. That is, the courts will not look favorably upon it and will attempt to avoid enforcing it if possible. Also, most courts will interpret a general prohibition as being only a promise not to assign. Therefore, a breach of the promise will give the obligor the right to sue for damages, but it will not make the assignment itself invalid.

Both the Restatement (§ 322) and the UCC (§ 2-210) provide that a prohibition against making an assignment, unless the circumstances clearly indicate otherwise, shall only prohibit the delegation of a duty by an obligee and not the assignment of a right by an obligor. Moreover, UCC § 9-318(4) says that a prohibition against the assignment of a right to receive payment for goods sold or leased, or for services rendered, is ineffective.

By comparison, UCITA § 503 provides that a contractual term prohibiting the assignment of a license, or the right to receive payment for a license, is enforceable, and "a transfer made in violation of that term is a breach of contract and is ineffective. . . ." The UCITA only requires that a prohibition in a mass-market license "be conspicuous."

For example, a provision in a software license that says "this software is transferred solely to the licensee and it may not be transferred or assigned to anyone else" is valid and enforceable. By comparison, a provision in a contract for the sale of goods that says "the seller may not assign the right to receive payment for these goods" is invalid and unenforceable.

Section 503 of the Uniform Computer Information Transactions Act is a highly controversial section and one of the main reasons why many have objected to the Act's adoption. Consider the following situation and then decide if you support the UCITA. Suppose that you buy a new computer from an online vendor, such as Dell Computer Corp. or Gateway, Inc.—one that comes fully loaded with operating system software, desktop software, office software, games, and everything else that you need to do whatever you do. Suppose, a year later that you want to sell the computer and buy a new one. You look at the licenses you signed for the software installed on the computer. Assume that all of them conspicuously forbid the transfer of the installed software to any third party. If the UCITA applies, and you want to *legally* sell your computer, you will have to strip off all of the software on the machine. Additionally, if the ROM on the processing chip contains a similar prohibition, you will have to remove or reprogram the chip. The UCC, of course, applies to the sale of the hardware (it is not "computer information"), and any prohibition against its transfer will likely be invalid and unenforceable.

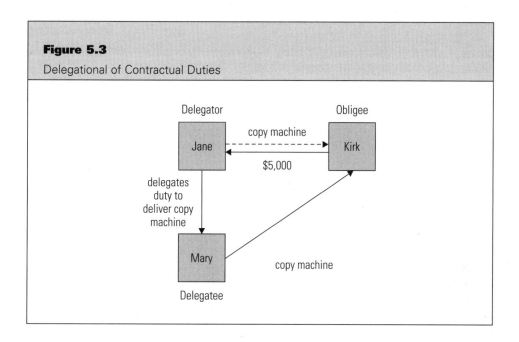

Figure 5.3
Delegational of Contractual Duties

Delegation of Contractual Duties

A **delegation of duties** is a transfer of contractual obligations to a third party. Continuing with our earlier example, if Jane were to ask a third party, Mary, to deliver the copy machine to Kirk in his place, this would not be an assignment of rights, but a delegation of duties. In this circumstance, Jane would be the *delegator,* Mary would be the *delegatee,* and Kirk would now be the *obligee.* Figure 5.3 illustrates this.

As a general rule, a delegation of duties is allowed. A delegation, however, will not be allowed under any of these conditions:

1. The nature of the duties is personal and the obligee has a substantial interest in having the particular obligor perform the contract.
2. The performance is expressly made nondelegable.
3. The delegation is prohibited by statute or public policy.

For example, if a skilled programmer is hired to write unique software for a client, he may not send someone else to do so in his place, even if that person is an equally good programmer, because this contract is personal in nature.

Cyberethics

- Are shrink-wrap licenses ethical?
- Is it ethical for a software vendor to forbid a licensee from transferring licensed software to another person?
- Is it ethical for a software vendor to include a provision in its license that requires a purchaser to agree in advance to buy future releases of other software?
- Is it ethical for someone who has entered into an online contract to attempt to avoid it because it is not in writing and does not contain a signature?
- Is it ethical for a software vendor to include a disclaimer provision in a pop-up window that is in small type and that cannot be printed out for reference and perusal by the purchaser?

Third-Party Beneficiaries

A contract may benefit persons who are not parties to it. Such persons are known as **third-party beneficiaries.** Generally, third-party beneficiaries have no interest in a contract and have no right to sue to enforce the contract or to get damages if it is breached. However, a third-party beneficiary may sue if the parties *intended* for him or her to benefit from the contract.

For example, assume that Nick owes the Online Bank $10,000. Nick enters into a contract to write a software program for Paula in exchange for $10,000. Rather than have Paula pay him, Nick arranges to have Paula pay off Nick's debt at Online Bank. In such a case, the Bank is a *creditor beneficiary,* as it was previously owed an obligation by Nick. If Paula does not pay the bank, the bank may sue either Paula, because the bank is a third-party creditor beneficiary, or it may sue Nick, because the bank is the obligee on the original debt.

If the parties to a contract intend to make a gift to a third person, that person is known as a *donee beneficiary.* Unlike a creditor beneficiary, a donee beneficiary may only sue the party who owes them performance under the contract, and not the party who contracted to make them a gift. The beneficiary of a life insurance policy is usually a donee beneficiary. Such a person, therefore, may sue the life insurance company if it fails to pay on the policy, but may not sue the party who purchased the policy.

Performance of Contracts

At the time that the parties enter into a contract they both assume an obligation to perform. That is, they both agree to deliver to the other the consideration they have promised. Such an obligation, however, may be conditioned on the occurrence of some event. Once the conditions have been satisfied, a failure to perform is treated as a *breach of contract,* which allows an injured party to sue to obtain performance, to rescind the contract, or to obtain damages.

Conditions

The parties to contracts often impose conditions on their performance. Conditions may be precedent, concurrent, or subsequent to the obligation to perform.

- *Condition precedent*—one that must occur before a party has an obligation to perform. For example, a contract that promises to replace or repair a defective computer establishes a condition precedent. Only if the computer is defective is there an obligation to repair or replace it.
- *Condition concurrent*—one that requires both parties to carry out some performance at the same time. The most common condition concurrent is one that is implied in all sales transactions: the buyer must pay and the seller must deliver the promised property or services at the same time. Of course, the parties may agree otherwise, but in the absence of such an agreement, payment is due at the time that delivery is due.
- *Condition subsequent*—is one that excuses performance if an event takes place. For instance, many international contracts provide that an obligation to perform will come to an end if war is declared between the countries where the parties are located.

Performance

The parties to a contract agree to fully perform their obligations. However, if a contract is complex, if events intervene, or if a party is obstinate, performance may not be complete. The courts generally recognize three degrees of performance.

- *Complete performance* is full and total performance as required by the contract. For example, if a party promises to pay $1,000, and he does so, he has completely performed. A party who completely performs may not be sued for breach of contract.
- *Substantial performance* is less than complete performance, but it is one that does not significantly affect the other party's rights under the contract. For example, if Roger contracts to deliver a desktop computer to Sam, and the computer that Roger delivers is missing a cover to one of its expansion slots, Roger will have substantially performed. The computer, even without the cover will do everything it is supposed to, and a missing cover can be obtained, either from Roger or from someone else. A party who substantially performs can demand performance from the other party, but he or she will be liable to supply whatever is deficient or to pay for the cost of obtaining the deficiency from another source.
- *Material breach* is an unjustified failure to substantially perform. In other words, it is a failure that significantly affects the other party's rights. In the preceding example, if Roger delivered a computer without its central processor, Roger will have materially breached the contract. This is because the computer will not do what it is supposed to do. In such a case, the nonbreaching party is excused from any further obligation to perform and the breaching party is liable for any damages relating to the breach.

Discharge of a Contract

A party to a contract is *discharged* when the party no longer has any obligation to perform. In most cases, discharge will happen because a party completely performs. Additionally, a nonbreaching party will be discharged from any obligation to perform when the other party commits a material breach.

Other circumstances when a party will be discharged are as follows:

- A condition precedent does not occur.
- A condition subsequent occurs.
- The parties mutually agree to rescind (cancel) their contract.
- The parties agree that one of them will be replaced by a third party and that the party so replaced will be discharged (this is known as a *novation*).
- One party waives the right to hold the other one to a promise to perform.
- The ability of a party to perform becomes impossible due to factors beyond that party's control (this is known as *impossibility of performance*).
- The ability of a party to perform becomes so impracticable that the party would suffer a substantial financial hardship (this is knows as *commercial impracticability*).

Remedies for Breach of Contract

If a party breaches a contract, the nonbreaching party is entitled to a remedy. The remedies available from a court are as follows:

1. *Specific performance*—a court order ordering a breaching party to perform as they originally promised to perform. For example, if a party promised to deliver certain software and does not, the court would order the party to do so. A court, however, will not order a party to specifically perform a contract for personal services, such as to finish a programming project. This is because it would be difficult for the court to determine if the services are satisfactorily performed.
2. *Injunction*—a court order prohibiting a party from doing a specific act. For example, if Anna has promised to work exclusively for Brigitte to write a new computer program by a certain deadline, a court could issue an injunction to keep Anna from working for another employer.
3. *Reformation*—a court order correcting the terms of a written contract to conform to the original intent of the parties.
4. *Rescission*—a court order to void the contract and require both parties to return any consideration they may have received.
5. *Compensatory damages*—payment of a monetary award to place the injured party in a financial position equivalent to the one he would have been in had the other party performed. For example, suppose Charles sells a laptop computer to Daniel and he promises that its operating speed is 100 percent faster than

Daniel's current laptop. However, as delivered the laptop is only 25 percent faster. If the laptop would have been worth $3,000 as it was promised but it is only worth $2,500 as delivered, Charles will recover the difference: $500.

6. *Consequential damages*—payment of a monetary award to compensate the injured party for unusual losses that the other party knew or ought to have known would have resulted from that party's failure to perform. For instance, assume that Ellen hires Fast Delivery Service (FDS) for $20 to deliver a software package to a client of hers and that delivery is to be made the next day. If FDS fails to do so, it will have to return the $20 as compensatory damages, because that is the only damages it knew that Ellen would suffer. Suppose, however, that Ellen tells FDS that the package has to be there or Ellen will lose a contract with her client worth $10,000. If FDS still agrees to deliver the package on time, and it fails to do so, it will have to compensate Ellen for both the delivery charge and her lost contract.

7. *Nominal damages*—a token award (often $1) given to an injured party to show that he was entitled to sue for a breach of contract when the other party's breach caused no financial injury to him. Suppose, for example, that Frank orders a word processor program from Giant Retailer for $250, but then Giant fails to deliver. If Frank is able to purchase the same program from another retailer at the same price and without incurring any additional costs, then the only damage he would be entitled to would be nominal damages. The damages would show that Giant had breached but that Frank had suffered no financial loss.

Ordinarily, these remedies are mutually exclusive. That is, an injured party would not be entitled to both specific performance and rescission. However, consequential damages are ordinarily awarded in addition to compensatory damages.

Summary

A contract is a legally enforceable promise. The parties must manifest by words or conduct their *mutual assent* to a contract. Usually this is done when one of them makes an offer and the other accepts it. Additionally, the contract must involve an exchange of *consideration;* the parties must have the legal *capacity* to contract; and the contract itself must be *legal.* Also, some contracts must be in *writing;* in the United States, the most common contracts that must be in writing are those involving a sale of goods for more than $500.

The making of contracts electronically has presented the law with the challenge of applying traditional legal concepts to new circumstances. Among the challenges are the use of click-wrap contracts and tying clauses in contracts made by large software vendors. Contracts made electronically present the parties with the unique problem of complying with writing and signature requirements. Recently enacted electronic signature acts are meant to solve this problem, but they have not been adopted in all states. Companies regularly engaged in electronic data interchange with other companies are advised to enter into EDI Trading Partner Agreements to ensure that their contracts meet the writing and signature requirements of the law.

One approach to simplifying the law governing contracts made electronically is the Uniform Computer Information Transactions Act (UCITA), promulgated in July 1999 by the National Conference of Commissioners on Uniform State Laws. The UCITA has proven to be very controversial, and consumer groups oppose it because it would preempt existing state consumer protection laws. Manufacturers and retailers support it because it simplifies and validates contracts made electronically.

Manager's Checklist

- Be aware that the Uniform Computer Information Transaction Act has not been adopted. If it is adopted, it will change many of the rules of electronic commerce.
- Be aware that an advertisement to sell or license goods on the Internet is only an offer that can be revoked. So, too, is an offer to sell goods through an online auction service.
- Be aware that the UCITA will allow the parties to one transaction to agree that the acceptance of a future offer may be done by inaction.
- Be aware that some courts as well as the UCITA regard shrink-wrap and click-wrap licenses as valid.
- Be aware that only merchants can make firm offers that are nonrevocable.
- Be aware that the law is unsettled as to whether a minor who misrepresents his age will be able to avoid a contract entered into online.
- Be sure to use EDI Trading Partnership Agreements if your company is regularly involved in entering into electronic data interchange contracts with another company.
- Be aware that the federal government and most (but not all) states have adopted electronic signature acts that give legal effect to electronic records and signatures.
- Be aware that the obligation to perform a service contract ordinarily cannot be delegated to a third person.
- While US law requires that contracts for the sale of goods for more than $500 must be in writing, this is not required for most international sales or for sales between merchants in other countries.
- Be aware that the UCITA will allow software licensors to limit the assignment of licensed software to third parties.

6

Taxation

"The Internet should not be taxed. The Internet is the greatest thing that's happened to the world . . ."

—Sen. John McCain
The Internet Newsletter, Dec. 1999, p. 6.

Introduction

According to the U.S. Department of Commerce, retail sales over the Internet in 1998 generated $2.6 billion. In an e-commerce sales transaction, a seller/vendor receives gross receipts from the buyer that represent enormous amounts of potential sales tax revenue to a taxing state. The state's sales tax and use tax on e-commerce is considered the most critical tax controversy confronting an e-business. When a sales or use tax is imposed by the state, vendor companies face a sales tax liability for failure to collect and remit to the state the sales tax on out-of-state sales.

Online services and products are generally sold from remote locations to consumers in a manner similar to a mail-order catalog purchase. The out-of-state e-business must have a **nexus,** or physical connection with the taxing state where the customer is located, before it has an obligation to collect and remit to the state the sales tax. E-tailors that have this physical connection (nexus) with the state are collectors of tax revenue from consumers.

For example, if you purchase a book at a Barnes & Noble brick-and-mortar bookstore in a state with a sales tax, you pay the tax at the point of sale. If you buy the same book online from Amazon.com in a state with no retail store or warehouse, you don't pay the sales tax.

Should an e-business without a retail store, doing business in a state with a sales tax, be exempt from collecting the tax from the online shopper and paying the state the sales tax? Should e-commerce retail transactions in the same state be treated any differently from Main Street bricks-and-mortar shops, simply because the e-commerce has no physical store in that state? Companies have often moved to a state or country because of its favorable tax treatment. This has always been a costly step involving an assessment of the foreign country's political stability, its labor market, infrastructure, and other considerations. A pure e-business can easily move from one state to another with no sales tax to avoid tax liability.

A startup e-business should always explore the tax consequences of the state where it will do business and consider selecting a desirable tax site. For example, an online consumer in Maryland purchases a computer from a New Hampshire e-business that is shipped from a New Hampshire warehouse. Since New Hampshire has no sales tax, the web merchant, with no physical presence in Maryland, has no obligation to collect a sales tax from the online consumer. If the same consumer purchased the computer in a retail store in Maryland, the local merchant would have to collect sales tax.

State governors have expressed a desire to tax electronic sales transactions by out-of-state Web merchants doing business in their state. Congress has been aware of this, and in order to study the impact of taxing the Net, it has enacted the Internet Tax Freedom Act of 1998 (ITFA), which will be discussed in this chapter. The Act calls for a moratorium on any new Internet taxes until 2001, and has established an Advisory Commission on Electronic Commerce (ACEC) to report its findings and legislative suggestions to Congress.

This chapter will emphasize the taxability of e-commerce transactions with special emphasis on sales and use taxes. It will also discuss how the U.S. Constitution's due process and commerce clauses place limitations on the state's authority to tax an e-business.

Taxation in Cyberspace

Taxation in cyberspace assumes various forms. The states may impose a sales tax or a use tax on a resident consumer and, provided it has sufficient nexus (i.e., a connection with the out-of-state e-business), compel the seller to collect the sales tax and remit it to the state. Both the sales and use tax are based on a flat rate, usually between 3 percent and 8 percent of the gross receipts of the sale. What would the Internet economy's tax base represent within this context?

Sales tax is a tax paid by the consumer at the point of purchase on tangible personal property, and is collected by the seller/vendor. It is charged on the gross amount of the sale or leased transaction and collected where the sales tax originated. Most states rely on sales tax for much of the state's revenue. The *Advisory Commission on Intergovernmental Relations* reports that about 6,600 state and local jurisdictions impose sales and use taxes.

Currently only five states do not charge a sales tax: Alaska, Delaware, Montana, New Hampshire, and Oregon. Forty-five states do have a sales tax, and eleven have applied it to Internet sales transactions prior to October 1, 1998. These eleven states may levy a sales tax on Internet transactions under a grandfather clause of the Internet Tax Freedom Act.

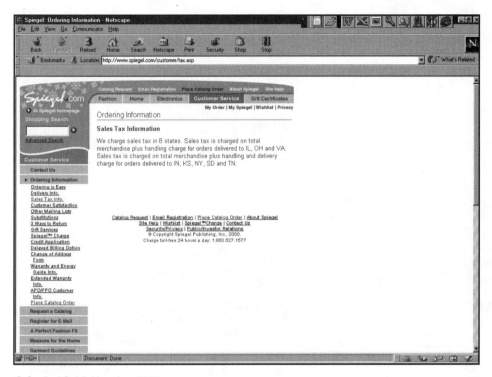

© Speigel Publishing, Inc. 2000.

Use tax is a tax imposed on the consumer for tangible goods purchased out of state for use within the taxing state. For example, if a resident of Massachusetts buys a computer in New Hampshire where there is no sales tax and intends to use the computer in Massachusetts, the purchaser should pay a use tax to the state of Massachusetts. Usually because this tax is self-assessed, it is generally *not* paid (see Figure 6.1).

The emerging and sustained conflict on Internet taxation revolves around the state's ability and willingness to tax sales transactions in e-commerce and the obstacle to e-commerce growth resulting from this taxation. In addition to the fifty states, various local counties would like to impose a sales tax on e-commerce transactions. As we already mentioned, this amounts to more than 6,600 tax jurisdictions. Imagine the confusion caused by the various tax rules and regulations imposed on an e-business with the obligation of charging and collecting a sales tax on its transactions. Violation of these tax statutes imposes a sales tax liability on the Web merchant and, if intentional, could result in criminal prosecution. Is this an unreasonable burden to impose on an out-of-state e-business that has no bricks-and-mortar store in the state and does not use the tax-supported infrastructure that offline stores rely upon?

Figure 6.1

Use Tax Form

FORM ST-11
(Rev. 4/96)

Massachusetts Department of Revenue
Individual Use Tax Return

Name _____   Social Security number _____

Address _____   State _____   Zip _____

Return is due with payment on or before April 15 for purchases made in the prior calendar year. Make check payable to the Commonwealth of Massachusetts. Mail to: **Massachusetts Department of Revenue, PO Box 7009, Boston, MA 02204.**

I declare under the penalties of perjury that this return has been examined by me and to the best of my knowledge and belief is a true, correct and complete return.

Signature _____   Date _____

1. Year purchases made **1**
2. Total purchases from line 9 on reverse **2**
3. Use tax (5% of line 2) **3**
4. Total credit for sales/use tax paid to other states or jurisdictions. From line 10 on reverse **4**
5. Balance. *Subtract line 4 from line 3.* Not less than "0" **5**
6. Penalty **6**
7. Interest **7**
8. Total amount due **8**

Date of purchase	Name of seller, city and state	Quantity and description of property purchased	A. Sales price	B. Sales/use tax paid to other jurisdictions or 5% of sales price — *whichever is less*

9. Total purchases. Add all of the purchase prices listed in column A. Enter the result here and in line 2 on the front. ▲ $

10. Total sales/use tax paid to other states or jurisdictions. Add all of the amounts listed in column B. Enter the result here and in line 4 on the front. ▲ $

Attach an additional statement if more space is necessary

9M 3/98 CRP0198

Figure 6.3

Commerce Clause Test for Tax Purposes

✓ E-business needs a substantial nexus with the taxing state
✓ The tax must be fairly apportioned
✓ Tax cannot discriminate
✓ Tax must be fairly related to the services provided by the state

---

Certain sales transactions are generally exempt by state statue from sales and use tax. They commonly include food, clothing, and nontangible transactions such as services. Because this differs from state to state, it is important to review the state tax statute to ascertain these exemptions.

State Tax Jurisdiction under the U.S. Constitution

Before a state may tax a sales transaction, it must have tax jurisdiction over the out-of-state merchant. Tax jurisdiction requires that a company have a physical presence in the state, referred to as a *substantial nexus*. The physical presence requirement usually takes the form of a retail store, warehouse, employees, or sales representatives doing business in the taxing state. The taxing state must prove this nexus before an out-of-state company is required to collect the tax from the buyer and remit it to the state. The tax jurisdiction requirement, that a company have some physical presence before a state can tax a sales transaction, has for years, prior to electronic commerce, given mail-order companies an advantage over local retail stores.

Mail-Order Transactions

Mail-order companies include catalog sales, direct marketing, and cable television shopping. Since they have no physical presence in an out-of-state sale, they generally do not have to collect and remit the sales tax. Mail-order forms usually list the states where the consumer must pay a sales tax and request h/her to submit it with the purchase order (see Figure 6.2).

Local Main Street retail stores find this unjust and discriminatory, since they have to charge and collect the sales tax while an out-of-state mail-order house or e-business with no physical presence in the state is exempt. A Web out-of-state merchant doing e-business in a foreign state where it has no physical presence is treated

Figure 6.2
Order Form

Sur La Table

Catalog Division
1765 6th Avenue South
Seattle, Washington
98134-1608

ORDER TOLL FREE
800 243-0852
24 HOURS A DAY

ORDERED BY:
Name and address should be that of person placing order. Please make corrections as necessary.

SHIP TO:
☐ Same   ☐ Different   ☐ See gift forms below

Name _____

C/o _____

Address _____

City, State, Zip _____

E-mail Address _____

▶ Day Phone (___) _____

Please fill in order form completely, including item numbers.

LINE	QTY	ITEM #	DESCRIPTION	✓ GIFT WRAP	UNIT PRICE	TOTAL
1						
2						
3						
4						
5						
6						

GIFT #1

Name				Gift Message		
Address						
City	State		Zip	Recipient's Phone ( )		

| 7 | | | | | | |
| 8 | | | | | | |

GIFT #2

Name				Gift Message		
Address						
City	State		Zip	Recipient's Phone ( )		

| 9 | | | | | | |
| 10 | | | | | | |

PAYMENT METHOD:
☐ Check or Money Order   ☐ VISA   ☐ MasterCard
☐ American Express   ☐ Novus

Expiration Date _____   Signature _____

Order $200 worth of items from our catalog and receive this pasta server FREE!
($9.95 value)

Merchandise Total	
Add $5 for each Gift Wrap	
Subtotal	
Add Delivery Charges per Address *(see ordering information)*	
Additional Shipping Charges *(AK, HI, 2nd day and overnight delivery)*	
State Sales Tax*	
GRAND TOTAL	

ORDER TOLL FREE 800 243-0852 • FAX 206 682-1026 • www.surlatable.com

for sales tax purposes like a mail-order business. It must charge and collect sales tax if its home state has a sales tax, but there is no obligation to do so if it has no physical presence there.

In *Quill v. North Dakota*, 504 U.S. 298 (1992), the court required an out-of-state merchant to have a physical presence in a state before it's obligated to collect a use tax and remit it to the state. In reaching this conclusion the court required

http://
See
www.ecommercetax.com
for sales tax information
and see
www.geocities.com/streamlined2000
for a state sales tax initiative proposal

satisfaction of both the commerce clause and the due-process clause of the United States Constitution.

Quill, a mail-order business, was a Delaware corporation that had offices and warehouses in Illinois, California and Georgia. It did not have any employees or signifi-cant property in the state of North Dakota. Quill had annual national sales of $200,000,000 of which $100,000,000 were made to about 3,000 customers in North Dakota. All of its office supply merchandise were delivered to its North Dakota customers by mail or out-of-state common carriers. The state wanted to compel it to collect a use tax from its North Dakota customers. Quill argued because it had no physical presence in the state it need not collect use taxes from the North Dakota customers. The state contends that the due process clause only requires that a company "do business" within the state for state tax jurisdiction pur-poses and need not have a physical presence within the taxing state. The Supreme Court disagreed and held that the commerce clause prohibits discrimination against interstate commerce and requires not only that the out-of-state business carry on business activity within the state but also, under the commerce clause, it have a physical presence within the state.

This case has special importance in the area of the state taxability of a pure e-business that does significant business within a state without having a physical presence. The commerce clause, according to the *Quill* case, requires a nexus or physical presence before a state has tax jurisdiction over a business. It remains to be seen if Congress will enact legislation that overrules this case. Main Street stores that are required to collect sales taxes from its customers will not then be discrimi-nated against by pure online companies.

Although the *Quill* decision explicitly allows Congress to enact legislation for the states to impose sales and use taxes on products sold by an out-of-state merchant, it has to date failed to do so.

In view of the enormous loss of state revenue, you can expect state representa-tives to continue their request to tax remote sales for mail-order and e-commerce transactions. The report to Congress from the Advisory Commission on Electronic Commerce will probably suggest the taxation of e-commerce transactions in some fashion.

Physical Presence Nexus Test for E-Commerce

An out-of-state Web merchant may have a physical presence for tax jurisdiction purposes without having a retail store in the taxing state.

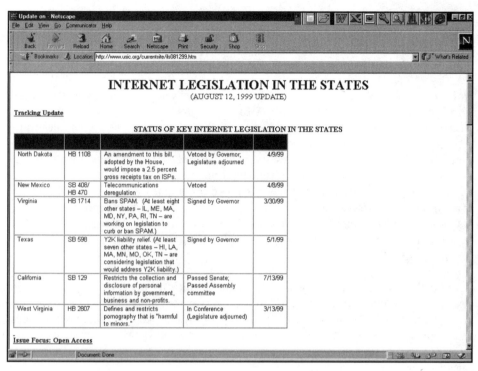

© United States Internet Council.

In order to avoid being subject to collecting and paying a sales tax to the taxing state, an online company should be aware of seven bases for establishing a tax nexus with the e-business.

1. Renting an office or a warehouse in the taxing state
2. Holding trade shows where employees or agents take orders from customers in the taxing state
3. Working with a server in the taxing state
4. Maintaining inventory in a taxing state
5. Licensing software to licensees in a taxing state
6. Hiring agents in the taxing state
7. Falling under the market maintainance theory

These seven bases are the foundation of the **physical presence test.** We will examine each one in the following paragraphs.

Renting an Office or Warehouse.   An e-business that leases office or warehouse space will be considered to have a "nexus" for tax purposes even if the office or warehouse is not used to generate sales. Since most e-commerce retailing requires the inventory to be stocked in a warehouse and often shipped by UPS or FedEx to the remote customer, this is an important consideration. An e-business should consider leasing an office or warehouse in one of the five states which does not impose a sales tax.

Holding Trade Shows.   Suppose your e-business sells software and you send a few employees to an e-commerce trade show to display and sell your products. If the state where the trade show is located has a sales tax, your employees or agents sales transactions at the trade show could result in a nexus for state tax jurisdiction. Tax nexus depends on how long the employees attended the trade show and how much revenue was generated. Managers should consult with their tax advisors to determine the tax effect of trade show attendance. Even though your company has no physical presence at the trade show in a taxing state, having agents who are sales representatives, employees, or independent contractors working on sales on behalf of your company may constitute a tax **nexus by attribution** and a resulting obligation to collect the sales tax.

Using a Web Merchant's Server.   One of the perplexing questions regarding state taxation of e-commerce is whether having a server in a state constitutes a physical and a substantial tax nexus. It may be possible for a Web merchant who owns, leases, or rents a server in a state with a sales or use tax to have a tax nexus in that state. If your server is in a jurisdiction where you fill orders, you may be subject to sales tax liability in that state.

Maintaining Inventory in a Taxing State.   An e-business that maintains a warehouse for inventory purposes can result in a tax nexus for those states imposing a sales or use tax. Warehoused property that is sold may result in a sales tax imposed by the state where the warehouse is located when the buyer is a resident of that state. For example, assume a book is purchased by an Arizona resident from Amazon.com located in the State of Oregon. If its *warehouse* were in Arizona, Amazon would have to collect the sales tax and remit it to the State of Arizona.

The sale of digital software products over the Internet creates special sales tax problems because software is not tangible personal property, and it can be sold and delivered electronically.

An online buyer of software will generally pay with a credit card number that does not identify the address of the buyer. Since the sale is made by allowing the buyer to download the software,

---

Cyberethics

Is it ethical for an out-of-state e-business, doing extensive business in a state with a sales tax, not to collect that tax merely because it lacks a tax nexus?

Is this fair to the bricks-and-mortar retail store in the taxing state that must collect the sales tax for selling the same product?

there is no physical delivery of a tangible product, and the e-business vendor may not know where the sale was made. This will prevent the e-business from complying with a sales tax in the state of purchase. Software stacked in a warehouse in a state with a sales tax may subject the vendor to collecting the sales tax. At issue is whether the software is tangible personal property. Nineteen states impose sales tax on the sale of intangible goods sold over the Internet. A company selling software online should try to avoid having a Web-based business in those states taxing the online sale of software.

Licensing Software to Licensees in a Taxing State.   Suppose a Web company develops software and licenses it in a state with a sales tax. Depending on the number of licensees in the taxing state, the licensor may have a tax nexus and be required to collect the sales tax. Failure to do so will result in a penalty tax on the licensor.

Hiring Agents in the Taxing State.   A Web merchant's agent (independent contractor or sales representatives) in the foreign state may create nexus for sales and use tax purposes. It is not necessary that the vendor's agents be its employees in order to create a tax nexus in the foreign state.

Falling Under the Market Maintenance Theory.   Tax nexus between an out-of-state vendor and the taxing state may be based on a theory of **market maintenance**. This occurs when the vendor's state activities are significantly associated with the taxpayer's ability to establish and maintain a market in the state for its sales. In *Tyler Pipe Industries, Inc. v. Dept. of Revenue,* 483 U.S. 232 (1987) the court ruled that through sales contacts, the representatives maintained and improve the name recognition, market share, goodwill, and individual customer relations of the company and therefore, subjects the company to the state's tax nexus.

Notice how in each of the seven tests of establishing a tax nexus for sales tax purposes, an e-business must be aware of subtle business associations that are very difficult to determine. The business must work closely with its tax advisor as it pursues expanding markets.

Internet Tax Freedom Act of 1998 (ITFA)

In an effort to prevent the states from overtaxing Internet transactions, Congress passed the **Internet Tax Freedom Act** (ITFA) in October 1998. (See Appendix excerpts from ITFA.) The Act prevents federal, state, and local governments from

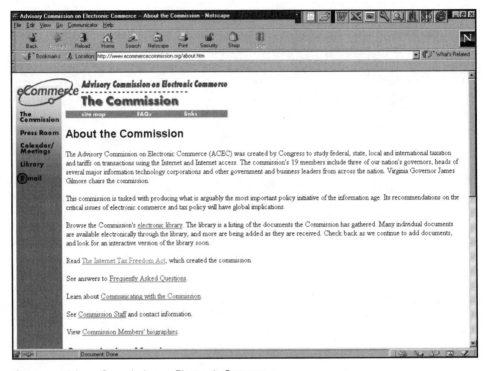

Courtesy Advisory Commission on Electronic Commerce.

imposing any new taxes on the Internet for a period of three years. However, existing Internet taxes, those enacted and enforced prior to October 1998, may continue to be imposed on Internet transactions. The act "establishes a national policy against state and local interference with interstate commerce on the Internet."

The Act created an **Advisory Commission on Electronic Commerce** that will study the implications of taxing e-commerce. A simple majority, rather than two-thirds majority required by the act to qualify as a "recommendation," reported to Congress in April 2000 that the current moratorium be extended for five years to 2006.

Recall that the U.S. Supreme Court *Quill* case, previously discussed, exempted mail-order catalog businesses from collecting sales tax in states where they do not have a physical presence. The ITFA provides Internet no-tax advocates with a similar tax exemption for e-business transactions. For example, Micron sells computers on the

http://
See Micron at
www.micron.com

Net without collecting sales taxes for any state except Idaho, where it maintains its only retail outlet store.

International Internet Taxation

Since many e-business transactions are international, the Web merchant's business contacts with a foreign country may subject the merchant to collecting and remitting taxes to the foreign country. Many foreign countries, such as the members of the European Union, impose a value-added tax (VAT) and custom duties on business transacted in their countries. Offshore e-businesses may sell and deliver software electronically, thereby avoiding taxes and custom duties. The taxation of international e-commerce is currently under review to consider how it should apply to online business.

In 1997 the White House issued a paper titled *Framework for Global Electronic Commerce* that endorsed minimal global taxation. The Organization for Economic Cooperation and Development (OECD) has expressed the view that it will be difficult to apply a value-added tax to the Internet. It issued a paper titled *Electronic Commerce: Taxation Framework Conditions* proposing that international tax authorities simplify their tax systems, especially for smaller e-commerce business. An e-business should be aware of the possible tax consequences of doing business in a foreign country and have its tax advisor constantly monitor developments in this area. See Chapter 13 for a discussion of the taxation of international eletronic commerce.

Summary

An out-of-state e-business with a tax nexus in the state must be aware of any local sales tax that obligates it to collect a sales tax from the buyer and remit it to the state. Failure to do so could result in the state collecting the taxes due from the e-business, plus imposing a penalty tax for late payment. If it has reason to believe the tax evasion was intentional, there could be criminal prosecution.

This is a daunting task for the e-business tax advisor because each state, and some local communities, have their own version of the amount to be taxed and what items may be exempt. It is no wonder that Congress in 1998 passed the Internet Tax Freedom Act that created a three-year moratorium on any new Internet taxes. Proponents for keeping the Internet tax-free argue that imposing taxes on the Internet will impede our electronic-driven economy. The opposition, consisting of some state governors and bricks-and-mortar businesses, complain of tax discrimination with a tax-free Internet advantage to the online merchant. The e-businesses argue that they do not use the infrastructure that the state tax base supports, and for the states to require them to charge and collect a sales tax on their behalf is unfair.

We can only be assured that the report and legislative suggestions to Congress, rendered by the Advisory Commission on Electronic Commerce, will continue to be vigorously debated.

Manager's Checklist

1. An e-business should determine in which states it has nexus for sales and use tax purposes. Managers should work with their tax advisors to discover what products and services are taxable and at what rate.
2. A Web company should determine if the products or services it sells are taxable in the nexus state. For instance, downloaded software is subject to sales and use tax in Alabama, Illinois, Louisiana, Nebraska, New York, North Dakota, Texas, Washington, and Wisconsin.
3. Be aware that the tax law in this area is subject to change and managers should work closely with their tax advisors. It is reasonable to expect that the Advisory Commission formed under the Internet Tax Freedom Act will report to Congress that Internet transactions should be subject to new taxes in some fashion. E-commerce companies should consider the ramifications of this decision.
4. Remember that noncompliance with tax law can incur substantial penalties to the e-business and an intentional violation may be criminal. A Web company that does not collect the sales tax from the buyer at the time of the sale will forever lose that opportunity.
5. A Web merchant who owns, leases, or rents a server in a state with a sale and/or use tax may be subject to a tax nexus in that state.
6. Attendance at e-commerce trade shows by a Web company's employees or sales representatives may establish a tax nexus in that state.

Additional Readings

- Grierson, R. Scott. "*State Taxation of the Information Superhighway: A Proposal for Taxation of Information Services,*" 16 **Loyola of Los Angeles Entertainment Law Journal** 200 (1995)

- Eisenstein, M. I. "*The Constitutional Limits on Sales Taxation of Cyberspace,*" **State Tax News** (Feb. 24, 1997)

- Frieden, Karl & Michael Porter. *The Taxation of Cyberspace: State Tax Issues Related to the Internet and Electronic Commerce,* 1996 St. Tax Notes 1363, 1367.

7

Online Securities Offerings

"As technology recasts our markets and helps attract more and more investors than ever before, the SEC's mission to protect investors and maintain market integrity remains absolute. We are prepared to do whatever is necessary to help protect investors."
—*SEC Chairman Arthur Levitt, in a speech May 4, 1999, at the National Press Club.*
www.sec.gov/news/presindx.htm (Release No. 99-43)

Introduction

This chapter discusses one of the methods for raising capital needed for business creation and expansion—the offering of security interests in businesses and how this is accomplished over the Internet. Out of such transactions, businesses receive infusions of cash for their operations, and the investor receives an interest in the business—a **security**—along with the hopes that the investment will produce dividends and that it will, over time, appreciate in value.

These transactions traditionally have been conducted by investment banks, which market the shares through brokerage firms and are registered to be traded by a stock exchange. This process is concurrently regulated by a panoply of federal and state laws, as enforced by the Securities and Exchange Commission (see www.sec.gov/), the various stock exchanges, as well as individual states, as represented by the North American Securities Administrators Association (NASAA) (see www.nasaa.org).

Although all of these laws are still applicable, the medium through which businesses sell shares to investors who thereby become shareholders has changed dramatically. The Internet's stunning ability to widely disseminate information and simultaneously demystify and democratize processes is now becoming a reality in investing. Wall Street is now a virtual highway.

The first part of this chapter is essentially a survey of securities laws. It addresses what is a security, what laws govern the issuance and administration of securities, the different types of securities offerings, and the ways these offerings traditionally have been made.

The second part of this chapter discusses the law that is developing for Internet securities offerings, and how the Internet has radically altered the traditional methods of capital formation. Also discussed is the reality that while the same laws govern traditional as well as Internet transactions, regulators have had to make adjustments to their conventional regulatory framework in order to govern capital formation over the Internet.

What Is a Security?

There are a number of ways for businesses to procure capital in order to improve and expand operations. Businesses may borrow money from institutional lenders, typically banks, and are then obligated to repay the loan plus interest. This method of raising capital is low-risk in nature, but it has some significant disadvantages. It is expensive, the business may not qualify for a loan, and if it gets the loan, it becomes burdened with loan and interest repayments. Businesses may also borrow money from *angels* (wealthy individuals who are not averse to investing in early-stage companies) or venture capitalists (those involved in funding emerging companies). Such investors, though, usually become involved in the business, which may or may not be favorable. Businesses also raise capital through the issuance of bonds, which has a similar effect on businesses as a bank loan. To the extent that the business is considered a high risk, the interest repayment burden is correspondingly high.

Therefore, one of the most attractive ways for businesses to procure capital is to allow investors to purchase a security interest in the business. In return, investors receive a certificate indicating the amount of ownership in the business. Under this method of capital formation, from the businesses' standpoint, it has succeeded in raising needed funds, yet it is under no obligation for any repayments. From the investors' standpoint, they perceive ownership of shares as a way to invest now, possibly receiving dividends in the hope that the business will become profitable as well as grow, so that their ownership in the company increases in value. It is, for the most part, a mutually beneficial arrangement.

As there are so many varied investment schemes, the first question that must be asked is whether the interest being sold by a business is actually a security interest. If it is, then the protection of the federal and state securities laws may be invoked for the benefit and protection of investors against fraudulent practices of those who solicit money under the guise of representing a plan as an investment.

The starting point for any discussion construing whether a purchased interest is a security is the **Securities Act of 1933.** Enacted following the historic stock market crash of 1929, this statute defines *security* in sufficiently broad and general terms to encompass many types of instruments. It thus recognizes the nearly limitless possibilities of schemes that promoters create. Section 3(a)(10) of the Securities Act states:

> "[t]he term 'security' means any note, stock, treasury stock, bond, debenture, certificate of interest or participation in any profit-sharing agreement or in any oil, gas, or other mineral royalty or

lease, any collateral-trust certificate, preorganization certificate or subscription, transferable share, investment contract, voting-trust certificate, certificate of deposit, for a security, any put, call, straddle, option, or privilege on any security, certificate of deposit, or group or index of securities (including any interest therein or based on the value thereof), or any put, call, straddle, option, or privilege entered into on a national securities exchange relating to foreign currency, or in general, any instrument commonly known as a "security'; or any certificate of interest or participation in, temporary or interim certificate for, receipt for, or warrant or right to subscribe to or purchase, any of the foregoing; but shall not include currency or any note, draft, bill of exchange, or banker's acceptance which has a maturity at the time of issuance of not exceeding nine months, exclusive of days of grace, or any renewal thereof the maturity of which is like-wise limited.

The SEC, as the administrator of securities laws, and federal courts have indicated that they do not intend to be bound by legal formalisms and instead will take account of the economics of the transaction. Congress's intent was to regulate investments in whatever form they are made, by whatever name they are given. The seminal case construing the definition of security is *Securities & Exchange Commission v. W.J. Howey Co.,* 328 U.S. 293 (1946). The U.S. Supreme Court was asked to determine whether an instrument was an "investment contract," in the form of a sale of an interest in Florida citrus groves. The Court created a sort of *risk capital* analysis and pronounced the interest a security because the transaction evidenced (1) an investment; (2) in a common enterprise; (3) with a reasonable expectation of profits; (4) to be derived from the efforts of others.

While this transaction—manifested shares in an undertaking—are the quintessence of a security, notes may, or may not be, a security. The Supreme Court recently considered this question in *Reves v. Ernst & Young,* 494 U. S. 56 (1990). The Court considered whether uncollateralized and uninsured promissory notes payable on demand that paid a variable rate of interest were securities. Concluding that they were, the Court declined to follow *Howey* in this instance and instead adopted a "family resemblance" test for determining if notes are securities. This begins with the presumption that they are securities, which may be rebutted only by showing that the note more closely resembles the family of instruments found *not* to be securities. The Court must assess (1) motivations of the buyer and seller; (2) the plan of distribution of the note; (3) the reasonable expectations of the buyer/investor; and (4) whether there were other laws regulating the transaction, rendering application of the Securities Act unnecessary.

Even though the definition of *security* seems to address every possible investment definition and variation, there continues to be litigation over whether an investment is legally a security.

The Laws That Govern the Issuance and Administration of Securities

Once it is determined that the offering made is actually a security, then a number of laws come into play, all with the purpose of ensuring disclosure of material relevant infor-

http://

A helpful Web site for securities law resources may be found at
www.legal.gsa.gov/legal5b.htm

mation on the part of the companies, as a means to protect investors. There are laws at both the federal level (applicable in all U.S. jurisdictions), and state level (applicable to that particular jurisdiction). The primary focus of discussion in this section is the federal laws, with some reference to state laws. Following the name of each act is a series of numbers and letters indicating the citation for the full text of each law. Accessible at libraries, over the Internet (at, for example, www.law.uc.edu/CCL/sldtoc.html), and through electronic databases such as WESTLAW or LEXIS/NEXIS, the U.S.C. (United States Code) cite is the actual law. The C.F.R. (Code of Federal Regulations) cite is to the SEC rules and regulations that interpret the statutory law. For examples of rules and proposals for new rules, see www.sec.gov/rulemake.htm.

Overall responsibility for enforcement of laws is the domain of the **Securities and Exchange Commission (SEC)**. This agency was created during the aftermath of the stock market crash of 1929, and it administers securities laws that the U.S. Congress has passed.

Securities Act of 1933 (Securities Act), 15 U.S.C. § § 77a-77aa (1999), 17 C.F.R. Parts 229, 230 (1999)

Congress has mandated a host of registration, delivery, and filing requirements for companies wishing to raise capital through the public offer and sale of securities. The Securities Act requirements detailed here are, for the most part, applicable to established companies seeking to raise at least $10 million. Other offerings are exempt from many of these Securities Act registration requirements. (Later in the chapter we discuss exemptions that Internet securities offerings are typically made through.) To start with, companies must file with the SEC a registration statement detailing relevant investment information. The intent of this statement is to make available to all prospective purchasers of securities all facts and information that an investor would find material and important in making an investment decision. The first part of the registration statement contains the **prospectus** detailing information regarding the following:

- Offering summary
- Issuing company
- Description and number of securities offered
- Underwriting—discounts, commissions, plan of distribution
- Use of proceeds
- Dilution, if any, of shares
- Dividend policy
- Risk factors, financial data

- Discussion of the business, including, property, plant and equipment, legal proceedings, and management (directors, officers, key personnel, board members, consultants and salaries)

The prospectus must be delivered to every purchaser of the security for the offer and sale to be valid. Companies usually issue first a preliminary prospectus, also known as a *red herring,* containing warnings in red ink about its initial incomplete form.

The second part of the statement contains all other materials the SEC requires. This is also a public document, and it may discuss

- Insurance and indemnification
- Bylaws
- Financial statements
- Large contracts

Alternatively, if a company qualifies as a small business (less than $25 million in previous fiscal year, and outstanding publicly held stock worth less than $25 million), it may file a simplified registration statement. This is done with either a Form SB-1 (to raise capital of $10 million or less), or a Form SB-2 (to raise capital in any amount). Audited financial statements must be filed with the SEC under either scenario. These filings have increased dramatically since the forms were revised in 1992. These forms may be found at www.law.uc.edu/CCL/33forms/index.html.

Should investors rely on any misstatements of material facts, civil and criminal liability may be imposed. In between the time that the materials are filed and before the securities offering is officially registered, companies typically undertake an advertising campaign to publicize the offering, called a *road show.* The underwriters have historically presented information to institutional customers such as mutual fund portfolio managers, as well as stock brokerage securities analysts. The oral and audiovisual representations made are likewise governed by the securities laws. It is crucial that every investor first receive an offering prospectus before investing. Finally, the securities are registered on an exchange, sold to investors, and then subsequently publicly traded between investors.

Securities Exchange Act of 1934 (Exchange Act), 15 U.S.C. § § 78a-78kk (1999), 17 C.F.R. Part 240 (1999)

The **Securities Exchange Act of 1934 (Exchange Act)** was originally passed to regulate the various exchanges. Largely unregulated heretofore, this legislation brought all of the various exchanges under control of the SEC. The Exchange Act essentially mandates accounting and recordkeeping procedures for domestic companies registered with the SEC. Thus, if a company (1) registers a securities offering with the SEC, or (2) has $10 million in assets, 500 or more shareholders, and lists its securities on an exchange, the Exchange Act requires company reports about the following:

- Operations
- Financial conditions
- Management
- Financial statements
- Elections
- Mergers, acquisitions, tender offers
- Beneficial ownership of shares
- Company securities transactions by officers, directors, and 10 percent shareholders
- Foreign Corrupt Practices Act (FCPA) overseeing accounting records

In addition to the two major acts, Congress has enacted other laws for the benefit of the investing public. Refer to Table 7.1 for a listing of these acts. You may also wish to refer to a securities law Web site posting these laws in full at www.seclaw.com/secrules.htm.

In addition to the patchwork of federal laws, each state also has its own securities laws and regulations. It is the final authority over which securities may be sold in its jurisdiction. These are known as *blue sky laws*. The blue sky laws disclose in which states the offerings will be registered. The North American Securities Administrators Association (NASAA) maintains a state members' Web site found at http://nasaa.org/regulator/memberlist.html.

Although this concludes the discussion of the major laws that regulate traditional large public offerings, it also raises questions. Traditional methods of raising capital are most appropriate for large-capital, publicly held companies with more than 500 shareholders that intend to raise over $10 million. The reality is that the vast majority of jobs created in the United States are in the small business sector, and small businesses urgently need capital and have faced extraordinary difficulties securing it. The amounts that such businesses need, in the range of $250,000 to $5 million, are too small to interest major investment banking or venture capital funds. The Small Business Administration refers to this gap as the *capital chasm* and estimates that $60 million is needed to meet the business and investment requirements of small businesses.

Recognizing this need, Congress developed exemptions to Securities Act and Exchange Act requirements in an effort to encourage the flow of capital to entrepreneurs.

> **http://**
> Exchange Act reporting forms may be found at
> **www.law.uc.edu/CCL/34forms/index.html**

Exemptions for Small Business Securities Offerings

Many factors have historically contributed to the constricted access of small businesses to capital markets. Compliance with federal regulatory requirements is complicated and costly; and the requisite cost of national publicity is prohibitively expen-

Table 7.1

Additional Investment Acts

Act	Code	Purpose
Investment Company Act of 1940	15 U.S.C. § § 80a-1 - 80a-58 (1999) 17 C.F.R. Part 270 (1999)	This act regulates mutual fund and other investment companies and attempts to mitigate conditions that adversely affect the investing public.
Investment Advisers Act of 1940	15 U.S.C. § § 80b-1 - 80b-20 (1999) 17 C.F.R. Parts 275, 279 (1999)	This act regulates investment advisers and seeks to check the power of advisers over company directors.
Private Securities Litigation Reform Act of 1995	15 U.S.C. § § 77k, 77l, 77z-1, 77z-2, 78j-1, 78t, 78u, 78u-4, 78u-5 (1999)	This act imposes certain limitations on private lawsuits imposing stricter pleading standards for class actions and limitations on discovery.
Public Utility Holding Company Act of 1935	15 U.S.C. § § 79 - 79z-6 (1999) 17 C.F.R. Part 250 (1999)	This act attempts to protect consumer interests and correct abuses in the holding company device, especially in the gas and utility industries.
Securities Investor Protection Act of 1970	15 U.S.C. § § 78 aaa - 77lll (1999) 17 C.F.R. § 200.30-3- .30-18 (1999)	This act attempts to stop the failure or instability of a significant number of brokerage firms; to restore investor confidence in capital markets; upgrade financial responsibility of registered representatives; and establish a fund for claims against firms.
National Securities Markets Improvement Act of 1996	15 U.S.C § 77r (1999)	Codifies rules giving SEC power in exempting SEC transactions from duplicative regulation.
Securities Litigation Uniform Standards Act of 1997	H.R. 1689, 105th Cong. (1997); S. 1260, 105th (1997)	Legislation proposing preemption of certain state securities fraud litigation and vesting exclusive jurisdiction of litigation over nationally traded securities in federal courts.
Trust Indenture Act of 1939	15 U.S.C. § § § 77aaa-77bbbb (1999) 17 C.F.R. Part 260 (1999)	This act attempts to eliminate fraudulent practices and improve disclosure of indenture provisions toinclude such features as financial condition and relationship with underwriters.

sive. Pursuant to this, in 1980 Congress passed the Small Business Investment Incentive Act (amending scattered sections of 15 U.S.C.) directing the SEC to develop a uniform exemption from the burdensome registration requirements. It is important to remember, however, that even if such offerings are exempt from the traditional registration requirements, the companies must comply with state requirements, and remain responsible for false or misleading statements, as well as the anti-fraud provisions of the securities laws. A useful Web site for exemption rules is the SEC's small business page, found at www.sec.gov/smbus/qasbsec.htm.

Essentially, a business that qualifies for one of the following exemptions enjoys a legal way to offer and sell securities without the registration requirement of the Securities Act. There are five major categories of exemptions: intrastate; Private Placement Regulations A; and D; SCOR; and California Limited Offerings. Each of these will be explained and described, but major emphasis will be placed on the Reg A offering exemption, since this is the exemption of choice currently for Internet stock offerings (ISOs).

Intrastate Offering Exemption

The **intrastate offering exemption** facilitates the financing of local business operations. Securities Act registration requirements are waived if the company

- is incorporated in the state where the securities are being offered;
- does a significant amount of business in this state; and
- makes offers and sales only to residents of this state.

There are no limits on the size/dollar amount of the offering. Purchasers must hold the securities for a period of time before reselling them.

Private Placement Offering Exemptions, 17 C.F.R. 230.251-.263 (1999)

Private placement offerings, made possible by regulatory reforms begun in the 1980s, simplify the capital-raising process to make it much easier for small businesses. For example, the federal registration requirements in some instances amount to filling out question and answer forms, and in some cases audited financial statements are not even required. Section 4(2) of the Securities Act exempts from federal registration requirements "transactions by an issuer not involving any public offering." Thus nonpublic offerings do not need to comply with the Securities Act. It has been construed that to qualify for any private placement offering exemption, certain general conditions must be met:

- Investors must be (i) sophisticated (having enough knowledge and experience in finance and business

http://
www.sec.gov/smbus/forms/formssb.htm

matters to evaluate the risks and merits of an investment), or (ii) be able to bear the economic risk of the investment.
- Investors must have access to the type of information normally provided in a prospectus.
- Investors must agree not to resell or distribute the securities to the public.

Section 3(b) of the Securities Act authorizes the SEC to exempt from federal registration requirements small securities offerings. Pursuant to this, the SEC created **Reg A offerings** that share many characteristics of registered offerings, yet feature streamlined and simplified procedures. Set forth here are the major characteristics of Reg A offerings, with a more complete discussion to follow:

- Businesses receive a conditional exemption to raise up to $5 million in a 12-month period.
- Solicitation or advertising is allowed prior to the offer and sale of securities.
- Companies may "test the waters" to first see whether there is sufficient investor interest before producing the offering circular and financial statements.
- SEC qualification is required.
- Offering format and paperwork is simplified and may be completed on Forms 1-A, SB-2, or U-7.
- The offering is available to all investors (accredited or non-accredited), including limited partnerships and businesses in the oil and gas industries.
- There is no limitation on the number of investors.
- There is no minimum share price requirement.
- There are few specific disclosure requirements.
- There is a provision for "bad-boy" disqualification.
- Resale of securities is not restricted.
- Two years of financial statements are required, and they need not be audited.

The SEC-sponsored Small Business Initiatives in 1992–1993 created this revitalized Reg A, making it applicable to many more small businesses. Formerly it exempted offerings of up to $1.5 million; this of course, has been raised to $5 million. Primarily, though, Reg A is known for its *test the waters* feature. By allowing businesses to determine if there is sufficient interest and demand for their security offering *prior* to the time of offer, issuers/businesses may avoid significant unnecessary costs. For example, in 1995, sixty-one issuers submitted testing solicitations to the SEC, and just twenty-six of those followed up with an actual Reg A offering. This feature is invaluable to businesses that are small and still relatively unknown. In this offering, businesses are allowed to use general solicitations and advertising *prior* to the offer and sale, but no money may be accepted until the SEC review is complete. Businesses must file with the SEC these solicitations of interest, and then they may be distributed. Twenty days must elapse between the last solicitation and the offering.

Should businesses find that there is sufficient interest in their offering, they have a choice of forms on which to file with the SEC. Investor qualifications are not an issue with Reg A, so anyone may purchase the securities. Other exempt offerings limit prospective purchases to those who are accredited, such as businesses, trusts, or benefits plans worth more than $5 million, or persons with high net worth or income. Likewise, other offerings may limit purchasers to sophisticated investors—those with sufficient knowledge and expertise enabling them to evaluate the merits of a prospective investment. Thus, relative to other exempt offerings, the potential class of Reg A investors is very large. Such a wide open structure as Reg A is especially well suited to the Internet medium in which access to postings is unrestricted.

Reg A contains a *bad-boy* provision, which has the effect of suspending the exemption if any person involved with the business or its offering has engaged in specified acts of misconduct, even if the acts do not lead to a conviction.

Although business financial statements need not be audited, most states' blue sky laws require audited financial statements anyway. Finally, there are no Exchange Act reporting obligations following the offering, unless the business has more than $10 million in assets and more than 500 shareholders.

Reg D, 17 C.F.R. 230.501-.508 (1999)

Within **Reg D,** there are three exemptions available from federal registration requirements. The three exemptions relating to raising capital are briefly discussed here. Note that as the exempt amount increases, so does the attendant risk. Consequently, there are greater restrictions imposed.

RULE 504 (known as the *seed capital exemption*)

- An exemption is given to raise up to $1 million in a 12-month period.
- There is no limitation on solicitation or advertising to public investors.
- The offering is available to all investors (accredited or non accredited).
- There is no limitation on the number of investors.
- There are no specific disclosure requirements (e.g., what the business intends to do with the capital).
- Audited financial information is not required.

RULE 505

- An exemption is given to raise up to $5 million in a 12-month period.
- Solicitation and advertising is completely limited.
- The offering is available to an unlimited number of accredited investors plus an additional 35 nonaccredited investors.
- There is a bad-boy disqualification provision (as it historically has been known, suspending the exemption if any person involved with the business or its offering has engaged in specified acts of misconduct, even if the acts did not lead to a conviction).
- Audited financial information is required.
- Securities are subject to resale restrictions.

RULE 506

- An exemption is given to raise over $5 million without regard to time restrictions.

- There is complete limitation on solicitation and advertising.
- The offering is available to an unlimited number of accredited investors plus up to 35 nonaccredited investors. Unlike Rule 505, the nonaccredited investors must be "sophisticated," defined as those with sufficient knowledge and experience rendering them capable of evaluating a prospective investment.
- There is no bad-boy disqualification provision.
- Audited financial information is required.
- Investors receive securities that have secondary sale restrictions and so may not be freely traded.
- The National Securities Markets Improvement Act of 1996, which gives the SEC the power to exempt securities transactions from duplicative regulation, applies to Rule 506 transactions (but not to Rule 504 or 505 transactions). Thus, Rule 506 preempts certain aspects of state securities regulation, so compliance with the capital-raising requirements are made much easier for business.

SCOR Offerings.   SCOR, the **Small Corporate Offering Registration** format, was adopted by the SEC in 1992. In some states it is known as a Uniform Limited Offering Registration. This offering is referred to as the seed capital exemption because it is for such a small amount and usually involves companies with early stage products or services:

- Exemption is given to raise up to $1 million in a 12-month period.
- There is no secondary offering.
- Businesses may use Form U-7, a less complicated form in a question-and-answer style.
- Offering is not available to all investors.
- SEC qualification is not required.
- There is no testing the waters.
- A minimum share price is required.
- Audited financial statements are required.

California Limited Offering Exemption, SEC Rule 1001, 17 C.F.R. § 230.1001 (1999), Cal. Corp. Code 25102(n) (West Supp. 1999).   The SEC adopted the **California Limited Offering Exemption** following its passage under California blue sky laws. It is most similar to Reg D exemptions. While this exemption is limited to businesses organized under California law, or to those attributing more than half their business to California, the SEC stated that it would provide exemptions for other states that enact such provisions. It provides the following:

- An exemption is given from state registration provisions of up to $5 million.
- Some types of general solicitation are allowed.
- The offering is available to "qualified investors" (similar to "accredited investors").

A few other notable exemptions, by way of example, include *Reg S* (exempting securities of qualified international offerings) (17 C.F.R. § 230.901-.905 (1999)); *Reg E* (exempting securities of small business investment companies) (17 C.F.R. § 230.601-.610 (1999)); and *SEC Rule 701* (exempting sales of securities through employee benefit plans of nonpublic companies) (17 C.F.R. § 230.701 (1999)).

With any of these offerings, it is extremely important to note that the exemption from federal registration requirements is conditioned on businesses meeting all of a program's provisions. Furthermore, there still remain state requirements to meet before an offer is qualified. For example, even while Rule 504 of Reg D does not mandate the production of audited financial statements, virtually every states' blue sky laws do, rendering audited financial statements a necessity. You may wish to refer back to the NASAA Web site, www.nasaa.org. Thus, this sometimes conflicting patchwork of federal and state laws impedes the full utility of these exemptions. States are currently inclined to adopt blue sky laws that are more stringent than the federal securities laws, which makes compliance with all of the relevant laws a daunting task.

Internet Securities Offerings (ISO)/ Direct Public Offerings (DPO)

It is an understatement to say that the Internet has radically altered small business capital formation. Internet technology advances during the 1990s enabled wide dissemination of information as well as the opportunity to target offerings directly to potential investors. By way of example of these changes, the SEC created an electronic database of corporate information, known as EDGAR (electronic database gathering, analysis, and retrieval)—see www.sec.gov/edgarhp.htm. This service allows for electronic filing and access to many documents heretofore available only to large institutions. Also, there are now Web sites providing market-influencing data on transactions previously available only to large institutions. (One such service is InsiderScores.com.) This has served to blur the line between financial professionals and the investing public, and most importantly for our purposes here, has further enhanced access to investing information and leveled the playing field between large and small investors, as well as between large and small businesses.

These direct marketing and sales options actuated by the Internet are in stark contrast to traditional investment banking, in which offerings are carefully and deliberately screened through many filtering systems before the offering is finally made to the public. Through the Internet, businesses may make information directly available to potential investors. They may also solicit, advertise, and market securities offerings at a greater speed and lower cost than any paper-based system generated by investment bankers. This occurrence is due to two phenomena: the relaxation of legal and regulatory requirements over the past twenty years; and the growing uses of the Internet. The Internet has popularized and democratized many facets of our life's activities, and by providing immediate and almost universal access

to business information for prospective investors, this has become true in the realm of securities offerings.

Companies typically seeking to raise capital through a direct exempt offering are usually at earlier stages of formation and product development and are oftentimes undercapitalized—all features of a higher risk investment. This is why a measure of caution is warranted. The traditional offerings (i.e., those that are made for an established business with seasoned management, attorneys, accountants, and underwriters who have arranged for distribution of equities and a transfer agent) generally have a better rate of success. Traditional underwriters still add value to the offering. The underwriters develop a valuation and set pricing accordingly; they aggressively sell the securities and offer support after the securities are initially sold in an attempt to minimize price volatility; they offer expertise in industry segments; and are (hopefully) capable of making a judgment about the ability of this company and its products or services to grow and thus attract investors. This acts as a sort of certification of market fitness and that the fundamentals of the business are sound. Such services act as checks in the process, beginning from when capital is needed to the actual receipt of capital through the sale of securities.

There is an inherent bias, though, in the traditional offering process in favor of established (name brand) companies and products. By way of example, it is much

Figure 7.1

Notice of Stock Offering for a Little Known Company

NOTICE OF STOCK OFFERING

Desserts by David Glass, Inc. is offering 650,000
shares of common stock (no par value) to the public
(offered only in CT, MA, NY, DC, and CA)
at a price of $3.00 per share (minimum purchase 100 shares).
A final offering circular may be obtained from the Company via
the Internet at www.davidglass.com or by calling
1–888–DAVID–IPO (toll-free) or by writing to the
Company at 140–150 Huyshope Avenue,
Hartford, CT 16106

easier to raise capital on Wall Street for Pepperidge Farms cakes than for David Glass's gourmet cakes. This is due to the fact that Pepperidge Farms has established product and distribution systems. The David Glass product is not as likely a candidate for a Wall Street-style paper-based offering (see Figure 7.1)

This is where ISOs/DPOs become a possibility—they represent a low-cost means to an end—raising capital for expansion and new businesses. **Internet securities offerings (ISOs)**—also called *direct public offerings (DPOs)*—offer efficient marketing to targeted investors, and they offer capital-raising possibilities that have historically not been available to small and startup businesses. Moreover, it is estimated that a successfully marketed offering reaps 10 to 15 percent more of the proceeds for the business than it would have received through a traditional paper-based offering. However, the Desserts by David Glass business does not have an established market, nor are its systems as institutionalized. And there is no established market for investors to trade shares of David Glass securities that they may already own. ISOs have thus far attracted a very high number of offerings from businesses that are startups, in which management is relatively inexperienced, the products and services are in the earliest stages of development without being time-tested, and channels of distribution are typically not yet secured. When the offerings are by way of the Internet, moreover, it is best characterized as a passive effort since bankers and brokers are not aggressively selling the securities, but rather the business is waiting for a 'hit' on its offering web site. In fact most of the investors in ISOs are from what is known as *affinity groups,* such as business suppliers, customers, employees,

http://

Learn more about IPOs and ISOs at
http://linux.agsm.ucla.edu/ipo/

distributors, and friends. The after-market price and valuation is an issue, too, and prices currently are subject to wide fluctuations.

In summary, an investment in an ISO is typically fraught

> **http://**
> A two-week advance listing of the IPO pipeline is at
> **www.ipo.com**

with many more risks than a security brought to market by a traditional investment banking team and listed on a major exchange. And although the cost of a direct offering is much less than that of a traditional offering, the success of the former offering is more precarious and uncertain. This will most certainly change as the ISO market matures, and investment banks adopt the Internet as the standard mode for marketing offerings and trading securities, but until then, it is still a developing and changing system.

This half of the chapter discusses the current business environment of securities offerings over the Internet and regulatory responses to Internet offering initiatives. It should be kept in mind that all of the securities laws, regulations, rules and SEC policies discussed earlier in this chapter, are applicable to all ISOs. Although the caselaw in this area is at the most preliminary stage, the SEC has issued reports, advice, interpretive releases, enforcement actions and final rules. The SEC has also in some instances taken no action (by the issuance of a *No-Action Letter*), and therefore the business may carry on with its Internet securities offering strategy. The SEC may also file complaints in court. This part of the chapter will be divided into four sections, addressing the major legal issues of ISOs/DPOs.

Requirements of Electronic Delivery of Offering Materials

In 1995, in a seminal statement, the SEC paved the way for conducting securities transactions over the Internet. In Release 33-7233 (www.sec.gov/rules/concept/33-7233.txt), the SEC stated:

> Given the numerous benefits of electronic media, the Commission encourages further technological research, development, and application . . . the use of electronic media should be at least an equal alternative to the use of paper-based media. Accordingly, issuer or third party information that can be delivered in paper under the federal securities laws may be delivered in electronic format.

Electronic delivery of offering materials was authorized by the SEC for the first time in 1995. The law firm Brown &

> **http://**
> Access the Federal Regulations in Internet Offerings Web site at
> **www.securitiesweb.com/fedreg.html**

Cyberethics

When an issuer posts its offering on a centralized service listing many different offerings, does the issuer have any responsibility to then monitor that Web site to ensure accuracy?

This practice could be compared to hiring an advertising firm to conduct a campaign. Ultimately, responsibility rests on the business seeking the services.

Wood, on behalf of its clients Merrill Lynch and Goldman Sachs, inquired whether prospectus delivery requirements were met by providing it via computer on a proprietary system for investors to download. In response, the SEC issued a **No-Action Letter** (1995 SEC No-Act. LEXIS 281 (April 17, 1995)) concluding that such a method meets Securities Act delivery requirements if certain conditions are met. A No-Action Letter is one way in which the SEC may respond to a company's inquiry about a proposed action. The SECs No-Action response allows the company to act upon its proposal and indicates that except for conditions in the letter, there will be no further action by the SEC in the matter. The actual substantive law requiring delivery of a prospectus has not changed, but the format of delivery has evolved, and so the law has evolved to accommodate electronic delivery of offering materials.

The first offering conducted over the Internet occurred in February 1996. Spring Street Brewing Company posted a Reg A IPO prospectus on its Web site with the approval of the SEC and went on to raise $1.6 million for its operations. No commissions were paid to any underwriters, exchanges, or brokers.

The three basic guidelines remain the same for the successful delivery of offering materials:

1. *Notice*—there must be timely and adequate notice of the delivery of information. For example, a passive medium such as a Web site does not offer investors notice, but a separate notice by e-mail or postal mail does constitute notice.
2. *Access*—there must be relatively easy-to-use electronic communication systems available, rather than a system so burdensome that access is effectively denied.
3. *Evidence of delivery*—there must be reasonable assurance that investors receive the information. Receipt is automatically presumed if sent by postal mail or facsimile. The materials may be sent partly by one medium and partly by another. To the extent electronic media are used, the question of delivery becomes more complicated. For example, if delivery is attempted by e-mail, the SEC requires (a) there be informed consent on the part of investors to receive that information through this medium, and (b) businesses must obtain evidence that investors actually received this information, such as through an e-mail return receipt.

These three components must each be met before delivery is accomplished. In an effort to assist issuers of securities in conforming to these requirements, the SEC has generated many examples of when delivery is, or is not, affected. The following two examples are excerpted from SEC Release No. 33-7233.

Example i

Company XYZ places its sales literature in a discussion forum located on the World Wide Web. The sales literature con-

http://
Read further about this venture at
www.entrepreneurmag.com/resource/money_1296.hts

tains a hyperlink to the company's final prospectus. While viewing the literature the individual can click on a box marked "final prospectus," and almost instantly the person will be linked directly to the company's Web site and the final prospectus will appear on the person's computer screen.

Sales literature, whether in paper or electronic form, is required to be preceded or accompanied by a final prospectus. The hyperlink function enables the final prospectus to be viewed directly, as if it were packaged in the same envelope as the sales literature. Therefore, the final prospectus would be considered to have accompanied the sales literature. Consequently, the placing of sales literature in a discussion forum on a Web site would satisfy delivery obligations provided that a hyperlink that provides direct access to the final prospectus is included.

Example ii

Company XYZ places its final prospectus on its Internet Web site. Company XYZ then confirms by mail the sale of securities to investors with a note stating that the final prospectus is available on its Web site and giving the Internet location of the Web site.

Unlike paper delivery of a final prospectus, where access to the document can be presumed with delivery, not all investors purchasing securities could be presumed to have the ability to access the final prospectus via an Internet Web site. Therefore, absent other factors such as express consent from the investor or an investor's actually accessing the document on the Web site, these procedures by themselves would not satisfy the delivery requirements under the Securities Act.

Web sites and their links must be continually monitored to ensure compliance with securities laws and that no inappropriate material is incorporated into the offering Web site. Business liability in such cases is analogous to the earlier paper-based cases where investors relied on third-party (such as analyst) forecasts in making an investment decision. After suffering losses, investors filed suit against the businesses in which they invested. Recent case law indicates that in order to be liable under federal securities laws businesses must have placed their imprimatur, express or implied, on the projections. [See *In re Syntex Corp.,* 95 F.3d 92 , (9th Cir. 1996); *Elkind v. Liggett & Myers, Inc.,* 635 F.2d 156 (2d Cir. 1980).] Thus, liability could attach for hyperlinks appearing in conjunction with an offering.

The use of the Internet in the delivery of offering materials for exempt offerings is more problematic, however. For Reg D offerings, as an example, general solicitation is restricted because the offering is private. General access to such Web sites and delivery of these materials may have the effect of disqualifying an offering from these private placement exemptions.

The SEC recently considered a company's request for a No-Action Letter (1996 SEC NoAct Lexis 642) in response to an online offering. The company wished to post a prospectus for a Reg D offering. Such offerings, however, are available only to accredited or sophisticated investors. The company proposed to post this offering on a password-protected page, accessible only to those who fill out the questionnaire and qualify. The SEC issued a No-Action Letter noting that all legal requirements were satisfied.

Since this SEC Release No. 33-7233, in which the SEC first published its views on the use of electronic media to deliver information to investors and others, much has changed. The SEC continues to support this framework for electronic delivery that it established. It recognizes however, that as new issues arise, continued guidance is necessary to clarify other regulatory issues relating to electronic delivery of offering materials.

The SEC recently issued an Interpretive Release in 2000, which represents an effort to keep pace with technological innovations relating to electronic delivery of communications. It recognizes that the "Internet has had a significant impact on capital-raising techniques and, more broadly, on the structure of the securities industry. Today, almost seven million people invest in the U.S. securities markets through online brokerage accounts."

This release provides further guidance by clarifying that:

- Investors may consent to electronic delivery telephonically. In today's markets, significant matters often are communicated telephonically. Since business can be transacted as effectively over the telephone as it can in paper, the SEC is of the view that an issuer may obtain an informed consent telephonically, as long as a record of that consent is retained.
- Intermediaries may request consent to electronic delivery on a 'global,' multiple-issuer basis. This means that an investor my give consent to electronic delivery of all documents of any issuer in which that investor buys or owns securities through a particular intermediary – so long as consent is informed.
- Issuers and intermediaries may deliver documents in portable document format, or PDF, with appropriate measures to assure that investors can easily access documents. The 1995 Release stated that a particular medium should not be so burdensome that intended recipients cannot effectively access the information. Many issuers interpreted this statement to preclude delivery of PDF documents, which cannot be accessed without special software. The SEC believes that this is not the correct interpretation, and so documents may now be delivered in PDF format if, for example, issuers provide investors with the necessary software and technical assistance at no cost.

- An embedded hyperlink within a prospectus or any other document required to be filed or delivered under the federal securities laws causes the hyperlinked information to be a part of that document. The SECs position is that issuers may be responsible for hyperlinked information. In such an inquiry, the SEC states that the placement and text surrounding the hyperlink is relevant, as is whether there is a risk of confusion as to the source of the hyperlinked information, and how the hyperlink appears within the layout of the page.

To give issuers a sense of what is permissible under these new guidelines, the SEC provides another series of examples.

EXAMPLE I

Investor John Doe gives XYZ Delivery Service his informed consent over the telephone using automated touch tone instructions (after accessing the service using a personal identification number). The automated instructions informed John Doe of the manner, costs and risks of electronic delivery. The consent related to electronic delivery of documents. Before delivering any electronic documents to Investor John Doe, XYZ Delivery Service sends Investor John Doe a letter confirming that he had consented to electronic delivery.

The confirming letter sent by XYZ Delivery Service provides assurance that John Doe consented to the same extent as if he had provided a written or electronic consent. Thus, XYZ Delivery Service's procedures would evidence satisfaction of delivery. We also note the XYZ Delivery Service has reason to be assured of the authenticity of John Doe's telephonic consent because of his use of a personal identification number.

EXAMPLE II

In seeking a global consent to electronic delivery from Investor John Doe, Broker DEF specifies that the electronic media that may be used to deliver documents will be CD-ROM, an Internet web site, electronic mail or facsimile transmission, and further advises John Doe that if he does not have access to all of these media he should not consent to electronic delivery. John Doe consents to electronic delivery from Broker DEF.

In this situation John Doe's consent would be informed regarding the manner of electronic delivery. The consent need not specify which form of media a specific issuer may use.

EXAMPLE III

Investor John Doe consents to delivery of all future documents of Company XYZ electronically via Company XYZ's Internet web site, including documents delivered in PDF. The form of consent advises John Doe of the system requirements necessary for receipt of documents in PDF and cautions that downloading time may be slow. Company XYZ places its proxy soliciting materials and annual report to security holders in PDF on its Internet web site, with a hyperlink on the same screen enabling users to download a free copy of Adobe Acrobat (software permitting PDF viewing) and a toll-free telephone number that investors can use to contact someone during Company XYZ's business hours for technical assistance or to request a paper copy of a document.

Company XYZ has satisfied its delivery obligations. Under these circumstances, John Doe can effectively access the information provided.

EXAMPLE IV

Company XYZ, which is engaged in a public offering of its securities, places its preliminary prospectus on its Internet web site. In the Business section of the prospectus, Company XYZ has placed a hyperlink to a report by a marketing research firm located on a third-party web site regarding Company XYZ's industry.

Because the hyperlink is embedded within the prospectus, the report becomes a part of the prospectus and must be filed with the Commission. In addition, Company XYZ must obtain a written consent from the person preparing the report in accordance with the Securities Act. This consent also must be filed with the SEC. Moreover, the report will be subject to liability under the Securities Act, as well as other anti-fraud provisions of the federal securities laws.

Beyond this Guidance that the SEC has provided to issuers, it has solicited comment from interested parties on a number of topics. For example, some issuers have suggested that it is time to shift from the present delivery model to an 'access-equals-delivery' model. Under this model, investors would be assumed to have access to the Internet, thereby allowing delivery to be accomplished solely by an issuer posting a document on the issuer's or a third-party's web site. Although the SEC does not believe that the time has come for this model, it has requested comment as to whether there are circumstances under which this might be appropriate.

In another instance, issuers have argued for changes to the consent requirement, and suggested that electronic delivery would be more forthcoming if they were permitted to use a form of implied consent to evidence satisfaction of delivery. The SEC was concerned, however, that investors would be adversely affected by this through their inadvertent failure to object. In these and other cases, there is a dialogue between interested parties and the SEC as to modifications to the rules based on a changing technological and user environment.

Electronic Delivery of Offering Materials: The Range of Transmittable Information

Businesses are now able to disseminate information instantaneously on a global scale. Prior to the advent of the Internet, business communications of investment-sensitive information were limited to the elite Fortune 500 and other highly capitalized institutions. Now small-cap, and even micro-cap businesses are able to participate in

ISOs/DPOs. The Internet has leveled the playing field by making capital raising possible for virtually all businesses. This technology has had the effect of bridging the capital gap between supply and demand for venture capital funds, and has thereby made the capital markets more efficient. It has also bridged the information gap between institutions and individual investors.

The usefulness of Internet technology in securities offerings is just being recognized and exploited. Of particular note for our purposes, and more fully discussed next, are: (1) Web site as well as CD-ROM prospectuses; (2) electronic roadshows; (3) electronic sales literature and (4) private offerings. Related Internet uses not central to our discussion include corporate communications; delivery of proxy materials; electronic voting; access to shareholder meetings; and access to securities analysts' conference calls to businesses.

In 1996, the SEC provided final rules for this issue in a directive called Use of Electronic Media for Delivery Purposes. The SEC expressly acknowledged the impact of the Internet observing the "strict compliance with requirements applicable to printed materials may not be possible in all electronic media." It issued specifications for formatting; graphic, image, and audio data; document delivery; and where filings are to be made.

Prospectuses—Web Site and CD-ROM

Prospectuses have been posted online since 1996—in some instances, for informational purposes only. Online delivery of prospectuses has just gained momentum. In 1997, Great Plains Software, Inc. was the first to post a Web site prospectus with audio and video components. The audio portion was provided by *streaming*, and viewers could hear the file before it was even downloaded, although this streamed information could not be printed or stored. The Web site prospectus consisted of textual disclosures, product overviews, photographs, audio, and a downloadable video with product demonstrations.

Also in 1997, the first multimedia CD-ROM prospectus was delivered to investors for an offering by Ameritrade. (K-Mart Corp. delivered a CD-ROM private placement offering circular for investors in 1996. The prospectuses were issued in both paper and CD-ROM formats.)

The SEC's position with regard to the inclusion of media images such as video clips is that while they cannot be filed with EDGAR or included in the paper prospectus, it requires "equivalent disclosure" between the e-prospectus, and the paper one. Thus, the EDGAR filing must include a "fair and accurate description" of presentation material that could not be included because of technological constraints. This description could be in the form of a graph explaining the media image, a transcript of the words spoken, an expla-

http://

See

www.sec.gov/rules/final/33-7289.txt

nation of the graphics, and so on. The SEC cautions that the issuer remains responsible for ensuring compliance with all securities laws.

Electronic Roadshows

Prior to the advent of the Internet, company management would conduct live presentations to small groups of high net-worth, sophisticated investors and institutional clients such as managers of mutual and pension funds. This gave money managers with billions of dollars to invest the opportunity to speak face to face with the management before making an investment in the business. This would be done during the waiting period between the prospectus delivery and registration/actual sale of securities, at which time written communications, but not oral communications, are restricted. During this period, roadshows are used and management may speak about issues raised in the written prospectus filed with the SEC, elaborating and clarifying information contained therein. Beginning the 1980s, the roadshows began to be broadcast live simultaneously to central points where interested investors could meet to listen to the roadshow. Now the term *roadshow* is an anachronism, in that management does not have to go "on the road" pitching the offering. With the advent of webcasting technology, anyone with an Internet connection may listen in on a conference call. The SEC does not require but rather allows businesses to offer this to investors. Advocates of this openness assert that even small investors deserve a chance to perform the same due diligence inquiry on offerings that large investors have always performed. The first **electronic roadshow** occurred in 1996 and was conducted by Primary Care Centers of America for a Reg D offering. It used video, slides with audio narration, interviews, and an online offering circular.

> **http://**
> For a brief discussion of these issues, see
> **http://smartbiz. com/sbs/columns/galkin20.htm**

Recently, NetRoadshow requested from the SEC a confirmation that its business method of posting a variety of road shows to qualified investors for public offerings on the Internet did not violate any securities laws; and that such road shows would not be considered prospectuses (1997 SEC No-Act, Lexis 864). NetRoadshow divulged its procedures for providing this service, detailing how it would ensure that only qualified investors could access presentations. Also that it would clarify to users that they were viewing not a prospectus, but rather a sales and marketing presentation about an investment opportunity. NetRoadshow also pointed out that its fees were not contingent on the degree of success of the offering. The SEC again issued a No Action letter noting that such practices do not violate any securities laws.

Internet Roadshows are now a commonplace ancillary feature to internet ipo's. You may wish to visit Net Roadshow's site at http://www.netroadshow.com. Additionally, some worthwhile sites to visit are: http://www.e-analytics.com/ipo/bplan3.htm; and http://www.srz.com/pub/iporoad.html.

Electronic Sales Literature

Under Section 5 of the Securities Act, three important time periods are set out with reference to the distribution of sales literature. First, there is the pre-filing period in which no statements regarding sales of securities may be made. Second, there is a waiting period between the registration and effective period when sales may commence, and only oral statements may be made at this time (such as is done in roadshows). Third, there is the post-effective period. At this time, the securities are already being traded. Oral and written offers and the dissemination of sales literature are allowed, but only if accompanied by a final prospectus. This is construed to mean that they must be in close proximity to each other on the same menu, or they must be linked to each other. Compliance with the Securities Act on this issue is a challenge because of the abilities to link and frame. The SECs position is that if there is direct access from one site to another, it associates the two pages as one document. This entangling could cause trouble if all of a business's links are to only favorable reports. It is therefore best to avoid linking a final prospectus with investor-sensitive materials, and instead it is advisable to limit links to routine product/service marketing information.

Private Placement Offerings

The ability of businesses to engage in ISOs is just being explored, and its potential has not yet been realized. For those offerings subject to bans on solicitation, businesses are developing password-protected Web sites accessible to only those investors who meet the legal requirements. This creation of proprietary networks is a necessity for many offerings in order to comply with the securities laws. The open and universal quality of the Internet is not well suited for those offerings that are private and where no solicitations are allowed. Therefore privacy protections must be built into the software.

In another instance, Lamp Technologies, a data processing and software company, asked the SEC to consider its systems for electronic private offerings. The SEC counsel wrote in 1997, and later restated, that "it would not recommend that

> **http://**
> See, for example, NetRoadshow's site at
> **www.netroadshow.com/site/main.html**

> **http://**
> For a Web site listing private placement offerings, see
> **www.dsm.com/offerings/private/default.htm**

the Commission take enforcement actions if Lamp posts information concerning private funds on a web site that is password-protected and accessible to subscribers who are predetermined by Lamp to be accredited investors."

[For the complete correspondence in this case, see Lamp Technologies, Inc., 1997 SEC No-Act. Lexis 638; *cf.* 1998 SEC No-Act. Lexis 615.]

Consolidation of Web Sites for Marketing Offerings, and Secondary Sales of Securities

As the possibilities expand for ISOs/DPOs, businesses increasingly utilize the Internet for at least a portion of their capital-raising efforts. At the beginning of this phenomenon during the period 1995–1997, each offering was a singular undertaking conducted independently. The next logical step was reached shortly after these lone offerings were made on the Internet. Investors in these securities soon realized that there was no secondary market for shares of these offerings, as these companies typically were not listed with the major exhanges. To alleviate this issue of illiquidity, in 1996 Spring Street Brewing Company asked, and received from the SEC, an okay for its plan to create an issuer-based Bulletin Board trading system called Wit-Trade. This established an e-marketplace for trading in such shares. [See Spring Street Brewing Company, 1996 SEC No-Act. LEXIS 435, April 17, 1996.]

Since this time, the use of the Internet for offerings has surged, and now there are a number of Web sites capitalizing on this convergence of Internet technology and the financial markets. Centralized Web sites offering a full range of corporate finance and investment banking services are now available. Their services are similar those available at any bricks-and-mortar banking firm. In no particular order, here are some of these sites:

Digital Capital Corp.
  www.digicap.com/

The Elysian Group
  www.elysiangroup.com/

Interactive Business Channel
  www.ibchannel.com/

StockTrans
  www.dpousa.com/

Millenium Capital
  www.millcapquest.com/

Venture Associates
  www.venturea.com/overview.htm

Financial Web
  www.financialweb.com

Direct Stock Market
  www.dsm.com/

Equity Analytics, Ltd.
  www.ipoalley.com

Direct IPO, Inc.
  www.directipo.com/

Wit Capital Group
www.witcapital.com/

Rule506.com
www.rule506.com/

FirsTrade.com
www.firstrade.com

ipo.com
www.ipo.com/

Yahoo!
biz.yahoo.com/ipo/

A Web site that offers comparisons of these services may be found at: www.cyber-invest.com/guides/ipodpo.dpo.guide.html.

Traditional firms have been scrambling to catch up with the e-securities firms, and sign up investors online. These include:

Morgan Stanley Dean Witter
www.online.msdw.com

Merrill Lynch & Company
www.mldirect.ml.com

E*Trade Group, Inc.
www.etrade.com

Powerstreet
www.fidelity.com

It is most instructive to connect to these Web sites or any similar listing sites that you may come across, and start right with the tombstone ad of the offering, and follow along with the information by connecting to the various hyperlinks. While doing so, it is helpful to bear in mind such issues of whether the offer is actually for a security; whether advertising is legal for that type of security; whether delivery of the prospectus has been accomplished; and so forth.

This consolidation of Web sites posting offerings bodes especially well for exempt offerings because there has never been an exchange or other national listing service for such securities. Heretofore the market for these investments has been fragmented, and investors have not had full access to the vast range of available offerings. Interestingly, SEC Chair Arthur Levitt spoke with great concern about the overall fragmentation of the securities markets. As the number of trading markets proliferates, oversight and visibility of them has declined. It is, in a sense, a conflict between centralization and competition.

In the headlong push to be part of the electronic medium, laws may have been overlooked. Securities regulations, meanwhile, have issued only guidance on using the Internet, through no-action letters, releases, proposed rules, notices, reports, and so on. It is the sort of process where business entities and regulators act and react to each other, thereby creating a dynamic, changing and largely unpredictable business environment.

One of the major concerns of ISOs is the illiquidity of the securities—and the related issue of the lack of an established centralized exchange for investors to trade securities of all of these offerings. Such securities are priced in negotiations between the selling shareholder and a broker/dealer firm that assesses demand for the security and is ultimately priced at close proximity to the most recent sale price of that security, which has been published at an exchange. The lack of markets for secondary sales of ISOs is a major concern. *Liquidity* is a key element to success for investors will remain cautious about purchasing indefinitely illiquid securities. The SEC issued in 1997 a Concept Release (Release No. 34-38672), addressing, in part, technology and securities trading, yet a workable system still needs to be developed.

The SEC has indicated each time that at a minimum, companies must do the following:

1. Keep records of all quotes entered into the system and make these available
2. Abide by all securities laws and prohibitions on advertising
3. Not receive any compensation for creating or maintaining, or the use of such system
4. Not provide any information on the advisability of any transaction
5. Not receive, transfer, or hold funds or securities from any transaction

For further information, see The Flamemaster Corp., 1996 SEC No-Act. LEXIS 972 (Oct. 29, 1996).

Virtual stock markets are now appearing in cyberspace. These systems include the Portfolio System for Institutional Trading (POSIT). The Arizona Stock Exchange exists on the Internet. The company, Niphix Investments, Inc., operates a trading system for Reg A offerings. The Pacific Stock Exchange received approval in 1995 by the SEC to list SCOR and Reg A offerings. Just as there is movement toward centralization and consolidation in the industry for ISO services, this process has begun for secondary sales of securities.

The Use of Internet Web Sites for Off-Shore Offerings

Because of this global reach of the Internet, the enforcement of U.S. securities laws is a challenge with regard to **off-shore offerings.** Off-shore transactions are defined as those where the offer or sale is not made to a person in the U.S.; and at the time, the buyer was outside the U.S. or the seller reasonably believed the buyer was outside the U.S. Alternatively, the transaction is off-shore if it is executed on the physical trading floor of a foreign securities exchange. (Recall that all U.S. offers and sales must be registered, or conducted under an authorized exemption.) As the Internet transcends geopolitical boundaries, an international posting of an offering *may* constitute an offering for purposes of U.S. securities laws. The relevant legal question here is whether such postings are offers *in the United States* that must be registered. If this is the case, then the U.S. has jurisdiction over the transaction and the power to regulate the offering to ensure it complies with the U.S. laws. (This, of course, brings up issues of jurisdiction, which is discussed in Chapter 2.)

There is not as yet a body of law targeting off-shore Internet transactions exclusively, but the SEC has published its views on this subject in the Statement of the Commission Regarding the Use of Internet Web Sites to Offer Securities,

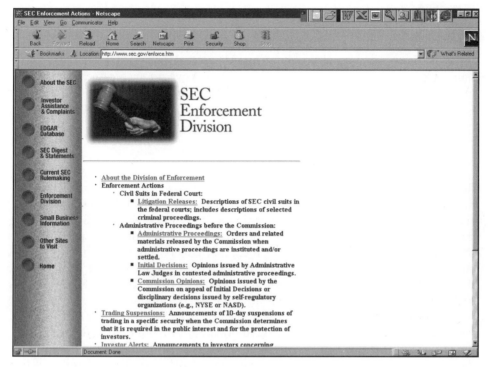

Courtesy of The Securities and Exchange Commission.

Solicit Transactions or Advertise Investment Services Offshore, found at www.sec.gov/rules/concept/33-7516.htm. The SEC wrote that if "offerors implement adequate measures to prevent U.S. persons from participating in an offshore Internet offer, we would not view the offer as targeted at the United States and thus would not treat it as occurring in the United States for registration purposes." The SEC elaborated on this standard and indicated that "such measures" include:

1. a Web site disclaimer statement making it clear that the offer is directed only to countries *other* than the United States, and
2. a Web site with procedures reasonably designed to guard against sales to U.S. persons.

Consider the following disclaimers and decide whether they are sufficiently meaningful:

"This offering is intended only to be available to residents within the European Union."
"The offer is not effective in any jurisdiction in which it could or would be illegal."

A few additional issues involving off-shore offerings deserve mention.

Off-Shore Offerings by U.S. Issuers

U.S. issuers may set up a Web site outside the United States and issue securities through it in an attempt to be exempt from U.S. securities laws. The SEC urges additional scrutiny beyond factors (1) and (2) listed above for such cases, recommending additional precautions such as the use of password-type procedures in an effort to ensure only non-U.S. persons are able to access the offer.

Exempt Offerings

Recall that some offerings are exempt from U.S. securities registration requirements. The main off-shore exemption is known as Reg S, and the SEC attempts to ensure that the exemption is available only for offers and sales be made in off-shore transactions. As for Reg D off-shore offerings, the SEC cautions that the ban on solicitation and advertising is still in force and issuers should not attempt to circumvent the law through the posting of an off-shore Web site. In a related issue, the SEC suggests businesses separate their postings of U.S. and off-shore offerings and provide no direct links between the two types of offerings.

In general, the SEC demands that Web site offerors act in good faith to screen U.S. persons from viewing off-shore offering information. As with every offering, though, the SEC states that it will enforce the anti-fraud and anti-manipulation laws if jurisdiction exists. The SEC has not taken a position in cases of whether it has jurisdiction over a non-U.S. person's off-shore offering. As the Internet technology evolves and more off-shore offerings compete for investor capital, further guidance can be expected.

This issue of the use of Web sites for off-shore offerings raises questions regarding the international regulatory environment of securities transactions. One such authority is the International Organization of Securities Commissions (IOSCO), www.iosco.org/iosco.html. Its mission is to establish common international standards for securities transactions, conduct effective surveillance of the transactions, and encourage mutual assistance and effective enforcement of the securities laws.

Enforcement of Securities Laws in Cyberspace

The SEC's Director of the Division of Enforcement states, "While the Internet has many benefits, a small group of thieves is trying to hijack unsuspecting investors on the information superhighway." (See www.sec.gov/news/press/98-69.txt.) In fiscal year 1998, the SEC received 1,114 complaints involving online securities firms, a 330 percent increase over the 259 complaints received in fiscal year 1997. The SEC will be hard-pressed to maintain effective enforcement of its laws because its budget for 2000 has been cut and the demands on this agency have increased. Even though the sheer volume of fraudulent cases has increased, the Internet nevertheless makes their detective work easier, as these Internet schemes are posted for everyone to see.

The first Internet-related securities case was brought in 1995 (*SEC v. Pleasure Time, Inc.,* 1996 SEC Lexis 3334 (Dec. 6, 1996)). It involved a scheme to sell unregistered securities in a worldwide telephone lottery over the Internet.

The SEC created within its agency an Office of Internet Enforcement in 1998, with the goal of keeping the Internet safe for investors. As in traditional investing, every imaginable scam (e.g., ponzi schemes, scalping, pyramid schemes) may be attempted electronically and is still a potential hazard of doing business. The current securities laws, for the most part, have parallel application to electronic fraud; and in fact, the Internet does not substantially change the nature of securities frauds (with the possible exception of frauds by off-shore business).

The cases usually involve multiple frauds, such as misrepresentation, failure to disclose payments to "independent advisors" who recommended investors to buy the securities while they themselves are receiving large fees from the offering company, and the like.

Other recent cases, are again, high-tech renditions of classic securities frauds. In one, Yun Soo Oh Park allegedly engaged in scalping. Park would purchase stock in a company and then post on his investment Web site materially false and misleading performance results for this company. He would then recommend others to buy shares in this company that he manipulated to create artificially inflated prices. Then he would profit by selling as soon as these investors were buying. See www.sec.gov/news/tokyojoe.htm. In another recent instance, the SEC settled charges against individuals who illegally offered to sell securities on the Internet auction site eBay. See www.sec.gov/news/press/99-138.txt. In the main, the fraudulent operations publicized by the SEC historically have had more to do with the false claims and misleading statements by promoters of the securities, than with the actual registration process and prospectus delivery issues. A useful Web site to visit for SEC enforcement actions is www.sec.gov/news/studies/techrp97.htm. (U.S. Securities and Exchange Commission, Report to the Congress: The Impact of Recent Technological Advances on the Securities Markets, Appendix C: Enforcement Actions Involving Internet-Based Activities).

As this chapter concludes its coverage of the legal environment of Internet ISOs/DPOs, it is worthwhile to consider the ethical issues surrounding ISOs as well. Would it be considered ethical of businesses to rush their ISO through because general market conditions are favorable—even though their products, while having good potential, are still in the process of being developed? Consider this question if the product was a complete AIDS vaccine, or a new generation of hand-held personal computers.

Recalling off-shore offerings, would it be considered ethical for a U.S. person to invest in an off-shore offering that, while purportedly aimed at non-U.S. persons, was not particularly clear about this point? Consider the investor's actions, and consider the issuer's actions, too.

Summary

As this is such a new area of law, there will continue to be a close interplay between businesses and regulators. Entrepreneurs in the business of ISOs are, in effect, creating the rules of the game by creating new systems, and then requesting no-action relief from the SEC. Gradually a body of law will develop from these letters, releases, interpretations and enforcement proceedings. It is a tremendously exciting time full of new, less expensive, and better-targeted opportunities for businesses to issue securities in exchange for expansion capital, and investors increasingly are able to participate in investment opportunities heretofore available to only large institutional entities. Many of these ISOs, however, carry somewhat higher investment and liquidity risks than traditional offerings, and so this must be factored in by investors purchasing these securities.

Manager's Checklist

- Issuers, even for those contemplating an ISO, should work closely with attorneys and accountants who are familiar with such offerings to ensure full compliance with securities laws.
- Issuers should work closely with the Web site managers to continually update the postings, keeping track of all materials and links, and waiting periods.
- Issuers must take steps to ensure that the Internet offering is targeted to only those investors who are eligible by law—this is particularly difficult because of the universality of the Internet, yet it is important to do.
- Issuers can keep "pushing the envelope," creating new systems to aid in their ISOs, and the SEC will offer a timely response.
- Issuers must comply with a patchwork of federal and state law requirements and must monitor the laws as they continually change.

Additional Readings

- Fisch, Jill E. "Can Internet Offerings Bridge the Small Business Capital Barrier?", 2 *Journal of Small & Emerging Business Law* (Northwestern University School of Law) 57 (1998).

- Arkebauer, James B. *Going Public* (Dearborn Financial Publishing, Inc. 1998).

- U.S. Securities and Exchange Commission, Report to the Congress: The Impact of Recent Technological Advances on the Securities Markets (1997), www.sec.gov/news/studies/techrp97.htm.

- For a good discussion of offering costs, see the following article: Stephen D. Solomon, "Follow the Money," *Inc. On Line* (June 1997), at 80, www.inc.com/incmagazine/archives/06970801.html.

- For a good discussion on the intrastate offering conducted for Ben & Jerry's ice cream, see Mark Kollar, "Do-It-Yourself Public Offerings: The Internet gives a new dimension to an old financing vehicle," *Investment Dealers' Digest* (Mar. 24, 1997), at 14.

- For a good discussion on the start-up of an Internet investment company, see Peter Truell, "Investment Maverick Navigates the Internet," *New York Times* (November 9, 1998), at C1.

PART 4

Social Issues
in Cyberspace

8

Privacy

"That the individual shall have full protection in person and in property is a principle as old as the common law; but it has been necessary from time to time to define anew the exact nature and extent of such protection."
— *Samuel D. Warren and Louis D. Brandeis* **The Right to Privacy,**
4 Harvard Law Review 193 (1890)

Introduction

At the time Warren and Brandeis talked about the concept of a "right to privacy," none had been recognized constitutionally or otherwise. This chapter discusses the evolution of this right and its application to cyberspace. We will explore some of the privacy laws related to the use of the Internet, with major emphasis on the workplace.

The enormous and continuing growth of the Internet, not only as a means by which we communicate with one another via e-mail, but also as a marketing vehicle for e-commerce and e-business, has given rise to growing concerns about the rights to privacy of more than 70 million Internet users (according to a 1998 Nielsen survey).

Every time we visit a Web site we leave a kind of footprint containing personal demographic information. To gather this information, businesses use computer files called *cookies* capable of tracking our visits to Web sites and depositing facts about us on our hard drives. What is bothersome, and has the potential for legal and ethical problems, is the use of this private information for commercial purposes without our permission. Later in this chapter, we will discuss one of the uses of this information—*spamming* (the bulk e-mailing of unsolicited advertisements)—and the privacy issues involved. This chapter will attempt to discuss our rights to privacy regarding these and similar issues related to cyberspace.

You should first be aware that if you to searched the Bill of Rights and all twenty-seven amendments to the United States Constitution, you would not find an express or *enumerated* right to privacy. The right to privacy is a *penumbral* or implied right under the Constitution. The sources of this right require us to consider the Fourth,

Fifth, and Ninth Amendments to the U.S. Constitution as applied to the states by the Fourteenth Amendment. Keep in mind, these amendments protect us from unwarranted government intrusions.

Sources of the Right to Privacy

United States Constitution

The **Ninth Amendment** provides:

> "The enumeration in the constitution of certain rights shall not be construed to deny or disparage others retained by the people."

This Amendment was probably the genesis used by the courts and legal scholars including Warren and Brandeis to create a kind of right to privacy. In addition, the Fourth and Fifth Amendments are also sources of the "right to privacy."

The **Fourth Amendment** provides:

> The right of the people to be secure in their persons, houses, papers, and effects, against unreasonable searches and seizures, shall not be violated; and no Warrants shall issue, but upon probable cause, supported by oath or affirmation, and particularly describing the place to be searched, and the persons or things to be seized.

In *Griswold v. Connecticut,* 381 U.S. 479 (1965), the U.S. Supreme Court declared unconstitutional a state law prohibiting the use of birth control devices and the giving of advice concerning their use. The Court also recognized that the Bill of Rights provided us with what it deemed to be "zones of privacy," or areas or locations where privacy is expected.

Later cases held that an important element of this right was to establish the existence of a "reasonable expectation of privacy" (discussed later in more detail) in the particular zone of privacy. The following are minimum requirements for establishing a "reasonable expectation of privacy:"

1. *A person exhibits an actual expectation of privacy.* Consider what you expect when entering an area or location, such as your bedroom, in which you desire to be "off limits" to others. Or consider what level of privacy an employee should anticipate with regards to his/her office, desk, file cabinet, or floppy disk.
2. *Society recognizes the expectation as reasonable.* In addition to your privacy expectation, what do others believe to be your expectation of privacy when you close the door to your bedroom or your office, enter a public phone booth, send an e-mail, or surf a Web site?

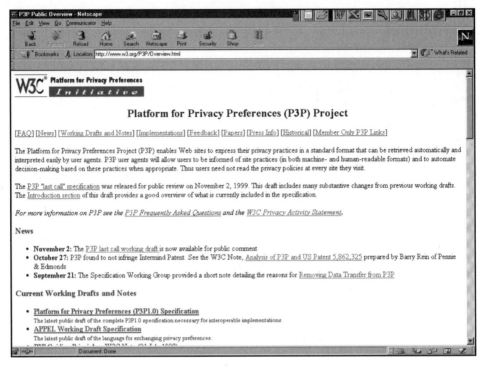

© 2000 World Wide Web Consortium.

For purposes of our discussion of establishing privacy rights associated with cyberspace, these requirements, at a minimum, will have to be satisfied concerning the mass of information, some of a personal nature, being disseminated and accumulated over the Internet.

We next focus on the provision of the **Fifth Amendment** that protects us from government actions that could result in self-incrimination. That provision reads in part:

> No person . . . shall be compelled, in any criminal case, to be a witness against himself.

This does not apply when a person voluntarily turns over documents, records, files, and papers to a law enforcement agency or official. Similarly, the public records of a corporation are not subject to this provision, even if they contain incriminating evidence.

An interesting cyberlaw application of the Fifth Amendment involves the act of *encrypting* a file that contains possible incriminating information. *Encryption* involves using encoding methods (using key codes and secured passwords) to block access to certain documents. In *Doe v. United States,* 487 U. S. 201 (1988), the Supreme Court held that an individual could "be forced to surrender a key to a strongbox containing incriminating documents, but not to reveal the combination to his wall safe . . . by word or deed." This case seems to imply that a law enforcement agency, pursuant to a valid search warrant, could obtain an encrypted file. However, the decision in *Doe* would likely prevent the agency from forcing a defendant to supply the private key, password, or code that could enable decryption or decoding, thereby allowing access. *Doe* raises issues regarding employees who store potentially criminal information on their employer's computers. If the information belongs to the employer and not the employee, it is possible a court would allow the employer to access it and use it not only to fire the employee but also to provide it to law enforcement officials. Of course, this presupposes that if the employee has encrypted the material sought, the company has the ability either through stated company policy or the law, to require the employee to allow access.

State Constitutions

In addition to the United States Constitution, state constitutions are a source of privacy rights. These rights mirror the Fourth Amendment in content and, similarly, apply only to public employees. However, some states afford greater protection to government violations of privacy. States have afforded privacy protection to electronic eavesdropping (wiretapping), medical, insurance, school records, credit and banking information, and so on. You should also recognize that the states, under the common law, grant privacy protection to what are called certain "privileged" communications. For example, with very limited exceptions, what a client tells an attorney or what a patient tells a physician is private and not available to anyone, including government officials, unless voluntarily disclosed by the client or patient.

Common Law Torts for Invasion of Privacy

Our focus next shifts to the four types of torts recognized as common law and by the Restatement (Second) of Torts. These provide monetary and injunctive relief for an unreasonable or unwarranted invasion of the right to privacy. Conceivably, they could also provide remedies for a cause of action in cases involving privacy rights in cyberspace. These torts are **Intrusion upon Seclusion; Public Disclosure of Private Facts Causing Injury to Reputation; Publicly Placing Another in a False Light; and Misappropriation of a Person's Name or Likeness Causing Injury to Reputation.**

http://
Check your state's government Web site to see what privacy rights are provided under state law from links at **www.law.cornell.edu/states/listing.html**

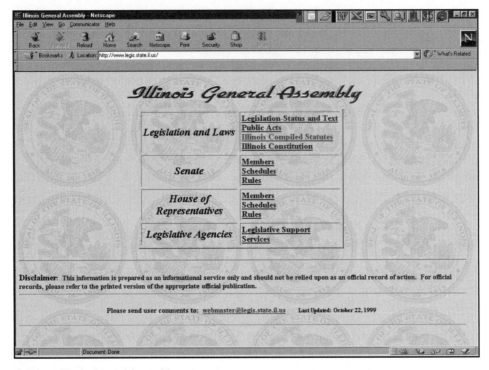

Courtesy Illinois General Assembly.

Intrusion upon Seclusion

On occasion, most of us have wished to enjoy what Brandeis recognized as a basic *"right to be let alone,"* to go to a place of seclusion. Of course, like most of our legal rights, this right is not absolute. However, when another individual, without permission or legal justification, violates that place of seclusion, this tort could provide a remedy. The Restatement (Second) of Torts defines Intrusion upon Seclusion as:

> "Intentionally intruding, physically or otherwise, upon the solitude or seclusion of another or his private affairs or concerns."

In order to succeed, a plaintiff would have to prove the following elements:

- There was intent to intrude or knowledge that the intrusion would be wrong.
- There was a reasonable expectation of privacy.
- Intrusion was substantial and highly offensive to a reasonable person.

Intent or Knowledge.   The tort of intrusion to seclusion, similar to the other three that follow, requires that the defendant acted with intent to intrude or violate the plaintiff's privacy or with knowledge that actions would result in a privacy intrusion.

Reasonable Expectation of Privacy.   Expanding on our earlier discussion, the level or amount of privacy we should expect depends on whether we are in what is usually considered to be a public or private place. What is done in the privacy of one's home should be entitled to more privacy than what one does in a public park or airport. However, laws may prohibit certain acts even if they occur in the privacy of one's home. Also, be aware that state laws can prohibit what consenting adults do in the privacy of their home. These laws usually refer to sexual activity deemed by the state to constitute "acts against nature."

Similarly, the fact that an individual is in a "public" place does not deprive the person of all rights to privacy. In fact, in right to privacy cases, courts have focused on protecting the person rather than the place.

Then, what level of privacy can we reasonably expect regarding our e-mail and other online communications? Currently, there are no strict prohibitions imposed for using the personal information we *voluntarily* disclose in e-mail and other cyberspace communications (later in this chapter, we will discuss the laws governing unauthorized use of this information). *Internet Service Providers (ISPs)* and others utilize channels of communication easily accessible by others. This is similar to the easy access to cellular phone conversations. Therefore, unless security measures are employed by the user to prevent access and ensure privacy, or a law recognizes a right to privacy exists, we should *not* expect any degree of privacy in the online information we volunteer or allow to be accessed. (*Note:* Again, the best method for insuring security is encryption). As far as the unauthorized or unjustified access by an employer of an employee's online communications resulting in an invasion of privacy, *Intrusion upon Seclusion* probably provides the best remedy.

Substantial and Highly Offensive to a Reasonable Person.   Most of the case law and the Restatement (Second) of Torts concerning this tort require that the defendant's conduct and resultant intrusion shock or outrage the conscience of a reasonable person. Monitoring telephone or e-mail messages without justification or consent would probably constitute an intrusion sufficient for this element. However in *Michael A. Smyth v. Pillsbury Company*, 914 F. Supp. 97 (E.D.Pa., 1996) the Defendant told its employees that their e-mail would be confidential yet it intercepted inappropriate and unprofessional e-mail messages sent by the Plaintiff to another employee. As a result, the Plaintiff was fired. The court held that despite the assurances of the employer, the Plaintiff should not have reasonably expected privacy rights in his e-mail, especially since he made the communications voluntarily over the company e-mail system. The court found there to be no privacy rights in inappropriate and unprofessional comments directed at the employer or other employees.

Cases like *Smyth* serve to teach us that in the workplace an employee can expect little or no privacy regarding work-related activities. Managers must seek to implement and publicize company privacy policies regarding e-mail and other computer use.

http://

For examples of privacy policies, see
**www.privacyrights.com/rights.htm,
www.geis.com/html/privacy.html (GE Information
Services),** and **www.ibm.com/privacy/(IBM)**

Public Disclosure of Private Facts Causing Injury to Reputation

This tort allows recovery when highly personal facts or information about another are publicly disclosed or transmitted whereby injury to reputation results. In some instances, this tort is associated with the tort of defamation, and both may be used as separate causes of action arising out of the same case.

In addition to the elements of "intent or knowledge" and "highly offensive to a reasonable person" previously discussed, the public disclosure of private facts causing injury to reputation requires the following:

- The facts must be of a private nature.
- Communication or publicity must be disclosed to a significant segment of the community.

Facts Must Be Private.   If the information disclosed were obtained with consent, voluntarily, or was already in the public domain, this tort likely will not be successful. This can result when we sign a consent form authorizing the release of personal information about us related to medical or insurance reports. It could also be true regarding highly personal information we volunteer to ISPs or companies operating online. This information ends up stored in their vast databases, available for any number of purposes, including the sale to others.

If the information is not obtained as described and subsequently is disclosed, the issue again focuses on establishing that the plaintiff had a reasonable expectation that the facts disclosed would be kept private.

Communication or Publicity to a Significant Segment of the Community.   Recovery here is based on disclosure to a large enough group of people so that the information about the plaintiff becomes common knowledge. Therefore, it would be insufficient "to communicate a fact concerning the plaintiff's private life to a single person or even a small group of persons." [Restatement (Second) of Torts].

Publicity Placing Another in a False Light

This tort also is associated with the tort of defamation and involves falsely connecting a person to an immoral, illegal, or embarrassing situation resulting in injury to one's reputation. In general, the elements of this tort mirror those already discussed. To date, it has not been the subject of much, if any, litigation involving the invasion of privacy in cyberspace.

Misappropriation of a Person's Name or Likeness Causing Injury to Reputation

This tort usually applies in cases where the name or picture of a *living* person is used for commercial (non-newsworthy) purposes without the person's permission or consent. In some states, such as New York, it can result in both criminal and civil liability.

Federal Privacy Laws

Congress began passing laws designed to protect privacy in the 1970s (see Table 8.1). These laws deal primarily with the requirements for keeping and using personal data about individuals by the government. The focus of this part of the chapter will be on the most significant of those acts, as well as those that affect nongovernment or private entities.

Privacy Protection Act (PPA) (1980), 42 U.S.C. § 2000

The **Privacy Protection Act (PPA)** applies to law enforcement agencies and allows Fourth Amendment protection against the unreasonable searches and seizures of:

> Work product materials possessed by a person reasonably believed to have a purpose to disseminate to the public, a newspaper, book, broadcast, or other similar form of public communication, in or affecting interstate commerce.

Table 8.1

Federal Privacy Laws

- Privacy Protection Act, 1980 (PPA)
- Privacy Act, 1994
- Cable Communications Protection Act, 1984 (CCPA)
- Video Privacy Protection Act, 1988 (VPPA)
- Telephone Consumer Protection Act, 1991 (TCPA)
- Fair Credit Reporting Act, 1970 (FCRA)
- Computer Fraud and Abuse Act, 1986 (CFAA)
- Electronic Communications Privacy Act, 1986 (ECPA)

The PPA could apply to those qualifying as electronic publishers who use the Internet for the interstate transmission of their messages. If there were probable cause to believe the materials sought from these publishers were being used for a criminal purpose, a court would likely uphold a search of them as long as Fourth Amendment requirements were met. The same would be true if the search were necessary to prevent a person's injury or death.

Privacy Act of 1994, 5 U.S.C. § 552a

The **Privacy Act** establishes requirements that must be satisfied before government agencies or departments can disclose records and documents in its possession that contain personal information about individuals. The act only applies to records and documents that identify an individual by name, identification number, or other means of personal identification such as a photograph, fingerprint, or voice print. Thus, in order for the act to apply to the Internet, personal information about a person would have to be stored in a file containing one of these identifying features. The individual's name alone would be insufficient for the act to apply.

In addition, the act requires the agency or department to do the following:

1. Obtain the written consent of the individual unless the purpose of the disclosure is consistent with that for which the records are being retained.
2. Furnish copies of the records to the individual upon request.
3. Allow the individual to correct any misinformation contained in the records.
4. Make a reasonable effort to inform the individual that their records have been disclosed.

In general, the exceptions to these requirements apply to certain government law enforcement activities, situations that concern the health or safety of an individual, and court-ordered disclosures. Violations of the act can result in lawsuits by the injured party against the agency for money damages, remedies at equity such as an injunction, or both.

Cable Communications Protection Act (CCPA) (1984), 47 U.S.C. § 551

The **Cable Communications Protection Act (CCPA)** applies to cable television operators and is concerned with the privacy rights a subscriber should expect regarding personal data or information about them that a cable television operator gathers. In general, the operator is required to do the following:

1. Obtain the permission of its subscribers before collecting personal data about them.

2. Notify subscribers annually regarding the extent to which personal information about them is used or disclosed, and the purposes for which it is gathered.
3. Allow the subscriber to examine the data and make corrections of any errors or mistakes.
4. Not disclose the data except as may be required by law or court order.

(*Note:* This requirement also applies to government requests for personal information about cable subscribers.)

Failure to follow these requirements can result in lawsuits by affected subscribers.

Seemingly, the CCPA could apply to the operator of a Web site that offers cable-like entertainment (adult or otherwise) or goods and services, and where its visitors wish to remain anonymous.

Video Privacy Protection Act (VPPA) (1988), 18 U.S.C. § 2710

This **Video Privacy Protection Act (VPPA)** expands the Cable Communications Protection Act. Specifically, it prohibits the use and disclosure of personal information about the videocassettes and related products an individual rents or purchases unless their written permission is obtained. This act could be applied to rentals and purchases of videos and related products via the Internet.

Telephone Consumer Protection Act (TCPA) (1991), 47 U.S.C. § 227

The **Telephone Consumer Protection Act (TCPA)** was passed as a direct result of the telemarketing activities arising from the transmission of telephone solicitations originating from automatic dialers. The TCPA directs the Federal Communications Commission (FCC) to promulgate and implement rules and regulations directed at these solicitations. Basically, the TCPA provides the following:

1. It is illegal to make a phone call by means of an automatic dialing system or pre-recorded (or artificial) voice that results in the party called being charged for the call. (This also applies to calls made to a cellular phone number).
2. It prohibits the use of any device to send an unsolicited advertisement to a telephone facsimile machine.
3. Companies engaging in telephone telemarketing are required to set up "do not call" lists for consumers who do not wish to receive these types of calls. Consumers also have the right to have their names removed from existing lists.
4. It prohibits making unsolicited telemarketing calls to police, fire, or other emergency phone numbers.

Thus far, the TCPA has not yet been applied to bulk e-mail solicitations. However, if it is to have any effect on the Internet, most likely it would relate to the act of spamming, which can be defined as the mass or bulk mailing of unsolicited e-mails containing advertisements for goods or services (also pertains to junk mail and chain letters). Spamming will be discussed in greater detail later in this chapter.

It should be noted that a federal district court has given exclusive jurisdiction to the states in suits brought under the TCPA. [*Erienet, Inc., et al. v. Velocity Net, Inc., et al.*, 1998 U. S. App. Lexis 23931 (3rd Cir., September 25, 1998)].

The Fair Credit Reporting Act (FCRA) of 1970, 15 U.S.C. § 1681

The purpose of the **Fair Credit Reporting Act (FCRA)** is to ensure that the credit reports furnished by consumer credit reporting agencies are accurate, impartial, and respect privacy. Also, in general, before an agency can release credit information about an individual, the individual's permission must be obtained.

The FCRA also gives consumers the right to obtain information about their credit status from credit bureaus. Failure to comply with the FCRA requirements can result in civil and criminal liability. The FCRA would apply to online requests for information made to credit agencies. The Federal Trade Commission has jurisdiction over the FCRA.

The Computer Fraud and Abuse Act (CFFA) of 1986 (Amended 1994), 18 U.S.C. § 1030

The primary purpose of the **Computer Fraud and Abuse Act** is to protect national security by prohibiting the intentional access of data stored in computers belonging to or benefiting the U.S. government. The CFFA makes it a felony for an individual to obtain this data without authority. Of significance to our discussion of privacy is another provision of the act that makes it a felony to intentionally access information about a consumer contained in the financial records of a financial institution or in a file of a consumer reporting agency.

The Electronic Communications Privacy Act (ECPA) of 1986, 18 U.S.C § 2510

The most important federal statute regarding privacy in cyberspace is the **Electronic Communications Privacy Act (ECPA)** of 1986. In 1968, no doubt influenced by cases including *Katz v. United States* (discussed earlier in this chapter) that demonstrated the ability of the government to monitor and record telephone conversations, Congress passed Title III of the Omnibus Crime Control and Safe Streets of Act (18 U.S.C. § 2510), the so-called *wiretap* statute. This statute established Fourth Amendment requirements that government agencies would have to satisfy in order to carry out legal wiretaps. These included obtaining a valid search warrant based on a showing of probable cause that the phone call to be intercepted was related to a criminal activity.

By the 1980s, advancements in technology and the creation of new and more sophisticated modes of wire and electronic communications, including e-mail, caused concerns that existing wiretap laws were inadequate to protect the rights of individuals. Congress responded by passing the ECPA, which amended the Omnibus Crime Control and Safe Streets Act. The ECPA applies to ISPs and other commercial online service providers engaged in the transmission, interception, and storage of electronic communications, including e-mail "to the public" that affects interstate or foreign commerce.

The meaning of *to the public* under the ECPA was a major issue before the court in *Andersen Consulting LLP v. UOP,* 991 Fed. Supp. 1041 (N.D. Ill. 1998). In *Andersen,* the defendant maintained an internal e-mail system and allowed the plaintiff to use it. The defendant disclosed some of the plaintiff's e-mail messages to a newspaper that published them. The plaintiff sued under the ECPA. The court dismissed the suit, interpreting the phrase "to the public" as meaning the "community at large." Here, the defendant intended its e-mail system to be for internal communication purposes and not for transmission to the public or community at large. The defendant certainly had not intended to affect interstate commerce. Therefore, the disclosure did not violate the ECPA.

After considering *Andersen,* you might be contemplating whether the ECPA would apply to the interception or access of electronic communications intended to be readily accessible to the general public. An example would be a message posted on a public bulletin board. It is likely that the ECPA would not apply because the message would not imply that the sender had a reasonable expectation of privacy.

Essentially, the ECPA contains two major provisions. Title I applies to the interception and disclosure of wire, oral, and electronic communications, and Title II applies to stored wire, transactional, and electronic communications. Violations of either title can result in criminal and civil liability. You should *note* that the ECPA does not, in the absence of an agreement to the contrary, prohibit disclosure of the contents of an e-mail message by the intended recipient.

Title I (§§ 2510–2522)—Interception and Disclosure of Wire, Oral, and Electronic Communications.   Title I prohibits the unauthorized interception and disclosure of wire, oral and electronic communications. The ECPA defines an electronic communication as:

> Any transfer of signs, signals, writing, images, sounds, data, or intelligence of any nature transmitted in whole or in part by a wire, radio, electromagnetic, photoelectronic or photooptical system that affects interstate or foreign commerce.

Examples include transmissions by radio paging devices (excluding "tone-only" devices), cellular phones, computer generated transmissions, and e-mail. The ECPA covers all communication carriers or persons who provide or operate facilities for communications that affect interstate or foreign commerce.

Specifically, Title I prohibits, with exceptions:

1. Any person from intentionally intercepting any wire, oral, or electronic communication;
2. Any person from intentionally using or disclosing the contents of any wire, oral, or electronic communication to another person;
3. An Internet service provider (ISP) from intentionally disclosing the contents of a communication to any person or entity other than the addressee or intended recipient.

In *McVeigh V. Cohen et al.*, 983 F. Supp. 215 (D.D.C., 1998), the plaintiff, Timothy McVeigh, was discharged from the United States Navy because he was gay, a fact disclosed to the Navy by America Online (AOL), an ISP. AOL had discovered McVeigh's sexual orientation after identifying him as the sender of an anonymous e-mail, and as an individual described in its membership directory as gay. In issuing a preliminary injunction preventing the Navy from discharging McVeigh, the Court of Appeals ruled the Navy was in violation of its "Don't Ask, Don't Tell" policy. The Court was also aided in its decision by the actions of AOL in intentionally disclosing information about McVeigh and his e-mail, resulting in a direct violation of the ECPA.

Note: The ECPA does not prohibit access or disclosure of electronic communications placed on a site intended to be readily accessible by the public.

There are four *major* exceptions to Title I:

1. Internet service providers (ISPs)
2. *Business Extension Rule,* or "Ordinary Course of Business"
3. Prior consent to interception of electronic communications
4. Government and law enforcement agencies—Interception and disclosure of electronic communications

1. Internet Service Providers (ISPs).   An online operator, officer, employee, or agent of a provider of wire or electronic communication service may, in the normal course of employment, intercept, disclose or use an electronic communication "which is a necessary incident to the rendition of" their service or to the "protection of the rights or property of the provider of that service." (*Note:* Random observing or monitoring of a communication are not allowed under this exception except for mechanical or quality control purposes.)

This exception would apply to outside e-mail service providers such as Prodigy, CompuServe, and America Online, as well as to an internal e-mail system operated by the employer.

In *United States v. Mullins,* 992 F.2d 1472 (9th Cir. 1992), an employee and agent of American Airlines was investigating discrepancies in reservations being made by a travel agent on an online travel reservations system maintained by American. The employee intercepted some of these reservations and the travel agent sued, arguing the employee's actions violated Title I of the ECPA. The court disagreed, deciding that American Airlines was a service provider acting to protect its rights and property interests. Therefore, the interception of the communication was allowable under the above exception and did not violate the ECPA.

2. Business Extension Rule or Ordinary Course of Business. The **business extension rule** focuses on the ECPA section that requires a plaintiff to prove the defendant used an "electronic, mechanical, or other devise," capable of intercepting an electronic communication. Specifically, it exempts from liability under the ECPA any devise furnished to the subscriber or user by a provider of wire or electronic communication service in the ordinary course of business and being used by the subscriber or user in the ordinary course of its business.

This exception would allow the interception of e-mail and other communications by an employer, provided certain qualifications are met. The employer would have to prove that it had established a monitoring policy and had made certain employees knew about it in advance of the interception, and that the interception was business related. Therefore, it appears that an employer could monitor an employee's phone calls or e-mail messages in order to make sure they were business related and not purely "personal" in nature.

Monitoring for this purpose is not without limits or conditions. In *Sanders v. Robert Bosch Corp.*, 38 F.3d 736 (4th Cir. 1994), the court deemed 24-hour-a-day monitoring of an employee's phone calls excessive and not in the ordinary course of business. This same rationale would likely be applied to a constant monitoring of an employee's e-mail absent a justification authorized by the ECPA. In *Watkins v. L.M. Berry and Co.*, 704 F.2d 577 (11th Cir. 1983), the court held that once an employer has discovered the employee has made personal calls, he must stop monitoring. The same would likely result if e-mail were involved.

3. Prior Consent. The interception of an electronic communication is permitted where one of the parties to the communication, either the sender or the recipient, has given prior consent to the interception unless the communication is intercepted for purposes of committing a crime or tort. The extent of prior consent regarding e-mail and other communications has yet to be defined or decided by a court under this exception. However, as discussed earlier, where an employer has informed its employees of its monitoring policy especially regarding personal calls, a court could find that an employee had given, at the least, *implied* consent to the employer to monitor and intercept e-mail and other communications. Actual or express consent would exist if the employee signed a consent form allowing the employer to monitor or intercept e-mail, and so on. (Recall the decision in *Smyth* discussed earlier in the chapter.)

4. Government and Law Enforcement Agencies—Interception and Disclosure of Electronic Communications. Here the ECPA distinguishes between an electronic communication accidentally intercepted by a service provider and those sought from an ISP or other provider by a government or law enforcement agency official.

A service provider who *accidentally* intercepts a communication containing evidence of an illegal act may, without liability under the ECPA, disclose the communication to the proper authorities. However, law enforcement officials must follow the provisions of the ECPA. Essentially, they require the official to apply to a judge for a court order, search warrant, or, in the case of private documents, a subpoena. In the application, the official will have to establish that there is sufficient probable cause to believe the person named in the application is, has, or is about to commit a crime.

If the communication sought is associated with an emergency situation that poses an *immediate* threat of death or serious injury to a person, a threat to national security, or involves criminal activity associated with organized crime, the interception may occur without the application and court order, warrant, or subpoena. However, within forty-eight hours after the interception, the agent must then comply with the above application procedure. If the application is not approved and a court order, warrant, or subpoena is not issued, the interception will be declared to have been obtained in violation of the ECPA and would be, most likely, inadmissible in a criminal prosecution brought against the person who was the subject of the application.

In most cases where the government has requested access to a subscriber's e-mail messages or other stored data, the ECPA requires the service provider to notify the subscriber of the request. The subscriber then has fourteen days from the date of the notice to challenge the request in a court proceeding. An interesting question is posed by an electronic communication containing a message that is encrypted. Obviously, a service provider could not accidentally intercept this type of message. What about a law enforcement agency seeking to intercept a message it believes contains evidence of a criminal activity? Currently, there is no law that expressly gives law enforcement officials the right to access encrypted messages *even with a court order*. The FBI and other law enforcement agencies have asked for laws requiring that encryption software be sold with key features (a kind of "backdoor") that would allow a message to be decrypted and accessible by the agency. Advocates of privacy rights are strongly opposed to restricting the use of encryption that would result were such laws passed.

Title II (§ 2701)—Unlawful Access to Stored Communications. The purpose of Title II is to protect data stored in transit and at the point of destination from being accessed and disclosed. This usually involves data stored in RAM (random access memory) or on computer discs and other similar devices.

Subject to exceptions similar to those under Title I, § 2701 basically does the following:

1. It prohibits any person from intentionally accessing without authorization a facility through which an electronic communication service is provided; or intentionally exceeding authorization to access that facility and thereby obtaining, altering, or preventing authorized access to a wire or electronic communication while it is in electronic storage in such a system.

In *Sega v. MAPHIA*, (857 F. Supp. 679, 1994), the court had to decide whether the defendant infringed Sega's copyrights in its video games by publishing them on their BBS which was accessible by the public by use of an alias or pseudonym. The court also had to decide if Sega's having its employees use a pseudonym to access and collect data stored on MAPHIA's BBS violated this section of the ECPA. The employees were able to gain access using information supplied by an informant who was an authorized user. The court decided that since MAPHIA's BBS was open to the public, Sega's actions were authorized and not in violation of the ECPA.

2. It prohibits a person or entity providing an electronic communication service to the public from knowingly divulging to any person or entity the contents of any communication while in electronic storage by that service.

3. A person or entity providing remote computing service to the public is prohibited from knowingly divulging to any person or entity the contents of any communication that is carried or maintained on that service.

Spamming

Your telephone rings and you answer it to discover it is another one of those direct marketing solicitations. For many, this is an annoying and unwanted business practice. As you already learned, the Telephone Consumer Protection Act governs companies using this marketing method and gives us the right not to be called. A similar practice has arisen on the Internet. In recent years and in increasing numbers, companies are using bulk e-mailings to send unsolicited advertisements for their goods and services. This marketing tool is called **spamming.** It is a relatively inexpensive method to reach huge numbers of prospective customers. Again for many, the spam serves only to annoy, invade privacy, and create a kind of online "traffic jam."

The Federal Trade Commission (FTC) is the federal administrative agency that regulates advertising. Therefore, it has jurisdiction and regulatory power over spamming. As such, concerned consumer groups, members of Congress, and ISPs have suggested that the FTC sponsor or support legislation to regulate spamming. Instead, the FTC has opted to leave it up to the computer industry to self-

http://
For more information, visit the FTC site at
www.ftc.gov

http://
Visit TRUSTe, an independent, nonprofit Internet privacy organization, at
www.etrust.org

Cyberethics

Cybermanners?

Netiquette is an unofficial attempt at self-regulation by businesses engaged in cyberspace. It proscribes a kind of ethical code of etiquette to be followed when dealing with customers or users online. Generally, it seeks to require courtesy and respect online. It also seeks to ensure that bandwidths are not clogged.

How can a company ethically justify spamming and yet adhere to the netiquette code?

regulate. As a matter of fact, in a report issued by the FTC in July 1999, it concluded that self-regulation was the least intrusive and most efficient means to ensure fair information practices online.

Of course, if self-regulation proves to be ineffective, expect an attempt at appropriate federal legislation. You should be aware that Nevada, Virginia, and California have passed anti-spamming legislation.

Other states have similar legislation pending.

You might be wondering where these e-commerce companies get our names and other personal information about us. Needless to say, the number of consumers shopping online in recent years has increased dramatically. Amazon.com reported receiving some 7 million hits during the 1999 holiday season. As we indicated in the introduction to this chapter, every time we visit a Web site we leave a "fingerprint" of information about ourselves in the form of a cookie. Not only is personal information about us stored on the cookie, but also other information such as our buying habits and preferences. E-businesses are willing to pay for this valuable information. Thus, the gathering of such data has evolved into big business for many companies specializing in the sale of it in the form of lists. The privacy concern arises because these lists and their contents are sold without our consent or knowledge. This problem and the potential legal liability for invasion of privacy that it portends have led to many e-businesses implementing consumer-friendly privacy policies. Recognizing the privacy issues associated with this practice is the recent industry attempt at self-regulation in the form of TRUSTe, an independent, non-profit Internet privacy organization sponsored by AOL and Microsoft and comprised of more than 600 member companies. Its major function is to monitor the Web sites of its members making sure their information practices are fair and sensitive to privacy rights. Members are also required to inform users about how personal information about them is used and to establish oversight and consumer complaint procedures. Those in compliance receive a *trustmark,* (a type of online "seal of approval").

For insight as to how federal courts have treated cases involving spamming, consider *Cyber Promotions v. America Online, Inc.,* 948 F. Supp. 436(E.D. Pa 1996) where Cyber Promotions sent unsolicited e-mail ads to AOL members and refused to stop them arguing First Amendment rights to freedom of speech and press. The court decided AOL was a private company and Cyber had no legal right to send the ads to AOL's members irrespective of the freedom of speech and press protections under the First Amendment.

Global Issues of Privacy in Cyberspace

Many foreign countries have enacted or are in the process of enacting laws or policies to protect privacy. One of the most significant of these is the ***European Union's (EU) Directive on Privacy Protection,*** which became effective on October 25, 1998. The Directive 95/46/EC of the European Parliament and the Council of 24 October 1995) requires the fifteen member states of the EU to adopt legislation that seeks to protect the "fundamental rights and freedoms" of an individual, particularly the right to privacy as it relates to the processing and collection of personal data. *Personal data* under the Directive would include "information that relates to an identified or identifiable *natural* person (corporations are not subject to the processing requirements of the directive). *Processing* under the Directive is defined as "any operation or set of operations performed upon personal data" and includes its collection, storage, disclosure, destruction, and so on. The provisions of the legislation also apply to nonmember states doing business with member states. Specifically, Article 6 of the Directive requires member states involved in the collection and possession of personal data to ensure that the data are:

- Processed fairly and accurately
- Collected for specified and legitimate purposes and not further processed in a way incompatible with those purposes
- Adequate, relevant, and not excessive for the purposes for which they are collected and/or further processed
- Accurate and, where necessary, updated
- Kept in a form that permits identification of data subjects for no longer than is necessary

Additionally, Article 7 of the Directive requires that personal data may only be processed if the person or corporation in control ("controller") of the data can prove at least one of the following:

- The consent of the data subject has been given unambiguously.
- The processing of the data is necessary for the performance or preparation of a contract to which the data subject is a party.
- The processing of the data is necessary for compliance with a legal obligation of the controller.
- The processing of the data is necessary in order to protect the vital interests of the data subject.
- The processing of the data is in the public interest or in the exercise of official authority of the controller or a third party.

> **http://**
> For the text of the EU Directive, see
> **www2.echo.lu/legal/en/dataprot/directiv/directiv.html**

- The processing is necessary for the legitimate interests of the controller or a third party except where the data subject's privacy rights are greater.

Of particular significance to the United States and other EU nonmembers, is Article 25 of the Directive. It prohibits the export of personal data to nonmember countries that do not have laws that "adequately protect" personal data. It should be noted the Directive does not define the meaning of *adequate*. This implies that such would have to be determined on a case-by-case basis "in light of all circumstances surrounding a data transfer operation or set of data transfer operations."

Currently, U.S. laws on privacy do not comply with the Directive's mandates. However, Article 26 of the Directive does provide exceptions that could facilitate the transfer of personal data to U.S. interests. Two of the more important business-related exceptions, already mentioned, provide that the data may be transferred if the subject of the data has unambiguously consented to its transfer, or the transfer is necessary for the execution of a contract.

In this chapter we have presented U.S. privacy laws that are applicable to personal data. However, there is no law that currently satisfies the requirements of the Directive. The U.S. Commerce Department has been involved in discussions with the European community in an effort to create an effective privacy policy or legislation aimed at satisfying the Directive.

It should be obvious that if a country fails to meet the exceptions provided, or does not have the required privacy legislation, the ability of its e-commerce businesses to access information and transmit information to the EU members will be adversely effected, along will their ability to compete globally. (For further discussion of global privacy issues, see Chapter 13.)

Summary

This chapter discussed the common law and constitutional sources of the right to privacy, applying them to cyberspace. It also discussed the many federal statutes that have been passed to protect this right. Major emphasis was placed on the Electronic Communications Privacy Act because of its importance to this chapter. Employee expectations of privacy, if any, were also explored. Spamming and its conflict with First Amendment rights were also highlighted. Finally, mention was made of the attempt by the European Union to establish privacy protection for personal data.

Manager's Checklist

- Make sure company use of the Internet and Web are mindful of rights to privacy.

- Establish and publicize company privacy policies regarding e-mail and computer usage. Make sure you establish a level of privacy employees should "reasonably expect."
- Take steps to protect privacy of company-related data, especially related to personnel.
- Make sure you and your employees are aware that there is very little privacy protection afforded to online communications.
- If your company gathers and stores information about its customers, make sure you tell them how this information is to be used. Consider adopting the TRUSTe seal of approval for your Web site and a code of courtesy and etiquette patented after *netiquette*.
- If your company is involved in global e-commerce that involves gathering and storing personal data, make sure it complies with the European Directive.
- Implement a policy of self-regulation regarding privacy rights, including the kind of netiquette that others have established.

Additional Readings

- Clark, Don. "Rivals Microsoft and Netscape Team Up to Protect Privacy on the Web," *Wall Street Journal,* (June 12, 1997) (*www.wsj.com*).
- Cohen, Alan. "Can the Spam: Bills Declare War on Junk E-Mail," *New York Law Journal* (Sept. 15, 1997) (*www.nylj.com*).
- Rothfelder, Jeffrey. "No Privacy on the Net," *PC World* (February 1997) (*http://pcworld.com*).

9

Obscenity

"Censorship reflects a society's lack of confidence in itself. It is a hallmark of an authoritarian regime. A book worthless to me may convey something of value to my neighbor. In the free society to which our Constitution has committed us, it is for each of us to choose for himself."

—U.S. Supreme Court Justice Potter Stewart dissenting in Ginzburg v. United States, 383 U.S. 463, 1966

Introduction

With the continuing growth of literally thousands of adult-oriented sexually explicit Web sites, concern and controversy have arisen regarding censorship and the legal issues surrounding it. Some of the statistics demonstrate just how enormous this market has become:

- In 1996, Americans spent in excess of 8 billion dollars on hard-core videos, adult cable programming, computer porn and other similar materials. This figure exceeded the combined total of Hollywood domestic box office receipts and all revenues from rock and country music recordings. (*U.S. News and World Report,* February 10, 1997).
- In 1998, 970 million dollars was spent on visits to adult Web sites, an amount that could rise to 3 billion dollars by 2003. (*U.S. News and World Report,* March 27, 2000).
- In January 2000, 17.5 million surfers visited porn sites from home (Nielsen NetRatings).
- There are currently over 72,000 sexually explicit Web sites (Log-On Data Corporation).
- In 1998, 25 percent of the U.S. teenagers visited Web sites containing nudity (PC Meter, Inc.).
- The FBI has documented over 4,000 cases of online child pornography.

Traditionally, governments and courts have found it difficult to define or distinguish prohibited obscene or indecent materials from those entitled to protection under First Amendment guarantees of freedom of expression. Courts have always taken a dim view regarding the dissemination of material considered to be harmful to children. A somewhat more fettered approach has been taken when dealing with the regulation of obscene material possessed by an adult for use in the privacy of one's home. As you read this chapter, keep

http://
For views on censorship and obscenity, visit
www.aclu.org, www.eff.org, www.cdt.org, and
www.cc.org

in mind that much of the difficulty concerning the transmission of **cyberporn** results from a lack of consensus as to how it should be defined. Public interest groups such as the American Civil Liberties Union (ACLU), the Electronic Frontier Foundation (EFF), and the Center for Democracy and Technology oppose Internet censorship and legislation. Other groups such as the Christian Coalition are the driving forces behind legislation directed at prohibiting obscenity and indecency on the Internet.

First Amendment Protection—Freedom of Expression

Before we discuss the test currently employed for determining whether questionable materials transmitted or displayed via the Internet are to be protected or prohibited, we should look at the First Amendment's provision regarding freedom of expression. It basically puts limitations on the government's ability to regulate our rights to freedom of speech and expression. However, as you have probably observed in other contexts, our rights under the Constitution or, for that matter those provided by other federal and state laws, are not absolute (as we will see in the next chapter, speech that is defamatory is not protected).

In the landmark case *Roth v. United States*, 354 U.S. 476 (1957), Roth, the defendant, operated a business involving the sale of books, photographs, and magazines, some of which were obscene. He was convicted under a federal obscenity statute for mailing obscene materials. In upholding Roth's conviction, the Supreme Court held that obscenity was not within the area of constitutionally protected speech or press. Specifically, the Court declared:

> The protection given speech and press was fashioned to assure unfettered interchange of ideas for the bringing about of political and social changes desired by the people. [All] ideas having even the slightest redeeming social importance—unorthodox ideas, controversial ideas, even ideas hateful to the prevailing climate of opinion—have the full protection of the guaranties, unless excludable because they encroach upon the limited area of more important interests. But implicit in history of the First Amendment is the rejection of obscenity as utterly without redeeming social importance.

The Test for Obscenity

Whether questionable materials transmitted via the Internet will be prohibited or protected may be determined by applying the three-prong test for obscenity announced in the landmark U.S. Supreme Court case, *Miller v. California*, 413 U.S. 15 (1973).

Applying the Three-Prong *Miller* Test to Material Transmitted Online (Cyberporn)

The three-prong *Miller* test resulting from the *Miller v. California* case defines obscene material as having the following attributes:

1. It arouses "Prurient interest" that does not conform to "contemporary community standards."
2. It is "patently offensive."
3. It "lacks serious literary, artistic, political or scientific value."

"Prurient" Interest and "Contemporary Community Standards". What did the Court mean by prurient interest and **contemporary community standards?** The courts have been inconsistent in providing predictable answers to this question, making it difficult, if not impossible, for transmitters of online materials to predict protection or prohibition of its materials. In *Roth,* mentioned earlier, the U.S. Supreme Court may have provided the *Miller* Court with some guidance in defining the terms. In arriving at its decision to affirm Roth's conviction, the Court found that the materials dealt with sex in a manner appealing to "prurient interest" in that they had a "tendency to excite lustful thoughts." The court also applied to the facts the definition of *prurient* found in Webster's *New International Dictionary* (Unabridged, 2d ed. 1949), deciding that the materials in question demonstrated an "Itching; longing; uneasy with desire or longing; of persons, having itching, morbid, or lascivious longings; of desire, curiosity, or propensity, lewd."

The Court further expanded the above by applying to it the definition of obscene as contained in the Model Penal Code Section 207.10(2) (Tent. Draft No. 6, 1957):

> A thing is obscene if, considered as a whole, its predominant appeal is to prurient interest, i.e., a shameful or morbid interest in nudity, sex, or excretion, and if it goes substantially beyond customary limits of candor in description or representation of such matters.

In addition to establishing this, *Miller* would require that the material be viewed in the context of the relevant local "contemporary community standards." A question that arises concerns which community's standards are to be used? With online transmissions, a court could either use the community standards where the transmission originated or where it was downloaded. The standards for each might be different, depending on the demographics or culture of the relevant community. Thus, material deemed obscene in one community might escape such a designation in another. Determining which community's standards are to be used is critical in establishing protection or prohibition for the material under scrutiny. Therefore, it is likely that operators of chat rooms, bulletin board services, and other Internet users will have difficulty in determining, with any predictability, whether a transmission would be deemed obscene or protected free speech or expression.

"Patently Offensive".   The second prong of the test is concerned with whether the material/transmission depicts or displays, "in a **patently offensive** way, sexual conduct specifically defined by the applicable state law." *Miller* would require the transmissions exhibit hard core "ultimate sexual acts, normal or perverted, actual or simulated" that include "masturbation, excretory functions, and lewd exhibition of the genitals." As with prurient interest, whether an online transmission would be prohibited or protected would have to be viewed in the context of local community standards, which would raise the same issue of predictability.

"Lacks Serious Literary, Artistic, Political, or Scientific Value".   Unlike the first two prongs of the test that view the material in the context of relevant local community standards, leaving it to a jury to decide, the third prong—**literary, artistic, political,** and **socially redeemable value**—would require a more objective determination based on a "reasonable person" test.

For example, in *Pope v. Illinois*, 481 U.S. 497 (1987), the Supreme Court ruled that the proper inquiry was not whether an ordinary member of any given community would find serious value in the allegedly obscene material but whether a reasonable person would find such value in it, taken as a whole. Thus, we should reiterate that the factors and standards for obscenity vary greatly, depending on the culture of the state, city or town, or, for that matter, foreign country. This makes it virtually impossible for a provider and others to determine, with any degree of predictability, whether the material they distribute, transmit, post, and so on would be deemed obscene.

Proving the Case

In earlier cases, if the material failed to satisfy the three-prong test and was deemed obscene, in order to establish liability the government had to prove the defendant had actual knowledge that the contents of the transmission were obscene and that the defendant was an adult who consented to view the material.

The Knowledge Requirement (Scienter).   Given the huge number of files and documents owned by a provider, establishing the knowledge requirement could be difficult and could provide a valid defense to prosecution. Thus, the later cases seem to reflect a less stringent burden of proof requiring the interstate transmission of the material together with proof the provider had knowledge of the character and nature of the material rather than knowledge that it was obscene.

The "Consenting Adults" Defense.   In *Paris Adult Theatre I v. Slaton* 413 U.S 49, 1973, the owners of two Atlanta theaters were charged under a Georgia statute that prohibited the showing of hard-core pornographic films. They raised the **consenting adults defense** that since their customers consented to viewing the films, they should be entitled to the same First Amendment and privacy protection they would enjoy as if they were at home. The Supreme Court did not agree with the analogy and reaffirmed its holding in *Roth*. Essentially, the Court upheld the right of a State to regulate, if it so chose, specifically defined sexual conduct between consenting adults as long as the regulation was within limits designed to prevent infringement of First Amendment rights.

If consenting adults viewed the pornographic films described in Slaton at home, would they be afforded First Amendment and privacy protection? The Supreme Court answered that question in *Stanley v. Georgia* 394 U.S. 557, 1969, where it created a zone of privacy in one's home. In that case, the defendant, Stanley, was suspected of bookmaking activities. With a warrant to search his home for evidence, the law enforcement authorities discovered pornographic films stored in his bedroom. In reversing the conviction for possession of obscene material and remanding the case, the Court extended freedom of speech, press and privacy protection to the right to receive information and ideas in one's home regardless of their social worth. In writing for the Court, Justice Thurgood Marshall stated:

> "If the First Amendment means anything, it means that a state has no business telling a man, sitting alone in his home, what book he may read or what films he may watch."

Government Regulation of Cyberporn

Once material has been declared obscene, our focus shifts to a review of some of the important laws that attempt to regulate it. These laws, both state and federal, have been challenged constitutionally, sometimes successfully, and in other instances, they have been the subject of controversy and criticism because of their impact on our personal freedoms.

The **Communication Decency Act (CDA) of 1996** (Title V of the Telecommunications Act of 1996; 47 U.S.C. § 223) was passed primarily to protect minors from pornography. The CDA makes it a crime for anyone to knowingly transport obscene material for sale or distribution either in foreign or interstate commerce or through the use of an interactive computer service. The CDA has been the subject of criticism as being overburdensome and overbroad in its attempt at regulation. As we shall see, parts of it have been declared unconstitutional while others have passed constitutional scrutiny.

The CDA provides for fines of up to $100,000 and imprisonment of up to five years for a first offense and up to ten years for each subsequent offense. The CDA specifically applies to what it terms *matter*—in particular, books, magazines, pictures, paper, film, videotape, and audio recordings.

Another provision of the CDA prohibits and makes it a crime for anyone to knowingly transmit obscene online communications that involve "comments, requests, suggestions, proposals, images, or other communication which is obscene, lewd, lascivious, filthy or indecent made with the intent to annoy, abuse, threaten, or harass another person."

A separate part of this provision makes it a crime to knowingly transmit the described material to a person under the age of eighteen, irrespective of whether the maker placed the call or initiated the communication.

Allowable Defenses

The CDA allows certain defenses to liability. One defense is based on the distinction between an *access software provider* and a *content provider.* Specifically, criminal liability is imposed on the content provider who transmits obscene materials to a minor, rather than on the Internet service provider who provides access or connection to a network and has nothing to do with content.

A second defense applies to a person who has made a good faith effort or attempt to restrict or prevent access by minors to the types of communications prohibited under the CDA. To successfully raise this defense, a defendant has to prove that it made use of available technology to block the transmission. This includes use of a "v" chip, verifiable credit card to gain access, a debit account, an adult access code, or adult personal identification number.

Similarly, it could be possible for a content provider to avoid liability by raising this defense. The content provider would have to prove that it took all available steps (e.g., warning labels, sign-on requirements, etc.) to restrict access to its site by minors.

Table 9.2

Defenses to Liability Under the Communications Decency Act

• Access service provider v. content provider	Criminal liability is imposed on content provider, rather than the ISP.
• Efforts to block access to the site	Defendant must prove it used technology to block transmission of cyberporn.
• Good Samaritan defense	Online provider or user is protected from publishing information provided by another content provider.
• Social value	Material with social value is protected against criminal liability.

Keep in mind that many argue that the responsibility for monitoring or preventing a minor's access to obscene Web sites is best placed on the minor's parent or guardian and not technology.

A third defense is the **Good Samaritan defense** for blocking and screening offensive material. It protects an online provider or user of an interactive computer service from civil liability as a publisher or speaker of any information provided by another content provider.

You should be aware that certain expressions involving ideas and information about sexuality, reproduction, and the human body could be afforded protection under the CDA even if received by a minor. A court could deem these to have social value, thereby eliminating liability for their transmission. Table 9.2 summarizes the defenses to liability under the CDA.

The CDA Under Constitutional Attack

Congress can regulate speech or expression that is harmful to minors. This may not include "indecent" speech or expression. The problem with Sections 223 (a) and (d) of the CDA is that they do not clearly define what is considered to be "indecent" speech or expression, nor do they sufficiently distinguish "indecent" from "obscene." The U.S. Supreme Court and the Federal Communications Commission (FCC) provide some assistance. The Supreme Court has defined *indecent* as referring to *"nonconformance with accepted standards of morality."* (See *FCC v. Pacifica Foundation*, 438 U.S. 726 1978, also mentioned in the *Reno* case that follows). The FCC, using the second prong of the *Miller* Test only, defines *indecent* as *"language or material that depicts or describes, in terms patently offensive as measured by contemporary standards in the broadcast medium, sexual or excretory activities or organs."*

In *Reno v. American Civil Liberties Union*, 521 U.S. 844 (1997), the U.S. Supreme Court declared §§ 223 (a) and (d) to be unconstitutional under the freedom of speech and expression protections of the First Amendment. The provision regarding "obscene" materials was left alone as far as minors were concerned. In Reno, one provision of § 223 of the CDA made it a crime to knowingly transmit "obscene" or "indecent" messages via the Internet to a person under the age of 18. Another of its provisions prohibited the "knowing" sending or displaying to a person under age 18 any message that depicted or described, "in terms patently offensive, as measured by contemporary community standards, sexual or excretory activities or organs." the Supreme Court declared the CDA's "indecent transmission" and "patently offensive" display provisions unconstitutional under the First Amendment because they were too vague and overbroad. The Court further stated that although the Government has an interest in protecting children from harmful materials, these provisions pursue that interest by suppressing a large amount of speech that adults have a constitutional right to send and receive.

Child Pornography

Federal and state laws regulating child pornography are very strict and generally make it a crime to create, distribute, sell, or possess child pornography. Similar to the CDA, these laws have been attacked on constitutional grounds, generally without success.

What follows is a discussion of important federal legislation that attempts to eliminate child pornography and to protect minors from sexual exploitation either as participants in producing child pornography or as being harmed from exposure to it online.

Federal Regulation

You will recall that in *Reno* the Supreme Court declared parts of the CDA unconstitutional, declaring that indecent materials directed at minors on the Internet medium was entitled to the same First Amendment protection afforded other modes of communication. The second of the two federal acts, the Child Online Protection Act of 1998 (COPA), was passed as a substitute to the parts of the CDA that were declared unconstitutional.

Child Pornography Prevention Act of 1996 (CPPA), 18 U.S.C. § 2256.   For our purposes, § 2256 is the most significant section of the **Child Pornography Protection Act.** It prohibits and criminalizes the use of computer technology to knowingly produce child pornography that contains both depictions of real children as well as "virtual" or fictitious children. Section 2256 defines child pornography as:

"any depiction, including any photograph, film, video, picture, or computer or computer-generated image or picture, whether made or produced by electronic, mechanical, or other means, of sexually explicit conduct, where—

(A) the production of such visual depiction involves the use of a minor engaging in sexually explicit conduct;

(B) such visual depiction is, or appears to be, of a minor engaging in sexually explicit conduct;

(C) such visual depiction has been created, adapted, or modified to appear that an identifiable minor is engaging in sexually explicit conduct; or

(D) such visual depiction is advertised, promoted, presented, described, or distributed in such a manner that conveys the impression that the material is or contains a visual depiction of a minor engaging in sexually explicit conduct."

This language, particularly the phrases "appears to be" and "conveys the impression," has created some problems of interpretation, resulting in a split in case decisions at the Federal Circuit Court of Appeals level. At issue is whether these terms are so vague and overbroad that a person of ordinary intelligence would find it difficult to determine the age of those depicted and to understand exactly

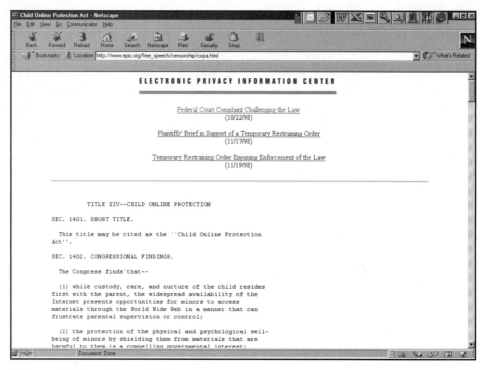

© Electronic Privacy Information Center.

what the CPPA prohibits, thereby rendering it unconstitutional. Some courts have ruled the language to be specific enough to fulfill the purposes of Congress to protect children from the evils of pornography. These courts have decided that the content of the language was sufficiently narrow to satisfy Congress's intention to eliminate child pornography by singling out and banning a particular category of expression, child pornography, based on its content. In *U.S. v. Hilton*, 167 F3d 61 (1st Cir. 1999), the court upheld the defendant's conviction for possession of child pornography, deciding that "child pornography was an unprotected category of expression identified by its content" and, therefore, was allowed to be "freely regulated." The decision did not distinguish between images of real children and those that were fictitious or imaginary.

A later Florida case, *U.S. v. Acheson,* No. 98-3559 (11th Cir. Nov. 12, 1999) reached a similar conclusion). However, in a California case, *Free Speech Coalition v. Reno,* No. 97-16536 (9th Cir. Dec. 17, 1999), the court reached an opposite conclusion. It viewed the definition of *child pornography* under the CPPA as vague and too broad because it applied to both real and fictitious depictions of children. Therefore, it held that the First Amendment prohibited Congress from enacting a statute that makes it a crime to create images of fictitious children engaged in imaginary but explicit sexual conduct. It would be virtually impossible for a person looking at the images to determine if the depiction was a minor or an adult with a youthful appearance. Furthermore, the court said that the CPPA represented a change in the original intent of Congress in enacting child pornography statutes. Originally, these statutes were aimed only at real children. The CPPA shifted from "defining child pornography in terms of the harm inflicted upon real children to a determination that child pornography was evil in and of itself, whether it involved real children or not." This, the court concluded, violated the First Amendment.

As you can see this area of the law is unsettled. Most likely, the U.S. Supreme Court will resolve the issue of the interpretation and applicability of the language.

Child Online Protection Act of 1998 (COPA), 47 U.S.C. § 231.   In passing the **Child Online Protection Act of 1998,** Congress expanded the provisions of the CPPA to include online transmissions by service providers and e-commerce site providers. It expressed the following rationale for this new legislation:

1. The Internet presents opportunities for minors to access materials through the Web in a manner that could frustrate parental control or supervision.
2. The protection of the physical and psychological well being of minors by shielding them from materials that are harmful to them presents a compelling governmental interest.
3. Industry attempts to provide ways to help parents and others restrict a minor's access to harmful materials have not been successful.
4. Prohibiting the distribution of material harmful to minors, combined with legitimate defenses, is currently the most effective and least restrictive means to protect minors.
5. Parents, educators, and industry must continue efforts to find ways to protect children from being exposed to harmful materials found on the Internet, notwithstanding protections that already limit the distribution over the Web of material that is harmful to minors.

COPA requires commercial site operators who offer material deemed to be "harmful" to minors to use bona fide methods to establish the identification of visitors seeking to access their site. Failure to do so can result in criminal liability with fines of up to $50,000 and six months in jail for each offense. Specifically, COPA provides:

> "Whoever, in interstate or foreign commerce, by means of the World Wide Web, knowingly makes any communication for commercial purposes that includes any material that is harmful to minors without restricting access to such material by minors pursuant to subsection (c) shall be fined not more $50,000, imprisoned not more than 6 months, or both.

Under COPA, Congress defined harmful material as:

"any communication, picture, image, graphic image file, article, recording, writing, or other matter of any kind that is obscene or that—

(A) the average person, applying contemporary community standards, would find, taking the material as a whole and with respect to minors, is designed to appeal to, or is designed to pander to, the prurient interest;

(B) depicts, describes, or represents, in a manner patently offensive with respect to minors, an actual or simulated sexual act or sexual contact, an actual or simulated normal or perverted sexual act, or a lewd exhibition of the genitals or post-pubescent female breasts; and

(C) taken as a whole, lacks serious literary, artistic, political, or scientific value for minors."

The constitutionality of COPA was challenged almost immediately after its enactment. In *ACLU et al. v. Reno* (referred to as *Reno II*), No. 98-CV 5591, 1999 U.S. Dist. LEXIS 735 (1999), the plaintiffs sought a temporary restraining order to enjoin implementation of the statute. The federal district court granted the injunction agreeing with the plaintiffs that COPA violated the First and Fifth Amendments, that the affirmative defenses provided by COPA were technologically and economically unavailable to many of the plaintiffs, and that it overly burdened speech that was protected as to adults. Additionally, the plaintiffs successfully argued that the impact of COPA could result in denying adults and older minors access to protected educational materials that could contain information about art, science, medicine, or sex.

The court was also concerned that commercial and noncommercial service providers and operators would be fearful of prosecution under COPA. This would result in self-censorship of their online materials. This would have a chilling effect on speech and would cause irreparable harm to the plaintiffs both constitutionally and economically.

Further, the court expressed concern that, although the public has an interest in protecting minors, that interest would not be served by enforcing an unconstitutional law. Instead, the court indicated that the public interest would be best served by maintaining the status quo until some time in the future when a more thorough examination of the constitutionality of COPA could be explored.

Protection of Children from Sexual Predators Act of 1998, Title 18 U.S.C. § 302. The **Protection of Children from Sexual Predators Act of 1998,** expands liability to those who attempt to use the Internet for purposes of child pornography. This statute specifically targets commercial pornographers and makes it a crime to knowingly make a communication for commercial purposes harmful to minors (sixteen years old and younger) or to use the Internet for purposes of engaging in sexual activities with minors.

(*Note:* Additional relevant federal statutes include The Protection of Children Against Sexual Exploitation Act of 1977, The Child Pornography Prevention Act of 1996, and other sections of Title 18 of the U.S. Code.)

State Regulation

In addition to federal regulations, BBS, online service providers and Web site operators may be subject to state statutes prohibiting the possession, distribution, and sale of child pornography. These laws usually mirror the federal standards with some modifications, particularly regarding the *Miller* test. In *New York v. Ferber* 458 U.S. 747 (1982), The U.S. Supreme Court upheld New York's strict standards concerning child pornography. In that case, the defendant owned a bookstore and was convicted of selling material depicting children under sixteen years of age in certain prohibited sexual activities. The U.S. upheld the constitutionality of the statute, stating that "the prevention of sexual exploitation of children constitutes a government objective of surpassing importance."

The Court also modified the *Miller* test, holding that:

1. The material need not appeal to the prurient interest of the average person.
2. The sexual activity need not be done in a patently offensive manner.
3. The material need not be considered as a whole.

Remember that the prosecution must still prove the defendant had knowledge (*scienter*) of the "character and content" of the material. Additionally, many states including New York allow a defendant to avoid liability if they can prove that they had a good faith and reasonable belief the actors in the materials were of legal age.

The Consenting Adults Defense in Child Pornography

In the case of child pornography, the fact it is viewed by consenting adults is not a defense.

As far as cyberspace is concerned, it should be obvious individuals who possess, sell, and distribute child pornography in e-commerce will be held criminally liable, irrespective of where or in what context the pornographic material is disseminated and accessed.

Employees and Workplace Access to Adult Web Sites

This part of the chapter focuses on the right of an employer to monitor an employee's use of a company-owned computer. The legal issues here involve an employee's rights under the United States Constitution, particularly the *right to privacy* and the freedom from unreasonable search and seizure.

Surfing the Web for non–work-related purposes is a major problem for employers and their goal to maximize employee workplace productivity. In 1996, a Nielsen survey determined the *Penthouse* magazine adult Web site was being visited, in the workplace, thousands of times monthly by employees of AT & T, IBM, Hewlett-Packard and other companies.

In 1999, a more telling study was conducted by Elron Software, Inc. Elron was hired to install monitoring software on computers used by employees working for some 110 corporations, educational institutions, and government agencies with employees numbering from 50 to 15,0000. The testing, lasting for three days, determined that 62 percent of the employees accessed adult-oriented, sexually explicit Web sites. Employers must be particularly wary of the possibility that such usage can sometimes result in cases of sexual harassment as prohibited under provisions of Title VII of the Civil Rights Act of 1964, as amended. One of the ways this could result is from the sending of unwelcome sexually charged messages or jokes to other employees, thereby creating a hostile work environment. Of course, using a computer to request sexual favors as a condition of employment, promotion, pay raise, and so on could also be considered a form of sexual harassment.

Employers' Monitoring of Employees' Use of Company-Owned Computers

The above study also indicated that more than 90 percent of businesses and organizations have adopted or intended to implement an Acceptable Usage Policy. Some have installed monitoring software. In order to uphold their right to monitor, remember that these companies should develop and publicize such policies in employee handbooks, memos, information sessions, and where relevant, union contracts. The Electronic Communications Privacy Act (ECPA) of 1986 (refer back to Chapter 8) gives employers, in the private sector, the legal right to monitor employee phone calls, e-mail messages, voice mail, computer files, and other communications made on company owned equipment in the "ordinary course of business."

The Right of Public Employees to Access Adult-Oriented Web Sites

In the public sector, governments have attempted to regulate and restrict the use of computers by their employees. In a Virginia Case, *Urosky, et. al. v. Gilmore,* 167 F.3d 191 (4th Cir., Feb. 10, 1999), under a state statute, state employees, in this case, university professors, needed state agency approval in order to use their state owned computers to access online sexually explicit materials. The employee would have to prove the materials were to be used for a "bona fide' research project. the court decided that the statute violated the First Amendment holding it to be overly inclusive because it restricted access to sexually explicit Web sites intended to be used for academic, artistic, literary, historical and philosophical purposes.

(Note: the Virginia House of Delegates amended the act in Urosky requiring the Virginia Department of Personnel and Training to adopt and implement an Internet acceptable use policy. In addition, the act now applies to material that is lascivious.)

Global Issues: Obscenity on the Internet

The nations of the world have each formulated laws governing forms of speech usually reflective of what they deem to be in the best interest of its culture and society. As is the case in the United States, in foreign countries the standards for obscenity vary, making it virtually impossible to establish predictability as to whether online material will be allowed or prohibited. Such issues surround the importation and exportation of pornography and attempts to regulate it. As you read this section, keep in mind the following factors that affect and determine the ability or inability to achieve a worldwide agreement on prohibiting obscene materials:

1. There is no body of international law governing the transmission or receipt of obscene material, nor any universal definition or set of standards regarding it.
2. Cultural, moral, and legal characteristics usually form the basis of a country's views on obscene and other forms of speech.
3. It is virtually impossible for one country to impose or enforce its laws on another country.
4. A provider in a country with strict obscenity standards may transmit materials to a country with more liberal standards, and from there it is accessible worldwide by a simple click.

It is worth making a brief note about the third factor as it relates to the U.S. and the **Act of State Doctrine.** Under this doctrine, one government is obligated not to judge the acts of another government committed within its own country or territory. Therefore, a U.S. court would lack jurisdiction and be powerless to rule on what occurs within the borders of a foreign country, even if it violates U.S. laws. For example, both the United States and Germany have laws protecting free speech. However, German law criminalizes speech that denies the existence of the Holocaust or that fosters Nazism, so-called *hate speech*. U.S. law would likely afford such speech First Amendment protection. Therefore, if these types of hate speech were received by a user in the United States, and challenges to their legality under U.S. law were raised, the Act of State Doctrine would prevent a U.S. court from prohibiting their dissemination, notwithstanding German law.

Similarly, a question arises as to whether a foreign court would have the power to regulate transmissions by a U.S. service provider that were prohibited under the laws of a foreign country. This was the issue in a 1995 case brought in a German court against CompuServe Germany, a wholly owned subsidiary of CompuServe USA. CompuServe Germany provided local dial-up access for German subscribers to CompuServe USA's facilities. As a result of an investigation, the German police found a list of almost three hundred Internet newsgroups stored on CompuServe USA's servers containing alleged images of pornographic materials illegal under German law. Some of these sites did not contain prohibited materials. Nevertheless, faced with prosecution, CompuServe USA blocked access to these sites by its over four million U.S. and worldwide subscribers. Subsequently, CompuServe made parental control software available to its subscribers and proceeded to unblock the sites. Later, the German police discovered the newsgroups still contained illegal materials. Felix Somm, the general manager of CompuServe Germany, was then indicted, tried, convicted, and sentenced to two years in jail for failing to block access to the sites. The court declared CompuServe USA an accomplice with Somm for its failure to block access and the financial benefits realized therefrom.

U.S. Views on the Importation of Cyberporn

Title 19 of the U.S. Code bans the importation of:

> Any obscene book, pamphlet, paper, writing, advertisement, circular, print, picture, drawing, or other representation, figure, or image on or of paper or other material, or . . . article which is obscene or immoral.

Liability under Title 19 could be imposed on a service provider who had knowledge of the contents of prohibited material originating in a foreign country yet who allowed it to be downloaded. The same liability may be imposed on a user who searches and downloads prohibited material from a foreign source.

U.S. Views on the Exportation of Cyberporn

Service providers are subject to the obscenity laws of those countries in which they solicit or obtain customers. As we have seen, these laws may be strict or liberal, except in the case of child pornography, where the laws are generally extremely strict.

We have already seen the restrictions Germany places on speech dealing with the Holocaust and Nazism. This same speech (hate speech) would be protected under the laws of some other countries. China and Singapore are even more restrictive than Germany.

Laws in China.   China's laws on obscenity prohibit access to Web sites including *Playboy, Penthouse,* etc. These sites are not considered obscene and, in general, are protected by the laws of the United States, the United Kingdom, Canada, and so on. China also restricts access to Web sites it believes contain materials that are politically incorrect. These include *The New York Times, The Wall Street Journal, Cable News Network (CNN),* Amnesty International, and the Taiwan Government Information Office. You should also be aware that before any ISP is allowed to transmit in China, approval must be obtained from the Chinese Ministry of Posts and Telecommunications.

Laws in Singapore.   In Singapore, any Web site containing pornographic material is banned, along with those containing issues related to political criticisms, religions, and race. Scrutiny is particularly strict regarding political parties whose Web sites must be approved by the agencies of the Singapore government. Also note that unlike the United States, libraries and schools are held to higher standards of supervision regarding access to the Internet.

Summary

This chapter discussed obscenity and the attempts at regulating its transmission via the Internet. It should be obvious that no matter how vigilant those in society are regarding censorship of what they believe to be questionable materials, there exists no foolproof methods for preventing or blocking their online transmissions.

From a legal liability perspective, the best way to avoid prosecution under state, federal, and international law is to take whatever steps are necessary to comply with all relevant laws. Parents or guardians are probably the first and best defense for protecting children from obscenity.

Manager's Checklist

- Employers should develop and publicize a written Acceptable Usage Policy outlining appropriate uses of computers in the workplace.
- Penalties and procedures for violations of the policy should be established and publicized.
- Determine if a policy is needed to monitor employee computer use.
- If such a policy is established, make sure it does not violate employees' rights to privacy or free speech. It should also be written and publicized.
- Policies adopted should not be overly restrictive so as to impact employee morale negatively.
- If an employee is suspected of computer misuse, make sure you verify the identity of the employee before taking any action.
- Determine whether installing appropriate software or other means could protect company computers from being downloaded with undesirable materials.
- From time to time, employer/employee open discussions may be helpful in establishing an acceptable, or at least comfortable, business environment regarding computer use.

Additional Readings

- Bilstad, Blake T. "Obscenity and Indecency in the Digital Age: The Legal and Political Implications of Cybersmut, Virtual Pornography, and the Communications Decency Act," *Santa Clara Computer and High Technology Journal,* 13 (1997).

- Wilks, Fred L. "The Community Standards Conundrum in a Borderless World: Making Sense of Obscenity Laws in Cyberspace," UCLA Online Institute for Cyberspace Law and Policy (1998) (*www.gseis.ucla.edu/clp/flwilks.htm*).

- "Internet Pornography—The Red Light District of Cyberspace," CWA Library, May 1999 (*www.cwfa.org/library/pornography/1990–05_pp_internet.shhhtml*).

10

Defamation

"Reputation, reputation, reputation! Oh, I have lost my reputation! I have lost the immortal part of myself, and what remains is bestial."

—William Shakespeare
Othello, Act II
Scene III

Introduction

As we have seen in earlier discussions, the First Amendment of the U.S. Constitution provides us with the rights of free speech and expression. However, as with other rights, these are not entitled to absolute protection. They can be limited if, in practice, they infringe or violate the rights of others. This chapter focuses on one such limitation, the common law tort of defamation as it relates to the reputations of individuals and e-businesses communicating in cyberspace. As you proceed through this chapter remember that not only do the laws we discuss pertain to the reputation of an individual, but also to that of a business or its product or service.

You should be aware that the laws regarding defamation differ from state to state and country to country. This fact poses some interesting questions of jurisdiction, conflict of laws, and choice of laws. In general, courts consider the impact and injurious effect of the statements on the plaintiff's reputation in the community where the plaintiff resides. Most likely, the damage to reputation would be greatest where others know the plaintiff. Therefore, a court could apply the law of that place. This may yield a just result for nonpublic figures. However, a different situation is presented if the plaintiff is a public figure whose fame extends domestically and internationally. Whose laws would be used? Where should the suit be brought? What if the laws of one state or country conflict with those of another? These difficult questions have yet to be answered, and the laws governing these cases are unsettled.

To date, not many cyberspace-related cases have been litigated. The likelihood of an increase of such cases in the future is inevitable, given the personal nature of electronic communications, publications, e-mail messages, and so on, and the relative ease by which it is possible to virtually instantaneously publish and transmit to millions of other online users worldwide. The potential for harm to one's reputation can be significant if these messages contain defamatory material. Complicating the issue is the fact that online users can communicate anonymously whether in chat rooms or in newsgroups.

In addition, those communicating online sometimes engage in what has become known as *flaming* (i.e., a kind of cyberspace online word battle where individuals engage in heated discussions directed at each other, sometimes rising to the level of defamatory language). These communications are not private, may be accessible by others, and may lead to potential liability for the *flamers*.

In order for us to understand the nature of defamation and its significance to cyberspace, we must first explore some background regarding the common law tort of defamation.

The Tort of Defamation

Defamation may be defined as oral or written false statements that wrongfully harm a person's reputation. The oral form is called **slander** and the written or published form is **libel**. (*Note:* If the defamatory remarks are directed against the goods or services of one's business, the tort is called *business* or *product disparagement*. In all cases, the harm to reputation must be severe enough so as to lower the esteem of the plaintiff in the community by subjecting the individual to ridicule, contempt, or even hatred.

Defamation in Cyberspace: Slander or Libel?

Since most material communicated on the Internet can be classified as published (bulletin boards, e-mail, chat rooms, etc.) and has a degree of permanence, if it satisfies the elements of proof needed for defamation, it will likely be classified as libel and not slander.

Elements of Proof Required for Defamation

In suits for the tort of defamation, the Restatement (Second) of Torts requires proof of certain elements (see Table 10.1). We will consider their applicability to libel in cyberspace.

First, a false and defamatory statement, usually of fact and not opinion, must be made about another's reputation or business. Direct evidence, innuendo, insinuation or reference may establish this. What is necessary to establish is that the statement made is understood by others as "of or concerning" the plaintiff. Note that this tort, like some others, is considered personal. Therefore, if the individual who is the subject of the defamation is deceased at the time it is published, no cause of action for defamation exists.

Second, an unprivileged publication is made to a third party. Generally, there is no liability if the defendant did not intend the publication to be viewed by anyone other than the plaintiff. However, it is common knowledge that very few online communications, especially those concerning e-mail, are considered private. They are accessible and capable of interception by literally millions of others worldwide. Therefore, it is unlikely that a defendant would be able to argue he did not intend others to view defamatory statements published online.

Third, depending on state law or whether the plaintiff is considered to be a public official or figure, the plaintiff may have to establish some degree of fault or negligence on the part of the defendant. As discussed later in more detail, a plaintiff who is a public official or figure will have to prove the defamatory remarks were made with *actual malice* (with knowledge the remarks were false or with reckless regard as to whether they were false or not). If the plaintiff is a private individual, one not famous in the community, then the burden of proof is less demanding, depending on the state's requirement for "fault" regarding this element. Typically, those states with such a requirement require a plaintiff to prove the defendant failed to exercise reasonable care in determining the truth or falsity of the statements published.

Fourth, the defamatory statements must result in actual or presumed damages. If the words qualify as libel, damages are presumed to exist. The permanent nature of a libelous statement, the ability, especially via the Internet, to distribute it widely, and the fact that, in general, written words require more premeditation than those spoken, have led courts to allow recovery for libel without proof of actual or special damages.

On the other hand if the words qualify as slander, a plaintiff will have to establish actual or special damages unless the false accusations fall into one of the following categories known as *slander per se* where damages are presumed to exist:

1. Accusing another of committing a serious crime
2. Accusing another of having a loathsome or communicable disease
3. Injuring another in their business or profession
4. In some states, accusing a woman of being unchaste

Table 10.1

Elements of Proof Required in a Suit for Defamation

- A false statement of fact, not opinion, about the plaintiff
- Publication of the statement without a privilege to do so
- Fault or negligence
- Damages—actual or presumed

Defenses to Defamation

There are defenses to defamation suits available to a defendant. *Truth* is an absolute or complete defense to defamation. If what is stated about the plaintiff is true, there is no basis for recovering damages, even where the defendant is motivated by malice (ill will, spite, or revenge) (see Table 10.2).

In certain situations, the law allows an individual an **absolute privilege** to speak freely about another without regard to liability for defamation. This defense usually extends to statements associated with the effective furtherance of the operations of government. Thus, members of the judicial, legislative, and executive branches of government are protected from liability for publishing false statements as long as they relate to their particular function. The law recognizes that these individuals must be free to express their opinions freely without fear of a lawsuit.

A **qualified privilege** attaches to other situations. Such is the case where an individual who is defamed by another publishes a reasonable rebuttal to the statements made about them. This defense is also recognized where the publisher and the third party have a common and legitimate interest in the plaintiff, as where a prospective employer seeks a reference from a prior employer of a prospective employee. The statements contained in the reference must relate to the employee's job performance. You should note that in some states, the privilege is lost if the former employer knows the information furnished is false or the employer is motivated by malice toward the employee.

When dealing with public officials or figures, the law imposes a stricter burden of proof than that required of private figures. Here, the law attempts to strike a balance between the right of individuals to protect their reputation and the right of the public to know about the newsworthy activities of public figures and officials.

Before discussing the burden of proof, it is necessary to define public officials and figures.

In *Rosenblatt v. Baer*, 383 U.S. 75 (1966), the Supreme Court defined public officials as *"those among the hierarchy of government employees who have or appear to have substantial responsibility over the conduct of governmental affairs."* Individuals elected to office and others such as police and fire chiefs will qualify under this definition.

The courts have found it more difficult to define who is a public figure. In *Gertz v. Robert Welch, Inc.*, 418 U.S. 323 (1974) held that in order to qualify as a public figure, a plaintiff would be required to show "clear evidence" they have established

Table 10.2
Defenses to Defamation
• Truth • Absolute privilege • Qualified privilege

fame or notoriety in the community. World-famous celebrities like Madonna or Michael Jordan would meet this test and, if defamed online, would be classified as *public figures.*

Turning our attention to liability and privilege, the press and other media have a *qualified privilege* to inform us about the activities of the famous. In the landmark case, *New York Times v. Sullivan,* 376 U.S. 254 (1964), the U.S. Supreme Court qualified this privilege by requiring that, in order to hold a defendant liable for defaming public officials, a plaintiff had to prove the defendant published the alleged defamatory material with *actual malice* (i.e., "with knowledge that it was false or with reckless disregard of whether it was false or not"). Three years later in *Curtis Publishing Co. v. Butts,* 388 U.S. 153 (1967), the Supreme Court extended the requirements of *Sullivan* to public figures seeking damages for defamation.

Liability of Online and Internet Service Providers for Defamation

For purposes of establishing liability for publishing defamation, a major issue involves a determination of whether online service providers (OSP) and Internet service providers (ISP) (hereinafter called service providers) are common carriers, distributors or publishers of the transmitted material.

Generally, courts have held that a *common carrier* (telephone or telegraph company) of published or transmitted material has virtually no control over the content of what is communicated over their service. Consequently, they are not liable for defamation.

Similarly, a *distributor* of published material such as a news vendor or bookstore does not exercise the degree of control over content necessary to establish liability for defamation. See *Smith v. California,* 361 U.S. 147 (1959) where the proprietor of a bookstore was convicted of possessing an obscene book in his store without knowledge of its contents. The Court reversed his conviction, holding that the freedom of expression and press guarantees of the First Amendment prohibits the prosecution of a distributor of an obscene book unless there is proof of "knowledge of the contents of the book."

On the other hand, a *publisher* of a book, newspaper, or television or radio broadcast can be liable for defamation since they exercise a sufficient degree of editorial control over what they publish. Therefore, it should follow that if a service provider or bulletin board operator controls the content of a publication or has knowledge of its contents, it can be liable if what is published over the service is defamatory.

Deciding exactly what is a publication has given courts some difficulty. Certainly, books, magazines, newspapers, journals, periodicals, and pamphlets will qualify. In *It's in the Cards, Inc. v. Fuschetto,* a Wisconsin case, 535 N.W. 2d 11 (Wis. Ct. App. 1995), the court had to decide whether a computer subscription service accessible anytime by its users could be considered a periodical and therefore a publication. In that case, the plaintiff and defendant were users of a bulletin board called *SportsNet* that involved the purchase and sale of sports memorabilia. A dispute arose between the plaintiff and defendant resulting in the defendant posting allegedly defamatory statements. A Wisconsin statute required that before a plaintiff could bring lawsuit for an alleged defamatory publication in a newspaper, magazine, or periodical, the plaintiff would have to give the defendant notice and an opportunity to retract the publication. The court defined *periodical* as a publication that appears on a regular basis. In this case, the posting was a random communication analogous to posting a written notice on a public bulletin board and, therefore, did not qualify as a publication as was required under the statute. Therefore, the notice and retraction requirements under the statute did not apply and the plaintiff could proceed with his lawsuit.

The following two cases provide some insight as to what factors a court can consider in order to determine the liability of a service provider for the publication of defamatory material. In *Cubby, Inc. v. CompuServe, Inc.* 776 F. Supp. 135 (S.D.N.Y. 1991), the defendant provided an "electronic" library service containing interest forums upon which daily newspapers were available to its subscribers on their computers. One of these newspapers was called *Rumorville* with which the defendant had no relationship nor any control over what it published. The plaintiff was the publisher of a competing publication called *Skuttlebut*. The plaintiff sued the defendant for allegedly publishing defamatory remarks about it on *Rumorville*. The court held that since the defendant had no control or knowledge of the contents of the publication, it could not be held liable as a publisher. The defendant was a distributor rather than a publisher.

Cubby presents a kind of dilemma for service providers and others. Seemingly, a service provider such as CompuServe, which makes no effort to check the contents of what is transmitted on its services, could escape liability as a publisher of libelous material. However, that lack of effort could result in the publication of material that could expose the service provider to liability in tort for negligence for allowing the publication. As a result of this negligence, the service provider could be liable for trademark and copyright infringement, invasion of privacy, fraud, violations of the laws against pornography, and in some cases, criminal activities.

In *Stratton Oakmont, Inc., v. PRODIGY Services Company*, 1195 N.Y. Misc. LEXIS 229, 1995 WL 323710 N.Y. Supp. Ct. (May 24, 1995), the defendant owned and operated *Money Talk*, the leading and most widely read financial bulletin board upon which members posted messages regarding stocks, etc. The facts indicated that the defendant exercised control over the content of the messages employing an agent and used software-screening programs to monitor content. Allegedly defamatory statements about the plaintiff were posted on *Money Talk* and the plaintiff sued, arguing that as a result of its control over content, the defendant should be held liable as a publisher rather than a distributor. The court agreed and the defendant was held liable for the defamatory messages.

The decisions in *Cubby* and *Stratton* clearly indicate that control over content is the key issue in holding a service provider liable for allowing the publication of defamatory statements on the Internet. However, it would be impossible for the provider to monitor every message posted. Furthermore, online users expect to communicate freely without censorship particularly on bulletin boards and in chat rooms. Therefore, it appears the most effective way for service providers to limit their liability as a publisher, is to engage the services of an independent contractor to control and edit messages and other publications. The result is that the **independent contractor** assumes sole responsibility for any defamatory publication. In the alternative, if the individual in charge of editing or controlling content is an employee or agent of the service provider, the service provider can be held liable along with the individual under the common law theories of **vicarious liability** and **"respondeat superior."** These theories hold an employer or principal liable for the torts of an employee or agent as long as the tort was committed within the "scope" of the terms of the employment.

The next section of this chapter discusses the efforts of Congress to ameliorate the effects of *Cubby* and *Stratton* on both Internet users and services providers.

Protection for 'Good Samaritan' Blocking and Screening of Offensive Material

Recall our discussion of the Communications Decency Act (CDA) in Chapter 9 (Obscenity). There we saw the Court in the *Reno* case declare certain provisions of the CDA to be unconstitutional. The CDA legislation manifests an intent by Congress to eliminate the potential liability of service providers and users for defamation whether they qualify as distributors under *Cubby* or as publishers under *Stratton*. Congress was concerned with the decision in *Stratton* contemplating that the liability as described would be a disincentive to service providers and others to develop technologies that would result in blocking and filtering devices and, ideally, in user control over what information is published and received by individuals, families, and others. **Section 230 of the Communications Decency Act** of 1996 (CDA 47 U.S.C. § 230(C)(1) was not only a reflection of that concern but also served to overrule the decision in *Stratton*.

Specifically § 230 provides that "no provider or user of an **interactive computer service** shall be treated as a publisher or speaker of any information provided by another information content provider." Further, § 230 eliminates potential civil liability where a provider or user takes a good faith, voluntary action to restrict access to or availability of material that the provider or user considers to be obscene, harassing, or otherwise objectionable, whether or not the material is constitutionally protected. The effect of these provisions is to protect a service provider (e.g., PRODIGY) from being classified as a publisher, particularly in cases where it attempts to exercise even a modicum of control over content.

In light of the immunity given to service providers under § 230, unless it is revoked or modified, success in libel suits against service providers will likely occur only where a plaintiff can establish that the service provider exhibited some degree

Cyberethics

Is it ethical to allow cyberspace to be free of restraints on defamatory speech that could help eliminate the potential of harm to a person's most valuable asset, their reputation?

http://

You can view the *Drudge Report* at
www.drudgereport.com

of editorial control over content. In *Sidney Blumenthal v. Matt Drudge and America Online*, 992 F. Supp. 44 (D.D.C. April 22, 1998), the defendant, Matt Drudge, published and sent alleged defamatory statements about the plaintiff through AOL, the co-defendant. The plaintiff sues AOL alleging they had editorial control over the content of the statements. Therefore, it could not claim immunity under § 230 of the CDA since Drudge was not anonymous when he sent the message through AOL with which he had a contractual relationship that allowed AOL to take an active part in controlling what Drudge was allowed to publish on AOL. The court granted AOL immunity from liability and decided that Congress' intent under § 230 was not to treat service providers like other information providers, e.g.,

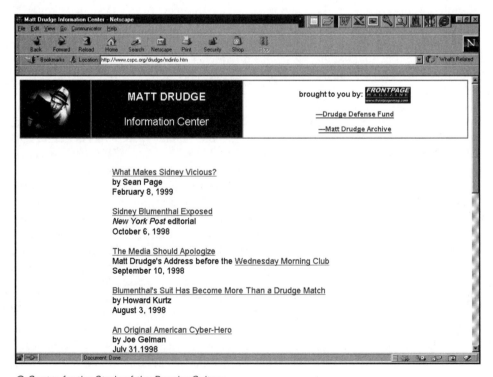

© Center for the Study of the Popular Culture.

newspapers, magazines, television, etc., but to allow them to self-police even if that proved to be ineffective. This result, the court believed, would help "preserve the vibrant and competitive free market" for services such as those provided by AOL.

Global Issues: Defamation on the Internet

In Chapters 8 and 9, we observed that the laws pertaining to privacy and obscenity could vary from state to state and from country to country. The laws regarding defamation are no different. They can differ among the more than 125 countries currently accessible on the Internet. The important issues and questions regarding defamation, primarily related to jurisdiction, are similar to those raised in the two previous chapters (see Table 10.3). They include the following:

1. Where does the publication of the defamation occur? Where it is sent or accessed? At common law, publication occurred when the defamatory material was communicated to the third party. Therefore, a publication of defamatory material in a newspaper would occur wherever a third party read it. Applying this to the Internet, a publication would occur each time at the location where the material was accessed.
2. Where would suit be brought? In the plaintiff's country or in the country where the publication occurred (where theoretically the laws could be different)? Or would the plaintiff engage in **"forum shopping,"** choosing the country whose laws were most favorable to the plaintiff?
3. If a plaintiff were successful in bringing a defamation suit in a U. S. court or one overseas, would the judgment be enforceable? For example, a U.S. court might not be willing to enforce a judgment rendered by a foreign court if it would result in a violation or denial of rights under the First Amendment. The same could result where a plaintiff is defamed in a foreign country and the laws there are not as favorable as those of the United States. As a result, the plaintiff opts to sue in a U.S. court. The United States could be powerless to impose its laws on the other country. (Recall the discussion of the Act of State Doctrine in Chapter 9).

Table 10.3

Questions Related to International Suits for Defamation

- In what country does publication of the defamation occur?
- In which country should the plaintiff file the lawsuit?
- Will the courts of one country enforce a judgment rendered by the courts of another country?

Keep in mind that a plaintiff suing for defamation published globally is most likely a world-famous figure. Consequently, if the person were libeled, the damages to be suffered would be without geographic boundaries and potentially enormous. Such a plaintiff with the financial ability could bring lawsuits seeking relief in many countries, each one with potentially different laws and procedures. Whereas, in most cases, the rest of us are probably known only within our immediate communities and would not be affected by defamation published online and accessible worldwide.

To date, few lawsuits dealing with global issues of defamation have been brought. However, with the expected continued growth in the numbers of users, and the relative ease and speed to communicate online, in many cases anonymously, the number of these types of suits will likely increase. It is also likely that foreign countries will embark on some sort of multicountry agreement patented after the European Directive on Privacy (discussed in Chapter 9). Some countries would oppose such an agreement, viewing it as an infringement upon their sovereignty. Others could desire to keep cyberspace free from restraints on speech and expression, opting instead for self-regulation and mutual cooperation.

Summary

The tort of defamation occurs when a person speaks or writes an unprivileged false statement about another's reputation or business that results in damages either actual or presumed. It takes one of two forms. If oral, it is called slander, and if written it is called libel. Defamation published online will be considered libel and not slander. The damages arise because the reputation of the plaintiff is diminished in the eyes of the community. The community may be relatively small, as in the case of a nonfamous or private individual, or it can be vast and without boundaries, as in the case of a public official or figure.

The defenses of truth, absolute privilege, and qualified privilege may be available to a defendant in a defamation suit.

If the plaintiff is a private, nonfamous person, the plaintiff may, depending on the applicable state law, have to prove the defendant was negligent in determining whether the statements were true or not. A plaintiff qualifying as a public official or figure will have to prove the defendant was motivated by actual malice, a reckless disregard as to the truth or falsity of the statements made. Prior to the passage of § 230 of the Communications Decency Act (CDA) of 1996, online and Internet service providers could face liability for defamatory materials posted on the services if, as a *publisher,* they exercised control of the contents of the material, or as a *distributor,* they knew or should have known the contents of the material was defamatory.

In an attempt to allow service providers to develop technology that could prevent the publication of online defamation and other objectionable material, and to foster self-regulation, Congress enacted § 230 of the CDA. This section immunizes service providers from liability for defamation where a third party not under the service provider's employ furnished the published material. Immunity also extends where a service provider attempts to restrict access to or availability of material considered to be defamatory or objectionable.

Global issues associated with online defamation involve issues of conflict of laws, forum selection, and enforcement of judgments.

Manager's Checklist

- As with privacy and obscenity, employers should establish a company policy regarding the sending and publishing of defamatory e-mail messages.
- Remind employees that they should not assume that others can not access their private e-mail messages even where such is not the intent of the employee. Remember that one speaks or publishes at his/her own peril.
- Monitor employee e-mail to insure they do not contain defamatory material that could lead to liability for the employer (as well as the employee).
- Make sure, that if you make statements of fact online about your competition or their goods or services, they do not contain defamatory material.
- If a defamatory message has been published on company e-mail online, remove it and issue a retraction or apology as soon as possible.
- If you are a service provider, engage the services of an independent contractor who will assume complete responsibility for controlling and monitoring the contents of all publications to be put online.
- Remember that in most cases of defamation, speaking or writing the "truth" is an absolute defense.

Additional Readings

- Caden, Marc L. and Stephanie E. Lucas. "Accidents on the Superhighway: On-Line Liability and Regulation," *Richmond Journal of Law and Technology*, 1996. *(www.richmond.edu/jolt/v2il/caden_lucas.html)*.

- Cavazos, Edward A. "Computer Bulletin Systems and the Right of Reply: Redefining Defamation Liability for a New Technology," *12 The Review of Litigation No. 1,* (1992). *(www.utexas.edu/students/trol/masthead.html)*.

- Sandberg, Jared. "Will the Threat of Libel Suits Chill Cyberspace Chatter?" *Wall Street Journal* (August 30, 1997). *(www.wsj.com)*.

11

Internet and Information Security

"The rapid growth of e-business has placed new demands on infosecurity. The 1999 Industry survey shows that in many ways, we're not equal to the challenge."
—*Cover Story, '99 survey Andy Briney, editor, www.infosecuritymag.com*

Introduction

We have transformed our economy into one in which information is as valuable an asset as physical assets. This information age has been made possible by the Internet. As individuals and businesses have migrated to the Internet, the urgent need for security of both information and information technology has rapidly gained momentum. This is due to the reality that while strengths are gained by this interconnectedness, the vulnerabilities of computer systems and information are greatly increased as well. The industry of computer and information security is thriving, as ever more transactions are conducted over the Internet. This chapter discusses the legal and ethical environment of Internet and information security.

The Challenges of Internet and Information Security

The U.S. Computer Emergency Response Team estimates that in 2000 there are two billion Internet users. The number of Internet host computers—those that store information and relay communications—is estimated in 2000 to number 200 million. Domain names, as well as World Wide Web sites, have increased astronomically.

This emergence of computer technologies has created new ways to access information—even such information that is not intended to be accessed. For example, even as early as 1995 the Pentagon reported suffering 250,000 attacks on its computers (www.us.net/softwar/gao.html); 65 percent of those represent attempts to gain entry to its network. In 1999 Microsoft had to shut down service for its 40 million Hotmail users after it was tipped off about a security vulnerability that left all of these accounts freely accessible (http://news.cnet.com/news/0-1005-200-114899.html). Despite legislative efforts to address many computer offenses, the global interconnection of computers overwhelms any individual country's efforts to completely secure computers and networks. Such an immense problem as Internet and information security is not lost on the general population, and is usually the principal impediment cited for not doing more business over the Internet.

The security of systems, information, and information technology is a goal for every network user. The efforts to secure information and transactions is an outgrowth of the law and values of privacy, in which there has developed a body of law protecting individuals from unauthorized access into certain confidential matters.

Information security is broadly defined as the ability to control access to computers, networks, hardware, software, and data. It includes the ability to protect computers and systems from intentional or accidental disclosure, modification, or destruction of proprietary systems or information. It also protects computers and systems from being used as an instrument for malicious or illegal activities. A Web site discussing computer security problems may be found at .

The challenge, of course, is how to ensure privacy and security of protected proprietary information when it is being sent/transmitted by way of the Internet, which is a public network. The problem of information security has come to the forefront of e-business concerns, and for good reason. A 1999 survey confirmed that companies conducting e-business are 57 percent more likely to experience a leak of proprietary information than are bricks-and-mortar businesses, and 24 percent more likely to experience a hacking-related breach. These complications, which did not pose problems heretofore, are directly related to the changes that have occurred in our communications systems. For example, business conducted 150 years ago was conducted in person, or by letter. After the telephone was introduced, this became another usual method of conducting business. Telephone calls, like letters, could be intercepted by third parties, but there was still an acceptable level of security. However with the advent of wireless communications and public networks, the ability to secure communications by ensuring their privacy and integrity is seriously compromised today.

In this era, persons conducting business with each other may not even know what the other person looks or sounds like—these are details from a bygone era. Now individuals are simply relying on perhaps a password or e-mail address as confirmation that the transaction took place and was valid. This is indeed a world away from the time when business was conducted face to face and consummated by a handshake. Now the Internet has developed into the medium of choice for so many transactions and communications. This migration to the Internet surely was not foreseen even by the original architects of

http://
See:
www.cert.org

http://
See:
www.info-sec.com/internet/99/internet_122799d_j.shtml
and **http://jaring.nmhu.edu/notes/security.htm**

the Internet. Developed a generation ago as a way for university researchers to communicate with each other, there was no consideration given to security matters. This open and public format, while perhaps the greatest public forum and democratizing force in history, is not at all well-suited to the communication of private information. In fact, it has been characterized as one big party line. The Internet is certainly not security-driven. Consequently, an industry whose mission is to find ways to keep information secure has been created to patch security measures onto the very public Internet. The size and magnitude of security issues will rise dramatically in this decade, as will the legal challenges to business and government and individual efforts to control information, as well as to access it.

The Goals of Internet and Information Security

It is important at the outset to understand that no means of communications is totally secure, and that there are some levels of risk to all of our communications. With this in mind, the goals of information security are to control communications to ensure the following:

- Confidentiality,
- Authenticity
- Integrity

of *each* electronic communication.

First, confidentiality, or privacy, of communications and data must be assured in order to maintain the value of the content and the system itself. Second, verifying the authenticity of users is critical, for otherwise the information and system has no value. Finally, maintaining integrity of the data is crucial—this ensures that the information is what it is supposed to be. For if these criteria are not met, there is no security and the risk of loss of proprietary information is unacceptably high. The business environment however, is changing faster than the security industry. In a recent article, Steven Foote wrote:

> In 1999, security management will take center stage. 1999 will be the year the traditional corporate walls crumble. To remain competitive, companies will need to have the ability to do business electronically with partners, remote employees and customers. With all of these users entering the enterprise from different points of entry, it will be nearly impossible to determine where one company ends and the next begins. The more virtual a corporation becomes, the greater its chances are of responding to market demands and succeeding competitively. The risk, of course, is that a virtual corporation will be dangerously insecure. *Get Ready for a Wild Ride,* www.infosecuritymag.com/nov/cover.html.

The goals of confidentiality, authenticity, and integrity of communications from "end-to-end"—that is, between users, Internets, intranets, extranets and ISPs—must be balanced with the reality of usability. People must be able to use a system and data efficiently and not be overly burdened with layers upon layers of computer security protections. Security thus must be balanced with usability.

Securing the Internet for business and personal use without sacrificing efficiency and usability is a major aspect of computer security discussed herein. But there is another, more public, issue involved—that of government security. Considered government's most basic role, law enforcement, military, and intelligence gathering functions rely on access to data and communications. A central problem, though, is that with everybody having access to information security products, most communications are becoming so secure as to render them impenetrable. Thus, highly secure programs and information used for illegitimate purposes thwart the rule of law and ultimately undermine the utility and desirability of the public Internet network. The reach of governmental entities into areas of computer surveillance and security such as encryption is an important and divisive subject in the field of computer and information security. The public aspects of computer security implicate constitutional rights, and there currently exists a conflict of opinion on these issues.

More complex personal and business uses of the Internet will grow only to the extent that usability and security are reasonably assured, but this level of security possibly impedes security and law enforcement functions of governments. It is therefore an understatement to say that the computer and information security industry faces enormous challenges.

Methods and Legal Challenges of Ensuring Security

A vast and increasingly sophisticated computer security industry has developed in response to the critical need to secure electronic information and systems. Its goals are to protect computers, systems and information from viruses, eavesdropping, hacking, theft, tampering, forgery, and interception. These needs are particularly important to the extent that the information is, for example, financial (such as credit card numbers), privileged (such as between attorneys and clients), or otherwise proprietary (such as business communications about products that are being developed). And while there might be security at the client level, this cannot be presumed at the system level.

The risks of security breaches are even greater as the public Internet network evolves into the standard mode for business communications. Table 11.1 lists the top ten security products. Two major categories, or bands, of security have evolved: firewall systems and commercial security systems.

Firewalls

Firewall security systems could be compared to the medieval security plan of a moat. The moat served to guard the inside of the building, while allowing entry only to authorized individuals through selected "gateways." A **firewall** acts as a barrier between the networked computers and the network, and it does just this for

Table 11.1

The Top Ten Security Products in 1999 (beginning with the most popular)

1. Firewalls
2. Access Controls
3. Client/Server Security
4. LAN/WAN Security
5. Web Security
6. Disaster Recovery
7. Network/Communications Security
8. Email Security
9. Encryption
10. Mainframe Security

computer systems. It allows for creation of private intranets and networks known as Virtual Private Networks (VPNs). In a typical business then, companies may use intranets to post information that only networked company employees may see. Although such a system is not effective against internal security threats, it does effectively secure the system from unauthorized external threats to entry and access.

Although there is not yet any litigation involving firewalls, it is foreseeable where the vulnerabilities are. A defective firewall system, like any other product, is a liability problem for the manufacturers, vendors, and users. Those who enter a computer system that is surrounded by a firewall may be liable for this unauthorized entry under both state and federal law. In fact, state and federal lawmakers have been continuously amending and updating laws to encompass liability for computers acts. The evolving state of laws is discussed later in this chapter.

Firewalls are invaluable at protecting a network of computers from outside intrusions, but to the extent that the security breach is from within the organization, the firewall offers no security.

Transactional Security Systems

While a firewall can be compared to a moat, a commercial security scheme could be compared to a truck going through checkpoints at every stage of its journey—from loading; to its driver; to its route; to its destination point; and finally, to unloading. A firewall could be considered security of the building itself, while transactional security systems could be considered checkpoints along the route

http://

For more on firewalls, see **www.clark.net/pub/mjr/pubs/fwfaq/index.htm, www.cs.purdue.edu/coast/hotlist/network/firewalls. html, or www.zeuros.co.uk/firewall**

while traveling to and from the building—it is a chain of security. There are currently a myriad of commercial security systems being developed, tested, and marketed, all of which attempt to secure data and information transmitted between businesses, service providers, and clients. The goal of transactional security systems is to protect information as it is being transmitted. The principal modes of ensuring commercial computer security are first discussed briefly, with major emphasis on cryptography and the legal issues it has created.

Password Protection/Script-based Single Sign-On (SSO).   Password protection is probably the primary form of security that we recognize. It is reflected in the ubiquitous name and password requests that appears in the workplace, and in e-commerce transactions, such as when purchasing goods online. This method for authenticating users is, in theory, generally considered easy. In practice, though, it is less so due to the phenomenon of forgotten names and/or passwords. This results in impediments to productivity as well as profits.

A **script-based single sign-on** (SSO) will learn and automatically apply the log-on processes for all existing applications. The limitation, however, is that SSOs generally are not workable as between external users such as clients and business partners.

Certificate Authorities (CAs) and Digital Certificates.   **Certificate authorities** (CAs) and **digital certificates** are another security method for authenticating users. They have the added benefit of being usable across multiple businesses. Certificate authorities issue and manage security credentials. CAs currently are centralized by industry and have a wide range of applications, such as e-mail, browsers, and VPNs. The digital certificates that CAs issue essentially permit the electronic identification of users to each other. They act as a digital ID or passport, and only those who can authenticate their identities over the Internet may access the secure data. The certificates authenticate the identities of users and then encrypt their transactions, much like a personal identification number (PIN) at an ATM machine. Moreover, attribute certificates can be created; thus, even authorized authentic users are limited to certain data. By way of example, a human resource manager may be authorized through his or her digital certificate to check on employee benefits information, but the attribute certificate would not allow access to employee job performance or salary history.

Biometrics.   **Biometrics** is a security method designed to authenticate users by employing technologies that capture human characteristics for use in computers and applica-

Cyberethics

Is there an ethical justification for hacking into your own company's computer systems?

> **http://**
> See
> **www.whatis.com/ca.htm or www.thawte.com** and
> **www.info-sec.com**

> **http://**
> Visit some Biometrics Consortium Web sites at
> **www.biometrics.org,** see also
> **www.zdnet.com/pcmag/features/biometrics,** or
> **www.icsa.com**

tions. Commercially available products at this time include recognition of face, iris, voice, or signature; scanning of fingerprints or retinas; palm prints; hand or finger geometry; and DNA.

Biometric technology has long been used in law enforcement, and most recently has been introduced by government agencies to process and verify welfare recipients. In 1999, British scientists established the uniqueness of ear cartilage patterns, and due to this a jury convicted a burglar who had put his ear to the window to listen inside the victim's home. Since authentication technology requires users to do more and reveal more, privacy concerns are heightened, even though such technologies greatly enhance Internet security.

For example, biometrics technology creates a record of a person's physical characteristics. This record in theory captures an immutable trait and so it cannot be used by someone else, or forgotten (unlike a password). There is a story that circulates—about a mugger, who came upon a person using an ATM that featured fingerprint ID technology—so the mugger simply chopped off the victim's finger to authenticate the transaction and access the money.

Other Ways to Secure Transactions. There are several other methods to secure transactions. These include tokens, smart cards, holography, processor serial numbers, time-stamping digital signatures, and electronic signatures.

Security tokens (sometimes referred to as *digipasses*) are another means to authenticate users and secure transactions. These usually augment common passwords by generating a random code number unique to each transaction. Available to interface with either software or hardware, the latter application has recently gained momentum as it supports PKI (discussed next). Taking advantage of the Universal Serial Bus (USB) port, a token the size of a house key is inserted. The computer "reads" the token that is embedded with passwords and certificates. It is thus a handheld password generator.

Smart cards are similar to tokens but have the added feature of portability—they store digital credentials, and can store and retrieve data. So, for example, an employee with a smart card could access the same secure data using an off-site computer as she could from her office computer. A smart card currently is similar to a credit card, and it contains an embedded processor and operating system. Smart cards are featured in more than 30 million cellular telephones to handle security information. Other possible applications include use in credit cards, bank cards, and as electronic purses.

http://
See for example,
www.vasco.com or www.shiva.com

Another security method is through the use of **holography.** Security holography products are in high demand at this time. Holographic images can be embossed or incorporated into a photopolymer process. They can be apparent, or they may be hidden—such as with the use of infared ink. Current applications include use on credit cards, ID badges, video-cassettes, and CDs. These are usually in the form of hot-stamped foil rainbow-colored wrappers. Tampering with these can immediately expose

http://
One industry organization's Web site is found at
www.scia.org.
See also **www.techtronics.com**

http://
See
www.holographx.com

trademark infringements, product piracy, and counterfeit or gray-market goods.

A security element that enhances control of information is the use of a **processor serial number in** every CPU. For example, current serial number technology, in which information is embedded into each computer's processing chip, has the potential to provide digital signing, time-stamping, secure archiving, and the feature of *nonrepudiation* (whereby the source of the message cannot be denied and so is traceable back to the physical device of the computer itself). This technology is being hailed by industry as a much-needed authentication element, when a simple password offers insufficient security. It has featured prominently in law enforcement efforts recently, yet consumer advocates assert that the use of such information further erodes personal privacy rights.

Public Key Infrastructure (PKI).   **Public Key Infrastructure (PKI)** refers to data encryption and associated technologies in the issuance and management of digital credentials certifying the identities of authorized users. This technology represents, currently at least, the culmination of the many security technologies thus far developed and discussed. It represents a system of collaboration between

http://
A few helpful Web sites on PKI include
www.opengroup.org/security/pki,
http://counterpane.com/pki-risks-ft.txt, and
http://jm.acs.virginia.edu/atg/techtalk/PKI/index.htm

the digital certificates; certificate authorities; registration authorities; and certificate management services, all in order to verify the identity and authority of each party involved in the transaction. Although layers of security are desirable and an effective way to control risk, there is an equally critical need for usability as well as interoperability between systems and users. PKI extends business systems securely so that clients, partners, and suppliers can function without problems of system incompatibility. Its potential uses include managing privacy, confidentiality, access control, and proof of transmission.

Cryptography.   The previous discussion of Internet and information security mainly dealt with authentification security. This discussion of **cryptography** necessarily focuses on the confidentiality aspect of security. Cryptography has been in use for at least 2,500 years. It does not hide the presence of data, but rather renders it incoherent, or unreadable, until the intended reader deciphers it. [This is in contrast to the field of steganography, which allows for the insertion of hidden information within data sources.] Cryptography is a system of coding, then de-coding the message. The first step in cryptography is the **encryption** of the data in which a program acts to take the data, known as plaintext, and, by use of a mathematical algorithm, stores the data in a different format known as *ciphertext*. Thus, the data are coded, or scrambled, for transmission. The data only become intelligible or readable to those possessing the means of **decryption** that will transform the ciphertext back to readable plaintext. Thus, the data are decoded with what is known as a *key* that solves the mathematical algorithm and reassembles the message.

It is important to understand a bit about the historical military applications of cryptography, in order to grasp the complexities of its legal regulation at the present time. Cryptography played an important role in the communication of messages by the Axis forces during World War II. The Allies' "Ultra" Project managed to break their code and thereby gain access to classified enemy information. Cryptography during this time had no civil or commercial applications and was classified until 1996 as munitions, under jurisdiction of the State Department's Office of Defense Trade Controls. Because cryptography was historically used for military applications to guard classified national security information, until recently the government totally controlled cryptography and possessed all of the keys to decode information. (See *Bernstein v. Department of State*, 974 F. Supp. 1288 (N.D. Cal. 1997.) Commercial applications of cryptography were underway by the 1980s as information became recognized as an increasingly valuable commodity, and it became possible to transmit it efficiently. Responding to this broader use of cryptography, then-President Clinton, through Executive Order 13026 (61 Federal Register 58767 (1996), transferred jurisdiction of non-

http://
For more on steganography, see
www.isse.gmu.edu/~njohnson/steganography

military commercial cryptographic products to the Commerce Department (see www.ssh.fi.tech/crypto).

The traditional government monopoly of encryption utilized a single key system (also known as private key or symmetric encryption) in which the same key was used to encrypt as well as decrypt communications. The U.S. government adopted a **Data Encryption Standard (DES)** in 1977, which is still in use today. (This standard, however, will be replaced by 2001 with the Advance Encryption Standard (AES), as the standard encryption algorithm for many official applications.) IBM originally developed the DES, which is done by encrypting plain text into blocks of 64 bits with 56-bit keys. This worked well when there was one supplier and few users—the government could securely dispatch and keep track of the keys. The obvious risk is that if the key is not well-guarded, there is no security. Technological advances have rendered the 1977 DES an anachronism. Today, 95 percent of major e-commerce sites use 512-bit strength encryption programs, although even now, experts favor a 1024-bit program as the standard for secure transactions.

This private key cryptography system became much less workable to the extent that a myriad of decentralized public commercial activities depend on the use of such security measures. The demand for encryption has clearly expanded from its origin in defense applications. Current uses include professional, commercial, and consumer markets needing secure computer communications about private, sensitive information between perhaps anonymous individuals—such as online credit-card purchases or securing loans. The government is simply unable to hand out keys for all of these activities, many of which are now commercial rather than military, and which have no relation to the government in any event.

In 1976, cryptographers Whitfield Duffie (now an engineer at Sun Microsystems) and Martin Hellman invented the theory that it is possible for someone to announce the precise method of coding a message, while at the same time retaining a secret private key for decoding it. Without this key, it is not possible for the receiver to decode the message, even knowing how it was coded. In 1977 three mathematicians at MIT (Ronald Rivest, Adi Shamir, and Leonard Adleman) patented their RSA-Algorithm, turning the Diffie-Hellman concept into a practical application: the public asymmetrical two-key encryption system in use today. The sender and receiver of information do not share the same key, but rather, the parties use their own keys that are mathematically related, but not discoverable to each other. Public key encryption systems work particularly well for the millions of anonymous commercial users, although secure key management rests with individuals instead of the government.

Encryption and decryption have improved in practice and have become extremely strong, or secure. This is done by increasing the complexity and thus the key length through the introduction of more bits. At this time encryption is the security standard of choice for the

http://

See

http://crsc.nist.gov/cryptval/des/des.txt, and
www.certicom.com/press/RSS-155.htm

Table 11.2

Creating a Secure Message Using Public-Key Cryptography

First: Sender defines message to be sent.

Second: Sender's software uses an algorithm (known as a hash function) to create a digital "freeze frame" of the message. This transformed message is known as a *hash result,* or a message digest.

Third: Sender's software combines the hash result with the sender's private key. This key creates a digital signature that is unique to that message and key.

Fourth: Sender transmits the message and digital signature over the Internet.

Fifth: Recipient's software receives the message and applies the same hash function as above, to the message. This produces a new hash result from the message. This result is compared to the hash result contained within the digital signature. If the two results are identical, the message has not been tampered with.

Sixth: Recipient uses the public key to verify that sender's digital signature was created with the corresponding private key. This confirms that the sender is authentic, and that the message originated from there.

For a try at decoding a message, see www.nara.gov/education/teaching/zimmermann/decode.html.

protection of transmitted information. Cryptography makes it possible to control access points and authorization of end users; transfer users; control the timing and length of access to data; track users; and vary the level of security within documents. This process of encryption and decryption is the technology behind the PKI technology and the **Secure Electronic Transactions** (SET) used by business. SET establishes industry standards governing commercial transactions (see www.setco.org).

This outstanding level of control through cryptography is all the more remarkable when you consider that the information is posted on a publicly accessible Web site, yet is off limits except to intended users (see Table 11.2).

Cryptography presents a host of fascinating legal questions, as it has become a standard protocol for securing information sent over the Internet. A number of legal issues have developed out of the commercial use of cryptography.

Most importantly, the question of whether cryptography is speech or mere computer source code implicates First Amendment rights. The second and related question is how much power the government has to regulate the export of cryptography software. Third, there is a heated controversy over Fourth Amendment rights of privacy and law enforcement efforts to control access to the recovery/decoding keys. Privacy and Fourth Amendment rights are at risk to the extent that there is unrestricted surveillance of private matters. Finally, government cryptography regulations implicate individual's Fifth Amendment rights. The legal and ethical environment of cryptography is dynamic, and an easy resolution of these issues, which are next discussed, is very much in doubt.

Is Cryptography "Speech"?

The importance of this question lies in the fact that speech or expression enjoys First Amendment protections from overly intrusive government regulation. Thus, if cryptography is considered speech or expression, the government may not unduly control the speech. Each type of speech merits varying levels of protection. For example, commercial speech is considered robust and therefore is not as protected as more fragile forms of expression such as political speech. In general, governments may impose neutral valid time, place and manner restrictions on speech, but these must be limited or carefully tailored, and must serve a substantial government interest. In construing speech cases, courts are more tolerant of *subsequent* punishment of speech than they are of *prior* restraints on that speech. In cryptography cases, the essential point being alleged is that these programs are protected speech and that they are all being regulated—academic as well as commercial programs—prior to their being used. Thus, they are classified as prior restraint cases. In essence, courts begin with the presumption that prior restraint of speech is invalid. Therefore, government infringements on prior speech are valid only if the regulation is narrowly tailored to the speech involved, and it demonstrates a compelling interest in regulating this speech. In contrast to these protections afforded in the U.S. by the First Amendment, in China for example, any information posted on Web sites "must obtain the inspection and approval of secrecy censorship." This is indeed a potent means to control speech.

The speech issue has special implications for the academic community, which is a true laboratory for this endeavor. Cryptographic research and information is routinely posted on Web sites for others to critique and comment on, and perhaps to decode. Such communications as these are stifled under current regulations. The authors submit that regulation of academic cryptographic research should be protected in a different way from commercial use and export of cryptographic programs. The case law on cryptography is in an extreme state of flux, since new regulations were enacted in January 2000. In fact, one case has been litigated for years, *Bernstein v. Department of State,* which in the future will be known as *Bernstein v. Department of Justice.* In May 1999 the Ninth Circuit held that encryption source code is expression, and therefore classified as speech deserving of First Amendment protections. Because of this the court invalidated federal regulations that allowed the government to restrain speech indefinitely with no articulated criteria for review. The U.S. government thereafter made a highly unusual request to withdraw this opinion, and so the Ninth Circuit has agreed to a new hearing in this case. The result reached in that May 1999 opinion stands somewhat contrast to the following case, which also resolves a First Amendment challenge to government export restrictions. The *Bernstein* case is mentioned here, not in the interest of confusion, but rather as a display of how the various courts reach different opinions, which oftentimes precedes a review by the United States Supreme Court or a change in the law by Congress.

http://

To access documents from the *Bernstein* case, see **www.eff.org/bernstein/**

A recent case is somewhat in agreement with the *Bernstein* opinion that was withdrawn. In *Junger v. Daley*, 209 F.3d 481 (6th Cir. 2000) a law professor posted encryption source code on his web site. Such source code is defined as an export under the Commerce Department's Export Regulations, thus in need of a license. The Sixth Circuit agreed with Junger that the First Amendemnt protects encryption source code because it is an expressive means for the exchange of ideas and information. The court noted, however, that its functional capabilities should be considered when analyzing the government's interests in regulating encryption source code. Using an intermediate level of scrutiny, the trial court will weigh whether Commerce's regulation of speech furthers an important or substantial interest that outweighs the interests in allowing the free exchange of ideas through the medium of encryption source code.

The *Junger* case has important ramifications. Given the vast number of commercial uses that are now recognized for encryption software, there will be many such cases as this. The court in this case found that while the posting of encryption source code is a form of speech protected by the First Amendment, such speech may be regulated by the government and thus curbed, under certain circumstances.

http://
Government cryptography policies may be found at
http://www.cybercrime.gov/crypto.html

Regulating the Export of Cryptography Products

This, the second major legal issue involving cryptography, is directly related to the previous First Amendment discussion. Recalling cryptography's historic military and Cold War applications, there has been an exaggerated effort on the part of the U.S. Government to maintain control of this technology. Even as recently as 1995, encryption was considered military technology, when the Wassenaar Accord reinforced this view. This represents an agreement among Western and former Soviet nations to increase stability and security through export controls on conventional arms and military technology. So-called dual-use commodities such as encryption are subject to the same controls as weapons.

The current civil, commercial uses of this technology have rendered military encryption export controls less relevant, according to business, consumers, freedom, and privacy experts. They assert that encryption is a necessary security tool in today's networked environment. Businesses, especially the software industry (which controls 90 percent of the worldwide software market), are discontent with U.S. government regulations, asserting that such controls place domestic companies at a severe global competitive disadvantage, because no other country has such a restrictive

http://
See
www.fas.org/spp/starwars/offdocs/a960717w.htm

export policy as the United States. Consequently, this has created an incentive for U. S. companies to set up separate businesses overseas for the express purpose of avoiding U.S. encryption export controls.

Countering these claims are assertions from law enforcement personnel that it must have some control over encryption products in order to effectively address crimes such as drug trafficking and terrorism. Strong encryption of data by individuals makes wiretapping and interception of such data virtually impossible for law enforcement officials.

In response to these charges and prompted by pressure from the software industry, many changes in encryption policy were made in 1999, representing the culmination of years of effort. Two important resources are the "Transcript of White House Crypto-briefing September 16, 1999" (www.info-sec.com/crypto/99/crypto_092199a_j.shtml) and the Revised U.S. Encryption Export Control Regulations January 2000, (www.epic.org/crypto/export_controls/regs_1_00.html). Also submitted to Congress with these regulations was the Cyberspace Electronic Security Act of 1999 (CESA). Refer to the discussion herein on the Fourth Amendment.

Specifically, the Clinton administration perceived that it had to balance four values relating to encryption policy: national security, public safety, privacy, and commerce. The policy attempts to allow industry to compete effectively while protecting national defense, security, and law enforcement interests. First, the new rules permit any 64-bit encryption product or software to be exported under a *license exemption* for commercial nongovernmental use, except to the following seven states that support terrorism: Cuba, Iran, Iraq, Libya, North Korea, Sudan, and Syria. Second, retail products exceeding 64-bits may be exported under a *license exception* to all users including governments, except to the seven states. Third, as per the Wassenaar Accord, the United States will support the modernization of multilateral encryption export controls. New to this policy is the introduction of a category of *retail* encryption, called *retail encryption commodities and software*. Also introduced is the requirement of supplying post-export reporting data for any products exceeding 64 bits. Clearly, an encryption product of any value exceeds 64-bits, and therefore Commerce will still be reviewing all export applications. As one expert observed, the good news is that products may now be exported; the bad news is that it's still a complicated compliance process, for which legal counsel is highly recommended. As a quick aside to U.S. policy, it is useful to compare developing policies with other countries. In China, for example, the law requires everyone who *uses* encryption software to register with the government.

Such a process favors highly capitalized operations, and becomes too expensive and cumbersome for many startups, however. This high-

> **http://**
> See also
> **www.pub.whitehouse.gov**

> **http://**
> For more on cryptography, see
> **www.info-sec.com**

lights the issues of speech and the fact that the new policies cater to business export of encryption, and still do not address academic and other use of encryption, and so all of the constitutional concerns still remain. The Electronic Privacy Information Center (www.epic.org), Electronic Frontier Foundation (www.eff.org), and American Civil Liberties Union (www.aclu.org) concur that defects remain in these new regulations that violate citizen's First Amendment rights. They allege that the new regulations, like the old ones, impose special requirements on Internet speech in violation of *Reno v. ACLU,* 521 U.S. 844 (1977), because they require the government be notified of any electronic export of publicly available encryption software. Yet, this same material may be freely sent anywhere on paper.

The export regulations are still a completely discretionary licensing scheme. They still require licenses for many communications protected by the First Amendment including source code. (The regulations state that applications are reviewed on a "case-by-case basis. . . .to determine whether the export or reexport is consistent with U.S. national security and foreign policy interest.") This standard is probably not sufficiently articulated or narrowly drawn to withstand First Amendment scrutiny.

- The new regulations appear to permit free posting of encryption source code, but states that it may be illegal if the poster of code has "reason to know" that it will be read by person in any of the seven terrorist-supporting states.
- The new regulations still ban the provision of information on how to create encryption technologies. These same provisions do not apply to other, non-encryption source code. (Notice how this is an equal protection issue as well as a First Amendment issue.)

These points are surely going to be among the next First Amendment challenges to the new law (see www.info-sec.com/crypto/00/crypto_011800a_j.shtml).

This final major legal issue of cryptography implicates Fourth and Fifth Amendment rights. This is the case because in the government's pursuit of security, it has a policy requiring that law enforcement agencies be given keys to decrypt messages. Such an escrowing, or key-recovery approach, is favored by among others, the FBI and National Security Agency (NSA). They assert that they should be given a key, likened to access through a back door, to decrypt messages that are now being encrypted with virtually unbreakable codes. In fact an NSA deputy director estimated that it would take a computer expert 100 quadrillion years to decrypt a message encrypted with a 128-bit algorithm. Their assertion is questionable though, in light of the fact that a 512-bit encrypted message may be decrypted in just a few days.

So while the growth of commercial activities over the Internet depends on this encryption technology to

> **http://**
> For cryptography issues and legislation see
> **www.cdt.org**

make such communications secure, the administration and government agencies are concerned with illegal activities that are conducted using these same secure encryption technologies. In fact, in January 2000, a National Plan for Information Systems Protection was presented. It calls for the creation of a centralized intrusion detection monitoring system that involves scanning millions of legitimate computer transactions by the government that is in search of potential cyberattacks. And so they support a system whereby the government has a copy of the decoding key. These crimes they refer to include money laundering, tax fraud, bribery, racketeering, terrorism, corruption, espionage, and economic crimes. The following excerpt is from the *Bernstein* case that was withdrawn, but the court's observations are particularly relevant to this next section addressing Fourth and Fifth Amendment issues with regard to cryptography and how they relate to privacy.

> We note that the government's efforts to regulate and control the spread of knowledge relating to encryption may implicate more than the First Amendment rights of cryptographers. In this increasingly electronic age, we are all required in our everyday lives to rely on modern technology to communicate with one another. This reliance on electronic communication, however, has brought with it a dramatic diminution in our ability to communicate privately. Cellular phones are subject to monitoring, e-mail is easily intercepted, and transactions over the Internet are often less than secure. Something as commonplace as furnishing our credit card number, Social Security number, or bank account number puts each of us at risk. Moreover, when we employ electronic methods of communication, we often leave electronic "fingerprints" behind, fingerprints that can be traced back to us. Whether we are surveilled by our government, by criminals, or by our neighbors, it is fair to say that never has our ability to shield our affairs from prying eyes been at such a low ebb. The availability and use of secure encryption may offer an opportunity to reclaim some portion of the privacy we have lost. Government efforts to control encryption thus may well implicate not only the First Amendment rights of cryptographers intent on pushing the boundaries of their science, but also the constitutional rights of each of us as potential recipients of encryption's bounty. Viewed from this perspective, the government's efforts to retard progress in cryptography may implicate the Fourth Amendment, as well as the right to speak anonymously, the right against compelled speech [a Fifth Amendment right], and the right to informational privacy. While we leave for another day the resolution of these difficult issues, it is important to point out that Bernstein's is a suit not merely concerning a small group of scientists laboring in an esoteric field, but also touches on the public interest broadly defined.

Fourth Amendment

Opponents of government escrowing of recovery keys contend that it is the functional equivalent of a warrantless search and seizure, which violates the Fourth Amendment rights of encryption users. Under the Fourth Amendment citizens enjoy a "reasonable expectation of privacy" from government searches. This standard was first enunciated in *Katz v. United States*, 389 U.S. 347 (1967). A legal challenge has

> **http://**
> For the Cyberspace Electronic Security Act see
> **www.cdt.org/crypto/CESA**

Table 11.3

Results of the fourth annual Computer Crime and Security Survey of Financial institutions, U.S. Companies, and Government Agencies.

- 26% reported theft of proprietary information
- 30% reported system penetration (increased for the third consecutive year—1997–1999)
- 55% reported unauthorized access by employees (also increased for the third consecutive year)
- 57% reported Internet connection as the source of security breach-(up from 37% in 1996)

Source: Computer Security Institute and the FBI

not yet been made to government key recovery systems. Under the rule of law, a search warrant is first required if the government suspects a crime has been committed and it wishes to conduct a search. After a hearing, a warrant may be issued, in which it will state, with particularity, the place to be searched and the items that the search expects to find. In general, a search without a warrant violates citizens' expectations of privacy and constitutes an unreasonable search and seizure, and any evidence collected from such a search is inadmissible in court.

If the government is merely *collecting*, rather than *using* the decrypting keys, however, it does not appear that the Fourth Amendment is violated. (Related to this point, in a recent case, two researchers found a way to crack the A5/1 encryption system used in 215 million cellular telephones worldwide. They discovered that this A5/1 algorithm used shorter keys than advertised. This prompted speculation that the algorithm was intentionally watered down to permit government eavesdropping.)

A byproduct of any Fourth Amendment discussion includes the issue of privacy. Computer and Internet technology is challenging the law to adapt to new realities and practices. Scholars question whether we have a reasonable expectation of privacy anymore, due to the advent of the Internet, Social Security numbers, tax filings, and other centralized recordkeeping activities. This is in stark contrast to the concept of privacy conceived of by the Constitution's framers. (An excellent discussion of the changes in privacy in our networked society may be found in the book, *Code and Other Laws of Cyberspace,* by Lawrence Lessig.)

There is a body of developing case law suggesting that citizens may in the future enjoy a lesser expectation of privacy—only for "intimate details." Courts face a significant burden to protect citizens' rights of privacy as technology, specifically surveillance capabilities, enhance the government's ability to conduct searches and seizures. The U.S. Department of Justice is planning to ask Congress for new authority to allow federal agents armed with search warrants to secretly break into homes and offices to obtain decryption keys, or to implant "recovery devices" that ensure any encrypted message can be read by the government. This alarming loss of privacy is a pervasive side effect of the information age where it is theoretically possible to collect data on everyone and everything. For example, Microsoft's 5.0 Internet

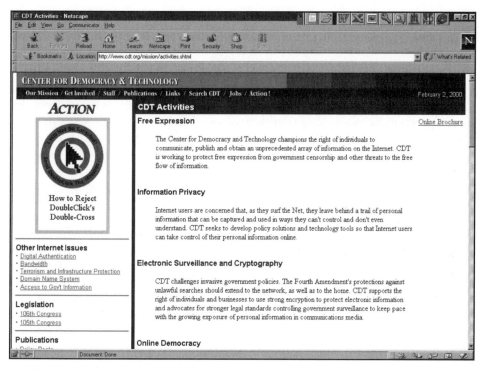

© 2000 The Center for Democracy & Technology.

Explorer automatically sent information to Web sites that users bookmarked. Recall that the Fourth Amendment protects our reasonable expectation of privacy, the question becomes, if this is the way transactions are conducted, do we even have an expectation anymore of privacy, and if so, how are we to articulate it?

The FBI and other government agencies make it clear that they wish to control escrow and recovery keys. Organizations supporting privacy and liberty rights assert that to allow this risks the centralization of government control and invites official abuse, while generally weakening the democratic system. The Wassenaar Accord working group on this issue rejected a key escrow/recovery system proposed by the United States. As cryptography products become ever more secure and sophisticated (i.e., with the advent of new products that use elliptical curve cryptography technology), the government will be sure to press its case even more vigorously. As a comparison, it is interesting to again compare U.S. cryptography policies with those in China. There, the government has the ability to read e-mail, and monitor the mail of known dissidents. This is clearly not a desirable practice in a democracy that values pri-

> **http://**
> For more on these topics, see the following sites:
> **www.unl.edu/lawcoll/library/encrypt.html;**
> **www.fbi.gov; www.usdoj.gov;**
> **www.cdt.org/crypto/risks98,** and
> **www2.epic.org/reports/crypto1999.html**

vacy. Businesses clearly need to know the encryption policies of other countries that they conduct commerce with, as it is regulated differently around the world.

Fifth Amendment

One of the Fifth Amendment's functions is to protect citizens from being compelled by the government to testify against themselves—it is otherwise known as the right against self-incrimination. This is a familiar feature of criminal legal proceedings and in practice, allows defendants to choose whether 'to take the stand' and defend themselves. The Fifth Amendment affords defendants this choice. The burden of proof rests solely with the prosecution. The question is whether in the government's law enforcement efforts, its policy of compulsory registration and disclosure of the algorithm keys violates the right against being compelled to give self-incriminating testimony. It is important, then, to first consider whether revealing an algorithm code key is testimony. On its own, a code key is similar to a house key—it does not in and of itself reveal information or represent testimony. A code key simply represents the means to access the information. The purpose of the Fifth Amendment is to prevent compelled self-incrimination, and does not act to protect other information that may be found as a result of using this key to discover incriminating evidence.

Pursuant to this, other cases have established that the government may lawfully and without being in violation of the Fifth Amendment order the production of accountants' working papers; defendants' blood tests; the appearance of defendants in line-ups; handwriting samples, and so on. The Fifth Amendment is not violated in such instances because nothing defendants have said or done is deemed sufficiently testimonial as to amount to compelled testimony. Under this standard, compulsory registration and disclosure of code keys would not be sufficiently testimonial to be afforded Fifth Amendment protections.

The Fifth Amendment affords other protections, too. Another issue raised in encryption export licensing cases is procedural due process. This inquiry is whether an official government decision denying a benefit violates the citizens' Fifth Amendment rights to a procedurally fair hearing and decision. Thus, a government decision that is deemed arbitrary, capricious, unreasonable, and irrational is held to deny individuals' rights to due process. This appears to be a difficult proof in encryption export licensing challenges, however, because government safety and security interests would appear to outweigh allegations of unreasonable, arbitrary, or capricious decision making. Finally, there are substantive due process claims involved in encryption export cases. This inquiry is whether the challenged law itself is flawed. The courts will closely scrutinize the effect of laws concerning important matters such as life or liberty. However, in such cases as encryption, where no fundamental right is at stake, courts will be more deferential to the laws that Congress enacted.

In *Karn v. Department of State*, 925 F. Supp. 1 (D.D.C. 1996), the court considered an export request—in the form of a diskette containing source code. (Previously Karn was allowed to export the same source code but in book form.) The

Department denied his request to export the diskette, and the court considered Karn's contention that such a denial violated his right under the Fifth Amendment. The court upheld the Department's denial of a license. The court considered that such an alleged economic harm should be analyzed using a rational basis analysis; and so the court deferred to the government. The court merely required that there be a reasonable fit between governmental purpose and the means chosen to advance that purpose.

The *Karn* case probably seems like a disappointing result. It has the effect of allowing the export of the materials in one form (book), but not in another form (diskette). The court seemed to understand this less-than-desirable result too, but under the analysis developed for substantive due process challenges, it was compelled to defer to the government because the challenge involved merely economic regulation. The Center for Democracy and Technology's crypto page provides updates on legislative activity in this area.

> **http://**
>
> See
> **http://www.cdt.org/crypto**

Privacy, Security, and Crimes: The Evolving Legal Environment

Hackers, crackers, snackers, computer forensics, internet filtering, malicious mobile code, macros and viruses, worms, logic bombs, computer voyeurism, eavesdropping, theft, tampering, forgery, interception—these are fast becoming the subject of government scrutiny and regulation (see Table 11.4; also see Chapter 12 for discussion of Internet crimes). By way of example, in a recent case crackers unlocked the decryption code for DVD-formatted movies. These programmers duplicated the software equivalent of a skeleton key and decoded the encryption program, known as a *content scrambling system,* and placed the software on the Internet for anyone to download. Such incidents as these will surely be the impetus for further legal and regulatory action, as well as cause businesses to explore next-generation security innovations. When these activities are considered, it becomes clear that the encryption debate, and associated constitutional challenges, is only part of the security puzzle.

The first sections of this chapter discuss the value of information security, the current methods for protecting this security, and corresponding legal challenges. This section of the chapter discusses the types of security breaches that now exist and the patchwork of laws that

> **http://**
>
> See
> **www.info-sec.com/crypto/99/crypto_110599a_j.shtml**

Table 11.4

Most Frequent Security Breaches (from most to least common)

1. Viruses
2. Employee access abuse
3. Unauthorized access by intruders
4. Theft and destruction of computer resources
5. Leak of proprietary information and trade secrets
6. Theft and destruction of data
7. Access abuse by employees who exceeded their right of access
8. Hacking of telecommunications equipment

apply. The interconnectedness of systems worldwide to the Internet poses unprecedented security and privacy challenges our current legal system generally is not well equipped to handle. Because we are all tied together by the Internet, we are all vulnerable to the same security breaches, and such a proposition demands coordinated security regulations at the international, federal, and state levels.

As with a home, security breaches occur because there are points of entry. Even though steps are taken to secure these points, they are still not 100 percent safe from intrusion. It is theoretically possible to make a 100 percent secure entry point, but if it features an overload of security devices, it probably would not be usable. Like much else, there are trade-offs between ease of use, privacy, and security. And so it is with information security and the Internet. The Internet was developed with free and open communications, rather than security, in mind. Yet as business has migrated to the Internet, security measures are, out of necessity, being patched onto the system, but with imperfect results. For if the Internet was to be made 100 percent secure, communications would be slowed to a halt, so the Internet is operating today with a relative level of security, in which the values of speed and usability have taken precedence over the value of security. Experts continually marvel that the Internet isn't brought to its knees more often.

The security problem inherent in protecting information on the Internet will never abate if the structure of the system remains the same. It is an open system, with intense commercial pressures to get products to market, where the vast majority of users are generally novices. The systems that are being created are typically *buggy*. Hardware, as well as software in many instances, is built on the fly and shipped half-formed, in beta-test mode, where customers become free software testers.

The following hypothetical case is an example of the liability issues that arise.

Infosec, Inc. created a software program that protects each data-

http://

See

www.zdnet.com

base with security perimeters that limit and control access to each business application. Hospital Care, Inc. is a company that manages the accounts receivables and payables for General Hospital. Hospital Care is located in another country from General Hospital, and so to communicate information, it forwards data over the Internet. World On-Line is the Internet service provider. Hospital Care leases the security software from Infosec. A number of things went wrong, however. Susan Jones, a Hospital Care benefits employee, discovered a weakness in the software, and so she broke through the perimeters and accessed Jane Smith's confidential medical records. Later, Susan inadvertently sent these records over the Internet to General Hospital and its medical suppliers. At the same time, a World On-Line employee was reading this information as it passed from one account to the other. This is in violation of World On-Lines' company policy.

Jane wishes to sue Susan for intentionally breaching a security perimeter; Hospital Care for negligent hiring and training oversight of Susan and of its computer systems; Infosec for negligent design of its product; General Hospital and its suppliers for their failure to detect this security breach and report it; and World On-Line and its employee for their actions. Hospital Care files suit against Infosec, claiming it merely leased the software and is not responsible for its poor quality. General Hospital files suit against Hospital Care, etc. . . .

The interconnected nature of the Internet multiplies, as well as blurs, liability in which victims are remote though connected parties, and nearly everyone else is a defendant. To prevail on a claim, however, there needs to be legal evidence of a break-in or breach, which may typically be found through an audit.

Breaches of security may be a civil or criminal offense, or both. (Please refer to chapters on substantive law, as well as to Chapter 12 on Internet crime.)

Computer security becomes further complicated because it is a global problem. Purely state or federal solutions are inadequate to deal with a problem that has no geographic borders, so an international strategy is best suited for Internet and information security. Such efforts are underway. For example, the Clinton administration issued "A Framework for Global Electronic Commerce" in 1997 to protect the Global Information Infrastructure (GII). Among other items, it addresses privacy and security, and the United States pledged to work closely with international governmental organizations to coordinate strategies. One such agency, the Organization for Economic Commerce and Development (OECD), issued a "Cryptography Policy: The Guidelines and the Issues." Interestingly, it focuses more on the goals of facilitating global commerce and ensuring the safety of data than on perceived safety and law enforcement concerns.

> **http://**
> See
> **www.ecommerce.gov/framework.htm** and
> **http://oecd.org/dsti/sti/it/secur/prod/GD97-204.htm**

Summary

Internet and information security will become a top priority of businesses as well as governments over the next few years. The concerns of security will always remain the same; however, the means of assuring it will constantly change and evolve. The tensions between cryptography, privacy, security, and law enforcement will be the subject of much public and congressional debate. Constitutional protections for encryption will be debated in courtrooms. The government clearly has a role in this process—it has the ability to regulate the marketplace of security technologies. It also has the fundamental responsibility to protect both privacy and security. The scope of legal responsibility for security and breaches will evolve through case law. The stakes are extremely high in these issues; businesses and governments have a keen interest in their outcome.

Manager's Checklist

- Businesses should engage the assistance of information security experts when any new business application is adopted.
- Businesses should conduct internal audits and additionally hire an outside auditor to monitor all electronic transactions.
- In conjunction with security experts, businesses should evaluate how to provide the best security for electronic transactions while maintaining efficient, private, and usable systems.
- Businesses must proceed with extreme caution in the use and sale of cryptographic programs, as their use and export remains highly regulated by the U.S. government.
- With regard to cryptographic programs, there are constitutional rights against government regulation implicated.

Additional Readings

- *Information Security.* This is the official publication of the International Computer Security Association. www.infosecuritymag.com/

- The U.S. Government's Center for Information Technology (a department in the National Institutes of Health) provides an excellent site providing information and links to other computer security sites. www.alw.nih.gov/security/security-www.html

- Penfold, R.R.C. *Computer Security: Businesses at Risk* (Robert Hale Ltd., 1999).

12

Internet and Computer Crime

"Who's stealing your information? In today's enterprise, the answer is everyone."
—Cover story, Industrial Espionage, April 1999, Dr. Dorothy E. Denning,
www. infosecuritymag.com

Introduction

The migration of government and business applications to computers has caused a corresponding shift from the commission of crimes, traditionally focused on physical assets, to the commission of crimes in cyberspace. Cybercrime has only recently begun to receive the attention that this massive problem warrants. The shift of crime to intangibles has a staggering impact on society, both socially and economically. This chapter material is best considered as a continuation of the Chapter 11. This chapter details the crimes made possible by breaching information and computer security. It describes the current legal environment of Internet and network computer crime.

The Nature of Computer Crime

Consider this scenario: Morris, a computer science graduate student, created a computer program to demonstrate the inadequacies of Internet security by exploiting security defects. He released a *worm* designed to spread, but at the same time draw little attention to itself. He discovered, though, that it replicated and infected machines at a much faster rate than anticipated. Many computers crashed as a result. He sent an e-mail message instructing programmers how to kill the worm and prevent reinfection, but this message could not get through because the network was too clogged. This negatively affected 6,200 computers at universities, military sites, and medical research facilities. The costs of repair exceeded $98 million. The student was found guilty and sentenced.

Moreover, all of this occurred in 1988, many computer generations ago, at a time when there were comparatively few computers and users. The damages are exponentially increased in this new millennium in which there are many more users and network applications that bring with them a high potential for a greater variety of crime.

Consider another set of scenarios, all hypothetical:

- One person meets with another for the express purpose of selling her a fake investment. The investor likes the plan, turns over her money, and the salesperson runs off with the proceeds.
- One person makes hundreds of telephone calls to sell that same investment. Some people like it and turn over their money; and the salesperson runs off with the proceeds.
- One person places an advertisement in a financial publication to sell shares of this same investment. Thousands of people read this ad; many of them invest; and the salesperson runs off with the proceeds.
- One person, with a laptop and a modem, logs onto the Internet and does a mass mailing of the investment deal to millions of people—a far greater number than could ever be efficiently reached by postal mailing. Millions read this; thousands of them invest; and the salesperson runs off with the proceeds.

The lessons here have not been lost on criminals, nor on law enforcement efforts. The means of committing crimes are now cheap and ubiquitous—a computer with an internet connection is all that is needed. Moreover, the number of potential victims is, in theory, limited by only one factor—the number of people connected to the Internet. It is clearly more efficient to conduct crime in cyberspace than in the physical world.

Computer crimes are made possible by the combination of computers with telecommunications abilities. The power to send data over communications equipment has transformed our society completely. This capacity to send data, however, does not operate in a perfect world. An analogy might be that ever since the first lock was invented, there have been criminals trying to pick the locks. And so it is in the information age. Even as data is being sent, criminals may be trying to steal or manipulate it; use it as ransom; spy on, or copy it. Even as early as 1998, the FBI considered that cybercrime was becoming epidemic.

In fact, the FBI thinks that these computer criminals, who are anonymous in a virtual world, will be the next significant wave of crime perpetrators. It is helpful to add some numbers to the discussion as a way of explaining the depth and breadth of the problem facing both governments and businesses. For example, half of Visa International, Inc.'s transactions from online sales were disputed, or full-fledged frauds. In 1999, federal agents investigated a credit-card billing scam—one man alone engineered $45 million of charges on hundreds of thousands of fraudulent transactions. More than 25 percent of all Fortune 500 corporations have been victimized by computer crime (see Figure 12.1).

> **http://**
> For articles dealing with cybercrime issues, see
> **http://emergency.com/techpage.htm**
> Visit the National Infrastructure Protection Center at
> **www.fbi.gov/nipc/welcome.htm**

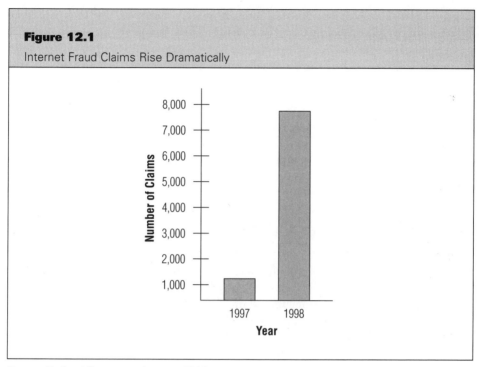

Figure 12.1

Internet Fraud Claims Rise Dramatically

Source: National Consumers League, 1998.

Most cybercrime goes unpunished. A survey by the Electronic Privacy Information Center on high-tech crimes found that 419 cases of alleged computer fraud were referred to federal prosecutors in 1998, but only 83 were prosecuted and the others were dismissed for lack of evidence. In that year, 47 people were actually convicted of federal computer crimes, 20 were sent to prison, and 10 were found not guilty. The average sentence for such crimes is four to eighteen months.

In addition to commerce crime, viruses are causing nearly incalculable damage. The Computer Emergency Response Team [CERT] at Carnegie Mellon's Software Engineering Institute rates Internet security breaches on a scale of 1 (the lowest) to 10. Historically, there was just one "Level 9" event per year. (The Melissa Virus was a level 9 alert—it was the fastest-growing virus in history, forcing the shutdown of servers around the world.) This is no longer the case; there are many such events per year now.

Such scenarios show no signs of abating, either. Businesses and governments have become dependent on the Internet, which as we mentioned in Chapter 11 could be characterized as one big party line. Systems and software traditionally have been developed with an emphasis on end-users' needs and their interest in ease of use. These have been the selling points, rather than the strength, of the products' security. The emphasis has never been on security features of systems or software. Consequently, there has not been a lot of discussion, or awareness, of risks, threats, contingency plans, and so on. And as more novices connect to the Internet, there becomes an overall declining expertise of users. There is an ever greater vulnerability, and comprehensive solutions do not yet exist.

> **http://**
> Visit CERT at
> **www.cert.org**

To more thoroughly understand the nature of computer crime and the current legal environment, this chapter is divided into sections, beginning with the definition of computer crimes and then the classification of such crimes. This will include discussion of relevant laws as well as cases on this subject.

What Is a Computer Crime?

Computer crime has been broadly defined as any illegal act that involves a computer, its systems, or its applications. It is any intentional act associated in any way with computers where a victim suffered or could have suffered a loss, and a perpetrator made or could have made a gain. The United States Department of Justice provides another definition, stating that computer crime is any illegal act for which knowledge of computer technology is essential for either its perpetration, investigation, or prosecution.

Computer crime, although perhaps not susceptible to a neat precise definition, is currently taken to include any crimes where knowledge of a computer is essential to commit the crime. This lack of precision in definitions is mainly due to the swift emergence of computers with telecommunications abilities, specifically with the appearance of the Internet. Prior to the Internet and computer networks, the number and variety of computer crimes were extremely limited. Such crimes usually consisted of illegal acts such as computer trespass and data manipulation or destruction. In any event, prior to the introduction of the Internet, crimes were defined and classified in terms of their relationship to physical objects. Most importantly, the ability to damage or trespass or steal computers or data was determined by physical constraints. Criminals could damage or take away only what was on that computer.

The Internet has changed much of this, of course. Computer crimes may just be high-tech variations of conventional crimes and consist of traditional crimes committed with the help of computers, such as the distribution of pornography. Other crimes are solely the product of the phenomenon of the Internet. Examples of this include the interception and re-routing of millions of Web users from their intended path to the domain name registration service InterNIC—to his own Web site, AlterNIC. Another example is the manip-

> **http://**
> Some general Web sites on Internet crime include
> **http://cyber.findlaw.com/criminal** and
> **http://cybercrimes.net**

ulation of a telephone switch by contestants to ensure that their call would be the winning telephone call. *United States v. Petersen*, 98 F.3d 502 (9th Cir. 1996).

It was not possible to commit this latter class of crimes

http://

Visit the Department of Justice at
www.usdoj.gov
A good site with computer crime links is found at
http://jaring.nmhu.edu/security.htm

prior to the Internet, and so the criminal laws are continually monitored and updated to address these novel criminal offenses.

This shift away from the tangible corporeal environment to the information economy made possible by the Internet and telecommunications capabilities is an enormous challenge for business, government and law enforcement. The physical constraints (e.g., traditionally a criminal could only steal that amount that he or she could carry away) do not exist in the commission of cybercrime. The lack of boundaries and physical constraints, combined with the speed in which these transactions take place, have changed many of the traditional paradigms of criminal law.

Defining what is a computer crime becomes further complicated by the fact that such illegal acts are subject to different laws—those at the state level, the federal level, and any applicable foreign countries. In fact, multiple prosecutions are possible for various offenses arising out of the same illegal act.

Common to the enforcement and prosecution for all crimes covered by federal and state criminal statutes are two required elements. First, it must be proven that there was a *criminal act*. Second, it must be shown that there was a *criminal intent*. Both elements must exist and be proven "beyond a reasonable doubt." It is helpful to keep these two elements in mind as you read through the cases. The second paradigm— criminal intent—is under fire in the realm of Internet prosecutions. For example, there have been a number of instances in the past five years where there are clearly criminal acts, such as illegally breaking into proprietary computers. The catch, though, is that the criminal intent element is not clear. In many instances, hackers gain entry just "for the fun of it." The Internet presents new law enforcement challenges such as these, and the law has not caught up to the realities of Internet criminal activity.

The next section attempts to help readers understand how Internet and computer crimes are classified. Additionally, recent cases are mentioned to give students a sense of the Internet crime that exists in our networked environment.

The Role of Computers in Crime: Crimes and Perpetrators

The advent of networked computers has created unprecedented opportunities for the anonymous perpetration of crimes. In fact, law enforcement experts perceive that the two most difficult problems they encounter are (1) establishing jurisdiction over alleged perpetrators; and (2) establishing the identities of the alleged perpetrators. This section addresses the latter issue, as the jurisdictional issue is discussed in Chapter 2.

This section first discusses how computers are used in crime. This is followed by a discussion of the sorts of crimes that are actually being committed with computers. Finally, there is a discussion of how it is that criminals are so easily able to mask their identities.

How Computers Are Used in the Commission of Crimes

Computers as the Target of Crime.   In this respect, the computer itself is the subject of the crime. The perpetrator uses the computer to obtain information or to interfere or damage operating systems or programs. Perpetrators access operations and systems through a *trap door* that exists for the bona fide reason of correcting faulty situations. As discussed in Chapter 11, any entry point is potentially exploitable for criminal purposes. For example, perpetrators may illegally take on the role of a systems manager (identity fraud) and access virtually everything in the system or network. Possible criminal offenses emanating from this activity include sabotage of any records such as hospital, government or business; theft of lists, intellectual property, intelligence reports; vandalism of Web sites; and even the introduction of computer viruses.

Computers as a Tool in the Commission of a Crime.   Computers can be used to facilitate crimes. The processes of the computer allow this to happen, and the result is usually a high-tech variation of a traditional criminal offense. By introducing new programming instructions, or manipulating computers' legitimate functions for illegal purposes, perpetrators exploit computers for the commission of crimes. This category includes the transmission of child or other pornography; fraudulent use of ATM or wire transfers; fraud in any e-commerce transaction; fraudulent electronic billing scams; and even murder (in one case, the suspect allegedly alerted medication information in the hospital's computer).

Computers as Incidental to a Crime.   The use of a computer is not absolutely necessary to the commission of this class of crimes. In fact, this class of crimes pre-dated computers. These are traditional crimes, such as money laundering, bookmaking, and drug-dealing. Essentially, computers are used in these crimes for recordkeeping purposes. These are still considered computer crimes, because perpetrators are thereby ren-

http://

See
www.usdoj.gov/criminal/cybercrime/crimes.html

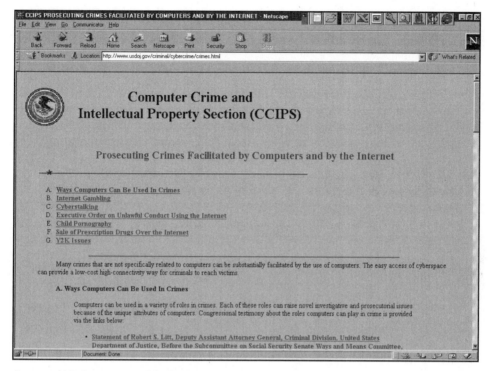

Courtesy U.S. Department of Justice.

dered more efficient by their use of computers, and so the frequency and magnitude of crime rise accordingly.

What Crimes Are Being Committed in Today's Networked Environment

While many of these crimes might sound familiar to you, the fact that they are being committed by or with a computer has highly significant ramifications, because computers inevitably produce high levels of accuracy and efficiency for whatever uses they are put to. And it is extremely difficult to identify alleged perpetrators and prosecute computer crimes. Although the previous discussion focused on classifying cybercrime by how computers were used, this section classifies cybercrime by its effect. The cybercrimes discussed herein are those most frequently occurring and have been classified here according to who, or what, is harmed by the illegal acts. We briefly examine the way the crimes are typically committed. Of course, in many instances there is an overlap among crimes and criminal charges. And in these descriptions, actual cases are mentioned. Since the vast majority of cases are resolved prior to trial, many of the reports of these cases are available only as news stories rather than in the form of court decisions. Three categories were created as an aid in understanding the material. You will find, however, that the categories overlap in that, for example, fraud may be perpetrated on persons or governments.

Crimes Against Persons or Businesses.

- **Pornography.** Pornography that involves children, or that is obscene, is a crime. This could involve the transmission or sale of such images. Also, law enforcement officials have found that pedophiles are turning to Internet chat rooms to pursue victims. See http://usdoj.gov/criminal/cybercrime/dagceos/html.
- **Harassment.** This would include communications of taunts, profanity, or demands. See www.kids-o-rama.com/items/qlitem6336.htm. In one case, an employee sent as many as fifty unwanted e-mails a day to a supervisor for the purpose of harassing him. This individual was charged with telecommunications harassment. See www.usdoj.gov/criminal/cybercrime/ngo_pr.htm.
- **Stalking.** In two similar recent cases, the stalkers assumed the women's identities in cyberspace and through their newsgroup messages, posted ads inviting strangers to the women's home. The messages included extremely detailed information about the women's schedules, telephone and address information, and even their social plans. See www.usdoj.gov/ag/cyberstalkingreport.htm.
- **Murder and death threats.** Threats of death via e-mail have been sent to President Clinton, as well as to the perpetrators' teachers, classmates, co-workers, and so on. There are reports of murder suspects who say that the availability of Internet pornography led them to kill. See www.kids-o-rama.com/quicklinks/ql990208.htm.
- **Fraud.** This includes fraud in the use of credit cards; e-commerce; auctions; and various scams such as Ponzi schemes. These are usually found through the offer of spurious business opportunities; or sales of Internet/computer-related goods or services. In one case, an online auctioneer took money for computers he never delivered. In another fraud case, the SEC froze the assets of a company that made false claims to investors. The National Fraud Information Center started the Internet Fraud Watch, found at www.fraud.org. See also www.scambusters.org.
- **Gambling.** Interstate gambling using the Internet is illegal unless (1) it is legal in all states involved and (2) adults only are participating. For the most part, however, it is difficult to verify such information, so it is rather easy to conduct an illegal gambling operation with impunity. In one recent case, the owners and operators of sports-betting companies based in the Caribbean were charged with the crime of conspiracy to transmit bets on sporting events via the Internet and telephone. See www.usdoj.gov/criminal/cybercrime/nypr.htm.
- **Hate crimes.** This is typically the communication of threatening hate-filled messages attacking people simply based on their traits of race, color, sex, religion, ethnicity, or sexual orientation. In one recent case, a college student pleaded guilty to sending derogatory e-mails to a number of people who had Hispanic last names. See www.usatoday.com/life/cyber/tech/ctf496.htm.

- **Spamming.** For marketers of unsolicited ads, the Internet offers incredible efficiencies. For recipients of these ads, though, they represent an unwelcome, but more importantly for our purposes, a controllable event. States such as Virginia (where AOL is headquartered) are increasingly taking the initiative and outlawing *spam,* as there is no federal law on this issue. More states will no doubt join the effort to outlaw this type of bulk unsolicited advertisement material. See www.infowar.com/law/99/law_022699b_j.shtml.

- **Sale of Controlled Items.** Prescriptive and non-prescriptive drugs, firearms, explosives, and so on have wide-ranging health and safety effects, and they may not be legal in every U.S. jurisdiction. In one recent case, an individual was charged with selling, without a prescription, the prescription drug Viagra over the Internet. This area of law is very unsettled at this time. There is some thought as to using the mail and wire fraud statutes for prosecuting such cases. It is also unclear whether these activities should be classified as civil or criminal. See www.usdoj.gov/criminal/cybercrime.

Crimes Against Property—Physical or Intangible.

- **Commercial espionage.** It is reported that 80 percent of illegal hacking into corporate computers originates from the inside. This is also considered the most costly source of cybercrime. Whether profits or "work rage" is the motive, companies are increasingly aware of the internal information security vulnerabilities. See www.businesswire.com.

- **Commercial extortion.** These are cases in which extortion, or blackmail demands, are made in return for something of value. The information economy is very susceptible to this crime, as vast amounts of valuable assets may be efficiently captured. In one recent case, a still unknown intruder gained access to all of the databases of Internet retailer CD Universe, and then demanded a $100,000 payment. After CD Universe refused this demand, the intruder started posting some of the credit-card files on the Internet. The extortionist is believed to be in Eastern Europe, beyond the reach of U.S. law enforcement officials. See www.nytimes.com.

- **Hacking.** Hacking into Web sites, also called *owning* them, is currently of epidemic proportions. Although security experts learn system vulnerabilities from hackers that post details of security holes they've uncovered (a practice known as *full disclosure*), there are still cost associated with these break-ins. With regard to whether the hacking is to be charged as a crime, the intent of the perpetrator is the critical issue to decide. See www.ncis.co.uk/newpage1.htm. There are sites devoted to advising Web users about hacking. See www.hackersclub.com.

- **Cracking.** This is a name given to malicious (i.e., criminal) hacking. The most infamous of these would be Kevin Mitnick, who was arrested and held without bail based on a $300 million estimate of the damage that he caused. He copied proprietary software from computers owned by cellular telephone manufacturers. He subsequently pleaded guilty and was sentenced to 46 months of detention. See www.wired.com/news/news/politics/story/18566.html.

http://

One trade group concerned with counterfeit software is the Software and Information Industries Association. Visit them at **www.siia.net**

- **Malware.** This is a type of harmful software that includes virus writing, transmission of worms, logic/time bombs, Trojan horses, and sniffer programs. **Virus-writing** programs have the ability to attach themselves to other programs and then cause damages, or hide and replicate (known as a **Trojan horse**). **Worms** infiltrate computers and destroy data but cannot replicate. **Logic bombs** remain essentially undetected until they "detonate." They might also used in conjunction with extortion schemes. See www.infosecuritymag.com (September and October 1999 editions).
- **Data manipulation.** This crime (also called *diddling*) involves the changing or erasing of existing information. This could consist of manipulation of work, or grades, or research, for example. See www.scit.wlv.ac.uk/~c9727436/page4.html.
- **Software and hardware piracy.** This crime involves the copying of protected (by copyright or trademark or service mark) programs. Such piracy is actionable even if no profits are made or contemplated. Hardware and peripherals can also be copied. In one recent case, government agents seized $56 million worth of counterfeit Microsoft software and product components. This is a particularly common problem for artists as well as designers and manufacturers of software programs, musical recordings, and DVD movies. See www.infosec.com/crypto/99/crypto_110599a_j.shtml.
- **Money laundering.** This crime has been made easier to commit based on new technologies such as Internet banking and smart cards. Banks are not in a position to monitor and report online transactions. For example, they are able to track fund flows and their origin and destination points, but they are unable to identify controlling parties. In one recent investigation, authorities are attributing erratic swings in European stock markets to an Internet money laundering scheme. See www.infowar.com and click on "Law & Legal Issues."
- **Trespass, vandalism, theft, data storms, denial of service.** These are committed by first breaking into computers. Vandalism and theft of data occur after the trespass. Data storms and denials of service are caused by the transmission of so many e-mails that the recipients' computers crash. In one recent case, four college students pleaded guilty to sending out more than 50 million spam e-mails in one day; the impact was felt most by the nearly clogged systems of e-mail providers AOL, AT&T, and Mindspring Communications.
- **Hardware weapons.** Although not as well-known as software and hardware piracy, these are equally malicious. They include: high-energy radio frequency (HERF) that may damage or destroy any system's electronic equipment; RF jamming or interception equipment; and electromagnetic pulse (EMP) weapons, which have a wider range but are less accurate than HERF guns. One Web site for example— www.spyking.com/herf.html—discusses these weapons in detail. The government's response to this threat is at www.house.gov/jec/hearings/cyber/vatis.htm.

Crimes Against Government or Government Functions.   In many cases the perpe-trators have underlying philosophical or political motivations for their actions.

- **Threats or disruptions to health and safety, shut-down of essential services, and extortion.** The potentially paralyzing effect of disruptions and shut-downs now has the attention of legislators. For example, the Legion of Doom hacking group gained the ability to alter, disrupt, or shut down local telephone service. In one incident, 40 percent of a patient's records were destroyed at a major medical center. In another incident, a teenager gained access to an airport's traffic control system and left it without telephone or data service. Hackers routinely vandalize government Web sites and deface or otherwise destroy them. See www.csis.org/pubs/pubsecur.html#cyber.
- **Espionage.** This involves the act of spying on government entities or officials. In one case, a hacker in Germany was being paid by the KGB to learn U.S. military secrets. In another case, it is alleged that a Los Alamos nuclear scientist used his computer to pass massive amounts of top-secret weapons data to China. See http://abcnews.go.com.
- **Terrorism.** This could by physical terrorism and attacks on the Internet, in the form of undermining or disabling entire countries, without ever firing a shot. In one such attack, a foreign hacker worked with two young U.S. collaborators to mount cyberattacks against Pentagon systems, a nuclear weapons research lab, and other targets. This was the subject of legislative hearings. Cyberterrorism could also involve nonphysical acts such as extortion and blackmail. See www.usdoj.gov/criminal/cybercrime/critinfr.htm.

It becomes clear, then how many criminal uses the Internet makes possible. The next section discusses in greater detail the legal framework for prosecuting cybercrime, with citation to presidential executive orders, as well as federal, state, and international laws.

Federal Laws Addressing Internet Crime

The federal laws are applicable in every U.S. jurisdiction, and may be implicated in prosecutions in which there is some nexus to the United States. Therefore, they are discussed in greater length than are the state or developing international laws. It is important to bear in mind, however, that even as this chapter discusses the legal response to criminal acts, there is also a body of law that addresses civil infractions for less serious acts. For example, a copyright infringement may be minor and so only civil fines are imposed. For more serious offenses, the criminal laws are invoked. Generally, civil actions are brought by either private individual parties or by a government agency, typically the Federal Trade Commission.

The criminal activity taking place with the aid of the Internet has not gone unno-ticed in Washington. There are a number of legislative proposals before Congress to regulate the Internet in many forms. Laws are constantly being amended to patch

http://
Visit the FTC at
www.ftc.gov
The FTC has authority over civil infractions of the law.

together protections for Internet users as well as victims. An example of an amendment to current law is the introduction of the NET Act to the copyright laws. In addition to the efforts by Congress, the executive branch has begun to address Internet crime. In 1999, then-President Clinton established by Executive Order 13133 the Working Group on Unlawful Conduct on the Internet. It brings together the varied agencies and law enforcement groups in an effort to assess the scope and applicability of current law to unlawful activity on the Internet. Finally, the judicial branch of government has spoken on the issue of Internet crime—in its interpretation of laws and disposition of criminal cases.

The next section mentions the laws that regulate criminal activities on the Internet—these laws are the basis for the prosecutions discussed earlier in the chapter. The salient features of each law are set forth, and in a few instances cases are presented to flesh out how it is that Congress's laws are applied to actual criminal prosecutions.

Computer Fraud and Abuse Act of 1986 (CFAA), 18 U.S.C. § 1030

http://
See
www.usdoj.gov/criminal/cybercrime/exeord.htm

This statute, first enacted in 1984, was the first legislation to treat computer-related crimes as distinct federal offenses. This made it unnecessary to individually amend nearly every federal law to include offenses committed with the use of computers. (This law was originally known as the Counterfeit Access Device and Computer Fraud and Abuse Act.) Most recently, in 1996, the **Computer Fraud and Abuse Act** was amended by the National Information Infrastructure Protection Act. Significantly, this Act protects all computers joined to the Internet, and all computer activities, whether they occur locally or nationally.

The CFAA has three goals, to protect the:

1. *confidentiality* of the data/communications.
2. *integrity* of the data/communications.
3. *availability* of the data/communications.

Pursuant to these goals, the CFAA prohibits using computers to commit any of the following seven crimes:

- To knowingly commit espionage by accessing information without authorization or exceeding authorized access (1030(a)(1))
- To access other information without authorization, or exceeding authorized access (1030(a)(2))
- To access any nonpublic government computer (1030(a)(3))
- To access any computer with an intent to commit fraud (1030(a)(4))
- To knowingly or intentionally damage a computer (1030(a)(5))
- To knowingly traffic in passwords (1030(a)(6))
- To threaten to cause damage to a computer with the intent to extort money or other things of value (1030(a)(7))

The CFAA is the one *general purpose* statute for prosecuting cybercrimes, and invariably it will be part of a prosecution. It may also be used in conjunction with any of the other statutes mentioned herein, as well as other statutes that are not directed at crimes made possible by the Internet. These include statutes covering embezzlement, malicious mischief, theft, false statements, accessory after the fact, and conspiracy to commit a crime. These statutes are found in Title 18 of the United States Code, and defendants may be charged with each or any of these additional crimes.

Fraud and Related Activity in Connection with Computers, 18 U.S.C. § 1030 (abridged version of a section of the CFAA)

- (a) Whoever -
  - ◊ (1) having knowingly accessed a computer without authorization or exceeding authorized access, and by means of such conduct having obtained information that has been determined by the United States Government pursuant to an Executive order or statute to require protection against unauthorized disclosure for reasons of national defense or foreign relations, or any restricted data, as defined in paragraph y. of section 11 of the Atomic Energy Act of 1954, with reason to believe that such information so obtained could be used to the injury of the United States, or to the advantage of any foreign nation willfully communicates, delivers, transmits, or causes to be communicated, delivered, or transmitted, or attempts to communicate, deliver, transmit or cause to be communicated, delivered, or transmitted the same to any person not entitled to receive it, or willfully retains the same and fails to deliver it to the officer or employee of the United States entitled to receive it;
- (2) intentionally accesses a computer without authorization or exceeds authorized access, and thereby obtains -
  - ◊ (A) information contained in a financial record of a financial institution, or of a card issuer as defined in section *1602*(n) of title 15, or contained in a file of a consumer reporting agency on a consumer, as such terms are defined in the Fair Credit Reporting Act (15 U.S.C. 1681 et seq.);

◊ (B) information from any department or agency of the United States, or

◊ (C) information from any protected computer if the conduct involved an interstate or foreign communication;

- (3) intentionally, without authorization to access any nonpublic computer of a department or agency of the United States, accesses such a computer of that department or agency that is exclusively for the use of the Government of the United States and such conduct affects that use by or for the Government of the United States;

- (4) knowingly and with intent to defraud, accesses a protected computer without authorization, or exceeds authorized access, and by means of such conduct furthers the intended fraud and obtains anything of value, unless the object of the fraud and the thing obtained consists only of the use of the computer and the value of such use is not more than $5,000 in any 1-year period;

- (5)

◊ (A) knowingly causes the transmission of a program, information, code, or command, and as a result of such conduct, intentionally causes damage without authorization, to a protected computer;

◊ (B) intentionally accesses a protected computer without authorization, and as a result of such conduct, recklessly causes damage; or

◊ (C) intentionally accesses a protected computer without authorization, and as a result of such conduct, causes damage;

- (6) knowingly and with intent to defraud traffics (as defined in section *1029*) in any password or similar information through which a computer may be accessed without authorization, if -

◊ (A) such trafficking affects interstate or foreign commerce; *or*

◊ (B) such computer is used by or for the government of the United States;

- (7) with intent to extort from any person, firm, association, educational institution, financial institution, government entity, or other legal entity, and money or other thing of value, transmits in interstate or foreign commerce any communication containing any threat to cause damage to a protected computer; shall be punished as provided in subsection (c) of this section.

A court recently interpreted provisions of the CFAA in *United States v. Czubinski*, 106 F.3d 1069 (1st Cir. 1997). Czubinski was employed by IRS. He routinely accessed information using his valid password, and was able to retrieve income tax information regarding virtually any taxpayer in the United States. IRS rules are clear that employees are not permitted to access data outside of the course of their official duties. Czubinski carried out numerous unauthorized searches of IRS files and accessed tax information on people, including: various political candidates; a woman he dated, and so on. He did not disclose or sell this information. The court reversed his conviction under the CFAA. It found that although the first element of the statute was met when he exceeded authorized access to a federal computer, the second element was not. He did not access such information in the furtherance of fraudulent scheme. Merely viewing unauthorized information cannot be deemed the same as obtaining something of value for the purposes of this statute.

The Computer Fraud and Abuse Act (CFAA) is enforced by a variety of government agencies. The main agency responsible for enforcement of

> ## http://
> See
> **http://www.cybercrime.gov/cccases.html.**
> Other agencies assisting with the prosecution of domestic crimes include: the FBI,
> **http://www.fbi.gov**
> and the U.S Secret Service, Electronic Crimes Branch,
> **http://www.treas.gov/usss.**

federal laws in this respect is the U.S. Department of Justice. They have an excellent web site, and a table of recent cases indexing which sections of the CFAA were violated.

Other Federal Laws

Computer and related crimes may be charged under a number of other statutes besides the CFAA. And while there may additionally be civil remedies for computer violations, this next section discusses the other major federal criminal statutes that complement federal enforcement of cybercrimes.

The first three cited statutes herein attempt to eliminate the transmission of child pornography, protect underage users from online pornography, and protect children from sexual predators on the Internet. Referring to the discussion in Chapter 9 on Obscenity, and the First Amendment discussion in Chapter 11, speech issues are implicated in these statutes. In fact, the principal challenge to prosecutions under these three statutes is that they violate defendants' First Amendment rights against government regulation of their free speech. The government's prior restraint on citizens' speech is presumptively invalid, and will withstand challenge only if the regulations are clearly and narrowly written, and not vague and overbroad. The state of the first two statutes is very unclear at this time, as different courts have reached different conclusions as to the constitutional validity of these laws. In these instances, this usually presages review by the U.S. Supreme Court, to clarify whether the law as written by Congress is constitutional.

Child Pornography Prevention Act, 18 U.S.C. §§ 2252A–2256 (1999).   The Internet is particularly susceptible to certain activities, and such is the case with trafficking in child pornography. Under the **Child Pornography Prevention Act,** Congress has prohibited the knowing sale, possession, or distribution of child pornography, whether of actual children or of computer-generated images of children, by any means, including by computer. This statute has two elements: (1) the requirement that it be done "knowingly"; and (2) that it be moved in interstate or foreign commerce by any means.

A violation of this Act may result in fines or imprisonment for up to fifteen years. Affirmative defenses include proof that the defendant possessed less than three images of child pornography; or took reasonable steps to destroy such images upon receipt of them. In 1998 this statute was amended by the Protection of Children From Sexual Predators Act (found at 18 U.S.C. section 2252(a)(4)(B)). It includes enhanced penalties for perpetrators using the computer to mislead the victims about their identities and committing sexual abuse. It also mandates that Internet service providers (ISPs) report communications of child pornography to authorities.

It is important to understand the current legal environment in which this case was decided. One court, in the opinion *United States v. Acheson,* 195 F.3d 645 (11th Cir. 1999) upheld the constitutionality of the CPPA. However, in a 2-1 decision, the Ninth Circuit in *Free Speech Coalition v. Reno,* 1999 U.S. App. Lexis 32704 (Dec. 17, 1999) disagreed with this line of decisions, and held that the First Amendment prohibits Congress from enacting a statute that makes criminal the generation of images of fictitious children engaged in imaginary but explicit sexual conduct.

Just hours after this *Reno* decision, federal law enforcement officials within the Ninth Circuit were compelled to release Patrick Naughton, a former Internet executive, who was convicted a few days earlier under this statute for possession of child pornography. The Naughton case presents extremely interesting questions. The charges stem from a government sting operation in which a federal agent posed as a thirteen-year-old in conversations with Naughton in an Internet chat room. Naughton traveled across state lines to meet with this supposed thirteen-year-old girl, where he was arrested. He was convicted of the possession of child pornography, but the jury deadlocked, along gender lines, on two other counts—soliciting sex with a minor over the Internet, and interstate travel to have sex with a minor. The novel aspect of this case is the argument by Naughton's lawyers to the jury that he lacked the requisite mental state (mens rea) to commit a crime. Instead, it is asserted on Naughton's behalf that he was merely participating in an Internet sex fantasy, and engaged in fantasy role playing. Naughton testified that there are probably millions of people carrying out sexual fantasies on the Internet, and they have no intention of actually following through on them. Referring back to how the jury split along gender lines, women believed the prosecution's version, while men believed Naughton's assertion that he was merely playing out a fantasy. This defense, if it prevails, will be a serious setback to law enforcement for such cases in which the FBI claims a 99 percent success rate. See www.infowar.com/law/99/.

Child Online Protection Act of 1998 (COPA) 47 U.S.C. section 231 (1999).   Like the other pornography laws, the **Child Online Protection Act (COPA)** restricts access to speech. Congress passed this act making it a crime to knowingly publish on the Internet any communication for commercial purposes of any material that is harmful to minors. Violations may result in imprisonment for up to six months, and fines of up to $50,000. This limited measure was passed after Congress's previous effort, the Communications Decency Act, failed. COPA has been successfully challenged in trial court, however, in *ACLU v. Reno*, 31 F. Supp.2d 473 (E.D. Pa. 1999), and it is doubtful whether this law will withstand appellate review.

It is instructive to bring up one further point about this act that shows how the development of the Internet is ahead of lawmakers and policy makers. In its definitions subsection, COPA defines the phrase "material that is harmful to minors" as any communication that is obscene, or that "the average person, applying contemporary community standards, would find, taking the material as a whole . . . is designed to appeal to, or is designed to pander to, the prurient interest. . . ." In years past, it was very easy and simple to determine a community standard. Now, however, we live in a global village in a sense—so should we use the community standards of, say, Iran—or China—or the United States? Is there a community standard of Internet users? These are interesting and ultimately difficult questions.

Federal Obscenity Laws, 18 U.S.C. §§ 371, 1462, 1465 (1999).   The **Federal Obscenity Laws** outlaw the interstate or foreign transportation for commercial purposes of any lewd, lascivious, book, or any other matter of indecent or immoral character. Violations may result in up to five years of imprisonment and/or fines. In a recent case, defendants were convicted under this statute in connection with their operation of an electronic bulletin board that posted pictures from sexually explicit magazines. (*United States v. Thomas*, 74 F.3d 701 (6th Cir. 1996)).

Intellectual Property Crimes

Patent, trademark, copyright, and trade secret laws have been amended over time to criminalize acts that previously were just civil infractions. (Please refer to Chapters 3 and 4 discussing trademarks and copyrights.) As our economy relies to an ever greater degree on digital information, the intellectual property practice area of law has exploded because the stakes have risen. In fact, in Internet start-ups, their intellectual property is their greatest asset.

Copyright Infringement Act, 17 U.S.C. § 501–512 (1999); 18 U.S.C. § 2319 (1999).   Such violations have been a particular concern for music and literary artists, and especially for software developers who have had their works pirated instead of resulting in legitimate sales. Under the **Copyright Infrigement Act** generally, any person who willfully reproduces or distributes, including by electronic means, copyrighted works shall be punished. Courts have the power to order forfeiture and destruction of such materials. Moreover, violations may result in

http://

See
www.usdoj.gov/criminal/cybercrime/levy2rls.htm

> http://
> See
> www.usdoj.gov/criminal/cybercrime/desktop.htm

imprisonment of up to ten years and fines in amounts relating to the retail value of the infringed-upon work. The pirated copies are subject to forfeiture and destruction.

The Copyright Infringement Act exempts, for the most part, Internet service providers from liability for infringements that are routed through their system or network. The copyright laws were amended in 1997, as a direct response to the phenomenon of the Internet. Then-President Clinton signed into law the No Electronic Theft (NET) Act. This law amends 17 U.S.C. section 506(a). Prior to the NET Act, the copyright laws were violated only when there was a commercial advantage, or private financial gain by the perpetrator. The NET Act closed this loophole that protected individuals who claimed they took no financial gain from uploading copyrighted materials for others to download at no charge. Sentences under this act are up to three years imprisonment and a fine of up to $250,000.

The first prosecution under the NET Act occurred in 1999. A 22-year-old University of Oregon senior, Jeffrey Gerard Levy admitted in a plea agreement that he illegally posted copyrighted products for the public to download, including software programs, musical recordings, entertainment software, and digitally recorded movies. He was sentenced to two years' probation with conditions.

Counterfeiting cases typically involve both criminal trademark and copyright infringements. Violations of federal trademark laws may result in up to ten years imprisonment and up to $2 million in fines per infringement. In one criminal trademark infringement case, a firm distributed computer memory boards in counterfeit IBM boxes. The company purchased memory chips and modules that were not manufactured by IBM and packaged them in counterfeit IBM boxes. Because the products appeared to be IBMs, the defendants were able to resell them at a premium price. In a plea agreement, the company agreed to a $2.2 million fine, and will repay IBM $1.1 million.

Economic Espionage Act (EEA), 18 U.S.C. §§ 1831–1839 (1999). The **EEA** criminalizes the theft or misappropriation of trade secrets by computer or other means. The first section specifically addresses the theft of trade secrets/economic espionage with the intent to benefit foreign governments. The second section addresses the theft of trade secrets/economic espionage more generally. This act further broadens the federalization of crimes that were historically the province of individual states. The EEA was enacted in 1996, following FBI Director Louis Freeh's request to Congress for more authority to combat economic espionage against U.S. companies. Congress, in its report, recognized that information may be as valuable as a factory is to a business. See www.ipcenter.com/0330tsecret.html. Offenses may result in up to fifteen years of imprisonment and/or fines up to $10 million, as well as forfeiture of the property or proceeds thereof. An impediment to the effectiveness of the EEA, however, is the possible reluctance of companies to cooperate with the government because of the risk of being forced to disclose sensitive data in discovery.

There have been few prosecutions under the EEA even though it has extremely important implications in the information age. In recognizing that a law of this breadth might be misapplied to criminalize the law of trade secrets, Congress insisted that for the first five years (1996–2001) any prosecutions must first be authorized at the highest level of the Department of Justice.

A recent case shows how difficult it is to reasonably prosecute economic crimes involving trade secrets. In *Unted States v. Hsu*, 155 F.3d 189 (3d Cir. 1998), the government became involved in uncovering an illegal operation. The defendants were interested in buying the processes, methods, and formulas for Taxol, a highly valuable anti-cancer drug created by Bristol-Myers. Defendants requested information on such a purchase from Hartmann, an undercover FBI agent who was posing as a technological information broker. During a meeting between the Defendants and Hartmann, FBI agents came in and arrested Defendants, charging them under the EEA with economic espionage, including theft and conspiracy to steal trade secrets. The case turned on whether there was an actual theft of trade secrets — or merely an attempted theft of trade secrets. Reasoning that it would be counterproductive for Bristol-Myers to reveal its trade secrets merely to prove that there were, in fact secrets to steal, the court did not agree to Defendants' request for Bristol-Myers to produce confidential company documents.

> ### http://
> There are a couple of excellent web sites to visit for further information on the EEA. They include the Department of Justice's page for Computer Crime and Intellectual Property, **http://www.usdoj.gov/criminal/cybercrime/eea.html** and Loyola's site devoted to Economic Intelligence issues, which may be found at **http://www.loyola.edu/dept/politics/ecintel.html.**

Electronic Communications Privacy Act (ECPA), 18 U.S.C. §§ 2521, 2701–2711 (1999). This act, discussed more in depth in the Chapter 8 material on privacy, essentially broadens privacy protections for computer users by expanding its definitions of communications as those affecting interstate and foreign commerce. This act otherwise updates existing laws prohibiting the interception of wire or electronic communications. The ECPA criminalizes this interception when the communication is obtained, altered, or rendered inaccessible to authorized users. Violations of the ECPA may result in imprisonment for up to two years and/or a fine. The ECPA also includes the Federal Wiretap Act, found at section 2511. This section criminalizes the intentional interception or use of any intercepted wire, oral or electronic communication. (Electronic communication is defined as any transfer of signals, images, data, etc. by does not include electronic storage of such communications.) There is no provision for a term of imprison-

Table 12.1

Top Ten Sources of Computer Fraud

1.	Auctions
2.	General merchandise sales
3.	Computer equipment and software
4.	Internet services
5.	Work-at-home offers
6.	Business opportunities
7.	Marketing schemes
8.	Credit-card offers
9.	Advance fee loans
10.	Employment offers

ment in this statute. Fines may be levied up to $5,000. This section is increasingly used in cybercrime cases as communications are migrating from wired to cellular equipment. In a recent case, a couple pleaded guilty to intentionally intercepting the radio portion of a cellular telephone call. They intercepted a conference call among then-Speaker of the U.S. House of Representatives Newt Gingrich and others. They were sentenced to a fine of $500 each. See www.usdoj.gov/criminal/cybercrime/177crm.htm.

Electronic Funds Transfer Act (EFTA), 15 U.S.C sec. 1693n (1999). Recognizing the benefits of electronic systems to transfer funds, this statute establishes the rights and responsibilities of the parties. The **Electronic Funds Transfer Act (EFTA)** criminalizes the giving of false or inaccurate or insufficient information. It also outlaws any transactions involving counterfeit, stolen, fictitious, or other debit instruments. Debit instruments include cards, codes, and so on that are used to initiate an EFT. Penalties include up to ten years imprisonment or up to $10,000 in fines.

Mail and Wire Fraud Statutes 18 U.S.C. § 1341 (1999) and 18 U.S.C. § 1343, 1346 (1999). **Mail and Wire Fraud Statutes** have wide-ranging application to computer and Internet crime. Under these acts, it is illegal to use the mails, interstate, or foreign communications to devise or further fraudulent schemes for obtaining money or property. These statutes, while not primarily regarded as cybercrime statutes, have application to many of the prosecutions for cybercrime. These statutes outlaw any computer-aided or enabled theft. Penalties include fines up to $1 million, and/or imprisonment for up to thirty years.

Wire fraud charges were brought against the defendant in the *United States v. Czubinski* case. The court found, however, that neither of the two elements of wire fraud: (1) the knowing and willing participation in a scheme to defraud and, (2) the use of interstate wire communications in furtherance of the scheme, were established beyond a reasonable doubt, since there was no underlying scheme to defraud (see Table 12.1).

National Stolen Property Act 18 U.S.C. 2314 (1999).   The National Stolen Property Act (NSPA) prohibits the transport or transmission in interstate or foreign commerce any goods over $5,000 in value, knowing that these goods have been stolen or taken by fraud. Note that this act applies to goods that are tangible (e.g., money, wares, merchandise, securities, etc.) and does not apply to items in an intangible form such as a software programs, which are considered intangible property (please refer back to the statutes regulating intellectual property). Sentences for violations of the NSPA may include fines and/or imprisonment for up to ten years.

State Laws Addressing Internet Crime

As a complement to federal law enforcement efforts, there are state as well as international laws, and so there may be multiple prosecutions arising out of the same occurrence. (International law enforcement is discussed at the end of this chapter and in Chapter 13 discussing global issues.)

Each state at this time has adopted, in some fashion, legislation that addresses computer and Internet crime. As a hypothetical example, should XXX Entertainment with offices in California wish to notify John Smith of Florida and others by way of an unsolicited e-mail of its newest child pornography materials for sale, it will send the e-mail through Smith's Internet Service Provider AOL. AOLs offices are located in Virginia. Perhaps not coincidentally, the state legislature of Virginia passed a bill in 1999 amending its Computer Crimes Act to make it illegal to send unsolicited bulk electronic mail. Thus, in addition to possible federal prosecution under the Child Pornography Prevention Act, the state of Virginia may exercise personal jurisdiction over XXX Entertainment. (Please refer to Chapter 2 discussing jurisdictional issues in detail.) In another instance, the state attorney general for Massachusetts has responded to recent terrorist threats. He has proposed a law making terrorist threats a crime by any form of communication to schools, courthouses, or places of worship.

The law enforcement efforts of individual states should not be underestimated. State laws are a potent complement to federal and international crime enforcement strategies. The preamble to California's Computer Crime legislation, Penal Code Section 502 expresses the issue well. It reads as follows:

> It is the intent of the Legislature in enacting this section to expand the degree of protection afforded to individuals, businesses, and governmental agencies from tampering, interference, damage, and unauthorized access to lawfully created computer data and

computer systems. The Legislature finds and declares that the proliferation of computer technology has resulted in a concomitant proliferation of computer crime and other forms of unauthorized access to computers, computer systems, and computer data. The Legislature further finds and declares that protection of the integrity of all types and forms of lawfully created computers, computer systems, and computer data is vital to the protection of the privacy of individuals as well as to the well-being of financial institutions, business concerns, governmental agencies, and others within this state that lawfully utilize those computers, computer systems, and data.

The U.S. attorney general has proposed an interstate compact to ensure enforcement of out-of-state subpoenas and warrants stemming from interstate investigations. This existence of both state and federal laws possibly covering the same criminal allegations raises issues of federalism. The co-existence of state and federal laws is a matter of constitutional concern. Under the supremacy clause and the doctrine of preemption, courts must conduct an exacting analysis of both the relevant federal and state laws to determine the applicable law. Thus, while it is helpful for law enforcement officers to have in their arsenal an array of federal and state laws, the laws are in some instances duplicative. This may result in wasting valuable court resources on preemption issues.

This situation arose in *Rosciszewski v. Arete Associates*, 1 F.3d 225 (4th Cir. 1993). The state of Virginia's Computer Crimes Act criminalized the use of a computer network without authority with the intent of obtaining property by false pretense. At issue was the reproduction of copyrighted computers programs. The federal trial court had to first decide which law applied: the state act or the federal Copyright Infringement Act—or whether both could co-exist—under the supremacy clause. In this case, the court held that the federal Copyright Infringement Act applied and therefore preempted the Virginia statute. Thus, with regard to this criminal allegation, only the federal government could prosecute it.

Corporate Forensics and the Impact of the Internet: Gathering and Preserving Evidence

Technology and crime go hand-in-hand at this time. Commentators believe that many of these crimes have to do with the perceived anonymity of the Internet. It has been said that the ability to act anonymously in large groups brings out the worst in human characteristics.

The Internet has brought this issue to the forefront of cybercrime management. For example, an employee of an Oregon company was recently accused of stealing equipment from his office. He immediately denied the charges and

---

Cyberethics

Is there an ethical justification for allowing government investigators to be able to access information from private companies' computers? What if the private company was engaged in some contract work for the government?

started covering his tracks, first by deleting incriminating e-mails and filed documents. When he learned that his computer was to be subpoenaed, he installed "scrubbing" software designed to wipe clean the computer's hard drive. See http:-//oregonlive.com/technw/99/05/tn051003.html.

When this perceived anonymity is coupled with tools such as encryption and scrubbing software to further ensure this identity cover, it becomes impossibly difficult to prosecute crime. The identity of the perpetrator may not be known, and the evidence may be destroyed.

Historically in the United States, a great deal of value has been placed on an individual's privacy from government intrusion (embodied in the Fourth Amendment), and more generally, on an individual's right to be left alone (embodied in such judicial decisions recognizing the right to marry without regard to race, and the right to control procreation, etc.). This has also been legislated to an extent. See the Privacy Protection, 42 U.S.C. section 2000aa (1999). The interest in being anonymous and the software that makes this feasible is an outgrowth of these values. In direct tension to and contrast with this, is society's demand for accountability—for individuals to be responsible for their actions—and for perpetrators to be made known and accountable for their conduct. The effect of the Internet on these basic societal values cannot be overstated.

Anonymous communications have great value in some instances, such as for corporate whistleblowers. There are many Web sites offering tools for anonymous communications (see, for example, www.anonymizer.com.) However, such a mode of communication incidentally benefits criminals who are able to avoid detection and arrest through the use of encryption, and other programs. It is possible to reconcile anonymity and accountability in a compromise environment of confidentiality. Users could remain anonymous, but there would be a third party—an escrow-key holder—who could, under agreed-upon circumstances (such as under a court order) reveal the user's identity. Law enforcement officials would naturally wish to be third-party escrow-key holders. The holders of such keys, though are the holders of valuable assets, which tempts abuse. The government's role in the investigation and prosecution of cybercrime is most basically to prove that a crime was committed, and that the person charged is guilty of that crime. There is a question of whether law enforcement efforts are equal to the challenges of cybercrime.

In order to prove the crime, evidence must be submitted to the court. The process of gathering this evidence by officials is known as a *search and seizure,* and is governed by the Fourth Amendment. Under the Fourth Amendment, the government in general is prohibited from conducting a search or seizure unless it is done pursuant to a search warrant. These warrants must be 'narrowly drawn' stating with particularity the items to be searched or seized. Should these rules not be observed, evidence from the defective search may not be inadmissible in court. Furthermore, in such a case the government may be liable for civil damages under the Privacy Protection Act.

For example, in one recent case, the government's search of an attorney's home office was challenged as overbroad, as not sufficiently particular. The warrant authorized seizure of "all computers . . . storage devices . . . software systems." It did not limit the search to the home office, or list the specific crimes for which the

http://
See
www.usdoj.gov/criminal/cybercrime/searching.html

equipment was sought. The court agreed with the defendant that his Fourth Amendment rights had been violated, but ultimately ruled that the evidence did not have to be excluded because the search team acted in good faith. (*United States v. Hunter*, 13 F. Supp. 2d 574 (D. Vt. 1998)).

The Department of Justice has issued guidelines for searching and seizing computers, and in particular there is discussion of ways in which searching computers are different from searching desks, filing cabinets, or automobiles. These guidelines also address seizing hardware as well as information, how to handle networks and bulletin board services, how to draft warrants, how to preserve evidence, and so on.

This detection and prosecution of cybercrime is aided in great part by recent developments in information security. In fact, within the professions of information security, law enforcement, and even accounting, there have emerged *cybersleuths,* computer forensics experts who specialize in electronic discovery through examination of deleted files, disks, Zip disks, backup tapes, and hard drives. This also involves reconstructing communications and data that are on systems or transmitted through ISPs.

The forensic examination process starts with making a duplicate image of the storage media under scrutiny, and then conducting a complete search for specific words, files, or documents. In fact, the Chicago office of Deloitte & Touche LLP has an entire department devoted to finding hackers, virus writers, and cyberspies. In one recent case, Deloitte & Touche was asked by a company to examine the financial records of another company it had recently purchased. Its concerns were confirmed after D&T revived all computer data that the acquired company thought it had erased. The deal was subsequently restructured.

In cases where a crime is suspected, the information is handed over to law enforcement authorities. When this information is transferred from person to person before being offered to the court as evidence, these transfers must comply with the legal doctrine of *chain-of-custody,* in which it must be shown that the evidence presented is exactly that which was taken from the crime scene. This becomes complicated by the fact that such evidence is easily altered and if this is so, the evidence may not be admissible. The gathering and preservation of computer evidence is indeed fraught with difficulties.

http://
Some companies specialize in computer evidence consulting, such as
www.secure-data.com

http://
See
http://cyber.findlaw.com/criminal/searchseiz.html

A final word about the application of Constitutional rights to Internet crime: The First and Fourth Amendments have been discussed in their relation to government action and criminal prosecutions. The Fifth Amendment is also a powerful safeguard against possible arbitrary government authority. In a criminal prosecution, the Fifth Amendment provides citizens with a number of important rights, such as the right to due process (the laws must be constitutional and procedures must be fair) and the right against self-incrimination (defendants cannot be compelled to testify against themselves). These were discussed in more detail in Chapter 11. The government must bring forward its case, proving beyond a reasonable doubt that the defendant was the one who committed the crime, and that each element of the crime was met. It must do so in a way that comports with the criminal statutes and constitutional jurisprudence.

International Aspects of Internet Crime

The Internet has made it almost more desirable to engage in international rather than domestic illegal activities. Simply put, in this era there is a greater probability of not being prosecuted for an international cybercrime. Boundaries are of no consequence to Internet crime. Previously, if a crime was committed and if the police thought that the alleged perpetrator was fleeing the country with the goods, law enforcement details were dispatched to all exit points in the country. Road, airport and train station details checking passports are quaint anachronisms in the information age. There are no borders, passports, or checkpoints on the Internet—it is one global universe online, and consequently domestic laws become inadequate to deal with the complexity of international Internet crime. Then-U.S. attorney general Janet Reno recognized these legal challenges in the following excerpt from a speech on this subject.

> [U]ntil recently, computer crimes has not received the emphasis that other international crimes have engendered. Even now, not all affected nations recognize the threat it poses to public safety or the need for international cooperation to effectively respond to the problem. Consequently, many countries have weak laws, or no laws, against computer hacking, a major obstacle to solving and to prosecuting computer crimes. [L]aw enforcement faces new procedural challenges, many of which are impossible to address without international consensus and cooperation. Consider, if you will, merely locating a hacker whose transmission passes from his computer to a local service provider, then through a telephone network, then crosses an ocean via satellite, and then passes through a university computer on its way to a corporate victim. To make matters worse, this hacker could be in his car, using wireless communications. How do we go about finding this individual? How do we collect the evidence and preserve it in a way that will be useful at trial? www.usdoj.gov/criminal/cyber-crime/agfranc.htm.

Clearly, intergovernmental cooperation is essential to address the unique law enforcement problems that the Internet presents. Countries

http://

See
www.coe.fr/index/asp and
www.oecd.org/dsti/sti/it/secur/prod/e_secur.htm

must each develop harmonious laws to combat cybercrime, for crime will migrate to the country with the weakest enforcement efforts. Second, treaties addressing the maintenance and sharing of information are critically important. Mutual assistance is necessary for law enforcement to have any effect. Third, there must be extradition treaties between nations that provide for the expeditious transfer of suspects and evidence. To an extent, progress has been made on these issues. The United States has pledged cooperation with the leaders of the seven other leading industrialized nations: England, France, Germany, Italy, Russia, Japan, Canada, altogether known as the Group of Eight (G-8). The Council of Europe has introduced recommendations relating to problems of criminal procedural law connected with information technology. Moreover, the Organization for Economic Cooperation and Development (OECD) has issued guidelines for the security of information systems. The OECD recommends that its member countries coordinate an international collaboration to develop compatible practices and procedures as well as to provide prompt mutual investigative assistance. Finally, international nongovernmental organizations (NGOs) might aid in law enforcement efforts. For example, the International Federation of the Phonographic Industry is coordinating a worldwide effort to remove illegal MP3 music files from the Internet.

International Internet and computer crime has a growth potential like no other type of crime. It will flourish until agreements between countries are enacted regarding extradition, evidence gathering, and preservation. This pressure for international cooperation among countries in an effort to combat cybercrime may even yield other unexpected dividends.

Summary

Internet and network computer crime are the unfortunate results of crime migrating to the places where the money is being made as well as used. Computers are used in different ways in the commission of crimes, ranging from fraud, to espionage, to terrorism. Federal, state, and international laws are constantly created or amended in an effort to keep up with the new and creative crimes being committed. Constitutional protections are in place for the accused, however, and include the First, Fourth, and Fifth Amendments. Individuals, businesses, and governments must be vigilant in their efforts to secure information, computers and networks against criminal activities.

Manager's Checklist

- Internal and external audits should be conducted on a regular basis.
- Office policies should be developed addressing all forms of computer use, including explanations and examples of what constitutes misuse.

- It is important to keep abreast of changes in the law—this is a particularly changeable time for Internet and computer legislation.
- Businesses must be prepared to work with law enforcement agents as most of the cybercrime is currently internal and external economic espionage.
- Businesses must take appropriate precautions regarding the protection of proprietary or trade secret information, and for the personnel responsible for its management.

Additional Readings

- Center for Strategic and International Studies, CYBERCRIME . . . CYBERTERRORISM . . . CYBERWARFARE; AVERTING AN ELECTRONIC WATERLOO (1998).

- Goldstone, David and Betty-Ellen Shave. "International Dimensions of Crimes in Cyberspace," 22 *Fordham International Law Journal* 1924 (1999).

- Charney, Scott and Kent Alexander. "Computer Crime," 45 *Emory Law Journal* 931 (1996).

PART 5

International Issues in Cyberspace

13

Global Issues

"There's no reason for governments to 'tarif-fy' e-commerce."
Richard Fisher, Deputy U.S. Trade Representative at WTO trade negotiations,
Seattle, Washington, November, 1999

Introduction

Both national and international laws govern cyberspace. Similarly, both national governmental agencies and international intergovernmental organizations enact, enforce, and adjudicate the laws governing cyberspace.

In this chapter, we will examine the organizations that regulate cyberspace internationally, the jurisdiction of national governments over electronic commerce and communications, and the national laws and international treaties that define and regulate international cyber-commerce and communications.

International Organizations

There are two kinds of international organizations: (1) public or intergovernmental organizations (IGOs) and (2) private or nongovernmental organizations (NGOs).[1] This section briefly highlights the principal IGOs and NGOs concerned with international electronic commerce.

Intergovernmental Organizations

An international **intergovernmental organization (IGO)** is a permanent organization set up by two or more member states to carry out activities of common interest to their members. Their activities may be wide ranging or narrowly focused. IGOs that engage in a wide range of activities (known as *general organizations*), include the

[1]*United Nations Charter*, Article 71.

United Nations, the European Union, the Council of Europe, and the Organization for Economic Cooperation and Development. Those that focus on particular activities (known as *specialized organizations*) include the World Trade Organization; the International Telecommunications Union; the United Nations Educational, Scientific and Cultural Organization; the International Labor Organization, the World Intellectual Property Organization; and the Wassenaar Arrangement.

United Nations.   The United Nations is the most important of international intergovernmental organizations. In addition to being a general organization, it is also a *universal organization* in that its membership is open to all the nations of the world, and nearly all are members. Its *Charter,* a multilateral treaty that came into force in 1945, defines the goals of the UN as the maintenance of peace and security in the world, the promotion of economic and social cooperation, and the protection of human rights. Underlying these goals is the idea that the relationships of nations should be based on the rule of law. In particular, the UN *Charter* requires member nations to treat each other as sovereign equals, to resolve their disputes peacefully and without resort to armed force, and to fulfill their international obligations in good faith.

The main organs of the United Nations include the General Assembly, the Security Council, the Secretariat, the International Court of Justice, and the Economic and Social Council. In addition, there are a great number of commissions, committees, working groups, and other subsidiary organs. Among these are the UN Commission on International Trade Law and the UN Conference on Trade and Development.

The United Nations Commission on International Trade Law (UNCITRAL) is charged with promoting the harmonization of international trade law. In the past, it was responsible for drafting the UN *Convention on Contracts for the International Sale of Goods,* the UNCITAL *Model Law on International Credit Transfers,* and the UNCITRAL *Model Law on Electronic Commerce,* among other international agreements. These are discussed in greater detail later in the chapter. Currently, UNCITRAL is drafting a set of uniform rules for the use of electronic signatures.

The United Nations Conference on Trade and Development (UNCTAD) is the UN General Assembly's main agency responsible for trade and development. In 1998, the General Assembly gave UNCTAD a special grant to pursue and develop electronic commerce initiatives. UNCTAD subsequently established an Electronic Commerce Section that began conducting workshops on helping developing nations expand into the area of electronic commerce.

European Union.   The European Union is a regional intergovernmental organization originally established in 1951 by six nations as a common market for the trade and exchange of coal and steel. Over the years it has expanded into a fifteen-nation[2]

[2]The current member nations are Austria, Belgium, Denmark, Finland, France, Germany, Greece, Ireland, Italy, Luxembourg, the Netherlands, Portugal, Spain, Sweden, and the United Kingdom.

common market for goods and services, and it is currently evolving into a monetary union with a common currency and banking system. The EU's principal organs are the European Commission, the European Council, the European Parliament, and the European Court of Justice.

The EU has taken an active role in consumer protection in the field of electronic commerce. In March 1997, the EU Council adopted a *Directive on the Protection of Consumers in Respect of Distance Contracts.*[3] This requires EU member states to implement legislation no later than March 2001 to protect consumers who purchase items by means of electronic commerce or other means of telecommunication. Specifically, the member state legislation must require sellers to give consumers accurate information in durable form about who they are, what they are offering to sell, the price of their goods or services, and the period of time during which their offer remains open. Consumers, additionally, will have a seven-day "cooling off" period during which they have the right to withdraw from any transaction without penalty.

Currently, the European Commission is proposing the adoption of a *Directive on Certain Legal Aspects of Electronic Commerce in the Internal Market* that would extend to electronic commerce most of the consumer protection rules that apply to traditional commercial transactions.[4] Sellers would be required to fully disclose information about themselves and provide consumers with a means for authenticating the seller's identity. Truth in advertising rules would apply to electronic commerce, and consumers would be allowed to filter unwanted e-mail. The directive would also define the kinds of contracts that may be made online and the point in time when they are concluded. Additionally, the directive would limit the liability on Internet service providers who act as intermediaries between sellers and consumers.

Another Commission proposal, to adopt a *Council Regulation on Jurisdiction and the Recognition and Enforcement of Judgments in Civil and Commercial Matters,*[5] would allow consumers to sue sellers who supply goods and services in the member state where the consumer is domiciled, regardless of any contrary agreement made by the consumer and seller.

http://

Links to the Websites of the international organizations and to the treaties described in this chapter can be found in the online International Law Dictionary and Directory posted at **august1.com/pubs/dict/**

Council of Europe. The Council of Europe is a regional IGO that works to strengthen democracy, human rights, and the rule of law within its forty-one member

---

[3]Directive 97/7/EC of the European Parliament and of the Council. *Official Journal* L 144 (May 4, 1997), pp. 19–28, posted at http://europa.eu.int/comm/dg24/policy/developments/dist_sell/dist01_en.html.

[4]Commission proposal COM (1999) 427 final, posted at www.ispo.cec.be/ecommerce/legal/documents/com1999-427/com427en.pdf.

[5]Commission Proposal COM (1999) 348 final, posted at http://europa.eu.int/eur-lex/en/com/reg/en_register_1920.html.

countries. Although it cooperates in many areas with the European Union, it is independent of, and should not be confused with, the EU. The Council's main organs are a Committee of Ministers, a Parliamentary Assembly, and a Congress of Local and Regional Authorities of Europe.

http://

The Council of Europe home page is at
www.coe.fr

http://

The text of the Convention is posted at
www.coe.fr./eng/legaltxt/108e.htm
The text of the Convention is posted at
www.coe.fr./eng/legaltxt/130e.htm

The main goal of the Council of Europe is the harmonization of its member countries' policies through the adoption of common practices and standards. It does this, in part, through the drafting and adopting of multilateral conventions in every area except defense. The Council had sponsored more than 160 conventions, including the *Convention for the Protection of Individuals with regard to Automatic Processing of Personal Data* and the Convention on Insider Trading.

Organization for Economic Cooperation and Development. One of the IGOs that most actively addresses issues of international electronic commerce is the Organization for Economic Cooperation and Development (OECD). The OECD is a consultative organization that seeks to help its member countries promote economic growth, employment, and standards of living through the coordination of their laws, regulations, and policies. Its twenty-nine member countries are the most economically developed, so it is sometimes referred to as the "rich countries club."[6]

Since 1997, the OECD has held annual conferences on electronic commerce aimed at developing a set of *Guidelines on Consumer Protection,* as well as ground rules for taxation of electronic sales.[7] Both the guidelines and the taxation ground rules should be completed and published sometime in the year 2000.

http://

www.oecd.org

[6]The 29 members are: Australia, Austria, Belgium, Canada, Czech Republic, Denmark, Finland, France, Germany, Greece, Hungary, Iceland, Ireland, Italy, Japan, Korea, Luxembourg, Mexico, the Netherlands, New Zealand, Norway, Poland, Portugal, Spain, Sweden, Switzerland, Turkey, United Kingdom, and United States.

[7]*See* the Report, OECD Forum on Electronic Commerce, October 1999, posted at www.oecd.org/dsti/sti/it/ec/act/paris_ec/pdf/forum_report.pdf.

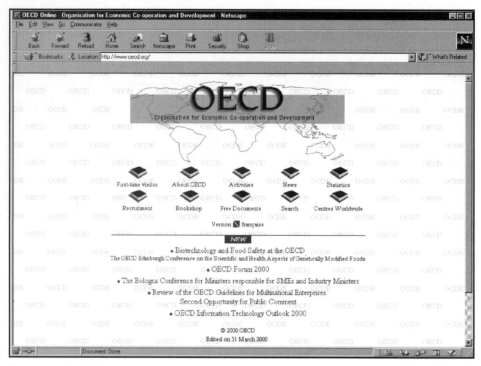

© 2000 Organisation for Economic Co-operation and Development.

World Trade Organization. The World Trade Organization (WTO) is a specialized intergovernmental organization responsible for administering various multilateral agreements, including the *General Agreement on Tariffs and Trade* (GATT), the *General Agreement on Trade in Services* (GATS), and the *Agreement on Trade-Related Aspects of Intellectual Property Rights* (TRIPS Agreement). Additionally, it functions as a forum for multilateral trade negotiations aimed at reducing tariffs and other restrictions on the free movement of goods and services, it reviews and reports on the trade policies and practices of its member states, and it serves as a tribunal for resolving trade-related disputes.

Established in 1995, the WTO currently has 135 member states. Its main organs are the Ministerial Conference, which meets at least every other year, and the General Council, which administers the WTO when the Ministerial Conference is not in session and also functions as the WTO's Dispute Resolution Body.

In May of 1998, the WTO Ministerial Conference issued a *Declaration on Global Electronic Commerce*[8] calling for the establishment of a comprehensive work program to examine all of the trade-related issues relating to global electronic commerce. In carrying out this program, the WTO has begun to establish policies relating to electronic commerce. It has concluded that goods bought and paid for

[8]WT/MIN(98)/DEC/2 posted at www.wto.org/wto/ecom/e_mindec1.htm.

over the Internet are subject to the existing WTO rules on trade in goods, including the GATT, if they are physically delivered to the purchaser. However, the WTO has yet to decide on the rules that apply when goods are delivered as digitalized information. It has also decided that services and many other products delivered over the Internet are subject to the GATS and the market-access commitments that members have made in complying with the GATS. The WTO, however, still needs to clarify how far particular activities are covered by those market-access commitments.[9]

International Telecommunications Union.   The International Telecommunications Union (ITU) is a specialized intergovernmental organization with state members and private organizational members. Representatives from member states make up its Plenipotentiary Conference and its Council. Representatives from both member states and organizations participate in three interest groupings, known as sectors: the Radiocommunications Sector, the Telecommunications Standardization Sector, and the Telecommunications Development Sector.

The ITU adopts international regulations and treaties governing all terrestrial and outer space uses of the electromagnetic frequency spectrum. Within the parameters set by these regulations and treaties, countries adopt their own national regulations. The ITU also develops and promulgates standards to facilitate the interconnection of telecommunication systems around the globe. For example, the ITU in 1998 issued the common technical standards for V.90, 56 kilobits-per-second PCM modem.[10] The ITU also promotes the expansion of telecommunication services and infrastructure in the developing world by recommending medium-term strategies and policies for national governments.

The ITU's e-commerce agenda is focused on developing a global information infrastructure. In doing so, it is developing standards for multimedia communications, system security, online privacy, digital certificates and certification, and the technical framework for electronic commerce. One of its highest current priorities is to assign the electromagnetic spectrum for a generation of satellite and cellular technologies that will provide wireless access to electronic commerce services around the globe.

http://
www.itu.int

United Nations Educational, Scientific and Cultural Organization.   The United Nations Educational, Scientific and Cultural Organization (UNESCO) works to

[9]*See* "Electronic Commerce and the WTO" posted at www.wto.org/wto/ecom/e_intro.htm. While the WTO's e-commerce policies are being developed, the WTO has imposed a temporary moratorium on the imposition of customs tariffs on e-commerce. *See* the Geneva Ministreal "Declaration on Global Electronic Commerce" of May 1998 posted at www.wto.org/wto/ecom/e_mindec1.htm.

[10]*See* "From Competition to Cooperation: The Road to e-Commerce" posted at www.itu.int/press/PP98/PressRel-Features/Feature3.html.

http://
Visit UNESCO at www.unesco.org, and the *Observatory* at
www.unesco.org/webworld/observatory

establish peace, security, and the common welfare of the world by promoting collaboration among nations in education, science, culture, and communications to further respect for justice, the rule of law, and human rights and fundamental freedoms.

In 1995, UNESCO established a project to address the ethical, legal, and societal challenges of the new information society. Included in this project are (1) an ethics program that promotes the importance of universal access to information, (2) a series of meetings of experts to advise UNESCO on what needs to be done to establish an ethical and legal framework for cyberspace and promote multilingualism and cultural diversity in this new environment, and (3) an online magazine, the *Observatory*, to supply news of developments in cyberspace.

At the conclusion of a UNESCO-sponsored meeting of experts on cyberlaw held in 1998, the experts recommended that UNESCO promote, as a fundamental human right, the right to communicate, and as a corollary to that right, that everyone should be entitled to access and to participate in the information society. This recommendation is currently being reviewed UNESCO's the secretary general for submission to it's General Conference.

International Labor Organization.   The International Labor Organization (ILO) is a specialized intergovernmental organization, founded in 1919, that became affiliated with the United Nations in 1945. The ILO works to formulate policies and develop programs that promote basic human rights, improve working and living conditions, and enhance employment opportunities. Toward that end, the ILO has assumed the role of monitor and analyst of the impact of information technologies on employment, enterprise development, work organization, working time arrangements, working conditions, and industrial relations. It is currently developing policies covering teleworking and the protection of worker's personal data and basic rights.[11]

World Intellectual Property Organization.   The World Intellectual Property Organization (WIPO) is responsible for promoting the protection of intellectual property throughout the world. WIPO administers the most important multilateral treaties dealing with the legal and administrative aspects of intellectual property, including the *Berne Convention for the Protection of Literary and Artistic Works* and the *International Convention for the Protection of Industrial Property* (or Paris Convention).

---

[11]*See* "Concluding Summary and Recommendations," XV World Congress on Occupational Safety and Health, April 1999 at www.ilo.org/public/english/90travai/cis/xvwc/conclu.htm.

WIPO is involved in the development of new international treaties dealing with intellectual property. Recently drafted treaties are the *WIPO Copyright Treaty,* which extends copyright protection to computer software, assures protection for databases, and forbids any tampering with

> http://
> **www.ilo.org**

> http://
> **www.wipo.int**

electronic coding identifying digitized intellectual property, and the *WIPO Performances and Phonograms Treaty,*[12] which defines the legal rights of performers, recording companies, and broadcasters and prohibits the circumvention of technological measures, including encryption, that protect those rights.

WIPO also offers a simplified and cost-effective means of filing and obtaining international protection for patents, trademarks, and industrial designs, and it plans to offer this service over the Internet in the near future.[13] Additionally, WIPO offers dispute-resolution services for private parties involved in international intellectual property disputes, including disputes over the assignment of World Wide Web domain names.[14]

Wassenaar Arrangement.   The Wassenaar Arrangement on Export Controls for Conventional Arms and Dual-Use Technologies came into being in July 1996, replacing the old Cold War-era Coordinating Committee on Multilateral Export Controls.[15] The Wassenaar Arrangement's goals are to promote the full and open disclosure of national export controls, the exchange of information, and greater responsibility in the transfer of conventional arms and dual-use goods and technologies. Member states are required to maintain export controls on a list of agreed upon items. Among the items included on this list are computers, software, telecommu-

> http://
> **www.wassenaar.org**

---

[12]Posted at www.wipo.int/eng/diplconf/distrib/95dc.htm.

[13]*See* the WIPO Digital Agenda at http://ecommerce.wipo.int/agenda/index.html.

[14]*See* Final Report of the WIPO Internet Domain Name Process (April 30, 1999), posted at http://ecommerce.wipo.int/domains/process/eng/processhome.html.

[15]Its current members are Argentina, Australia, Austria, Belgium, Bulgaria, Canada, Czech Republic, Denmark, Finland, Greece, France, Germany, France, Germany, Hungary, Ireland, Italy, Japan, Luxembourg, the Netherlands, New Zealand, Norway, Poland, Portugal, Republic of Korea, Romania, Russia, Slovak Republic, Spain, Sweden, Switzerland, Turkey, Ukraine, the United Kingdom, and the United States.

nications devices, electronics, lasers, and sensors. The lists are posted on the Internet at www.wassenaar.org/docs/index1.html.

Nongovernmental Organizations

Nongovernmental organizations (NGOs) are nonprofit organizations whose members are individuals and domestic organizations that reside in two or more countries. NGOs that have taken an interest in developments in cyberspace and cyberlaw include the Alliance for Global Business, the Global Business Dialog on Electronic Commerce, the International Chamber of Commerce, the International Electrotechnical Commission, and the International Organization for Standardization.

Alliance for Global Business.   The Alliance for Global Business (AGB) is a coordinating organization for international trade associations, including the Global Information Infrastructure Commission (GIIC), the International Chamber of Commerce (ICC), the International Telecommunications Users Group (INTUG), and the World Information Technology and Services Alliance (WITSA). It functions as the business community's advocate in developing regulatory policies for information technology and electronic commerce. Its position is set out in its *Global Action Plan for Electronic Commerce.* This calls for minimal government regulation and emphasizes business self-regulation as the most effective way of building confidence in transactions over open networks. In particular, it opposes government restrictions on encryption, security, advertising, and marketing. The plan, however, does support government action in specific areas, such as intellectual property protection, taxation, and the removal of barriers to competition. It urges governments to adopt the UNCITRAL *Model Law on Electronic Commerce,* and it supports the drafting of an international digital signature treaty.[16]

Global Business Dialog on Electronic Commerce.   The Global Business Dialog on Electronic Commerce (GBDe) is a forum for Internet businesses and a coordinating agency for expressing their views on the regulation of electronic commerce. Like the AGB, it advocates a minimalist role for government and the promotion of a market-driven environment for the future development of the Internet

```
http://
www.giic.org/agb
```

```
http://
www.gbde.org
```

---

[16]The Global Action Plan is posted at www.giic.org/focus/ecommerce/agbecpaln.html.

and global electronic commerce. A 1999 position paper addressed to the World Trade Organization calls on the WTO to adopt a permanent moratorium on customs duties on electronic commerce, and it calls on WTO member states to promptly adopt and faithfully enforce the WTO's *Agreement on Trade-Related Aspects of Intellectual Property Rights.*[17]

International Chamber of Commerce.   The International Chamber of Commerce (ICC) is an NGO representing businesses engaged in international transactions. It promotes open international trade, an open investment system, and the market economy. It issues a wide range of voluntary rules applicable to international business, such as the rules defining international commercial trade terms (or *Incoterms*) and its rules governing letters of credit. The ICC's International Court of Arbitration is the most widely used arbitral body for resolving international commercial disputes.

The ICC has established a Commission on Telecommunications and Information Technologies. This Commission is responsible for drafting technical guidelines on information technology and formulating the ICC's policy on issues such as computer security, telecommunications standards, and competition. The Commission also functions as an advocate for these policies in meetings with IGOs involved in the development of electronic commerce regulations, including the International Telecommunications Union, the European Union, and the World Trade Organization.

Another program of the ICC is its Electronic Commerce Project. This project is aimed at creating trust in electronic trade transactions by developing uniform business codes. One such code, issued in November 1997, is the GUIDEC, which contains rules for the use of electronic signatures and other digital authentication techniques. Other codes currently being drafted are a code of electronic commerce trade terms (*e-terms*) analogous to the ICC's *Incoterms*, and a code of rules for the electronic trade and settlement of securities.

International Electrotechnical Commission.   The International Electrotechnical Commission (IEC) is an international NGO that prepares and publishes international standards for all electrotechnologies. Electrotechnologies include electronics, magnetics and electromagnetics, electroacoustics, telecommunication, and energy production and distribution (i.e., all of the

http://
www.iccwbo.org

http://
www.iec.ch

---

[17]*See* "The Perspective of the Global Business Dialogue on Electronic Commerce (GBDe) on the WTO and Its Relationship to E-Commerce" posted at www.gbde.org/gbde.html.

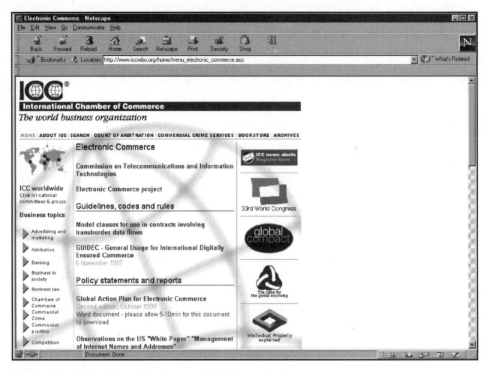

electronic equipment that makes technologies such as the Internet work). The IEC is also concerned with related aspects, including terminology and symbols, measurement and performance, dependability, design and development, safety, and the environment. Standards for other technologies are the responsibility of the International Organization for Standardization.

International Organization for Standardization. The International Organization for Standardization (ISO) is a worldwide federation of national standards bodies. Its mission is to promote the development of standardization in order to facilitate the international exchange of goods and services. It also promotes cooperation in the fields of intellectual, scientific, technological, and economic activity.

The ISO, in cooperation with the International Electrotechnical Commission, is responsible for developing many of the standards used in information technologies. For example, the ISO/IEC's Moving Picture Experts Group (MPEG) the digital recordings standards known as MPEG1, MPEG2, and so on.

http://
www.iso.ch

Jurisdiction

Jurisdiction, as we discussed in Chapter 2, defines the power of a government agency (national, state, provincial, and municipal) or international organization to act. Because jurisdiction defines powers, it also imposes limits on those powers. Within the territorial boundaries of a nation, national constitutions and laws define those limits. When government agencies seek to act beyond or across national boundaries, their jurisdiction is additionally defined and limited by rules of international law. That is, in order for a governmental agency to have the power to act internationally, both its national constitution *and* international law must allow it to do so. Similarly, when an international organization takes action, it must do so in accordance with its charter and with the rules of international law.

Jurisdiction of Governmental Agencies

The rules of international law that define the jurisdiction of governmental agencies are different with respect to criminal conduct and noncriminal (or civil) conduct.

Criminal Jurisdiction.   In order for a legislative assembly to adopt, an executive to enforce, or a court to adjudicate criminal sanctions internationally, there must be some *nexus,* or connection, between the agency or organization and the crime or criminal. Five such connections may be used to justify an exercise of international jurisdiction. Legal commentators refer to these connections as *principles*.

1. The **territoriality principle of jurisdiction** holds that the place where an offense is committed to determines jurisdiction.
2. The **nationality principle** looks to the nationality or national character of the person committing the offense to establish jurisdiction.
3. The **protective principle** provides for jurisdiction when a significant national or international interest is injured by the offender.
4. The **universality principle** allows for taking the offender into custody.
5. The **passive personality** holds that jurisdiction arises from the nationality or national character of the person injured by the offense.

For example, a person engaged in the unauthorized broadcasting of radio or television signals from a ship on the high seas may be arrested and tried by the state whose flag the ship is flying (this is a form of the territoriality principle); or, if the ship is not flying a flag, by any state (this being based on the universality principle); by any state whose radio communications are being affected (this is based on the protective principle); by any state where the transmission can be received (the passive personality principle); and by the state of which the person involved is a national (the nationality principle). See United Nations *on the Law of the Seas,* Articles 109 (3) and (4), and 110 (1982).

Not all of these principles are used in all cases. In fact, the territoriality principle is the jurisdictional nexus most commonly relied upon in legislation, and often it is the only such connection. For example, Britain's *Obscene Publications Act of 1959* only imposes criminal sanctions on offenders who publish obscene materials in the United Kingdom. A British defendant in the case of *Crown v. Waddon*[18] attempted to avoid liability under that act, accordingly, by posting pornographic materials on a server located in the United States. A British court, however, found that publication had occurred in the United Kingdom. It had, the court said, because the defendant transmitted the pornographic materials from his computer in the United Kingdom to the U.S. server, and those materials were downloaded from the U.S. server for viewing on a computer in the United Kingdom.

Civil Jurisdiction.   In order for a government agency to exercise jurisdiction over civil (noncriminal) matters, there must be a nexus between the persons or property involved and the territory (nation, state, province, municipality, and so on) where the agency is located—known as the *forum.* This is known as jurisdiction over persons (*in personam*) and jurisdiction over property (*in rem*) jurisdiction.

• *Jurisdiction over Persons.*   *In personam* **jurisdiction** is the power of a government agency to regulate matters involving natural and juridical persons. Natural persons are human beings. Juridical persons are legal entities created by national or international law and granted the privilege of carrying on many of the functions of natural persons, such as engaging in business, suing, and being sued. The included business firms, nonprofit organizations, international organizations, and governmental agencies.

The basis for *in personam* jurisdiction is consent, which may be actual or implied. Actual consent can be given in a **forum selection clause** in a contract, in which the parties designate the forum where disputes will be settled, and a **choice of law clause** in a contract, wherein the parties designate the forum whose law will govern their relationship. For example, Netscape Communications includes the following forum selection and choice of law provisions on its Web site:

> This web site (excluding linked sites) is controlled by Netscape from its offices within the state of California, United States of America. It can be accessed from all 50 states, as well as from other countries around the world. As each of these places has laws that may differ from those of California, by accessing this web site both you and Netscape agree that the statutes and laws of the state of California, without regard to the conflicts of laws principles thereof, will apply to all matters relating to use of this web site.

[18]BBC News, July 1, 1999, posted at http://news.bbc.co.uk/hi/english/sci/tech/newsid_382000/382152.stm.

You and Netscape also agree and hereby submit to the exclusive personal jurisdiction and venue of the Superior Court of Santa Clara County and the United States District Court for the Northern District of California with respect to such matters. Netscape makes no representation that materials on this web site are appropriate or available for use in other locations, and accessing them from territories where their contents are illegal is prohibited. Those who choose to access this site from other locations do so on their own initiative and are responsible for compliance with local laws.[19]

In addition to these clauses, actual consent can also be given by incorporating or otherwise registering to do business in a forum, and by bringing suit in a court. Consent can be implied from (1) having the nationality of the forum, (2) being domiciled in the forum, (3) being physically present in the forum, or (4) having minimum business contacts with the forum.

This last form of consent to *in personam* jurisdiction—having minimum business contacts with the forum—is generally only used in countries that have a common law tradition (that is, in countries that inherited their legal system from England). Most of the rest of the countries of the world follow a civil law tradition (one derived from legal system of ancient Rome). In civil law countries, generally, engaging in business in a forum without having a physical presence there, is not enough to establish *in personam* jurisdiction.

In common law countries, jurisdiction over a person based on minimum business contacts requires a showing that (1) the person purposefully availed itself of doing business in the forum and (2) the person reasonably could have anticipated that it would have to defend its actions there.

An example of a case that applied this minimum business contact criteria to an Internet dispute is *BrainTech, Inc. v. Kostiuk* (British Columbia Court of Appeal, BCCA 0169, 1999). In that case, BrainTech, a British Columbia company, alleged that Kostiuk, a British Columbia resident, published defamatory information about it on an Internet bulletin board maintained by a Texas company. BrainTech subsequently brought suit in Texas and the Texas court issued a judgment for damages in BrainTech's favor. BrainTech then sought to have a British Columbia court issue a judgment enforcing the Texas court's judgment. Because Kostiuk was a British Columbia resident and all his assets were there, the Texas judgment was of little effect. A trial court granted BrainTech its request and Kostiuk appealed, arguing that the Texas court lacked jurisdiction to hear any dispute between BrainTech and himself and therefore that its judgment was ineffective. The British Columbia Court of Appeal agreed. To assume *in personam* jurisdiction over a nonresident defendant, the court said, a defendant must have "minimum contacts" with the forum, the claim against the defendant must arise out of those contacts, and the overall exercise of jurisdiction must be reasonable. With respect to Kostiuk there was no "real and substantial connection" between Texas and the alleged wrongdoing. Kostiuk's

---

[19]Posted at http://home.netscape.com/legal_notices/laws.html.

only connection with Texas was the posting of the allegedly defamatory statement on the bulletin board maintained by the Texas company. He had no other contacts. Accordingly, the British Columbia Court of Appeal dismissed the trial court's judgment enforcing the Texas court's judgment.

Although countries that follow the civil law do not recognize *in personam* jurisdiction based on minimum business contacts, one mostly civil law territory, the European Union, recognizes a similar sort of adjudicative jurisdiction. This allows a court in one EU member state to assume *in personam* jurisdiction over consumer sales involving sellers from other member states. To establish this jurisdiction, the consumer would have to show that (1) the sale took place in the consumer's state of domicile; (2) the seller solicited the sale through advertising directed to the consumer or agree to accept payments in installments; (3) the seller is domiciled in, or has a branch, agency, or other establishment in another member state; and (4) the suit is brought in the consumer's state of domicile.[20] If the consumer can do this, a court in the consumer's state of domicile will have jurisdiction, even if the contract signed by the consumer has a forum selection clause giving a different state exclusive jurisdiction.

A recently proposed EU regulation would extend this consumer jurisdiction to Internet transactions. Instead of requiring proof that the seller has directed advertising to, or provided financing for, the consumer, the consumer would only have to show that the seller entered into sales transactions over the Internet in the consumer's state of domicile.[21]

Jurisdiction over Property.   *In rem* **jurisdiction** is the power to determine the ownership rights of all persons with respect to particular property located within the territory of the forum. For example, legislation may define certain property as being illegal to export (such as encryption software) or as contraband (such as CAD software used in developing missiles and nuclear weapons).[22] The ownership of real property (i.e., immovable property, such as land and buildings) is deter-

---

[20]Brussels Convention on Jurisdiction and the Enforcement of Judgments in Civil and Commercial Matters (1968), as amended, *Official Journal* C 027, pp. 0001-0027 (Jan. 26, 1998). The Convention is posted on the Internet at http://europa.eu.int/eur-lex/en/lif/dat/1998/en_498Y0126_01.html.

[21]Commission Proposal COM (1999) 348 final, posted at http://europa.eu.int/eur-lex/en/com/reg/en_register_1920.html. See Working Party on the Revision of the Brussels and Lugano Conventions, EU Document No. 7700/99 (April 30, 1999).

[22]To avoid infringing U.S. export controls, Netscape Communications includes of following provision on the Web site from its software can be downloaded.

> Software available on the Netscape Web site is subject to United States export controls. No software from this site may be downloaded or otherwise exported or re-exported (1) into (or to a national or resident of) Cuba, Iraq, Libya, Sudan, North Korea, Iran, Syria, or any other country to which the United States has embargoed goods; or (2) to anyone on the U.S. Treasury Department's list of Specially Designated Nationals or the U.S. Commerce Department's Table of Denial Orders.
>
> By downloading or using the software, you are agreeing to the foregoing and you are warranting that you are not located in, under the control of, or a national or resident of any such country or on any such list.

mined in an *in rem* court proceeding. Similarly, if the ownership of personal property (or movable property, such as computers and software) is contested, it would be determined in an *in rem* court proceeding in the state where the property is physically located.

Refusal to Exercise Jurisdiction.   A governmental agency, even if it has the power to enact legislation, enforce laws, or adjudicate disputes, does not have to do so. For legislative and executive bodies, this is a matter of discretion. So, for example, national and state legislatures have chosen—for the present—not to impose taxes on e-commerce sales. Courts, by comparison, may only refuse to hear a dispute over which they have jurisdiction if the doctrine of ***forum non conveniens*** applies. In essence, this allows a court to decline to hear a case if it is either inconvenient or unfair to do so. In determining this, a court will consider (1) the private interests of the parties (i.e., the ease and cost of access to documents and witnesses) and (2) the public interests of forum (i.e., the interests of the forum in the outcome of the dispute, the burden on the court to hear the case, and whether another forum has a much greater interest in the outcome of the dispute).

It should be noted that not all courts recognize the doctrine of *forum non conveniens*. For example, the state of Texas has forbidden its courts from applying the doctrine. When that is the case, a court must hear every dispute brought before it, so long as it has jurisdiction. This, in part, explains the decision of the Texas court in *Braintech, Inc. v. Kostiuk* to hear a dispute involving a Canadian plaintiff and a Canadian defendant. Because the Texas court had jurisdiction—even if it was the least amount of jurisdiction a court can have—the court had to hear the case.

Jurisdiction of International Organizations

By participating in many organizations, the members consent to observe and respect the executive decisions, legislative enactments, or judicial pronouncements of the organization.[23] That is, they consent to the jurisdiction of the organization. For example, member nations of the United Nations agree to abide by the UN Security Council's decisions on preserving peace and security. Member states of the European Union agree to observe its directives and regulations and the decisions of its Court of Justice. Member countries of the World Trade Organization agree to abide by the decisions of its Dispute Settlement Body.

Commonly, however, the jurisdiction of international organizations is granted on a case-by-case basis. For instance, the UN's International Court of Justice is most commonly granted jurisdiction in an *ad hoc* agreement between nations outlining the dispute they want the court to resolve. Similarly, the jurisdiction of international arbitration tribunals, such as the ICC's International Court of Arbitration, is almost always granted in a forum selection clause in a commercial contract.

---

[23]*See* http://home.netscape.com/legal_notices/export.html. Members of intergovernmental organizations, which are created by treaty, are expected to comply with their commitments in "good faith." *Vienna Convention on the Law of Treaties,* Art. 26 (1980).

Choice of Law

Most governmental agencies and intergovernmental organizations apply their own laws when enacting legislation, enforcing rules and regulations, and deciding disputes. For example, the procedural rules that a legislature will follow in enacting legislation will be its own procedural rules. This is true, as well, for the procedures an executive will follow in enforcing the law. It is not necessarily the case, however, for courts deciding disputes.

Choice of Law in International Courts and Tribunals

When an international court or tribunal is asked to decide a dispute, the parties must designate the applicable law at the time they choose the particular court or tribunal. This may be done expressly or by implication. For example, if the parties decide that the International Court of Justice should decide a dispute, they can say nothing and the Court will apply all of the applicable rules of international law. However, if the parties wish, they can also designate the applicable international laws they want the Court to use. International courts, such as the ICJ, will only use international laws. By comparison, international arbitral tribunals, such as the ICC's International Court of Arbitration, must be expressly instructed as to the laws to apply. The laws, however, may be international laws, the laws of any nation, the laws of several nations, or any combination of these.

Choice of Law in National Courts

When an international case is brought before a national court (including municipal, provincial, and state courts), the court must choose the applicable law governing the dispute. If the dispute involves a public right or a public injury (as is the case in a criminal proceeding or a tax dispute), the court will apply its own national law, or the applicable international law recognized by its national government. For example, in 1998, a German court applied German law in holding a CompuServe executive criminally liable for allowing pornographic materials to be posted on a CompuServe Web site that could be viewed in Germany.[24]

By comparison, if an international dispute involves a private right or a private injury (such as enforcing a contract or bring a complaint in tort), the court will apply the law of the nation most affected or concerned with the outcome of the dispute. It does so, because private parties take actions based on the assumption that

[24]The case is described in "Morning Briefcase," *Dallas Morning News* (May 29, 1998), at p. 2D.

[25]*See* Peter P. Swire, "Of Elephants, Mice, and Privacy: International Choice of Law and the Internet," posted August 23, 1998 at www.ohio-state.edu/units/law/swire1/elephants.htm.

a particular set of laws will apply. If a court were to apply a different set of laws, the effect would be to discourage international trade.[25]

In determining the applicable law in a private international dispute, a court will follow a two-step procedure. First, if the parties have agreed to application of the law of a particular country, the court will apply that law (unless forbidden from doing so by a statutory choice-of-law code). Such an agreement is commonly found in a choice of law clause, such as the one used by Netscape, quoted earlier. Second, if the parties have not agreed to the applicable law, then the court will determine for itself the law it should apply. In determining the applicable law for itself, courts follow one of three rules:

1. It will follow the dictates of a statutory choice-of-law code.
2. It will determine the country that has the most significant relationship with the dispute.
3. It will look for the country that has the greatest governmental interest in the outcome of the state.

Statutory Choice-of-Law Codes.   Most civil law countries have adopted private international law codes that contain choice-of-law rules. Commonly these choice-of-law rules apply what is known as the **vesting of rights doctrine.** This doctrine says that the court is to apply the laws of the country where the parties' rights vested (that is, where they legally became effective).

Choice-of-law codes commonly set out a rule that covers the general case, and then provide rules for particular cases. For example, the Japanese choice-of-law rule provides that, in most cases, "if the intention of the parties is uncertain, the law of the place of the act shall apply."[26]

Beyond the general case, the codes usually direct a court to look to the subject matter of the suit. Thus, if a dispute involves a tort, the applicable law is the law of the place where the wrong was committed. If the suit is based on a contract, the place where the contract was made governs questions of its validity, and the place where the contract was to be performed govern questions of its performance.

Sometimes, as we mentioned earlier, statutory choice-of-law rules forbid the parties from make a choice as to the application of certain laws. For example, the European Commission's proposed *Council Regulation on Jurisdiction and the Recognition and Enforcement of Judgments in Civil and Commercial Matters,*[27] states that consumers may sue sellers who supply goods and services in the EU member state where the consumer is domiciled even if the parties were to expressly disclaim the application of this regulation. In other words, if it were adopted, an online software

---

[26]Japan, *Law Concerning the Application of Laws in General,* Article 7(2).

[27]Commission Proposal COM (1999) 348 final, posted at http://europa.eu.int/eur-lex/en/com/reg/en_register_1920.html.

license that required disputes to be settled in a French court applying French law would be ineffective in the EU.

Most Significant Relationship Test.   Most common-law countries apply what is known as the **most significant relationship test.** This has courts apply the laws of the country that has the most real and significant "contacts" with the parties and their transactions. For example, in a tort case, a court will look at (1) the place of the injury, (2) the place of the act, (3) the nationality, domicile, residence, or place of incorporation of the parties, and (4) the place where the relationship between the parties was centered. In a contract case, a court will look at (1) the place of contracting, (2) the place of negotiation, (3) the place of performance, (4) the location of the subject matter, and (5) the nationality, domicile, residence, or place of incorporation of the parties.

This test, however, is hard to apply to disputes arising in cyberspace, and before very long courts may be forced to revise it. For example, suppose an American buys and downloads a musical recording from a company located in Canada, and they do not agree as to the law to apply in the event of a dispute. If the American later sues for breach of contract, the factors that the court will consider in determining the law to apply may leave it unable to do so. The place of contract, the place of negotiation, and the place of performance are all in cyberspace. The subject matter is a recording that is downloaded in Canada from a Web server in the United States. The plaintiff is from Canada and the defendant is from the United States. There is no clear-cut indication that either Canada or the United States has a more significant relationship with any element of this dispute. In such a case, a court will probably apply its own law (because that is the law it is most familiar with). But until a decision is handed down in a case such as this, we will not know for sure.

Governmental Interest Test.   A few courts, both in civil-law and common-law countries, follow a **governmental interest test.** This test has a court determine the countries that have a legitimate interest in the outcome of the dispute. If only one country has a legitimate interest, then the court is to apply the law of that country. If none do, then the court is to apply its own national law. If two do, and one of those countries is the court's own, then it shall apply its own country's law. If two others do, then the court is to apply the country's law that it believes is the soundest or that is most like its own country's law.

Substantive Laws Affecting Electronic Commerce

The substantive laws that define and regulate traditional international commerce also regulate electronic commerce. In the materials that follow we will examine those particular laws that have had, or are likely to have, the most impact on goods and services sold in cyberspace: intellectual property law, the law of contracts, capital transfer regulations, and tax law.

International Intellectual Property Law

Intellectual property—including copyrights, patents, and trademarks—is primarily a creature of national law. Although international law does not create intellectual property, it does set down guidelines for its uniform definition and protection, and it sets up ways to make it easier for owners to acquire rights in different countries. In the following materials we will look at the principal international treaties governing intellectual property and how they apply to materials posted in cyberspace.

The treaties that apply to intellectual property used in cyberspace are the *Agreement on Trade-Related Aspects of Intellectual Property Rights,* the *International Convention for the Protection of Industrial Property,* the *Berne Convention for the Protection of Literary and Artistic Works,* the *International Convention for the Protection of Performers, Producers of Phonograms,* and *Broadcasting Organizations,* the *Treaty on Intellectual Property in Respect of Integrated Circuits,* the *WIPO Copyright Treaty, and the WIPO Performances and Phonograms Treaty.*

Agreement on Trade-Related Aspect of Intellectual Property Rights.   The *Agreement on Trade-Related Aspects of Intellectual Property Rights*—the **TRIPS Agreement**—is one of the World Trade Organization's multilateral agreements. Like the other WTO multilateral agreements, the WTO member countries are automatically members of the TRIPS Agreement.

The TRIPS Agreement is meant to establish a comprehensive set of rights and obligations governing international trade in intellectual property. To accomplish this, the agreement establishes a common minimum of protection for intellectual property rights within the territories of all WTO member countries. The main points of the TRIPS Agreement are these:

1. WTO members countries are required to observe the substantive provisions of the following multilateral intellectual property agreements: the *International Convention for the Protection of Industrial Property* (Paris Convention), the *Berne Convention for the Protection of Literary and Artistic Works* (Berne Convention), the *International Convention for the Protection of Performers, Producers of Phonograms, and Broadcasting Organizations* (Rome Convention), and the *Treaty on Intellectual Property in Respect of Integrated Circuits* (IPIC Treaty).

2. The TRIPS Agreement supplements these multilateral intellectual property agreements. For example, the Agreements

http://
www.wto.org/wto/legal/27-trips.wpf

sets the minimum term of copyrights at fifty years, patents at twenty years, and trademarks at seven years.

3. The Agreement establishes criteria for the effective enforcement of intellectual property rights, and, because WTO member countries are bound by the WTO's *Dispute Resolution Understanding,* it establishes a mandatory mechanism for settling intellectual property disputes between WTO member countries.

4. The Agreements extends the basic international trade principles established in the General Agreement on Tariffs and Trade to the field of international intellectual property rights. First, the *national treatment principle* requires each member country to extend to nationals of other members treatment "no less favorable" than that which it gives its own nationals regarding intellectual property rights. Second, the *transparency principle* requires member countries to publish and to notify the WTO's TRIPS Council of all relevant laws, regulations, and practices, and to promptly respond to other member countries' requests for information about its intellectual property rules. Third, the *most-favored-nation treatment principle* requires a member country to grant to the nationals of all other member countries the most favorable treatment that it grants to the nationals of any one of them.

5. Finally, there is a transition period for less-developed member countries to bring their intellectual property rules into compliance with the TRIPS Agreement. Developing members and those transitioning to a market economy had to be in full compliance by January 1, 2000. The least developed member states have until January 1, 2006, to do so.

International Convention for the Protection of Industrial Property.   The *International Convention for the Protection of Industrial Property* (Paris Convention) establishes a "union" of countries responsible for protecting industrial property rights. Industrial property rights include patents, trademarks, and industrial designs. Member countries are required to comply with three principles:

1. *National treatment* (is the same principle set out in the TRIPS Agreement).
2. *Right of priority* provides that an applicant for protection in one country has up to twelve months to file an application in other countries, and that those other countries must then treat the application as if it were filed on the same day as the original application.
3. *Common rules* establish basic minimum criteria and procedures for granting industrial property rights.

---

http://
The text of the Paris Convention is posted at
www.wipo.int/eng/iplex/wo_par0_.htm

Berne Convention for the Protection of Literary and Artistic Works. The *Berne Convention for the Protection of Literary and Artistic Works* (Berne Convention) creates a union of countries responsible for protecting literary and artistic rights (i.e., copyrights). Four principles define the members' obligations:

http://

The text of the Berne Convention is posted at
www.wipo.int/eng/iplex/wo_ber0_.htm

1. *National treatment.*
2. *Nonconditional protection* means that no formalities (such as the use of the copyright symbol ©) may be required to protect artistic property.
3. *Protection independent of the country of origin* means that artistic property that is protected in one member country is protected in all.
4. *Common rules* (as with the Paris Convention) establish basic minimum criteria and procedures for granting literary artistic rights.

Many of the cyberlaw cases that are heard by courts around the world involve claims of copyright infringement in violation of the national laws that implement the Berne Convention. Examples include the case of *Wang Meng v. Century Internet Communications Technology Co.*, in which a court in Beijing, China, held that the defendant had violated the copyrights of several authors by posting their works on a Web site without their permission, and the case of *Int'l Federation of the Phonographic Industry v. Olsson,* in which a Swedish court held that a teenager had not infringed any copyrights by posting links to copyrighted recordings on his Web site.[28]

International Convention for the Protection of Performers, Producers of Phonograms, and Broadcasting Organizations.   The *International Convention for the Protection of Performers, Producers of Phonograms, and Broadcasting Organizations* (Rome Convention) establishes protection for performing artists, recording companies, and broadcasters. Artists are protected from the unauthorized recording of their original performances and from the use of authorized recording for a purpose different than what they agreed to. Recording companies are protected from the direct or indirect recording of their phonograms.[29] Broadcasters are protected from the unauthorized recording, rebroadcast, and other use of their broadcasts.

World Intellectual Property Organization Performances and Phonograms Treaty.   The *WIPO Performances and Phonograms Treaty* supple-

http://

www.wipo.int/eng/iplex/wo_ber0-.htm

---

[28]Summaries of these cases are posted at www.perkinscoie.com/resource/ecomm/Netcase/Cases-14.htm.
[29]A phonogram is defined in the Rome Convention, Article 3, as "any exclusively aural fixation of sounds of a performance or of other sounds." It is defined in the *WIPO Performance and Phonograms Treaty,* Article 2, as the "fixation of the sounds of a performance or of other sounds, or of a representation of sounds, other than in the form of a fixation incorporated in a cinematographic or other audiovisual work."

ments the Rome Convention, expanding the legal rights of performers, recording companies, and broadcasters granted in that Convention. Most significantly, it prohibits the circumvention of technological measures, such as encryption, that protect those rights.

World Intellectual Property Organization Copyright Treaty.   The *WIPO Copyright Treaty* extends copyright protection provisions of the Berne Convention to computer software. It also requires member countries, independent of the Berne Convention obligations, to protect databases and to outlaw any tampering with electronic information of digitized intellectual property that identifies the author, the owner of the work, and the conditions for its use.

Treaty on Intellectual Property in Respect of Integrated Circuits.   The *Treaty on Intellectual Property in Respect of Integrated Circuits* (IPIC Treaty) requires member countries to protect the designs used in integrated circuits (such as the designs on computer chips). Like the Berne and Paris Conventions, the IPIC Treaty contains a statement of the national treatment principle, and it provides for common rules. The common rules require members to outlaw the making of unauthorized copies and the importing of contraband copies.

Although the WTO's members are required to observe the IPIC Treaty, the treaty itself is not currently in force.

> **http://**
> Summaries of these cases are posted at
> **www.perkinscoie.com/resource/ecomm/**
> **netcase/Cases-14.htm**

> **http://**
> **www.wipo.int/eng/iplex/wo_rom0_.htm**

> **http://**
> **www.wipo.int/eng/diplconf/distrib/95dc.htm**

> **http://**
> **www.wipo/int/eng/diplconf/distrib/94dc.htm**

> **http://**
> **www.wipo.int/eng/iplex/wo_top0_.htm**

Application of Intellectual Property Treaties to Cyberspace

The TRIPS Agreement, together with the Berne, Paris, and Rome Conventions, and the IPIC Treaty, define the kinds of intellectual property that are protected by national and international law. The two WIPO treaties make it clear that the intellectual property protected by the other treaties is also protected in cyberspace. The *WIPO Copyright Treaty* (Article 8) states that "authors of literary and artistic works shall enjoy the exclusive right of authorizing any communication to the public of their works by wire or wireless means." And the *WIPO Performances and Phonograms Treaty* (Article 10 and 11) extends the same exclusive rights to performers, and grants to producers of phonograms "the exclusive right of authorizing the direct or indirect reproduction of their phonograms, in any manner or form."

The Law of Contracts

The law of contracts governs the buying and selling of all kinds of property. Internationally, the making of contracts is governed by both international and national laws. The main international law is the United Nations *Convention on Contracts for the International Sale of Goods* (CISG). In force since 1988, most of the world's largest trading nations are parties to the CISG. However, despite the importance of the CISG, national laws govern most contracts made internationally.

U.S. contract law, and, by analogy, the contract law of other common-law countries, was discussed in Chapter 5. Civil-law countries, however, apply a contract law that has many distinguishing features, and we will briefly examine those features in the following materials. We will also examine the CISG and UNCITRAL's *Model Law on Electronic Commerce*. The UNCITRAL law is important because it provides that national and international contract law applies to transactions in cyberspace.

The Law of Contracts in Civil-Law Countries

Among the most important of the national law codes in the civil law world are the *Napoleonic Codes* of France, adopted during the reign of Napoleon Bonaparte. These codes, including the *Civil Code* adopted in 1804 and the *Code of Commerce* of 1807, have influenced later similar codes in most of the non-English speaking world. For comparative purposes, we shall focus on the French codes here.

Commercial transactions are looked at differently in France than they are in common-law countries. The *Code of Commerce* not only defines who merchants are and the procedures they must follow (which are not as formal as those of nonmerchants), it also establishes separate Commercial Courts to hear disputes between and against them.

Despite these differences, many of the requirements for the formation of a French contract—especially French sales of goods contracts—are nearly identical to the requirements found in common-law countries. There are differences, of course, including the rules governing firm offers, acceptance with additional terms, formalities, and definiteness.

Firm Offers.   In France, both merchants and nonmerchants may make firm or irrevocable offers. That is, if an offer specifies a time for acceptance, it must be kept open during that time. If an offer says that it will be kept open for a period of time, but does not say how long, then it must be kept open for a reasonable time.

For instance, if an individual in France posts a promise on a Web site to sell a music video for 5 francs anytime during the next six months, the promise is enforceable, even if the individual later removes the promise from the Web site or posts a retraction. By comparison, in a common-law country a private individual is not bound to such an offer, and a merchant would only be bound if the offer were in a signed writing.

Acceptance with Additional Terms.   French law follows the **mirror image rule** for the making of all kinds of contracts. That is, an offer to buy or sell goods, real property, and other things must be accepted unequivocally. Any modification is treated as a rejection and a counteroffer.

By comparison, in common-law countries, merchants frequently engage in what is called the *battle of the forms,* with one making an offer containing one set of terms and another accepting with slightly different terms. As long as they are substantially alike, a contract is formed. This is not the case in France and other civil-law countries. An acceptance there usually consists of the words "I accept" and nothing more.

Formalities.   The form that a French contract must take depends on its subject matter. Contracts for the sale of real property have to be in a writing authored by a notary. The form of a French sales contract depends on whether a merchant is involved. If the party being sued is a merchant, an oral contract, regardless of the price involved, is enforceable (France, *Code of Commerce,* Article 109). However, if the party being sued is a nonmerchant, oral contracts are only enforceable if they are for less than 5,000 francs, while contracts for more than 5,000 francs must be evidenced by a written memorandum signed by the party being sued (France, *Civil Code,* Article 1341).

The civil law's elimination of formalities in contracts between merchants greatly simplifies international contracts and contracts made on the Internet. Unlike merchants in the United States, who have to enter into Trading Partner Agreements to ensure that their Electronic Data Interchange and other cyber contracts are legally enforceable, this is unnecessary in civil-law countries. Indeed, the fact that formalities are not required is one reason why some merchants from civil-law countries who enter into contracts with American companies insist upon a choice of law clause that adopts their own country's contract law.

Definiteness.   In order for a French sales contract to be enforceable, its terms must be definite. The only term that needs to be described, however is the price (France, *Civil Code,* Article, 1591), and it must be expressed as an amount of money. (Articles 1591 and 1592.) Other terms may be left for the determination of the parties or the courts.

UN Convention on Contracts for the International Sale of Goods

The United Nations *Convention on Contracts for the International Sale of Goods* (CISG) applies to contracts involving international sales between merchants. That is, the buyer and seller must both be merchants and they must both have places of business in different countries. Additionally, either: (1) both countries must be contracting states to the convention, or (2) the rules of private international law must "lead to the application of the law of a contracting state" (CISG, Article 1).

The CISG automatically applies when these prerequisites are met. However, Article 6 of the CISG expressly allows the parties to exclude or modify the CISG's application. That is, by the addition of a choice of law clause, the parties may provide that their contractual relationship will be governed in whole or in part by another contract law.

Coverage of the CISG.   The CISG only governs the *formation* of sales contracts and the *rights* and *obligations* of the parties that arise from such contracts. National laws govern other contractual considerations. Excluded from the coverage of the CISG are the following:

1. Questions concerning the validity of contracts
2. Questions of products liability
3. Sales to consumers
4. Sales commonly subject to special regulation, including sales: (a) by auction, (b) on execution or otherwise by authority of law, (c) of stocks, shares, investment securities, negotiable instruments, or money, (d) of ships, vessels, hovercraft, or aircraft, and (e) of electricity
5. Sales of services

Comparison of the CISG to the UCC and the French Civil and Commercial Codes. For the most part, the CISG is modeled on the provisions of the French *Civil Code* and *Code of Commerce* and similar civil law codes. Most of the differences between U.S. sales law, which is found in the *Uniform Commercial Code* (UCC) and the CISG, as a consequence, parallel the differences between the UCC and the French codes. There are, nonetheless, some differences between the CISG and the French codes. The most important concerns the requirement for definiteness.

http://
www.cisg.law.pace.edu/cisg/text/cisgtoc.html

The CISG (Article 14(1)) provides that a contract is definite "if it indicates the goods and expressly or impliedly fixes or makes provision for determining the quantity and the price." In other words, the CISG adopts requirements from both the common law and the civil law. Like the UCC, the CISG requires parties to specify the quantity of the goods being sold, and like the French *Civil Code,* the CISG requires them to specify the price.

UNCITRAL Model Law on Electronic Commerce

The purpose of the UNCITRAL *Model Law on Electronic Commerce* is to encourage the use of electronic commerce and to provide nations with model legislation "governing the use of alternatives to paper-based methods of communication and storage of information" (UN General Assembly Resolution 51/62 of 16 December 1996).

The Model Law is only meant to supplement existing contract laws. It does not define the elements of making and enforcing contracts. Rather, it describes how existing laws should be modified so that contracts can be made electronically.

In particular, the Model Law provides the following:

1. Electronic messages are to have legal effect.
2. Electronic messages may incorporate information by reference.
3. An electronic message is a writing for legal purposes if it is accessible for later reference.
4. An electronic message includes a signature if it identifies the person sending the message and indicates that the person approves of the information it contains.
5. An electronic message is an original document if it reliably retains its information in its original form.
6. An exchange of electronic messages can constitute an offer and an acceptance and thereby create a valid contract.

In other words, in countries that implement the provisions of this law, an electronic contract signed with an electronic signature will be just as valid and just as enforceable as a paper contract signed with a pen.

Regulation of the International Movement of Capital

The intergovernmental organization that has taken the leading role in regulating the international movement of capital is the OECD. Its *Code of Liberalization of Capital Movements,* first adopted in 1961 and last amended in 1989, requires the OECD

http://
www.uncitral.org/english/texts/electcom/ml-ec.htm

member countries to progressively abolish their restrictions on the movement of capital. That is, it encourages member countries to let foreigners invest locally and to allow residents to invest abroad. The code applies to all kinds of investments, including investments in equity and debt securities, such as stocks, bonds, money market transactions, and even swaps, options, and

> ## Cyberethics
>
> 1. Is it proper to post materials on a foreign Web server that violate local intellectual property laws or defamation laws?
> 2. Is it ethical to require a foreign consumer to agree to settle disputes in your country using your local law?
> 3. Is it ethical to sue a local competitor in a foreign court based solely on the fact that both of you have Web sites that can be accessed in the foreign country?

other derivative instruments. Although the OECD Code allows member states to retain controls that existed when the Code was first adopted, by the early 1990s, all the OECD member country had abolished all significant restrictions on the international movement of capital.[30]

The consequence of this elimination of restrictions has been the dramatic growth in recent years of international stock trading—nearly all of it done on intranets. The two international clearinghouses that arrange for the transfer of stocks internationally are Euroclear in Brussels and the Cedel Bank in Luxembourg. Euroclear currently handles more than 100,000 securities from more than eighty countries and has daily transactions that exceed $125 million. Cedel Bank deals in an equal number of diverse securities and has daily transactions of more than $60 million.

The other IGO that has taken an interest in capital movements is the Council of Europe. Its 1989 *Convention on Insider Trading* establishes a cooperative mechanism for supervising securities markets. In particular, "because of the internationalization of markets and the ease of present-day communications," the *Convention* focuses on uncovering insider trading activities "on the market of a state by persons not resident in that state or acting through persons not resident there."[31] Insider trading is the use of nonpublic information by a company insider (such as a corporate officer or director) about a company or the securities market to buy or sell

> **http://**
> www.oecd.org/lclaf/cmis/codes/elemart.htm

> **http://**
> www.coe.fr/eng/legaltxt/130e.htm

---

[30]*See* Pierre Poret, "The Experience of the OECD with the *Code of Liberalization of Capital Movements*" posted at www.oecd.org//daf/cmis/CODES/oecdexp.htm.

[31]*Convention on Insider Trading*, Preamble.

securities for personal gain. The *Convention,* in essence, allows the regulatory agencies in one country to request the assistance of those in another country to uncover conduct by an individual or individuals that constitutes insider trading in the requesting country.

Aside from the Council of Europe's multilateral *Convention on Insider Trading,* the other international efforts to stop insider trading are found in bilateral "memorandums of understanding" (MOUs) between the U.S. Securities and Exchange Commission and its counterpart in seventeen other, mostly European, countries.[32] The MOUs provide a mechanism for exchanging information and for mutual cooperation in the investigation of securities violations.

Taxation of International Electronic Commerce

The questions of how countries should tax electronic commerce, especially international electronic commerce, is under discussion at the Organization for Economic Cooperation and Development and the World Trade Center.

The OECD's Committee on Fiscal Affairs has proposed that "the taxation principles that guide governments in relation to conventional commerce should also guide them in electronic commerce." With respect to consumption taxes (such as sales taxes and value added taxes), the committee proposes "that taxation should occur in the [place] where consumption occurs." However, as for the sale of digitized products, such as digitized books, music, and software, the sale should be treated differently from the sale of other products. How differently, however, is still under consideration.[33]

The WTO at its Ministerial Conference in 1998 established a work program to study the trade-related issues of global electronic commerce, including the question of how it should be taxed. In the meantime, at the request of the business community, the WTO called on its member countries to maintain a temporary moratorium on the imposition of taxes on electronic commerce.[34] The business community, through such advocacy groups as the Global Business Dialog on Electronic Commerce, is urging the WTO to make this temporary moratorium permanent.[35]

---

[32]The countries are Argentina, Australia, Brazil, Chile, Costa Rica, France, Hungary, Italy, Japan, Luxembourg, Mexico, the Netherlands, Norway, Spain, Sweden, Switzerland, and the United Kingdom. In addition, the U.S. Securities and Exchange Commission has agreements with the Canadian provinces of British Columbia, Ontario, and Quebec.

[33]*See* OECD Tax, "Electronic Commerce," posted at www.oecd.org/daf/fa/e_com/e_com.htm.

[34]*Declaration on Global Electronic Commerce,* WT/MIN(98)/DEC/2 posted at www.wto.org/wto/ecom/e_mindec1.htm.

[35]"The Perspective of the Global Business Dialogue on Electronic Commerce (GBDe) on the WTO and Its Relationship to E-Commerce" posted at www.gbde.org/gbde.html.

Summary

This chapter provides an overview of the international organizations and international regulations that affect international electronic commerce.

International organizations may be intergovernmental or nongovernmental. The membership of intergovernmental organizations, such as the United Nations, the World Trade Organization, and the European Union, are limited to nation states. They function primarily to promote and harmonize relationships between those states, and to negotiate international conventions of mutual interest to the member states. Nongovernmental organizations, especially those with an interest in electronic commerce, primarily function as advocates for the private business firms seeking to influence the drafting of international rules and regulations.

National, state, provincial, and municipal government agencies as well as international organizations may exercise jurisdiction over electronic commerce. Government agencies may do so when their interests are affected or when companies or individuals give their consent. International organizations may only exercise jurisdiction when the parties involved give their consent. The same criteria also apply when national or international courts are asked to determine the law that governs an international dispute.

A number of international conventions, such as the Agreement on Trade-Related Aspects of Intellectual Property Rights, establish common rules applicable to the ownership of intellectual property. The United Nations Convention on Contracts for the International Sale of Goods (CISG) automatically governs most international sales contracts between merchants, and its rules are more like the contract law of civil-law countries than that of the United States or other common-law countries. In particular, the CISG does not require the contracts be evidenced by a signed writing.

Manager's Checklist

- Be aware that the membership of most intergovernmental organizations, such as the United Nations, the World Trade Organization, and the European Union, is made up of national governments and not companies or private individuals.
- Be aware that only countries may appear as parties before the International Court of Justice and most other tribunals sponsored by intergovernmental organizations.
- Be aware that the International Chamber of Commerce's International Court of Arbitration is the most widely used arbitral body for resolving international commercial disputes between private parties.
- Be aware that parties to an international commercial contract may agree upon the court that will hear their disputes concerning that contract and the law the court will apply.

- Be aware that a foreign court may assume jurisdiction over a dispute based on the most minimal contacts with the forum country.
- Be aware that, in the absence of an agreement between the parties, a court hearing an international dispute will probably apply the law of the country that has the most interest in the outcome of the dispute.
- Be aware that international agreements, such as the *Berne Convention for the Protection of Literary and Artistic Works* and the *Agreement on Trade-Related Aspects of Intellectual Property Rights,* establish minimum common rules that all their member countries must adopt.
- Be aware that the contract laws in civil-law countries treat consumer sales and sales between merchants differently.
- Be aware that a signed writing is not required to create an enforceable contract if a civil-law country's contract law applies.
- Be aware that the UNCITRAL *Model Law on Electronic Commerce* is a model law that must be adopted by local legislation before it will become effective.
- Be aware that the OECD's *Code of Liberalization of Capital Movements* is generally observed by the developed countries that are OECD members, and that capital movements to and from less-developed countries may be subject to a variety of local restrictions.
- Be aware that international guidelines for taxing electronic commerce transactions are only now being formulated.

Appendix A: Amendments to the United States Constitution

Amendment I

Congress shall make no law respecting an establishment of religion, or prohibiting the free exercise thereof; or abridging the freedom of speech, or of the press; or the right of the people peaceably to assemble, and to petition the government for a redress of grievances.

* * * * * * * * * *

Amendment IV

The right of the people to be secure in their persons, houses, papers, and effects, against unreasonable searches and seizures, shall not be violated, and no warrants shall issue, but upon probable cause, supported by oath or affirmation, and particularly describing the place to be searched, and the persons or things to be seized.

Amendment V

No person shall be held to answer for a capital, or otherwise infamous crime, unless on a presentment or indictment of a grand jury, except in cases arising in the land or naval forces, or in the militia, when in actual service in time of war or public danger; nor shall any person be subject for the same offense to be twice put in jeopardy of life or limb; nor shall be compelled in any criminal case to be a witness against himself, nor be deprived of life, liberty, or property, without due process of law; nor shall private property be taken for public use, without just compensation.

* * * * * * * * * *

Amendment IX

The enumeration in the Constitution, of certain rights, shall not be construed to deny or disparage others retained by the people.

* * * * * * * * * * *

Amendment XIV

Section 1. All persons born or naturalized in the United States, and subject to the jurisdiction thereof, are citizens of the United States and of the state wherein they reside. No state shall make or enforce any law which shall abridge the privileges or immunities of citizens of the United States; nor shall any state deprive any person of life, liberty, or property, without due process of law; nor deny to any person within its jurisdiction the equal protection of the laws.

Appendix B: Digital Millennium Copyright Act of 1998

www.dfc.org/issues/graphic/2281/2281.html

Section 1. Short Title

This Act may be cited as the "Digital Millennium Copyright Act."

Sec. 2. Table of Contents

Title III—Computer Maintenance or Repair Copyright Exemption

Title IV—Miscellaneous Provisions

Title V—Protection of Certain Original Designs

Appendix C: Excerpts from the Anticybersquatting Consumer Protection Act of 1999

http://techlawjournal.com/cong106/trademark/s1255is.htm

S. 1255 To protect consumers and promote electronic commerce by amending certain trademark infringement, dilution, and counterfeiting laws, and for other purposes.

Section 1. Short Title

This Act may be cited as the "Anticybersquatting Consumer Protection Act."

Sec. 2. Findings

Congress finds that the unauthorized registration or use of trademarks as Internet domain names or other identifiers of online locations (commonly known as 'cyber-squatting')—

(1) results in consumer fraud and public confusion as to the true source or sponsorship of products and services;

(2) impairs electronic commerce, which is important to the economy of the United States; and

(3) deprives owners of trademarks of substantial revenues and consumer good-will.

Sec. 3. Trademark Remedies

(a) RECOVERY FOR VIOLATION OF RIGHTS- Section 35 of the Act entitled 'An Act to provide for the registration and protection of trade-marks used in commerce, to carry out the provisions of certain international conventions, and for other purposes,' approved July 5, 1946, (commonly referred to as the 'Trademark Act of 1946') (15 U.S.C. 1117) is amended by adding at the end the following:

'(d)(1) In this subsection, the term 'Internet' has the meaning given that term in section 230(f)(1) of the Communications Act of 1934 (47 U.S.C. 230(f)(1)).

'(2)(A) In a case involving the registration or use of an identifier described in subparagraph (B), the plaintiff may elect, at any time before final judgment is rendered by the trial court, to recover, instead of actual damages and profits under subsection (a)—

'(i) an award of statutory damages in the amount of—

'(I) not less than $1,000 or more than $100,000 per trademark per identifier, as the court considers just; or

'(II) if the court finds that the registration or use of the registered trademark as an identifier was willful, not less than $3,000 or more than $300,000 per trademark per identifier, as the court considers just; and

'(ii) full costs and reasonable attorney's fees.

'(B) An identifier referred to in subparagraph (A) is an Internet domain name or other identifier of an online location that is—

'(i) the trademark of a person or entity other than the person or entity registering or using the identifier; or

'(ii) sufficiently similar to a trademark of a person or entity other than the person or entity registering or using the identifier as to be likely to—

'(I) cause confusion or mistake;

'(II) deceive; or

'(III) cause dilution of the distinctive quality of a famous trademark'.

(b) REMEDIES FOR DILUTION OF FAMOUS MARKS- Section 43(c)(2) of the Act entitled 'An Act to provide for the registration and protection of trade-marks used in commerce, to carry out the provisions of certain international conventions, and for other purposes', approved July 5, 1946, (commonly referred to as the 'Trademark Act of 1946') (15 U.S.C. 1125(c)(2)) is amended by striking '35(a)' and inserting '35 (a) and (d)'.

Sec. 4. Criminal Use of Counterfeit Trademark

(a) IN GENERAL- Section 2320(a) of title 18, United States Code, is amended—

(1) by inserting '(1)' after '(a)';

(2) by striking 'section that occurs' and inserting 'paragraph that occurs'; and

(3) by adding at the end the following:

'(2)(A) In this paragraph, the term 'Internet' has the meaning given that term in section 230(f)(1) of the Communications Act of 1934 (47 U.S.C. 230(f)(1)).

'(B)(i) Except as provided in clause (ii), whoever knowingly and fraudulently or in bad faith registers or uses an identifier described in subparagraph (C) shall be guilty of a Class B misdemeanor.

'(ii) In the case of an offense by a person under this paragraph that occurs after that person is convicted of another offense under this section, that person shall be guilty of a Class E felony.

'(C) An identifier referred to in subparagraph (B) is an Internet domain name or other identifier of an online location that is—

'(i) the trademark of a person or entity other than the person or entity registering or using the identifier; or

'(ii) sufficiently similar to a trademark of a person or entity other than the person or entity registering or using the identifier as to be likely to—

'(I) cause confusion or mistake;

'(II) deceive; or

'(III) cause dilution of the distinctive quality of a famous trademark.

'(D)(i) For the purposes of a prosecution under this paragraph, if all of the conditions described in clause (ii) apply to the registration or use of an identifier described in subparagraph (C) by a defendant, those conditions shall constitute prima facie evidence that the registration or use was fraudulent or in bad faith.

'(ii) The conditions referred to in clause (i) are as follows:

'(I) The defendant registered or used an identifier described in subparagraph (C)—

'(aa) with intent to cause confusion or mistake, deceive, or cause dilution of the distinctive quality of a famous trademark; or

'(bb) with the intention of diverting consumers from the domain or other online location of the person or entity who is the owner of a trademark described in subparagraph (C) to the domain or other online location of the defendant.

'(II) The defendant—

'(aa) provided false information in the defendant's application to register the identifier; or

'(bb) offered to transfer the registration of the identifier to the trademark owner or another person or entity in consideration for any thing of value.

'(III) The identifier is not—

'(aa) the defendant's legal first name or surname; or

'(bb) a trademark of the defendant used in legitimate commerce before the earlier of the first use of the registered trademark referred to in subparagraph (C) or the effective date of the registration of that trademark.

'(iii) The application of this subparagraph shall not be exclusive. Nothing in this subparagraph may be construed to limit the applicability of subparagraph (B).'

(b) Sentencing Guidelines

(1) IN GENERAL- Pursuant to the authority granted to the United States Sentencing Commission under section 994(p) of title 28, United States Code, the United States Sentencing Commission shall—

(A) review the Federal sentencing guidelines for crimes against intellectual property (including offenses under section 2320 of title 18, United States Code); and

(B) promulgate such amendments to the Federal Sentencing Guidelines as are necessary to ensure that the applicable sentence for a defendant convicted of a crime against intellectual property is sufficiently stringent to deter such a crime.

(2) FACTORS FOR CONSIDERATION- In carrying out this subsection, the United States Sentencing Commission shall—

(A) take into account the findings under section 2; and

(B) ensure that the amendments promulgated under paragraph (1)(B) adequately provide for sentencing for crimes described in paragraph

(2) of section 2320(a) of title 18, United States Code, as added by subsection (a).

Sec. 5. Limitation of Liability

Section 39 of the Act entitled 'An Act to provide for the registration and protection of trademarks used in commerce, to carry out the provisions of certain international conventions, and for other purposes,' approved July 5, 1946, (commonly referred to as the 'Trademark Act of 1946') (15 U.S.C. 1121) is amended by adding at the end the following:

'(c)(1) In this subsection, the term 'Internet' has the meaning given that term in section 230(f)(1) of the Communications Act of 1934 (47 U.S.C. 230(f)(1)).

'(2)(A) An Internet service provider, domain name registrar, or registry described in subparagraph (B) shall not be liable for monetary relief to any person for a removal or transfer described in that subparagraph, without regard to whether the domain name or other identifier is ultimately determined to be infringing or dilutive.

'(B) An Internet service provider, domain name registrar, or registry referred to in subparagraph (A) is a provider, registrar, or registry that, upon receipt of a written notice from the owner of a trademark registered in the Patent and Trademark Office, removes from domain name service (DNS) service or registration, or transfers to the trademark owner, an Internet domain name or other identifier of an online location alleged to be infringing or dilutive, in compliance with—

'(i) a court order; or

'(ii) the reasonable implementation of a policy prohibiting the unauthorized registration or use of another's registered trademark as an Internet domain name or other identifier of an online location.'

Appendix D: Uniform Domain Name Dispute Resolution Policy (the "Policy")

http://www.icann.org/udrp/udrp.htm

Approved by ICANN: October 24, 1999

1. **Purpose.**
   This Uniform Domain Name Dispute Resolution Policy (the "Policy") has been adopted by the Internet Corporation for Assigned Names and Numbers ("ICANN"), is incorporated by reference into your Registration Agreement, and sets forth the terms and conditions in connection with a dispute between you and any party other than us (the registrar) over the registration and use of an Internet domain name registered by you. Proceedings under Paragraph 4 of this Policy will be conducted according to the Rules for Uniform Domain Name Dispute Resolution Policy (the "Rules of Procedure") and the selected administrative-dispute-resolution service provider's supplemental rules.

2. **Your Representations.**
   By applying to register a domain name, or by asking us to maintain or renew a domain name registration, you hereby represent and warrant to us that
   a. the statements that you made in your Registration Agreement are complete and accurate;
   b. to your knowledge, the registration of the domain name will not infringe upon or otherwise violate the rights of any third party;
   c. you are not registering the domain name for an unlawful purpose; and
   d. you will not knowingly use the domain name in violation of any applicable laws or regulations.

   It is your responsibility to determine whether your domain name registration infringes or violates someone else's rights.

3. **Cancellations, Transfers, and Changes.**
   We will cancel, transfer or otherwise make changes to domain name registrations under the following circumstances:

a. subject to the provisions of Paragraph 8, our receipt of written or appropriate electronic instructions from you or your authorized agent to take such action;

b. our receipt of an order from a court or arbitral tribunal, in each case of competent jurisdiction, requiring such action; and/or

c. our receipt of a decision of an Administrative Panel requiring such action in any administrative proceeding to which you were a party and which was conducted under this Policy or a later version of this Policy adopted by ICANN. (See Paragraph 4(i) and (k) below.)

We may also cancel, transfer or otherwise make changes to a domain name registration in accordance with the terms of your Registration Agreement or other legal requirements.

4. **Mandatory Administrative Proceeding.**

This Paragraph sets forth the type of disputes for which you are required to submit to a mandatory administrative proceeding. These proceedings will be conducted before one of the administrative-dispute-resolution service providers listed under Providers.

a. Applicable Disputes. You are required to submit to a mandatory administrative proceeding in the event that a third party (a "complainant") asserts to the applicable Provider, in compliance with the Rules of Procedure, that

   i. your domain name is identical or confusingly similar to a trademark or service mark in which the complainant has rights; and

   ii. you have no rights or legitimate interests in respect of the domain name; and

   iii. your domain name has been registered and is being used in bad faith.

In the administrative proceeding, the complainant must prove that each of these three elements are present.

b. Evidence of Registration and Use in Bad Faith. For the purposes of Paragraph 4(a)(iii), the following circumstances, in particular but without limitation, if found by the Panel to be present, shall be evidence of the registration and use of a domain name in bad faith:

   i. circumstances indicating that you have registered or you have acquired the domain name primarily for the purpose of selling, renting, or otherwise transferring the domain name registration to the complainant who is the owner of the trademark or service mark or to a competitor of that complainant, for valuable consideration in excess of your documented out-of-pocket costs directly related to the domain name; or

   ii. you have registered the domain name in order to prevent the owner of the trademark or service mark from reflecting the mark in a corresponding domain name, provided that you have engaged in a pattern of such conduct; or

   iii. you have registered the domain name primarily for the purpose of disrupting the business of a competitor; or

   iv. by using the domain name, you have intentionally attempted to attract, for commercial gain, Internet users to your web site or other on-line location, by creating a likelihood of confusion with the complainant's mark as to the source, sponsorship, affiliation, or endorsement of your web site or location or of a product or service on your web site or location.

c. How to Demonstrate Your Rights to and Legitimate Interests in the Domain Name in Responding to a Complaint. When you receive a complaint, you should refer to Paragraph 5 of the Rules of Procedure in determining how your response should be prepared. Any of the following circumstances, in particular but without limitation, if found by the Panel to be proved based on its evaluation of all evidence presented, shall demonstrate your rights or legitimate interests to the domain name for purposes of Paragraph 4(a)(ii):

   i. before any notice to you of the dispute, your use of, or demonstrable preparations to use, the domain name or a name corresponding to the domain name in connection with a bona fide offering of goods or services; or

   ii. you (as an individual, business, or other organization) have been commonly known by the domain name, even if you have acquired no trademark or service mark rights; or

   iii. you are making a legitimate noncommercial or fair use of the domain name, without intent for commercial gain to misleadingly divert consumers or to tarnish the trademark or service mark at issue.

d. Selection of Provider. The complainant shall select the Provider from among those approved by ICANN by submitting the complaint to that Provider. The selected Provider will administer the proceeding, except in cases of consolidation as described in Paragraph 4(f).

e. Initiation of Proceeding and Process and Appointment of Administrative Panel. The Rules of Procedure state the process for initiating and conducting a proceeding and for appointing the panel that will decide the dispute (the "Administrative Panel").

f. Consolidation. In the event of multiple disputes between you and a complainant, either you or the complainant may petition to consolidate the disputes before a single Administrative Panel. This petition shall be made to the first Administrative Panel appointed to hear a pending dispute between the parties. This Administrative Panel may consolidate before it any or all such disputes in its sole discretion, provided that the disputes being consolidated are governed by this Policy or a later version of this Policy adopted by ICANN.

g. Fees. All fees charged by a Provider in connection with any dispute before an Administrative Panel pursuant to this Policy shall be paid by the complainant, except in cases where you elect to expand the Administrative Panel from one to three panelists as provided in Paragraph 5(b)(iv) of the Rules of Procedure, in which case all fees will be split evenly by you and the complainant.

h. Our Involvement in Administrative Proceedings. We do not, and will not, participate in the administration or conduct of any proceeding before an Administrative Panel. In addition, we will not be liable as a result of any decisions rendered by the Administrative Panel.

i. Remedies. The remedies available to a complainant pursuant to any proceeding before an Administrative Panel shall be limited to requiring the cancellation of your domain name or the transfer of your domain name registration to the complainant.

j. Notification and Publication. The Provider shall notify us of any decision made by an Administrative Panel with respect to a domain name you have registered with us. All decisions under this Policy will be published in full over the Internet, except when an Administrative Panel determines in an exceptional case to redact portions of its decision.

k. Availability of Court Proceedings. The mandatory administrative proceeding requirements set forth in Paragraph 4 shall not prevent either you or the complainant from submitting the dispute to a court of competent jurisdiction for independent resolution before such mandatory administrative proceeding is commenced or after such proceeding is concluded. If an Administrative Panel decides that your domain name registration should be canceled or transferred, we will wait ten (10) business days (as observed in the location of our principal office) after we are informed by the applicable Provider of the Administrative Panel's decision before implementing that decision. We will then implement the decision unless we have received from you during that ten (10) business-day period official documentation (such as a copy of a complaint, file-stamped by the clerk of the court) that you have commenced a lawsuit against the complainant in a jurisdiction to which the complainant has submitted under Paragraph 3(b)(xiii) of the Rules of Procedure. (In general, that jurisdiction is either the location of our principal office or of your address as shown in our Whois database. See Paragraphs 1 and 3(b)(xiii) of the Rules of Procedure for details.) If we receive such documentation within the ten (10) business-day period, we will not implement the Administrative Panel's decision, and we will take no further action, until we receive

  i. evidence satisfactory to us of a resolution between the parties;

  ii. evidence satisfactory to us that your lawsuit has been dismissed or withdrawn; or

  iii. a copy of an order from such court dismissing your lawsuit or ordering that you do not have the right to continue to use your domain name.

5. **All Other Disputes and Litigation.**
   All other disputes between you and any party other than us regarding your domain name registration that are not brought pursuant to the mandatory administrative proceeding provisions of Paragraph 4 shall be resolved between you and such other party through any court, arbitration or other proceeding that may be available.

6. **Our Involvement in Disputes.**
   We will not participate in any way in any dispute between you and any party other than us regarding the registration and use of your domain name. You shall not name us as a party or otherwise include us in any such proceeding. In the event that we are named as a party in any such proceeding, we reserve the right to raise any and all defenses deemed appropriate, and to take any other action necessary to defend ourselves.

7. **Maintaining the Status Quo.**

We will not cancel, transfer, activate, deactivate, or otherwise change the status of any domain name registration under this Policy except as provided in Paragraph 3 above.

8. **Transfers During a Dispute.**

   a. Transfers of a Domain Name to a New Holder. You may not transfer your domain name registration to another holder

      i. during a pending administrative proceeding brought pursuant to Paragraph 4 or for a period of fifteen (15) business days (as observed in the location of our principal place of business) after such proceeding is concluded; or

      ii. during a pending court proceeding or arbitration commenced regarding your domain name unless the party to whom the domain name registration is being transferred agrees, in writing, to be bound by the decision of the court or arbitrator.

   We reserve the right to cancel any transfer of a domain name registration to another holder that is made in violation of this subparagraph.

   b. Changing Registrars. You may not transfer your domain name registration to another registrar during a pending administrative proceeding brought pursuant to Paragraph 4 or for a period of fifteen (15) business days (as observed in the location of our principal place of business) after such proceeding is concluded. You may transfer administration of your domain name registration to another registrar during a pending court action or arbitration, provided that the domain name you have registered with us shall continue to be subject to the proceedings commenced against you in accordance with the terms of this Policy. In the event that you transfer a domain name registration to us during the pendency of a court action or arbitration, such dispute shall remain subject to the domain name dispute policy of the registrar from which the domain name registration was transferred.

9. **Policy Modifications.**

We reserve the right to modify this Policy at any time with the permission of ICANN. We will post our revised Policy for at least thirty (30) calendar days before it becomes effective. Unless this Policy has already been invoked by the submission of a complaint to a Provider, in which event the version of the Policy in effect at the time it was invoked will apply to you until the dispute is over, all such changes will be binding upon you with respect to any domain name registration dispute, whether the dispute arose before, on or after the effective date of our change. In the event that you object to a change in this Policy, your sole remedy is to cancel your domain name registration with us, provided that you will not be entitled to a refund of any fees you paid to us. The revised Policy will apply to you until you cancel your domain name registration.

Additional information regarding the Uniform Domain Name Dispute Resolution Policy & Rules may be found at www.icann.org/udrp/udrp.htm.

Appendix E: Federal Trademark Dilution Act

www4.law.cornell.edu/uscode/15/ch22.html

United States Code TITLE 15, CHAPTER 22, SUBCHAPTER III

(c) Remedies for dilution of famous marks

(1) The owner of a famous mark shall be entitled, subject to the principles of equity and upon such terms as the court deems reasonable, to an injunction against another person's commercial use in commerce of a mark or trade name, if such use begins after the mark has become famous and causes dilution of the distinctive quality of the mark, and to obtain such other relief as is provided in this subsection. In determining whether a mark is distinctive and famous, a court may consider factors such as, but not limited to—

(A) the degree of inherent or acquired distinctiveness of the mark;

(B) the duration and extent of use of the mark in connection with the goods or services with which the mark is used;

(C) the duration and extent of advertising and publicity of the mark;

(D) the geographical extent of the trading area in which the mark is used;

(E) the channels of trade for the goods or services with which the mark is used;

(F) the degree of recognition of the mark in the trading areas and channels of trade used by the mark's owner and the person against whom the injunction is sought;

(G) the nature and extent of use of the same or similar marks by third parties; and

(H) whether the mark was registered under the Act of March 3, 1881, or the Act of February 20, 1905, or on the principal register.

(2) In an action brought under this subsection, the owner of the famous mark shall be entitled only to injunctive relief unless the person against whom the injunction is sought willfully intended to trade on the owner's reputation or to cause dilution of the famous mark. If such willful intent is proven, the owner of the famous mark shall also be entitled to the remedies set forth in sections 1117(a) and 1118 of this title, subject to the discretion of the court and the principles of equity.

(3) The ownership by a person of a valid registration under the Act of March 3, 1881, or the Act of February 20, 1905, or on the principal register shall be a complete bar to an action against that person, with respect to that mark, that is brought by another person under the common law or a statute of a State and that seeks to prevent dilution of the distinctiveness of a mark, label, or form of advertisement.

(4) The following shall not be actionable under this section:

(A) Fair use of a famous mark by another person in comparative commercial advertising or promotion to identify the competing goods or services of the owner of the famous mark.

(B) Noncommercial use of a mark.

(C) All forms of news reporting and news commentary.

Appendix F: Uniform Commercial Code, Article 2–Sales

For full text, see www.law.cornell.edu/ucc/2/overview.html

Part 1. Short Title, General Construction and Subject Matter

Part 2. Form, Formation and Readjustment of Contract

Part 3. General Obligation and Construction of Contract

Part 4. Title, Creditors and Good Faith Purchasers

Part 5. Performance

§ 2-501. Insurable Interest in Goods; Manner of Identification of Goods.
§ 2-502. Buyer's Right to Goods on Seller's Insolvency.
§ 2-503. Manner of Seller's Tender of Delivery.
§ 2-504. Shipment by Seller.
§ 2-505. Seller's Shipment Under Reservation.
§ 2-506. Rights of Financing Agency.
§ 2-507. Effect of Seller's Tender; Delivery on Condition.
§ 2-508. Cure by Seller of Improper Tender or Delivery; Replacement.
§ 2-509. Risk of Loss in the Absence of Breach.
§ 2-510. Effect of Breach on Risk of Loss.
§ 2-511. Tender of Payment by Buyer; Payment by Check.
§ 2-512. Payment by Buyer Before Inspection.
§ 2-513. Buyer's Right to Inspection of Goods.
§ 2-514. When Documents Deliverable on Acceptance; When on Payment.
§ 2-515. Preserving Evidence of Goods in Dispute.

Part 6. Breach, Repudiation and Excuse

§ 2-601. Buyer's Rights on Improper Delivery.
§ 2-602. Manner and Effect of Rightful Rejection.
§ 2-603. Merchant Buyer's Duties as to Rightfully Rejected Goods.
§ 2-604. Buyer's Options as to Salvage of Rightfully Rejected Goods.
§ 2-605. Waiver of Buyer's Objections by Failure to Particularize.
§ 2-606. What Constitutes Acceptance of Goods.
§ 2-607. Effect of Acceptance; Notice of Breach; Burden of Establishing Breach After Acceptance; Notice of Claim or Litigation to Person Answerable Over.
§ 2-608. Revocation of Acceptance in Whole or in Part.
§ 2-609. Right to Adequate Assurance of Performance.
§ 2-610. Anticipatory Repudiation.
§ 2-611. Retraction of Anticipatory Repudiation.
§ 2-612. "Installment contract"; Breach.
§ 2-613. Casualty to Identified Goods.
§ 2-614. Substituted Performance.
§ 2-615. Excuse by Failure of Presupposed Conditions.
§ 2-616. Procedure on Notice Claiming Excuse.

Part 7. Remedies

Appendix G: Internet Tax Freedom Act of 1998

www.techlawjournal.com/congress/s442itfa/s442es.htm#mor

Title I—Moratorium on Certain Taxes

Sec. 101. Moratorium

(a) Moratorium.—No State or political subdivision thereof shall impose any of the following taxes during the period beginning on October 1, 1998, and ending 3 years after the date of the enactment of this Act—

(1) taxes on Internet access, unless such tax was generally imposed and actually enforced prior to October 1, 1998; and

(2) multiple or discriminatory taxes on electronic commerce.

(b) Preservation of State and Local Taxing Authority.—Except as provided in this section, nothing in this Act shall be construed to modify, impair, or supersede, or authorize the modification, impairment, or superseding of, any State or local law pertaining to taxation that is otherwise permissible by or under the Constitution of the United States or other Federal law and in effect on the date of enactment of this Act.

(c) Liabilities and Pending Cases.—Nothing in this Act affects liability for taxes accrued and enforced before the date of enactment of this Act, nor does this Act affect ongoing litigation relating to such taxes.

(d) Definition of Generally Imposed and Actually Enforced.—For purposes of this section, a tax has been generally imposed and actually enforced prior to October 1, 1998, if, before that date, the tax was authorized by statute and either—

(1) a provider of Internet access services had a reasonable opportunity to know by virtue of a rule or other public proclamation made by the appropriate administrative

agency of the State or political subdivision thereof, that such agency has interpreted and applied such tax to Internet access services; or

(2) a State or political subdivision thereof generally collected such tax on charges for Internet access.

(e) Exception to Moratorium.—

(1) In general.—Subsection (a) shall also not apply in the case of any person or entity who in interstate or foreign commerce is knowingly engaged in the business of selling or transferring, by means of the World Wide Web, material that is harmful to minors unless such person or entity requires the use of a verified credit card, debit account, adult access code, or adult personal identification number, or such other procedures as the Federal Communications Commission may prescribe, in order to restrict access to such material by persons under 17 years of age.

(2) Scope of exception.—For purposes of paragraph (1), a person shall not be considered to engaged in the business of selling or transferring material by means of the World Wide Web to the extent that the person is—

(A) a telecommunications carrier engaged in the provision of a telecommunications service;

(B) a person engaged in the business of providing an Internet access service;

(C) a person engaged in the business of providing an Internet information location tool; or

(D) similarly engaged in the transmission, storage, retrieval, hosting, formatting, or translation (or any combination thereof) of a communication made by another person, without selection or alteration of the communication.

(3) Definitions.—In this subsection:

(A) By means of the World Wide Web.—The term "by means of the World Wide Web" means by placement of material in a computer server-based file archive so that it is publicly accessible, over the Internet, using hypertext transfer protocol, file transfer protocol, or other similar protocols.

(B) Engaged in the business.—The term "engaged in the business" means that the person who sells or transfers or offers to sell or transfer, by means of the World Wide Web, material that is harmful to minors devotes time, attention, or labor to such activities, as a regular course of trade or business, with the objective of earning a profit, although it is not necessary that the person make a profit or that the selling or transferring or offering to sell or transfer such material be the person's sole or principal business or source of income.

(C) Internet.—The term "Internet" means collectively the myriad of computer and telecommunications facilities, including equipment and operating software, which comprise the interconnected world wide network of networks that employ the Transmission Control Protocol/Internet Protocol, or any predecessor or successor protocols to such protocol, to communicate information of all kinds by wire or radio.

(D) Internet access service.—The term "Internet access service" means a service that enables users to access content, information, electronic mail, or other services offered over the Internet and may also include access to proprietary content, information, and other services as part of a package of services offered to consumers. Such term does not include telecommunications services.

(E) Internet information location tool.—The term "Internet information location tool" means a service that refers or links users to an online location on the World Wide Web. Such term includes directories, indices, references, pointers, and hypertext links.

(F) Material that is harmful to minors.—The term "material that is harmful to minors" means any communication, picture, image, graphic image file, article, recording, writing, or other matter of any kind that—

(i) taken as a whole and with respect to minors, appeals to a prurient interest in nudity, sex, or excretion;

(ii) depicts, describes, or represents, in a patently offensive way with respect to what is suitable for minors, an actual or simulated sexual act or sexual contact, actual or simulated normal or perverted sexual acts, or a lewd exhibition of the genitals; and

(iii) taken as a whole, lacks serious literary, artistic, political, or scientific value for minors.

(G) Sexual act; sexual contact.—The terms "sexual act" and "sexual contact" have the meanings given such terms in section 2246 of title 18, United States Code.

(H) Telecommunications carrier; telecommunications service.—The terms "telecommunications carrier" and "telecommunications service" have the meanings given such terms in section 3 of the Communications Act of 1934 (47 U.S.C. 153).

(f) Additional Exception to Moratorium.—

(1) In general.—Subsection (a) shall also not apply with respect to an Internet access provider, unless, at the time of entering into an agreement with a customer for the provision of Internet access services, such provider offers such customer (either for a fee or at no charge) screening software that is designed to permit the customer to limit access to material on the Internet that is harmful to minors.

(2) Definitions.—In this subsection:

(A) Internet access provider.—The term "Internet access provider" means a person engaged in the business of providing a computer and communications facility through which a customer may obtain access to the Internet, but does not include a common carrier to the extent that it provides only telecommunications services.

(B) Internet access services.—The term "Internet access services" means the provision of computer and communications services through which a customer using a computer and a modem or other communications device may obtain access to the Internet, but does not include telecommunications services provided by a common carrier.

(C) Screening software.—The term "screening software" means software that is designed to permit a person to limit access to material on the Internet that is harmful to minors.

(3) Applicability.—Paragraph (1) shall apply to agreements for the provision of Internet access services entered into on or after the date that is 6 months after the date of enactment of this Act.

Sec. 102. Advisory Commission on Electronic Commerce

(a) Establishment of Commission.—There is established a commission to be known as the Advisory Commission on Electronic Commerce (in this title referred to as the "Commission"). The Commission shall—

(1) be composed of 19 members appointed in accordance with subsection (b), including the chairperson who shall be selected by the members of the Commission from among themselves; and

(2) conduct its business in accordance with the provisions of this title.

(b) Membership.—

(1) In general.—The Commissioners shall serve for the life of the Commission. The membership of the Commission shall be as follows:

(A) 3 representatives from the Federal Government, comprised of the Secretary of Commerce, the Secretary of the Treasury, and the United States Trade Representative (or their respective delegates).

(B) 8 representatives from State and local governments (one such representative shall be from a State or local government that does not impose a sales tax and one representative shall be from a State that does not impose an income tax).

(C) 8 representatives of the electronic commerce industry (including small business), telecommunications carriers, local retail businesses, and consumer groups, comprised of—

(i) 5 individuals appointed by the Majority Leader of the Senate;

(ii) 3 individuals appointed by the Minority Leader of the Senate;

(iii) 5 individuals appointed by the Speaker of the House of Representatives; and

(iv) 3 individuals appointed by the Minority Leader of the House of Representatives.

(2) Appointments.—Appointments to the Commission shall be made not later than 45 days after the date of the enactment of this Act. The chairperson shall be selected not later than 60 days after the date of the enactment of this Act.

(3) Vacancies.—Any vacancy in the Commission shall not affect its powers, but shall be filled in the same manner as the original appointment.

Appendix H: Securities Act of 1933 (Excerpts)

See www.law.uc.edu/CCL/33Act/index.html for full text.

Section 1—Short Title
Section 2—Definitions; Promotion of Efficiency, Competition, and Capital Formation
Section 3—Classes of Securities under this Title
Section 4—Exempted Transactions
Section 5—Prohibitions Relating to Interstate Commerce and the Mails

(a.) Sale or delivery after sale of unregistered securities.
Unless a registration statement is in effect as to a security, it shall be unlawful for any person, directly or indirectly—

1. to make use of any means or instruments of transportation or communication in interstate commerce or of the mails to sell such security through the use or medium of any prospectus or otherwise; or
2. to carry or cause to be carried through the mails or in interstate commerce, by any means or instruments of transportation, any such security for the purpose of sale or for delivery after sale.

(b.) Necessity of prospectus meeting requirements of section 10.
It shall be unlawful for any person, directly or indirectly—

1. to make use of any means or instruments of transportation or communication in interstate commerce or of the mails to carry or transmit any prospectus relating to any security with respect to which a registration statement has been filed under this title, unless such prospectus meets the requirements of section 10; or
2. to carry or cause to be carried through the mails or in interstate commerce any such security for the purpose of sale or for delivery after sale, unless accompanied or preceded by a prospectus that meets the requirements of subsection (a) of section 10.

* * * * * * *

Section 6—Registration of Securities
Section 7—Information Required in Registration Statement
Section 8—Taking Effect of Registration Statements and Amendments Thereto

Section 8A—Cease-and-Desist Proceedings
Section 9—Court Review of Orders
Section 10—Information Required in Prospectus
Section 11—Civil Liabilities on Account of False Registration Statement
Section 12—Civil Liabilities Arising in Connection with Prospectuses and Communications

(a.) In General. Any person who—
1. offers or sells a security in violation of section 5, or
2. offers or sells a security (whether or not exempted by the provisions of section 3, other than paragraph (2) of subsection (a) of said section), by the use of any means or instruments of transportation or communication in interstate commerce or of the mails, by means of a prospectus or oral communication, which includes an untrue statement of a material fact or omits to state a material fact necessary in order to make the statements, in the light of the circumstances under which they were made, not misleading (the purchaser not knowing of such untruth or omission), and who shall not sustain the burden of proof that he did not know, and in the exercise of reasonable care could not have known, of such untruth or omission, shall be liable, subject to subsection (b), to the person purchasing such security from him, who may sue either at law or in equity in any court of competent jurisdiction, to recover the consideration paid for such security with interest thereon, less the amount of any income received thereon, upon the tender of such security, or for damages if he no longer owns the security.

Section 13—Limitation of Actions
Section 14—Contrary Stipulations Void
Section 15—Liability of Controlling Persons
Section 16—Additional Remedies
Section 17—Fraudulent Interstate Transactions
Section 18—Exemption from State Regulation of Securities Offerings
Section 18A—Preemption of State Law
Section 19—Special Powers of Commission
Section 20—Injunctions and Prosecution of Offenses
Section 21—Hearings by Commission
Section 22—Jurisdiction of Offenses and Suits
Section 23—Unlawful Representations
Section 24—Penalties
Section 25—Jurisdiction of Other Government Agencies over Securities
Section 26—Separability of Provisions
Section 27—Private Securities Litigation
Section 27A—Application of Safe Harbor for Forward-Looking Statements
Section 28—General Exemptive Authority
Schedule A
Schedule B

Appendix I: Securities Exchange Act of 1934 (Excerpts)

See www.law.uc.edu/CCL/34Act/index.html for full text.

Section 1—Short Title
Section 2—Necessity for Regulation as Provided in This Title
Section 3—Definitions and Application of Title
Section 4—Securities and Exchange Commission
Section 4A—Delegation of Functions by Commission
Section 4B—Transfer of Functions with Respect to Assignment of Personnel to Chairman
Section 5—Transactions on Unregistered Exchanges
Section 6—National Securities Exchanges
Section 7—Margin Requirements
Section 8—Restrictions on Borrowing by Members, Brokers, and Dealers
Section 9—Prohibition Against Manipulation of Security Prices
Section 10—Regulation of the Use of Manipulative and Deceptive Devices

It shall be unlawful for any person, directly or indirectly, by the use of any means or instrumentality of interstate commerce or of the mails, or of any facility of any national securities exchange—

(a.) To effect a short sale, or to use or employ any stop-loss order in connection with the purchase or sale, of any security registered on a national securities exchange, in contravention of such rules and regulations as the Commission may prescribe as necessary or appropriate in the public interest or for the protection of investors.
(b.) To use or employ, in connection with the purchase or sale of any security registered on a national securities exchange or any security not so registered, any manipulative or deceptive device or contrivance in contravention of such rules and regulations as the Commission may prescribe as necessary or appropriate in the public interest or for the protection of investors.

Section 10A—Audit Requirements
Section 11—Trading by Members of Exchanges, Brokers, and Dealers

Appendix J: Children's Online Privacy Protection Act of 1998

www4.law.cornell.edu/uscode/15/ch91.html#PC91

United States Code TITLE 15, CHAPTER 91

Sec. 6501. Definitions

In this chapter:

(1) Child
The term "child" means an individual under the age of 13.

Sec. 6502. Regulation of unfair and deceptive acts and practices in connection with collection and use of personal information from and about children on the Internet

(a) Acts prohibited
(1) In general
It is unlawful for an operator of a website or online service directed to children, or any operator that has actual knowledge that it is collecting personal information from a child, to collect personal information from a child in a manner that violates the regulations prescribed under subsection (b) of this section.
(2) Disclosure to parent protected
Notwithstanding paragraph (1), neither an operator of such a website or online service nor the operator's agent shall be held to be liable under any Federal or State law for any disclosure made in good faith and following reasonable procedures in responding to a request for disclosure of personal information under subsection (b)(1)(B)(iii) of this section to the parent of a child.
(b) Regulations
(1) In general
Not later than 1 year after October 21, 1998, the Commission shall promulgate under section 553 of title 5 regulations that—
(A) require the operator of any website or online service directed to children that collects personal information from children or the operator of a website

or online service that has actual knowledge that it is collecting personal information from a child—

(i) to provide notice on the website of what information is collected from children by the operator, how the operator uses such information, and the operator's disclosure practices for such information; and

(ii) to obtain verifiable parental consent for the collection, use, or disclosure of personal information from children;

(B) require the operator to provide, upon request of a parent under this subparagraph whose child has provided personal information to that website or online service, upon proper identification of that parent, to such parent—

(i) a description of the specific types of personal information collected from the child by that operator;

(ii) the opportunity at any time to refuse to permit the operator's further use or maintenance in retrievable form, or future online collection, of personal information from that child; and

(iii) notwithstanding any other provision of law, a means that is reasonable under the circumstances for the parent to obtain any personal information collected from that child;

(C) prohibit conditioning a child's participation in a game, the offering of a prize, or another activity on the child disclosing more personal information than is reasonably necessary to participate in such activity; and

(D) require the operator of such a website or online service to establish and maintain reasonable procedures to protect the confidentiality, security, and integrity of personal information collected from children.

(2) When consent not required

The regulations shall provide that verifiable parental consent under paragraph (1)(A)(ii) is not required in the case of—

(A) online contact information collected from a child that is used only to respond directly on a one-time basis to a specific request from the child and is not used to recontact the child and is not maintained in retrievable form by the operator;

(B) a request for the name or online contact information of a parent or child that is used for the sole purpose of obtaining parental consent or providing notice under this section and where such information is not maintained in retrievable form by the operator if parental consent is not obtained after a reasonable time;

(C) online contact information collected from a child that is used only to respond more than once directly to a specific request from the child and is not used to recontact the child beyond the scope of that request—

(i) if, before any additional response after the initial response to the child, the operator uses reasonable efforts to provide a parent notice of the online contact information collected from the child, the purposes for which it is to be used, and an opportunity for the parent to request that the operator make no further use of the information and that it not be maintained in retrievable form; or

(ii) without notice to the parent in such circumstances as the Commission may determine are appropriate, taking into consideration the benefits to the child of access to information and services, and risks to the security and privacy of the child, in regulations promulgated under this subsection;

(D) the name of the child and online contact information (to the extent reasonably necessary to protect the safety of a child participant on the site)—

(i) used only for the purpose of protecting such safety;

(ii) not used to recontact the child or for any other purpose; and

(iii) not disclosed on the site, if the operator uses reasonable efforts to provide a parent notice of the name and online contact information collected from the child, the purposes for which it is to be used, and an opportunity for the parent to request that the operator make no further use of the information and that it not be maintained in retrievable form; or

(E) the collection, use, or dissemination of such information by the operator of such a website or online service necessary—

(i) to protect the security or integrity of its website;

(ii) to take precautions against liability;

(iii) to respond to judicial process; or

(iv) to the extent permitted under other provisions of law, to provide information to law enforcement agencies or for an investigation on a matter related to public safety.

Appendix K: Electronic Communications Privacy Act of 1986

www4.law.cornell.edu/uscode/18/ch119.html#PC119

US CODE TITLE 18, PART I, CHAPTER 119

Sec. 2510. Definitions

As used in this chapter -

(1) "wire communication" means any aural transfer made in whole or in part through the use of facilities for the transmission of communications by the aid of wire, cable, or other like connection between the point of origin and the point of reception (including the use of such connection in a switching station) furnished or operated by any person engaged in providing or operating such facilities for the transmission of interstate or foreign communications or communications affecting interstate or foreign commerce and such term includes any electronic storage of such communication;

(2) "oral communication" means any oral communication uttered by a person exhibiting an expectation that such communication is not subject to interception under circumstances justifying such expectation, but such term does not include any electronic communication;

(3) "State" means any State of the United States, the District of Columbia, the Commonwealth of Puerto Rico, and any territory or possession of the United States;

(4) "intercept" means the aural or other acquisition of the contents of any wire, electronic, or oral communication through the use of any electronic, mechanical, or other device.

(5) "electronic, mechanical, or other device" means any device or apparatus which can be sued to intercept a wire, oral, or electronic communication other than -

  (a) any telephone or telegraph instrument, equipment or facility, or any component thereof,

      (i) furnished to the subscriber or user by a provider of wire or electronic communication service in the ordinary course of its business and being used by the subscriber or user in the ordinary course of its business or furnished by such subscriber or user for connection to the facilities of such service and used in the ordinary course of its business; or

      (ii) being used by a provider of wire or electronic communication service in the ordinary course of its business, or by an investigative or law enforcement officer in the ordinary course of his duties;

    (b) a hearing aid or similar device being used to correct subnormal hearing to not better than normal;

  (6) "person" means any employee, or agent of the United States or any State or political subdivision thereof, and any individual, partnership, association, joint stock company, trust, or corporation;

  (7) "Investigative or law enforcement officer" means any officer of the United States or of a State or political subdivision thereof, who is empowered by law to conduct investigations of or to make arrests for offenses enumerated in this chapter, and any attorney authorized by law to prosecute or participate in the prosecution of such offenses;

* * * * * * * * * * * * * *

(12) "electronic communication" means any transfer of signs, signals, writing, images, sounds, data, or intelligence of any nature transmitted in whole or in part by a wire, radio, electromagnetic, photoelectronic or photooptical system that affects interstate or foreign commerce, but does not include -

    (A) the radio portion of a cordless telephone communication that is transmitted between the cordless telephone handset and the base unit;

    (B) any wire or oral communication;

    (C) any communication made through a tone-only paging device;

    (D) any communication from a tracking device (as defined in section 3117 of this title); or

(13) "user" means any person or entity who-

    (A) uses an electronic communication service; and

    (B) is duly authorized by the provider of such service to engage in such use;

(14) "electronic communication system" means any wire, radio, electromagnetic, photooptical or photoelectronic facilities for the transmission of electronic communications, and any computer facilities or related electronic equipment for the electronic storage of such communications;

(15) "electronic communication service" means any service which provides to users thereof the ability to send or receive wire or electronic communications;

(16) "readily accessible to the general public" means, with respect to a radio communication, that such communication is not   -

    (A) scrambled or encrypted;

    (B) transmitted using modulation techniques whose essential parameters have been withheld from the public with the intention of preserving the privacy of such communication;

(C) carried on a subcarrier or other signal subsidiary to a radio transmission;

(D) transmitted over a communication system provided by a common carrier, unless the communication is a tone only paging system communication;

(E) transmitted on frequencies allocated under part 25, subpart D, E, or F of part 74, or part 94 of the Rules of the Federal Communications commission, unless, in the case of a communication transmitted on a frequency allocated under part 74 that is not exclusively allocated to broadcast auxiliary services, the communication is a two-way voice communication by radio;
(17) "electronic storage" means

(A) any temporary intermediate storage of a wire or electronic communication incidental to the electronic transmission thereof; and

(B) any storage of such communication by an electronic communication service for purposes of backup protection of such communication;

* * * * * * * * * *

Sec. 2511. Interception and disclosure of wire, oral, or electronic communications prohibited

(1) Except as otherwise specifically provided in this chapter any person who—

(a) intentionally intercepts, endeavors to intercept, or procures any other person to intercept or endeavor to intercept, any wire, oral, or electronic communication;

(b) intentionally uses, endeavors to use, or procures any other person to use or endeavor to use any electronic, mechanical, or other device to intercept any oral communication when—

(i) such device is affixed to, or otherwise transmits a signal through, a wire, cable, or other like connection used in wire communication; or

(ii) such device transmits communications by radio, or interferes with the transmission of such communication; or

(iii) such person knows, or has reason to know, that such device or any component thereof has been sent through the mail or transported in interstate or foreign commerce; or

(iv) such use or endeavor to use (A) takes place on the premises of any business or other commercial establishment the operations of which affect interstate or foreign commerce; or (B) obtains or is for the purpose of obtaining information relating to the operations of any business or other commercial establishment the operations of which affect interstate or foreign commerce; or

(v) such person acts in the District of Columbia, the Commonwealth of Puerto Rico, or any territory or possession of the United States;

(c) intentionally discloses, or endeavors to disclose, to any other person the contents of any wire, oral, or electronic communication, knowing or having reason to know that the information was obtained through the interception of a wire, oral, or electronic communication in violation of this subsection; or

(d) intentionally uses, or endeavors to use, the contents of any wire, oral, or electronic communication, knowing or having reason to know that the information was obtained through the interception of a wire, oral, or electronic communication in violation of this subsection; shall be punished as provided in subsection (4) or shall be subject to suit as provided in subsection (5).

(2)(a)

(i) It shall not be unlawful under this chapter for an operator of a switchboard, or an officer, employee, or agent of a provider of a wire or electronic communication service, whose facilities are used in the transmission of a wire communication, to intercept, disclose, or use that communication in the normal course of his employment while engaged in any activity which is a necessary incident to the rendition of his service or to the protection of the rights or property of the provider of that service, except that a provider of wire communication service to the public shall not utilize service observing or random monitoring except for mechanical or service quality control checks.

* *

(3)(a) Except as provided in paragraph (b) of this subsection, a person or entity providing an electronic communication service to the public shall not intentionally divulge the contents of any communication (other than one to such person or entity, or an agent thereof) while in transmission on that service to any person or entity other than an addressee or intended recipient of such communication or an agent of such addressee or intended recipient.

(b) A person or entity providing electronic communication service to the public may divulge the contents of any such communication—

(i) as otherwise authorized in section 2511(2)(a) or 2517 of this title;

(ii) with the lawful consent of the originator or any addressee or intended recipient of such communication;

(iii) to a person employed or authorized, or whose facilities are used, to forward such communication to its destination; or

(iv) which were inadvertently obtained by the service provider and which appear to pertain to the commission of a crime, if such divulgence is made to a law enforcement agency.

(4)(a) Except as provided in paragraph (b) of this subsection or in subsection (5), whoever violates subsection (1) of this section shall be fined under this title or imprisoned not more than five years, or both.

* * * * * * * * * * * * * *

CHAPTER 121.   STORED WIRE AND ELECTRONIC COMMUNICATIONS AND TRANSACTIONAL RECORDS ACCESS

Sec. 2701. Unlawful access to stored communications

(a) Offense. Except as provided in subsection (c) of this section whoever—

(1) intentionally accesses without authorization a facility through which an electronic communication service is provided; or

(2) intentionally exceeds an authorization to access that facility; and thereby obtains, alters, or prevents authorized access to a wire or electronic communication while it is in electronic storage in such system shall be punished as provided in subsection (b) of this section.

(b) Punishment. The punishment for an offense under subsection (a) of this section is—

(1) if the offense is committed for purposes of commercial advantage, malicious destruction or damage, or private commercial gain—

(A) a fine of not more than $ 250,000 or imprisonment for not more than one year, or both, in the case of a first offense under this subparagraph; and (B) a fine under this title or imprisonment for not more than two years, or both, for any subsequent offense under this subparagraph; and

(2) a fine of not more than $ 5,000 or imprisonment for not more than six months, or both, in any other case.

(c) Exceptions. Subsection (a) of this section does not apply with respect to conduct authorized—

(1) by the person or entity providing a wire or electronic communications service;

(2) by a user of that service with respect to a communication of or intended for that user; or

(3) in section 2703, 2704 or 2518 of this title.

Sec. 2702. Disclosure of contents

(a) Prohibitions. Except as provided in subsection (b)—

(1) a person or entity providing an electronic communication service to the public shall not knowingly divulge to any person or entity the contents of a communication while in electronic storage by that service; and

(2) a person or entity providing remote computing service to the public shall not knowingly divulge to any person or entity the contents of any communication which is carried or maintained on that service—

(A) on behalf of, and received by means of electronic transmission from (or created by means of computer processing of communications received by means of electronic transmission from), a subscriber or customer of such service; and

(B) solely for the purpose of providing storage or computer processing services to such subscriber or customer, if the provider is not authorized to access the contents of any such communications for purposes of providing any services other than storage or computer processing.

(b) Exceptions. A person or entity may divulge the contents of a communication—

(1) to an addressee or intended recipient of such communication or an agent of such addressee or intended recipient;

(2) as otherwise authorized in section 2517, 2511(2)(a), or 2703 of this title;

(3) with the lawful consent of the originator or an addressee or intended recipient of such communication, or the subscriber in the case of remote computing service;

(4) to a person employed or authorized or whose facilities are used to forward such communication to its destination;

(5) as may be necessarily incident to the rendition of the service or to the protection of the rights or property of the provider of that service; or

(6) to a law enforcement agency, if such contents—

(A) were inadvertently obtained by the service provider; and (B) appear to pertain to the commission of a crime.

Appendix L: Child Pornography Prevention Act of 1996

www4.law.cornell.edu/uscode/18/2251.html

United States Code TITLE 18, PART I, CHAPTER 110

Sec. 2251. Sexual exploitation of children and other abuse of children

(a) Any person who employs, uses, persuades, induces, entices, or coerces any minor to engage in, or who has a minor assist any other person to engage in, or who transports any minor in interstate or foreign commerce, or in any Territory or Possession of the United States, with the intent that such minor engage in, any sexually explicit conduct for the purpose of producing any visual depiction of such conduct, shall be punished as provided under subsection (d), if such person knows or has reason to know that such visual depiction will be transported in interstate or foreign commerce or mailed, if that visual depiction was produced using materials that have been mailed, shipped, or transported in interstate or foreign commerce by any means, including by computer, or if such visual depiction has actually been transported in interstate or foreign commerce or mailed.

(b) Any parent, legal guardian, or person having custody or control of a minor who knowingly permits such minor to engage in, or to assist any other person to engage in, sexually explicit conduct for the purpose of producing any visual depiction of such conduct shall be punished as provided under subsection (d) of this section, if such parent, legal guardian, or person knows or has reason to know that such visual depiction will be transported in interstate or foreign commerce or mailed, if that visual depiction was produced using materials that have been mailed, shipped, or transported in interstate or foreign commerce by any means, including by computer, or if such visual depiction has actually been transported in interstate or foreign commerce or mailed.

(c) (1) Any person who, in a circumstance described in paragraph (2), knowingly makes, prints, or publishes, or causes to be made, printed, or published, any notice or advertisement seeking or offering —

(A) to receive, exchange, buy, produce, display, distribute, or reproduce, any visual depiction, if the production of such visual depiction involves the use of a minor engaging in sexually explicit conduct and such visual depiction is of such conduct; or

(B) participation in any act of sexually explicit conduct by or with any minor for the purpose of producing a visual depiction of such conduct; shall be punished as provided under subsection (d).

(2) The circumstance referred to in paragraph (1) is that -

(A) such person knows or has reason to know that such notice or advertisement will be transported in interstate or foreign commerce by any means including by computer or mailed; or

(B) such notice or advertisement is transported in interstate or foreign commerce by any means including by computer or mailed.

(d) Any individual who violates, or attempts or conspires to violate, this section shall be fined under this title or imprisoned not less than 10 years nor more than 20 years, and [1] both, but if such person has one prior conviction under this chapter, chapter 109A, or chapter 117, or under the laws of any State relating to the sexual exploitation of children, such person shall be fined under this title and imprisoned for not less than 15 years nor more than 30 years, but if such person has 2 or more prior convictions under this chapter, chapter 109A, or chapter 117, or under the laws of any State relating to the sexual exploitation of children, such person shall be fined under this title and imprisoned not less than 30 years nor more than life. Any organization that violates, or attempts or conspires to violate, this section shall be fined under this title. Whoever, in the course of an offense under this section, engages in conduct that results in the death of a person, shall be punished by death or imprisoned for any term of years or for life.

Appendix M: Communications Decency Act of 1996

www4.law.cornell.edu/uscode/47/223.html

United States Code TITLE 47, CHAPTER 5, SUBCHAPTER II

Sec. 223. Obscene or harassing telephone calls in the District of Columbia or in interstate or foreign communications

(d) Sending or displaying offensive material to persons under 18
    Whoever—
    (1) in interstate or foreign communications knowingly—
      (A) uses an interactive computer service to send to a specific person or persons under 18 years of age, or
      (B) uses any interactive computer service to display in a manner available to a person under 18 years of age, any comment, request, suggestion, proposal, image, or other communication that, in context, depicts or describes, in terms patently offensive as measured by contemporary community standards, sexual or excretory activities or organs, regardless of whether the user of such service placed the call or initiated the communication; or
      (2) knowingly permits any telecommunications facility under such person's control to be used for an activity prohibited by paragraph (1) with the intent that it be used for such activity, shall be fined under title 18 or imprisoned not more than two years, or both.

(e) Defenses
    In addition to any other defenses available by law:
    (1) No person shall be held to have violated subsection (a) or (d) of this section solely for providing access or connection to or from a facility, system, or network not under that person's control, including transmission, downloading, intermediate storage, access software, or other related capabilities that are incidental to providing such access or connection that does not include the creation of the content of the communication.

(2) The defenses provided by paragraph (1) of this subsection shall not be applicable to a person who is a conspirator with an entity actively involved in the creation or knowing distribution of communications that violate this section, or who knowingly advertises the availability of such communications.

(3) The defenses provided in paragraph (1) of this subsection shall not be applicable to a person who provides access or connection to a facility, system, or network engaged in the violation of this section that is owned or controlled by such person.

(4) No employer shall be held liable under this section for the actions of an employee or agent unless the employee's or agent's conduct is within the scope of his or her employment or agency and the employer (A) having knowledge of such conduct, authorizes or ratifies such conduct, or (B) recklessly disregards such conduct.

(5) It is a defense to a prosecution under subsection (a)(1)(B) or (d) of this section, or under subsection (a)(2) of this section with respect to the use of a facility for an activity under subsection (a)(1)(B) of this section that a person—

(A) has taken, in good faith, reasonable, effective, and appropriate actions under the circumstances to restrict or prevent access by minors to a communication specified in such subsections, which may involve any appropriate measures to restrict minors from such communications, including any method which is feasible under available technology; or

(B) has restricted access to such communication by requiring use of a verified credit card, debit account, adult access code, or adult personal identification number.

Appendix N: UNCITRAL Model Law on Electronic Commerce

[Original: Arabic, Chinese, English, French, Russian, Spanish]

Part one. Electronic commerce in general

CHAPTER I. GENERAL PROVISIONS

Article 1. Sphere of application*

This Law** applies to any kind of information in the form of a data message used in the context*** of commercial**** activities.

* The Commission suggests the following text for States that might wish to limit the applicability of this Law to international data messages:

"This Law applies to a data message as defined in paragraph (1) of article 2 where the data message relates to international commerce."

** This Law does not override any rule of law intended for the protection of consumers.

*** The Commission suggests the following text for States that might wish to extend the applicability of this Law: "This Law applies to any kind of information in the form of a data message, except in the following situations: [. . .]."

**** The term "commercial" should be given a wide interpretation so as to cover matters arising from all relationships of a commercial nature, whether contractual or not. Relationships of a commercial nature include, but are not limited to, the following transactions: any trade transaction for the supply or exchange of goods or services; distribution agreement; commercial representation or agency; factoring; leasing; construction of works; consulting; engineering; licensing; investment; financing; banking; insurance; exploitation agreement or concession; joint venture and other forms of industrial or business cooperation; carriage of goods or passengers by air, sea, rail or road.

Article 2. Definitions
For the purposes of this Law:

(a) "Data message" means information generated, sent, received or stored by electronic, optical or similar means including, but not limited to, electronic data interchange (EDI), electronic mail, telegram, telex or telecopy;

(b) "Electronic data interchange (EDI)" means the electronic transfer from computer to computer of information using an agreed standard to structure the information;

(c) "Originator" of a data message means a person by whom, or on whose behalf, the data message purports to have been sent or generated prior to storage, if any, but it does not include a person acting as an intermediary with respect to that data message;

(d) "Addressee" of a data message means a person who is intended by the originator to receive the data message, but does not include a person acting as an intermediary with respect to that data message;

(e) "Intermediary," with respect to a particular data message, means a person who, on behalf of another person, sends, receives or stores that data message or provides other services with respect to that data message;

(f) "Information system" means a system for generating, sending, receiving, storing or otherwise processing data messages.

Article 3. Interpretation

(1) In the interpretation of this Law, regard is to be had to its international origin and to the need to promote uniformity in its application and the observance of good faith.
(2) Questions concerning matters governed by this Law which are not expressly settled in it are to be settled in conformity with the general principles on which this Law is based.

Article 4. Variation by agreement

CHAPTER II. APPLICATION OF LEGAL REQUIREMENTS TO DATA MESSAGES

Article 5. Legal recognition of data messages

Information shall not be denied legal effect, validity or enforceability solely on the grounds that it is in the form of a data message.

Article 5 *bis*. Incorporation by reference

Information shall not be denied legal effect, validity or enforceability solely on the grounds that it is not contained in the data message purporting to give rise to such legal effect, but is merely referred to in that data message.

Article 6. Writing

Article 7. Signature

Article 8. Original

Article 9. Admissibility and evidential weight of data messages

(1) In any legal proceedings, nothing in the application of the rules of evidence shall apply so as to deny the admissibility of a data message in evidence:

    (a) on the sole ground that it is a data message; or,

    (b) if it is the best evidence that the person adducing it could reasonably be expected to obtain, on the grounds that it is not in its original form.

(2) Information in the form of a data message shall be given due evidential weight. In assessing the evidential weight of a data message, regard shall be had to the reliability of the manner in which the data message was generated, stored or communicated, to the reliability of the manner in which the integrity of the information was maintained, to the manner in which its originator was identified, and to any other relevant factor.

Article 10. Retention of data messages

CHAPTER III. COMMUNICATION OF DATA MESSAGES

Article 11. Formation and validity of contracts

(1) In the context of contract formation, unless otherwise agreed by the parties, an offer and the acceptance of an offer may be expressed by means of data messages. Where a data message is used in the formation of a contract, that contract shall not be denied validity or enforceability on the sole ground that a data message was used for that purpose.

(2) The provisions of this article do not apply to the following: [. . .].

Article 12. Recognition by parties of data messages

(1) As between the originator and the addressee of a data message, a declaration of will or other statement shall not be denied legal effect, validity or enforceability solely on the grounds that it is in the form of a data message.

(2) The provisions of this article do not apply to the following: [. . .].

Article 13. Attribution of data messages

(1) A data message is that of the originator if it was sent by the originator itself.

(2) As between the originator and the addressee, a data message is deemed to be that of the originator if it was sent:

    (a) by a person who had the authority to act on behalf of the originator in respect of that data message; or

    (b) by an information system programmed by, or on behalf of, the originator to operate automatically.

(3) As between the originator and the addressee, an addressee is entitled to regard a data message as being that of the originator, and to act on that assumption, if:

(a) in order to ascertain whether the data message was that of the originator, the addressee properly applied a procedure previously agreed to by the originator for that purpose; or

(b) the data message as received by the addressee resulted from the actions of a person whose relationship with the originator or with any agent of the originator enabled that person to gain access to a method used by the originator to identify data messages as its own.

(4) Paragraph (3) does not apply:

(a) as of the time when the addressee has both received notice from the originator that the data message is not that of the originator, and had reasonable time to act accordingly; or

(b) in a case within paragraph (3)(b), at any time when the addressee knew or should have known, had it exercised reasonable care or used any agreed procedure, that the data message was not that of the originator.

(5) Where a data message is that of the originator or is deemed to be that of the originator, or the addressee is entitled to act on that assumption, then, as between the originator and the addressee, the addressee is entitled to regard the data message as received as being what the originator intended to send, and to act on that assumption. The addressee is not so entitled when it knew or should have known, had it exercised reasonable care or used any agreed procedure, that the transmission resulted in any error in the data message as received.

(6) The addressee is entitled to regard each data message received as a separate data message and to act on that assumption, except to the extent that it duplicates another data message and the addressee knew or should have known, had it exercised reasonable care or used any agreed procedure, that the data message was a duplicate.

Article 14. Acknowledgement of receipt

Article 15. Time and place of dispatch and receipt of data messages

Part two. Electronic commerce in specific areas

CHAPTER I. CARRIAGE OF GOODS

Article 16. Actions related to contracts of carriage of goods

Without derogating from the provisions of part one of this Law, this chapter applies to any action in connection with, or in pursuance of, a contract of carriage of goods, including but not limited to:

    (a) (i) furnishing the marks, number, quantity or weight of goods;
        (ii) stating or declaring the nature or value of goods;
        (iii) issuing a receipt for goods;
        (iv) confirming that goods have been loaded;
    (b) (i) notifying a person of terms and conditions of the contract;
        (ii) giving instructions to a carrier;

(c) (i) claiming delivery of goods;
    (ii) authorizing release of goods;
    (iii) giving notice of loss of, or damage to, goods;
(d) giving any other notice or statement in connection with the performance of the contract;
(e) undertaking to deliver goods to a named person or a person authorized to claim delivery;
(f) granting, acquiring, renouncing, surrendering, transferring or negotiating rights in goods;
(g) acquiring or transferring rights and obligations under the contract.

Article 17. Transport documents

Glossary

Absolute privilege: Defense to a suit in defamation demation granted to those involved in legislative or judicial proceedings.

Act of State Doctrine: Doctrine that one government will not judge the legality of acts of another government committed within the latter's territory.

Adhesion contract: A contract that is unilateral and nonnegotiable. It is legal as long as it is "reasonable and fair."

Advisory Commission on Electronic Commerce: A commission established by the Internet tax freedom act to study the implications of taxing e-commerce.

Agreement on Trade-Related Aspects of Intellectual Property Rights (TRIPS): International agreement (one of the World Trade Organizations's multilateral agreements) that establishes a comprehensive set of rights and obligations governing international trade in intellectual property.

Anticybersquatting Consumer Protection Act (ACPA): Protects registered trademark holders from online cyberpiracy (registering as domain names another person or company's trademark).

Assignment of contractual rights: The voluntary transfer of a contracting party's rights to a third person.

B

Biometrics: Security technology designed to authenticate users by capturing human characteristics.

Business extension rule: The ECPA section that requires a plaintiff to prove the defendant used a devise capable of intercepting an electronic communication. It exempts from liability any devise furnished to the subscriber or used by a service provider in the ordinary course of business.

C

Cable Communications Protection Act (CCPA) of 1984: Deals with the privacy rights a subscriber to cable television should expect regarding personal data that the cable television operator gathers.

Cache: Temporary storage space on the hard drive.

California Limited Offering Exemption: Similar to Reg D offerings, it is limited to businesses organized under California law.

Certificate authorities (CA): They issue and manage digital certificates and are centralized by industry with a wide range of applications, such as e-mail, browsers, and VPNs.

Child Online Protection Act (COPA) of 1998: Expanded the provisions of the Child Pornography Protection Act to include online transmissions by service providers and e-commerce site providers.

Child Pornography Protection Act (CPPA) of 1996: Prohibits and criminalizes trafficking in child pornography.

Choice of law clause: Clause in a contract that designates the law that will govern any contractual dispute.

Click-wrap license: A license that appears on a computer screen when software is first being installed; and which the purchaser must accept before the installation will proceed.

Commerce clause: For tax purposes, the clause means that a tax must be fairly apportioned, it cannot discriminate, and it must be fairly related to the services provided by the state. The business must have a substantial nexus with the taxing state.

Communication Decency Act (CDA) of 1996: Makes it a crime for anyone to knowingly transport obscene material for sale or distribution either in foreign or interstate commerce or through the use of an interactive computer service. Parts of it have been declared unconstitutional.

Computer crime: Broadly defined as any illegal act that involves a computer, its systems, or its applications.

Computer Fraud and Abuse Act (CFAA) of 1986: The pre-eminent statute used in prosecuting the range of computer crimes.

Consenting adults defense: Defense against an obscenity charge; in most cases, people are entitled to First Amendment and privacy protection for actions involving consenting adults in the privacy of their home.

Consideration: The main reason for a person to enter a contract; a legal obligation assumed or a legal right surrendered.

Contemporary community standards: As part of the first prong of the three-prong *Miller* test, these are the standards that a local community holds with regard to its tolerance of obscenity.

Contributory infringement: The tort of contributing to the direct infringement of another by a party who knew of the direct infringement and could have taken simple measures to prevent further damages.

Cookies: Small text files that a server can store on the user's machine to track the user's Web-viewing habits.

Copyright Infringement Act: This act prohibits the reporduction or distribution of protected works even if there is no profit derived from such efforts.

Cracking: This is the name given to intentional, malicious hacking, and is a crime.

Cyberporn: Obscene material transmitted over the Internet or through e-mail.

Cyberspace: Term originally used by William Gibson in his 1982 novel *Neuromancer.* The totality of all the world's computers, represented as a visual virtual three dimentional domain in which a user may move and act with the consequences in the real world.

D

Data Encryption Standard (DES): The U.S. government's data security standard for cryptography.

Data manipulation: This is the crime of changing or erasing existing information.

Decryption: The second step in cryptography, whereby ciphertext is decoded and thus translated back into readable text.

Defamation: Oral or written false statements that wrongfully harm a person's reputation.

Delegation of duties: The transfer of a contracting party's obligations to a third person.

Denial of service attacks: Overloading a server to keep others from gaining access.

Derivative work: A work based on one or more preexisting copyrighted works.

Digital certificates: Digital ID or passport, so that only those who can authenticate their identities may access the secure data.

Digital Millennium Copyright Act (DCMA) of 1998: Act that provides "safe harbors" from infringement liability to online service providers.

Direct infringement: Action that violates a copyright owner's exclusive statutory rights with or without a specific intent to infringe.

Direct Public Offering (DPO): See Internet Securities offerings.

Domain name: A business address on the Internet.

Domain name system (DNS): a text name matched to the Internet protocol that makes it easier for users to access sites.

Due process clause: A constitutional requirement for personal jurisdiction based on two criteria: the nonresident e-business has sufficient minimum contacts in the forum state where the case is being tried, and jurisdiction in that court will not offend traditional notions of fair play and justice.

E

Economic Espionage Act (EEA): This makes it a crime to steal or misappropriate trade secrets by computer.

EDI Trading Partner Agreement: Agreement written on paper and signed by trading partners to validate electronic transactions with the intent of making them as enforceable as paper contracts.

Electronic Communications Privacy Act (ECPA) of 1986: This act outlaws the unauthorized interception, access, and disclosure of wire or electronic communications.

Electronic Data Interchange (EDI): Transfer of electronic data between companies.

Electronic Funds Transfer Act (EFTA): This act outlaws the giving of inaccurate or insufficient information in an EFT, or transactions involving counterfeit, stolen, or fictitious debit instruments.

Electronic roadshow: A management presentation to qualified investors following delivery of prospectuses. Content is limited to materials in the prospectus but it is (usually) good publicity.

Encryption: The first step in cryptography, whereby plaintex data is encoded by use of a mathematical algorithm to create cipher text stored in a different format known as ciphertext.

Espionage: Involves the act of spying or monitoring, and includes the theft or misappropriation of secrets by computer or other means.

European Union's (EU) Directive on Privacy Protection: Requires the fifteen member states of the EU to adopt legislation that seeks to protect the fundamental rights and freedoms of an individual, particularly the right to privacy as it relates to the processing and collection of personal data.

Exclusive statutory rights: Rights of copyright owner to reproduce and distribute works, prepare derivative works based on the work, and perform and publicly display the copyright work.

Extortion: This involves a ransom demand (blackmail) in exchange for something of value, usually directed at a business or government.

Extranet: Access of the company intranet by a limited number of customers, suppliers, or business partners.

F

Fair Credit Reporting Act (FCRA) of 1970: Ensures that the credit reports furnished by consumer credit reporting agencies are accurate, impartial, and respect privacy.

Fair use doctrine: Statutory limitation on exclusive rights of a copyright owner, allowing for free speech, use of material and is subject to guidelines.

Fifth Amendment: Amendment to the U.S. Constitution providing that no person shall be compelled in any criminal case to be a witness against himself.

File transfer protocol (FTP): System that moves files from one computer to another.

Firewall: A computer between the networked computers and the network, that secures this system from unauthorized access.

First sale doctrine: Limits the copyright owner's exclusive right to distribute publicly a copy of the work when the copyright material was lawfully acquired by another.

Fixed creative work: One that is sufficiently permanent to permit it to be perceived, reproduced, or otherwise communicated for a period of more than transitory duration.

Forum: the court or locale wherein causes are judicially tried.

Forum non conveniens: Doctrine that a court will decline to hear a dispute when it can be better or more conveniently heard in a foreign forum.

Forum selection clause: A provision in a contract that designates the forum where disputes will be settled.

Fourth Amendment: Amendment to the U.S. Constitution providing that the people have the right to be protected against unreasonable searches and seizures conducted by the government.

Fraud: An illegal act involving deception of identity or purposes, in order to gain something of value.

G

Gambling: Discussed here in a criminal context involving participation either in a jurisdiction where it is illegal; or with an underage person; or one who has diminished capacity.

Good Samaritan defense: A defense against the Communications Decency Act protecting an online service provider or user of an interactive computer service from civil liability as a publisher or speaker of any information provided by another content provider.

Government interest test: A test that directs a court if it must determine the laws that apply to a dispute, to apply the laws of the country that has the most interest in determining the countries that have a legitimate interest in the outcome of the dispute.

H

Hacking: The process of gaining access to computers or sites where no access was intended—this may be a crime in some jurisdictions.

Harassment: The communication of taunts, profanity, or demands.

Hardware weapons: These include radio frequency or electromagnetic pulse weapons that knock out a system's electronic equipment.

Hate crimes: Discussed here in a criminal context as the communication of threatening, hate-filled messages attacking people based on their traits of national origin, race, color, sex, religion, ethnicity, or sexual orientation.

Holography: An authentification technology involving the use of images incorporated into a photopolymer process.

Hypertext markup language (HTML): Platform-independent language that makes the Internet accessible on any type of computer.

I

In personam **jurisdiction:** The power of a court or other government agency to determine the rights of natural and judicial persons appearing before it.

In rem **jurisdiction:** The power of a court or other government agency to determine the ownership rights of persons with respect to particular property located within the territory of the forum.

Inherently distinctive trademarks: Suggestive, arbitrary, and fanciful trademarks.

Interactive Web site: A Web site that actively seeks business from customers.

Intergovernmental organization (IGO): An organization set up by two or more countries to carry out activities of common interest to them.

Internet Corporation for Assigned Names and Numbers (ICANN): A nonprofit public-benefit nongovernment organization with an international board of directors. Its mission is to create new top-level domain names. Selected by the U.S. government to manage the domain name system.

Internet protocol (IP): a unique computer address that consists of four series of three numbers allowing communication between computers.

Internet securities offerings (ISO): This refers to any equity offering done via the Internet.

Internet service provider (ISP): Company that connects users to the Internet.

Internet Tax Freedom Act of 1998: Act that prevents federal, state, and local governments from imposing any new taxes on the Internet for three years. Some existing taxes were grandfathered in.

Intranet: Use of the Internet within an organization.

Intrastate offering exemption: Helps finance local business by waiving requirements on securities offerings.

Intrusion upon Seclusion: One of four types of common law torts for the invasion of privacy; defined as intentionally intruding on the solitude or private affairs of another person.

J

Java: Universal computer language run by a program built into browsers.

Jurisdiction: The authority of a court or other government agency to hear and resolve a dispute.

L

Libel: Written or published defamation.

Literary, artistic, political, and socially redeemable value: The third prong in the three-prong *Miller* test; material that has redeemable or socially acceptable value is not considered obscene.

Logic bombs: Programs that remain essentially undetected until they detonate, set off by the onset of an event or a date.

Long-arm statue: State law that allows courts to claim personal jurisdiction over a nonresident defendant whose principal business is outside the state.

M

Mail and Wire Fraud Statutes: These statutes make it a crime to use the mails, interstate, or foreign communications to fraudulently obtain money or property.

Malware: Any harmful software or hardware, including viruses, worms, logic bombs, and so on.

Market maintenance theory: When vendors' state activities are significantly associated with the taxpayers' ability to establish and maintain market in the state for its sales.

Mass-market license: A provision in a license that allows consumer purchasers to return software if the terms of the license are unacceptable.

Minimum contacts: Legal measure of a nonresident defendant's purposeful use of the benefits of a state's economic market.

Mirror image rule: Rule that a contractual offer will not be accepted, and a contract will not be formed, unless the terms of the acceptance adhere exactly to the terms of the offer.

Misappropriation of a Person's Name or Likeness Causing Injury to Reputation: One of four types of common law torts for the invasion of privacy; defined as use of the name or picture of a living person for commercial purposes without that person's consent.

Money laundering: The act of flowing funds through various financial institutions so that the original source of the funds cannot be determined.

Most significant relationship test: Test that directs a court, if it must determine the laws that apply to a dispute, to apply the laws of the country that has the most real and significant "contacts" with the parties and their transactions.

Motion to dismiss: A legal maneuver to have a case dismissed because of lack of personal jurisdiction. The case may be then tried before the appropriate court that has jurisdiction.

N

Nationality principle of jurisdiction: Doctrine that a court has criminal jurisdiction if the victim is a national of the forum state.

Netiquette: An unofficial attempt at self-regulation by businesses engaged in cyberspace; a kind of ethical code that requires courtesy online and respect for bandwidth capacity.

Network Solutions, Inc.: A private company that, until recently, held a monopoly on second-level domain name registration.

Nexus: Physical connection with the taxing state where the customer is located.

Nexus attribution: For state tax purposes can occur by having agents who are sales representatives, employees, or individual contractors working on sales on behalf of a company in another state.

Ninth Amendment: Amendment to the U.S. Constitution providing that the rights not enumerated or expressed in the Constitution are retained by the people.

No-action letter: SEC method of responding to company's inquiry and that it will not take enforcement action on the matter.

No Electronic Theft Act (NET Act) of 1997: Amending the Copyright Infringement Act establishing that there is infringement, even without economic gain to the user, when the copyrighted material has a total retail value of more than $2,500.

Nongovernmental organization (NGO): An international organization whose members are persons other than countries.

O

Off-Shore offerings: Offers for sale of securities that are made outside of the U.S. to non-U.S. persons.

P

Packet: Bundle of data traveling on the Internet.

Parol evidence rule: Rule that parties to a complete and final written contract cannot introduce evidence in court of prior or contemporaneous agreements to to contradict the meaning of the contract.

Passive personality principle of jurisdiction: Jurisdiction based on the nationality or national character of the person injured by the offense.

Passive Web site: A Web site that transmits information only and doesn't solicit business.

Patently offensive: The second prong of the three-prong *Miller* test; material that is obviously offensive in its exhibition of sexual activity.

Physical presence test: Elements that can determine for tax purposes whether a company is subject to state tax jurisdiction.

Pornography: Any depictions of persons that are obscene.

Principal Register: Publication of the PTO that lists registered trademarks.

Privacy Act of 1994: Establishes requirements that must be satisfied before government agencies or departments can disclose records and documents in its possession that contain personal information about individuals.

Privacy Protection Act (PPA) of 1980: Applies to law enforcement agencies and allows Fourth Amendment protection against unreasonable searches and seizures of work product materials used to disseminate some form of public communication, or affecting interstate commerce.

Private key: Encryption of messages using a key known only to the communicating parties.

Private placement offering exemptions: Simplifies capital raising process for businesses. Offerings are available only to certain investors.

Processor serial number: An authentification technology wherein a unique number is embedded in every central processing unit of computers.

Prospectus: SEC-mandated statement delivered to each investor, and it details financial conditions and business the company is engaged in.

Protection of Children from Sexual Predators Act of 1998: This act expands liability to those who attempt to use the

Internet for purposes of child pornography; commercial pornographers are specifically targeted.

Protective principle: Doctrine that a court has criminal jurisdiction if the victim is a national of the forum state.

Prurient interest: The first prong of the three-prong *Miller* test; prurient material has a "tendency to excite lustful thoughts."

Public Disclosure of Private Facts Causing Injury to Reputation: One of four types of common law torts for the invasion of privacy; defined as revealing highly personal facts or information about another, leading to damage to their reputation.

Public Key Infrastructure (PKI): Encryption and associated technologies in the issuance and management of digital credentials to provide multi-layered security.

Public performance: Performance of a copyrighted work in a place open to the public or where a substantial number of people outside a normal circle of family and social acquaintances are gathered.

Publicly Placing Another in a False Light: One of four types of common law torts for the invasion of privacy; defined as falsely connecting a person to an immoral, illegal, or embarrassing situation resulting in damage to their reputation.

Q

Qualified privilege: Defense to a suit in defamation usually granted to statements made in good faith to others who have a legitimate interest in the information contained in the statement. Examples include employer references and recommendations.

R

Reg A offerings: Streamlined procedures of registered offerings for small business.

Reg D offerings: Investment offerings exempt from federal registered offerings requirements for small business including rules 504, 505, and 506.

Rule 504: A Reg D exemption allowing businesses to raise up to $1 million in 12 months.

Rule 505: A Reg D exemption allowing businesses to raise up to $5 million in 12 months.

Rule 506: A Reg D exemption allowing businesses to raise up to $5 million without time restrictions.

S

Sales tax: Tax paid by consumer and collected by the merchant at point of purchase on tangible personal property.

Scienter (Latin for "knowledge"): Refers to the requirement that defendant knew an act would result in a wrong.

Secondary meaning: A characteristic that permits a general word to acquire distinctiveness that makes it registrable as a trademark.

Section 230 of the Communications Decency Act: Provides that an Internet service provider would not be treated as publishers or distributors, and would thus not be held liable for defamation posted by the service provider.

Secure Electronic Transactions (SET): Industry standards of cryptography governing commercial transactions.

Securities Act of 1933: Law passed by Congress in response to the stock market crash of 1929 that set regulations for trading in securities.

Securities Act of 1934 (Exchange Act): Regulates accounting and recordkeeping of domestic companies registered with the SEC.

Securities and Exchange Commission (SEC): Government agency that regulates securities trading and administers U.S. securities laws.

Security: An interest in a business; this can take many forms, but should include an investment in a common enterprise with a reasonable expectation of profit derived from the work of others.

Security tokens: Also called digipasses; another means to authenticate users.

Service mark: Words, phrases, logos, or other graphic symbols that promote services and are also granted legal protection.

Shrink-wrap license: Terms of a contractual license that are not available for review until after the product is opened and the shrink-wrap is removed.

Signature: A person's name, initials, or symbol, used by that person to authenticate a writing.

Slander: Oral defamation.

Slander per se: Categories of oral defamation in which damages to reputation are presumed to exist.

Small Corporate Offering Registration: An exemption (called seed capital exemption) usually involved with companies in the early stages of product or service development.

Smart cards: Similar to tokens, they have the added feature of portability; users may access data even at offsite computers.

Software piracy: This is the act of duplicating and distributing copyright-protected materials without authorization from or payment to the copyright owner.

Sonny Bono Copyright Term Extension Act: A 1998 act that extended the term of copyright protection from 70 years to 90 years after the author's death.

Spamming: Sending unsolicited bulk e-mail advertisements.

Spoofing: Setting up sites to look like other sites.

Stalking: The act of shadowing or menacing a person.

Statutory damages: Payment entitled by plaintiff in lieu of actual damages.

Supplemental Register: Publication of the PTO that provides constructive notice of ownership to companies in all fifty states that you are using a trademark not yet registrable.

T

Telephone Consumer Protection Act (TCPA) of 1991: Extends privacy rights to several aspects of telephone marketing activities.

Territoriality principle: Doctrine that a court has criminal jurisdiction if an offense is committed within the forum state.

Terrorism: The act of undermining or disabling systems, and may involve extortion or blackmail.

Third party beneficiary: A person who benefits from a contract without being a party to it.

Trade dress: A colored design or shape associated with a product.

Trademark: A word, name, or device or any combination thereof, including a sound, used by any person to identify and distinguish goods from those of others.

Trespass: The act of breaking into computers or networks either without authorization or in excess of one's authorization.

Trojan horses: Programs that have the ability to hide and replicate themselves.

U

U.S. Patent and Trademark Office (PTO): The U.S. government agency where trademarks are registered.

Uniform resource locator (URL): the name of a file stored on a Web server.

Universality principle: Doctrine that a court has criminal jurisdiction if the forum state has the defendant in custody.

Use tax: Tax paid by consumer on tangible goods purchased out of state for use within a taxing state.

V

Vesting of rights doctrine: Doctrine that direct a court, if it must determine the laws that apply to a dispute, to apply the laws of the country where the parties' rights become legally effective.

Vicarious infringement: Occurs when a company receives direct financial benefit from the infringement by another and had the right and ability to supervise the infringement activity.

Video Privacy Protection Act (VPPA) of 1988: Expands the CCPA to prohibit the use and disclosure of personal information about the videocassettes and related products an individual rents or buys.

Virus writing: The act of writing programs that have the ability to attach themselves to other programs in other computers and thereby replicate themselves.

W

Worm: A program designed to infiltrate systems and destroy data.

Index

A

Acceptance, of offer, contract formation
and, 76–77
Caspi v. The Microsoft Network,
L.L.C., 78
ACEC. *See* Advisory Commission on
Electronic Commerce
ACPA. *See* Anticybersquatting Consumer
Protection Act
Address, internet, 4
Adult web sites, employees, workplace
access to, 175–177
Advisory Commission on Electronic
Commerce, 98, 108
Advisory Commission on
Intergovernmental Relations, 98
Affinity groups, securities, 124–125
AGB. *See* Alliance for Global Business
Agreement on Trade-Related Aspect of
Intellectual Property Rights, 363–364
Alliance for Global Business, 252
Amazon, 3
America Online, 3
Anticybersquatting Consumer Protection
Act of 1999, 44–45, 46
Arbitrary marks, 37
ARPANET, 3
Assent, mutual, contract formation
and, 73–77, 95
Assignment, of contractual rights, 88–90
Authorship, original work of, copyrights,
52–53

B

Bandwidth, 4

Bensusan Restaurant Corporation
v. King, 25
Berne Convention for Protection of Literary
and Artistic Works, 264–265
Berners-Lee, Tim, 3
Bilateral contract, 73, 89
Biometrics, information security and, 197–199
BrainTech, Inc. v. Kostiuk, 257–258
Brandname equity, 36
Business systems security, 9–10
encryption schemes, types of, 10
firewalls, to control access, 9–10
Internet Communications Management
Protocol, 10
ping, 10
ping of death, 10
private key encryption, 10
public key encryption, 10
service attacks, denial of, 10

C

CA. *See* Certificate authority
Cable Communications Protection Act,
152–153
Cache, 9
California Limited Offering Exemption,
121–122
Capacity to contract, 73
Capital, international movement of,
270–272
Caspi v. The Microsoft Network, L.L.C.,
78
CCPA. *See* Cable Communications
Protection Act

About the Authors

GERALD R. FERRERA received a B.S. from Boston College, an M.S. in taxation from Bentley College, and a J.D. from New England School of Law. He has co-authored texts in business law and legal environment and has written numerous law review articles. He was granted the Gregory H. Adamian Law Professorship, the first endowed chair of the law department at Bentley College. Publication awards include the Ralph C. Hoeber award given by the Academy of Legal Studies in Business, numerous Bentley College publication awards and the Bentley College Scholar of the Year Award. Teaching awards include the Charles M. Hewitt Excellence in Teaching Award granted from the Academy of Legal Studies in Business, and from Bentley College, the Gregory H. Adamian Teaching Award, and the Innovative Teaching Award.

He was President of the North Atlantic Regional Business Law Association and currently serves on the board of editors of the Business Law Review. He was chair of the Bentley College Law Department and is presently a research fellow at the Center for Business Ethics at Bentley College. He is also a member of the Massachusetts and Federal Bars.

STEPHEN D. LICHTENSTEIN has a B.S. from Boston College, a J.D. from Suffolk University Law School and a Certificate in Mediation. He has authored and co-authored numerous law review articles on many business law related topics. In 2000, he received the prestigious Bentley College Adamian Award for Excellence in Teaching. Professor Lichtenstein is past president of the North Atlantic Business Law Association, is a legal consultant to businesses and individuals and is a member of the Massachusetts and Federal Bars. Currently, he is Chair of the Bentley College Law Department and a Professor of Law.

MARGO E. K. REDER, ESQ. was graduated from the University of Massachusetts (B.A.); the London School of Economics and Political Science (Dipl.); and Suffolk University Law School (J.D.). She has served as a professor of law, a research associate at Bentley College, a prosecutor, and counsel for a start-up business venture. She has served as President of the North Atlantic Business Law Association, and is currently on its Executive Committee. Ms. Reder is a frequent contributor to legal texts, and has published numerous law review articles and the recipient of many publication awards. She is widely cited in the areas of civil rights in employment, arbitration, securities, punitive damages, and international law. Ms. Reder is a member of the Massachusetts and Federal bars.

RAY AUGUST holds a J.D. from the University of Texas at Austin, an LL.M. in international law from the University of Cambridge, and a Ph.D. in legal history from the University of Idaho. He is a professor of business law and coordinator of the business law program for the School of Accounting, Information Systems and Business Law at Washington State University. His courses make extensive use of online materials and feature animated online lectures that students watch over the Internet. He is the webmaster for the International Law Section of the Academy of Legal Studies in Business as well as the webmaster for the Pacific Northwest Academy of Legal Studies in Business. He is the author of books on international business law and public international law and articles on comparative law, legal history, and intellectual property law.

WILLIAM T. SCHIANO is an Assistant Professor and Chair of the MIS department at Bentley College. He developed and taught two graduate IS courses, Information Technology Management and Policy, and Electronic Commerce in the Global Economy, and has written numerous articles, papers, and Harvard Business School cases. He is a VanDuyne Scholar from the Williams College Department of Economics, with other honors and awards that include Participant in the 1995 Ernst & Young Foundation ICIS Doctoral Consortium and a Harvard University Fellowship.